A Chanticleer Press Edition

Taylor's Guide to Gardening Techniques

Houghton Mifflin Company Boston

Library of Congress
Cataloging-in-Publication Data
Taylor's guide to gardening techniques.
1st ed. — (Taylor's guides to gardening)
Based on: Taylor's encyclopedia of gardening.
4th ed. 1961.
Includes bibliographical references and index.
ISBN 0-395-56403-4
1. Gardening—Encyclopedias. I. Taylor's
encyclopedia of gardening. II. Series.
SB450.95.T38   1991   635—dc20   90-21863
CIP

Prepared and produced by Chanticleer Press,
New York
Typeset by Graphic Arts Composition,
Philadelphia
Printed and bound by Dai Nippon, Tokyo, Japan
Cover photograph by Saxon Holt

Series designed by Massimo Vignelli
Photography by Saxon Holt
First Edition.

DNP   10 9 8 7 6 5 4 3 2 1

Contents

Contributors

Jim Borland, author of the essay on propagation, owns Native Concepts, a consultation firm specializing in private, government, and commercial landscapes. One of his specialties is propagating and growing native plants of the western United States. His articles have appeared in many trade and scientific journals.

Rita Buchanan, who contributed the essay on preparing the soil, writes and edits for a number of garden books and magazines. She is an active home gardener, and she has worked as a grower for wholesale nurseries.

Nancy Carney wrote the essay on planting. She contributes articles to *Fine Gardening* magazine, lectures on gardening in the eastern United States, and works with home gardeners in Fairfield County, Connecticut.

Sheila Daar is the author of the chapter "Managing Pests Safely." She is Executive Director of the Bio-Integral Resource Center (BIRC), a nonprofit organization that provides technical information on integrated pest management. She frequently contributes to publications and training materials covering least-toxic pest management.

Roger Holmes acted as the editorial consultant for this book. The former editor of *Fine Gardening* magazine, which he helped to launch, he is currently a freelance writer and editor.

Saxon Holt, a San Francisco-based commercial photographer, took all the photographs for this book and has contributed to other *Taylor's Guides*. He specializes in photography of agricultural, ornamental, and native plants. His work has appeared in Ortho Books and in publications of The Nature Conservancy.

Edward Lam created all the black-and-white illustrations for this volume. He is a regular contributor to all the *Taylor's Guides*.

Dr. John W. Mastalerz, author of the essay on fertilizing, is Professor Emeritus of Horticulture at Pennsylvania State University. He has also taught horticulture classes at the University of Massachusetts.

Robert Parnes wrote the essay on compost. For ten years he served as director of a soil-testing service and is the author of a book on organic and inorganic fertilizers. He currently is a consultant, freelance writer, and workshop leader in the areas of soil fertility and plant nutrients.

Dr. H. Brent Pemberton contributed the essay "How Plants Grow." He is an Associate Professor at the Texas A&M University Agricultural Research and Extension Center. He is regularly involved in helping ornamental-plant producers solve production problems and in activities sponsored by the Tyler Rose Society and other garden clubs.

Warren Schultz, author of the essay on lawns, is editor in chief of *National Gardening Magazine.* He is currently working on a book about the gardens of the Soviet Union.

Lauren Springer contributed the chapter on creating a new garden bed. She writes a weekly gardening column for *The Denver Post.* An experienced traveler, she has maintained gardens in the British Isles, the northeast United States, and now in Northern Colorado, where she designs gardens and grows over 800 kinds of perennials, alpines, annuals, shrubs, and trees.

Guy Sternberg, author of the essay on pruning, is a landscape architect for the Illinois Department of Conservation. He has written articles for *Fine Gardening* and *American Nurseryman* magazines.

Gayle Weinstein wrote the essay on watering. She is the owner of ELETES, a botanical/horticultural firm in Denver that specializes in regional and water-conserving landscape design, education, and research. For more than ten years she has directed the horticultural programs and applied research at Denver Botanic Gardens.

Preface

Of all our many pastimes, gardening is perhaps the most accessible. It doesn't require a workshop full of tools, a wallet full of money, or hours of practice; plant a few seeds in a bit of earth, and you are on your way.

How your garden grows after those first steps depends on your enthusiasm, your resources, and your whims. A garden can be as small as a windowbox or as large as a meadow; it may be a carefully planned composition of colors, textures, and forms, or a naturalistic, unpremeditated mixture of favorite plants. Regardless of size or design, all successful gardens have one thing in common—healthy plants. Helping you to grow healthy plants is the purpose of this book.

Few of us are blessed with good soil, a benign climate, and a green thumb. To grow healthy plants, you will probably need to augment what nature has provided, by improving the soil or by supplementing rainfall and nutrients. Sometimes you will need to temper nature, shading plants from the heat, insulating them from the cold, or protecting them from insects and disease. You will also need to know your plants' natures. Understanding their preferences and differences will help you find the right place for them in the garden and keep them happy once they are there.

Start Off Right

Growing healthy plants means giving them a good start. A well-prepared garden bed is as important to a plant as a good home is to a child. If you buy plants from the nursery, the way you transplant them to the bed can make a big difference in how they will perform as they mature. You can also propagate plants yourself. Growing new plants from seeds, cuttings, or division can greatly increase the number and variety of plants in your garden.

Once established in the garden, plants need to be looked after in order to stay healthy. Delphiniums have to be staked, daylilies deadheaded, shrubs pruned, old clumps of bearded irises rejuvenated by division. Some tasks are seasonal; others, such as watering and weeding, are (or seem to be) continual.

Like the other titles in this series, this is a handbook. It provides clear and concise explanations, in words and pictures, of how to accomplish a wide range of gardening techniques. But good gardening is not so regimented as any "how-to" book might suggest; like child-rearing, gardening has its dos and don'ts, but there is great room for individual approaches and styles, depending on the kind of plants you choose.

Many plants tolerate a wide range of conditions; others are more particular, even fussy. Each garden is also unique. The soil, drainage, light, and temperature in your garden may be distinctly different from those in a friend's garden just down the block.

Given all the possibilities, this book is designed to help you understand why something is done as well as telling you how to do it. If you grasp the principles underlying the techniques, you will be less likely to be frustrated when something puzzles you in the garden. With an understanding of the processes governing plant growth, you can adapt procedures to suit circumstances. And learning about the interactions of plants, soil, water, and sunlight can enhance your enjoyment of gardening.

Which brings us back to the beginning. Ornamental gardens are grown only for the pleasure they give. Many gardeners count among those pleasures the hours spent in sowing, weeding, planting, and pruning; others consider the hours of such work to be the price of the delights of the end result—beautiful plants and flowers. But whether you enjoy every moment spent in your garden, or whether you groan through the chores of a weekend morning, this book is designed to enhance your pleasure and your skill.

A beginning gardener may wonder how the techniques for a supposedly accessible pastime can fill so many pages. Don't be daunted. Remember that this volume is a handbook, not an owner's manual. Your garden is your own creation. Skim the book and pick out the topics that pertain to what you want to do—start a new bed, grow plants from seed, transplant a seedling you bought at a nursery. Then go do it. A gardener's most important knowledge comes from actually growing plants and experimenting in the garden. This book should help you start out on the right path to great enjoyment.

How to Use

No two gardens are alike—a fact that makes gardening one of the most expressive, challenging, and joyful pursuits of modern living. No single guide to gardening techniques, therefore, can provide answers and advice for the infinite variety of questions that will arise. There are as many possibilities for the active gardener as there are landscapes and climates, cultivars and varieties, tastes and preferences.

Every good gardener, however, will want to acquire and perfect certain basic skills. This book is intended to help with those aims; to provide beginners with a fundamental understanding of the hows and whys of successful gardening, and to help more advanced gardeners sharpen and improve their outdoor skills.

How This Book Is Organized

Taylor's Guide to Gardening Techniques contains ten chapters, each an essay that deals with a basic horticultural skill or garden component.

The key to successful gardening is understanding the building blocks of plant life; to grow healthy plants, you must know what they need in the way of light, water, and nutrition. The first chapter, "How Plants Grow," offers an essential introduction to the rudiments of botany. This essay brings together the information that you will meet, in greater detail, in the rest of the book. Starting with reproduction, the discussion moves through the life cycle of a plant, so you will comprehend how your actions will affect the vigor and appearance of your garden.

Each of the nine chapters that follow is an individual discussion of specific topics critical to growing healthy plants: preparing and testing your soil; making a garden bed; planting; propagation; fertilizing; watering; pruning; controlling pests; and planting and maintaining a lawn. All the themes are covered in sufficient detail to provide a sturdy introduction for beginners, but the chapters are also designed to give direction to more ambitious or experienced gardeners.

Every chapter includes basic step-by-step instruction designed to help beginning gardeners master the techniques under discussion. No single volume, of course, can cover the limitless possibilities that exist; but with a solid grounding in these basics, you will be off to a good start.

The essays are supplemented by black-and-white drawings that will expand your grasp of the techniques discussed. In some cases, such as the chapter on lawns and the chapter on fertilizing, the experts have included charts designed to provide basic facts at a glance; more detailed information is found in the accompanying text sections.

This Guide

The Color Plates
Throughout the book, adjoining the relevant chapters, are color
photographs illustrating the successful use of the techniques
described within that essay. The photos were taken in various areas
of the country, in all types of climate, and in gardens large and
small; they have been carefully selected to offer you a general idea of
the possibilities you may unlock in your garden when you have
learned to apply these techniques. Some of the photographs show
the results of exercising fundamental skills; others show what may
be accomplished by acquiring more advanced knowledge.
The photos provide vibrant and colorful examples of the some of
the best types of plants that beginning gardeners can choose to
work with; the lush, full-color illustrations add a brilliant and
realistic dimension to the "how-to" black-and-white drawings of
the text section.

Captions
The captions that accompany the photos provide information at
a glance: which techniques have been applied, what factors of
garden life (such as soil or climate) are illustrated, and how certain
effects are achieved. The photo captions do not offer step-by-step
instruction (which is found in the text and line art); instead, the
captions are intended to serve as a basic jumping-off point and a
source of ready inspiration.

The Plant Charts
The charts beginning on page 416 allow you to see at a glance some
of the plant varieties that are best suited to your location and your
esthetics. These charts, similar to plant charts in the single-subject
Taylor's Guides, are intended to provide beginning gardeners with a
very general idea of the kinds of plants that they may wish to begin
with. Within each category, the flowers or shrubs included in the
chart were chosen for their availability, durability, and ease of
maintenance. (For the same reason, most of the plants in these
charts were also selected for inclusion in *Taylor's Pocket Guides to
Gardening.*) For detailed instructions regarding the cultivation of
these and other plants, turn to the single-subject *Taylor's Guides* or
to *Taylor's Pocket Guides to Gardening.*

A Lifetime of Pleasure
Few hobbies delight like successful gardening. This guide is offered
not as a rule book but as a source of inspiration and a means of
helping you to handle your garden plants with the attention and
understanding they deserve. They, in turn, will give back to you a
lifetime of gratification.

How Plants

The first challenge of gardening is to grow healthy plants.
Elsewhere in this book you will learn about techniques for creating
conditions in which plants thrive. This chapter, however, will give
an overview of the ways plants transform the light, water, and
nutrients that you work so hard to provide into healthy growth.
The more you know about how plants grow, the easier it will be
for you to use the information in the rest of the book to help them
thrive.

How Plant Life Begins

Asked how plant life begins, most people will say with a seed. A
gardener might add a panoply of other beginnings—bulbs, corms,
cuttings, divisions, and so on. But for our purposes, a seed is a good
place to start.

Seeds and Meristems

When you purchase a seed, you are buying an embryonic plant and
enough stored food to see it through its initial growth. Growth
starts with the elongation and rapid division of cells at two points,
called meristems, on opposite ends of the embryo. One meristem
forms a root, called a radicle; the other forms a shoot. The
emergence of the radicle signals the beginning of germination. The
shoot follows shortly after, and its emergence from the soil usually
is the gardener's first sign of germination.

As the young shoot grows, specific cells of this meristem
differentiate and produce leaves. Likewise, cells on the other
meristem differentiate to produce the first branches of the root
system. At the juncture, or axil, of each leaf and shoot, a new
meristem forms. All of the plant's subsequent growth and the
development of its wide variety of specialized structures—shoots,
branches, leaves, thorns, flowers, fruit, root hairs, tubers, even the
growth in diameter of woody plants—are the result of the
formation and differentiation of meristems.

Apical Dominance and Plant Form

The growing point of a shoot, root, or other structure is called the
apical meristem. Meristems behind it on the same structure, such
as those in the leaf axils on a shoot, for example, are called lateral
meristems. The growth relationship between apical and lateral
meristems, called apical dominance, is an important one that
governs many gardening practices. Simply put, the apical
meristem inhibits the growth of the lateral meristems behind it by
means of complex chemical signals. If the apical meristem is
damaged or removed, the chemical signals change and the buds in
the leaf axils begin to grow. Thus, a gardener's pinching or
pruning of shoot tips promotes branching and produces bushy,

Grow

more compact plants. Likewise, pinching or pruning root tips produces a fibrous root system that makes transplanting easier. Apical dominance also influences plant form. Plants with strong apical dominance generally are upright and pyramidal or conical. Corn, for example, shows strong apical dominance, and axillary buds are seldom produced. Plants with weak apical dominance are broad and spreading. In roots, a taproot indicates strong apical dominance; a fibrous root system, weak dominance.

Flower and Fruit Development
After the growth of roots, stems, and leaves, the development of meristems into flowers followed by fruits and seeds completes the life cycle of a plant. Most species are monoecious; that is, they produce flowers with both male and female parts. Dioecious species, such as spinach and date palms, however, produce only male or female flowers on any individual plant. Holly is dioecious, and this is why you must plant at least a few male holly plants to ensure pollination and berry development on the female plants. Some monoecious species, such as corn and squash, produce both male and female flowers at different places on the same shoot. This is why squash fruits do not develop on the first flowers of the plant, which are male, but form only on the female flowers that soon follow.

The opening of flowers ready for pollination, called anthesis by botanists, can be a memorable event. But for those gardeners who look forward literally to the fruits of their labors, flowering is simply a necessary phenomenon leading to pollination and fruit development. When pollen lands on a receptive stigma, a pollen tube is formed, which leads to fertilization of the ovules in the female part of the flower. Seeds then begin to develop, which in turn stimulates the development of the fruit. If the seeds do not develop properly, neither will the fruit.

As in apical dominance, a competition exists between a plant's vegetative growth (its leaves) and its reproductive growth (flowers and fruit). Chemical signals produced by young flowers and fruits draw mineral nutrients, sugars, and amino acids to them, while leaves and other flowers or fruits on the plant also compete for these needed substances. This is why you remove dead flowers to encourage more flowering, or thin young apple fruit so that those that remain will be larger at harvest.

The Five Factors of Plant Growth
Though desirable conditions for plant growth vary from species to species, they all fall into five broad environmental categories: water, gases, light, temperature, and soil and nutrition.

Water and Transpiration

Water is the lifeblood of plants, delivering nutrients to and removing wastes from individual cells. The movement of water through a plant starts (or ends, depending on your point of view) with transpiration. Plants transpire, or lose water vapor to the air, through microscopic pores, called stomata, usually located on the underside of each leaf. Loss of water through a stoma causes additional water to evaporate from the surface of tissue in a sub-stomatal chamber in the leaf. To replace this lost water, more is drawn into the cells from the conducting tissues of the plant, which are called the xylem. The xylem forms a continuous system down the stems and into the roots, where water and nutrients are drawn in from the surrounding soil.

A combination of forces moves the water through the plant. One is the tendency of water and water vapor to move from areas of high to low pressure. Transpiration provides one example. Water is drawn from inside the leaf, where the vapor pressure is high, to the air surrounding the leaf, where the vapor pressure is low. This creates a chain reaction of vapor-pressure differentials down through the plant and, ultimately, between the roots and the surrounding soil. The movement of water is also aided by the ability of water particles to cohere to each other and to adhere to other particles, such as the tissue of the xylem. As water particles move from high to low pressure, cohesion pulls the particles behind them along. Cohesion, adhesion, and differences in pressure can move water particles hundreds of feet, from roots deep beneath the soil surface to the top of the tallest redwood tree.

Plants, like many animals, cool themselves by making use of another of water's properties. Water requires an unusually high amount of energy to change from a solid (ice) to a liquid, and from a liquid to a gas (water vapor). As water changes from liquid to gas, it consumes heat energy, which cools the surface (your skin or a leaf) from which it evaporates. When the process is reversed, as when liquid water freezes, heat energy is released. Thus, orchardists protect fruit trees from mild freezes by sprinkling them with water. The heat released as a thin sheet of ice forms on the buds will keep the temperature of the buds from falling much below that of their icy envelope, even though the surrounding temperatures may drop much lower.

Plants can experience stress if the water content of the soil is low. In response, the plant closes its stomata and adjusts physiologically in other ways. When the stomata are closed, however, transpiration and its cooling effects decrease dramatically and the plant's internal temperature can rise. In addition, gas exchange is greatly reduced and nutrient uptake slows considerably. The degree of stress that different plants can tolerate varies, and species have developed various mechanisms to deal with drought. These range from

Chlorophyll in the leaves converts sunlight to carbohydrates; this food then flows through the plant. Leaves also "breathe," drawing in air, extracting carbon dioxide, and releasing oxygen. The bark acts as a protective layer around the cambium, or growing layer. The roots not only anchor the plant in place, but also draw in nutrients and water from the soil.

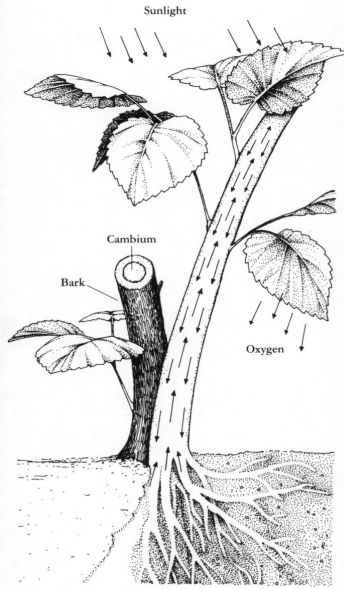

Sunlight

Cambium

Bark

Oxygen

Root tips

How Plants Grow

anatomical (spines instead of leaves, for example) to metabolic (cells can still function despite a very low water content).

Gases and Photosynthesis
Another very important function of stomata is to permit carbon dioxide to enter the leaf. Once inside, this gas is combined with water in the presence of sunlight to form sugars. This process, called photosynthesis, is unique to plants and forms the basis of life on earth.

Sugars produced by photosynthesis move through the circulatory system in the plant known as the phloem. The water- and nutrient-conducting xylem is in the central part of a stem, while the phloem usually is on the periphery near the surface, where it can easily be damaged. Gardeners fight aphids because they harm plants by inserting their stylets into the phloem of plants to suck the sweet juices for nourishment. Gardeners also avoid damaging tree bark because when the surface bark and underlying phloem of a tree are damaged, sugars cannot reach the roots. The trunk begins to swell above the wound. Gradually, the starving roots cease nutrient and water uptake, and the tree dies a slow death.

Directed by chemical signals, the products of photosynthesis move to many plant parts, where they are stored for later use or are immediately consumed for growth. Very young developing leaves may actually import sugars, while fully developed leaves will be very active exporters of photosynthetic products. The rate of photosynthesis will slowly decline in older, mature leaves, which, in many plants, will gradually yellow and drop from the plant. Developing seeds, as well as storage organs of perennial plants, such as bulbs and roots and the stems of woody plants, can be active importers of sugars during specific times of the year.

Most people know that plants produce oxygen from photosynthesis, but few realize that plants consume oxygen as well. In order to use sugars for growth, plants must break them down into small units. This process, called respiration, requires oxygen. Oxygen is rarely in short supply for aboveground shoots. But waterlogged soil can starve roots of the oxygen they need for respiration. This is why well-drained, well-aerated soil is crucial to the healthy growth of so many plants.

Light and Chlorophyll
Pigments in plant leaves absorb sunlight and transform it into the chemical energy needed to make sugars. The most important of these pigments is chlorophyll, which absorbs all the wavelengths of light in the visible spectrum except green—hence the characteristic color of leaves.

Different species have different requirements for maintaining healthy chlorophyll. Nitrogen and iron help produce chlorophyll in

Carefully pruned boxwood hedges and flowering plum trees grace this formally designed backyard garden in Virginia. Although home garden styles can vary widely— from this type of patterned, controlled layout to much more natural, free-flowing arrangements—all should be thoughtfully planned and cared for.

The informality of this small southwestern meadow garden matches the style of the adobe house it flanks. The yarrow, rudbeckia, gaillardia, evening primrose, and flax require annual reseeding and weeding to keep the meadow full and healthy.

The shrub border in a traditional, easy-to-care-for garden in the Pacific Northwest combines a white-flowering deutzia, pink rhododendrons, and a blossoming box-elder tree. The well-manicured lawn sets off the border while enticing visitors into the backyard.

Once established, a
mixed bed of well-chosen
perennials, annuals,
and roses can be
surprisingly easy to
maintain. Included here
are sages, veronica,
hollyhocks, and grasses.

Wise choices for a shady
garden include ferns,
some types of azaleas,
and small understory
trees like the Japanese
maples seen here.
Growing plants in
shade requires some
special tasks, but
appropriate plant
selection is the most
important factor.

The shadows cast by the ornamental plum, birch, and laburnum trees in the Canadian garden below provide a perfect environment for hostas, polygonum, and other shade-loving perennials.

Built on a hillside, the shrub and tree garden shown at right surrounds the deck with foliage of varied shapes and colors.

A patio parterre, or geometric arrangement of beds and paths, holds tulips, boxwood hedges, and dogwood trees. Such a design is perfectly suited to small, level areas close to a house, where it can be enjoyed from inside as well as out. This garden also serves to supply cut flowers for indoor arrangements.

Dramatic wisteria vines and a pink dogwood tree fill an entryway with springtime color. Both plants are adaptable to many climates, given good garden soil. Wisteria may also be grown as a small weeping tree or as a ground cover. It does require several years to reach blooming stage.

A flowering shrub garden in the Pacific Northwest features the azaleas, rhododendrons, viburnums, and other species that grow so well in the cool, moist climate. This climate closely matches that of Japan, where many of these plants originated. It is always a good idea to choose plants whose requirements can be met naturally by the local climate.

Shrub roses are used as foundation plants in this profusely blooming front-yard landscape, while climbing roses grace the side-yard trellis. Plants in the perennial beds, seen in the foreground, include echium, stachys, and foxglove. The neat, healthy lawn serves to set off the profuse flower beds.

In dry climates, using plants native to the area—and to those where conditions are similar—is the best way to save water and time and to ensure success. The native and Mediterranean plants thriving in this Southern California garden are agave, wallflowers, rock rose, and lavender.

The plants in this coastal California yard bloom throughout the winter and spring months and require no water beyond what falls as rain in the area.

A prairie-style garden in the Midwest incorporates natives such as coneflowers, gay-feather, bee balm, and black-eyed susans in a regional variation on the English-style border.

A garden of native plants in Northern California blends in nicely with the surrounding scenery. Native plants are becoming more easily available through local *or mail-order nurseries, and their natural look is gaining popularity with many gardeners.*

leaves, and leaves that are deficient in them often turn yellow. Too little light can result in too little photosynthesis, but too much light can destroy the pigments by photooxidation. Unfortunately, shading plants to control light levels does not always work. Not all of the light energy absorbed by the chlorophyll is transformed into chemical energy. Some is lost as heat, so the effects of light are complicated by temperature. Many plants need high light levels but cannot cope with the high leaf temperatures that accompany the light in many parts of the world. This is why a Texas gardener cannot grow alpine species in a rock garden.

Chlorophyll is not the only light-absorbing compound in plants. A pigment called phytochrome is believed to play a major role in the sensing of day length by plants. The effect of day length on plants is termed photoperiodism, and one of the most common uses gardeners make of it is to control flowering. Some plants, such as chrysanthemums, are short-day plants, so called because they flower only if the day length, or photoperiod, is shorter than a certain length of time. Thus, they bloom in fall. Others, such as rudbeckias, are long-day plants, requiring a long photoperiod (long summer days) in order to flower. Day-neutral plants, such as roses (which bloom spring, summer, and fall) will flower regardless of photoperiod.

Photoperiodism also influences flower development, stem elongation, leaf growth, and the formation of storage organs such as bulbs, as well as dormancy and cold-hardiness. This phenomenon helps explain the difference in development and flowering times of plants in the garden, but it is seldom useful for manipulating growth and flowering in your backyard. Techniques for controlling light are widely used, however, in greenhouse production of cut flowers and flowering potted plants.

Temperature and Growth Cycles

Each plant species has a minimum, a maximum, and an optimum temperature for growth. If the temperature is too low, the enzymes that aid chemical reactions in plant cells cannot work, and growth ceases or does not start. If the temperature is too high, the enzymes can actually be destroyed. Temperatures below optimum can slow growth and delay flowering and fruit development.

Temperature is also important to other aspects of plant development, often in conjunction with photoperiod. Plants needing several weeks of cool temperatures to flower are said to require vernalization. In the nonflowering stage, these plants typically form rosettes, which are clumps of leafy growth on shortened stems. In the flowering phase, the stem rapidly elongates and flowers form, a process called bolting. Many winter annuals, such as bluebonnets, need vernalization and must be planted and germinated in the autumn in order to flower the following spring. Biennials produce only foliage during their first growing season and must be exposed to cold temperatures in order to flower the second season. Many perennials also require vernalization, though they may not form rosettes. For many species of all types, the increasing photoperiods of spring and summer after winter cold are also required. Frequently, however, long photoperiods can substitute for exposure to cold temperature.

Like species that have adapted to survive high summer temperatures, many species have adapted to survive the rigors of winter. In general, these hardy plants are able to stop active growth or become dormant when the days shorten in late summer and early autumn and resume it again when days lengthen in the spring. One way that plants survive winter is by storing food in special underground structures such as bulbs, tubers, corms, or rhizomes. A bulb is an enlarged, modified bud containing a vertical stem surrounded by a dense mass of scale-like leaves such as a tulip. Tubers are usually modified stem tissue such as in sweet potato or dahlia. A corm is a swollen, vertical stem base enclosed by dry scale-like leaves such as a gladiolus or crocus. And a rhizome is a specialized stem with a main axis that grows horizontally at or just below ground level as in lily-of-the-valley or many types of grasses. Other mechanisms that plants use to survive cold winters include the shedding of tender aboveground parts, hardening of others, and changes in metabolism. Many nursery plants are commonly dug and stored for late shipment during the dormant period.

Although it may look as if nothing is happening in a dormant plant, it is still respiring, albeit at a much slower rate. For this reason, it is better to buy larger bulbs or perennial crowns, which have larger stored reserves to draw on during dormancy and subsequent growth. Many dormant plants must be exposed to cold temperatures for a specific length of time before they will resume growth. In this way, a plant responds to the changing seasons and adapts for survival.

Plant Hardiness Zones

Hardiness zones provide a convenient way to assess whether a plant will survive the cold temperatures in your area. A hardiness zone groups together locations whose average annual minimum temperatures fall within a certain range. The United States Department of Agriculture produces the most frequently cited hardiness-zone map (see pages 36–37), which includes 10 main zones. The temperature that can kill a hardened plant is a characteristic of each species. These minimum temperatures have been determined by experiment and experience for many species and have been correlated with the hardiness zones. A species said to be hardy to zone 5, for example, can be expected, in general, to survive winter temperatures between −20° and −10° F. You can sometimes extend a plant's hardiness by a zone or more by screening it from the winter wind, by mulching, or by other techniques that mitigate local conditions.

Soil and Nutrition

Soil provides a medium in which plant roots can grow, retains a solution of water and nutrients that can be absorbed by roots, and supports the plant's aboveground growth. Most water and nutrient uptake is in the extensive network of root hairs developed by young, actively growing roots. As roots age, they lose their root hairs and become covered with a material that repels water. They continue to absorb soil solution, although at a much reduced rate, through gaps in this covering and through the holes left when branch roots die. For a plant to grow vigorously, it must maintain an actively growing root system. Well-aerated soil, which supplies oxygen to the young roots, is essential. There are, of course, plants that have become specially adapted for growing in heavy or waterlogged soils.

Because we cannot see most of the organisms in it, it is easy to forget that soil is a living system. Healthy soil is home to many living organisms. Large ones, such as earthworms, are vastly outnumbered by small ones, such as bacteria and fungi. Some of these organisms form symbiotic, or mutually beneficial, relationships with plants. Some fungi, for example, grow into plant roots, where they benefit from the sugars the plant produces; at the same time, the extensive growth of the fungus in the soil increases the uptake of nutrients into the plant.

Experimenting in the Garden

As you go about your gardening chores, be observant and don't be afraid to experiment. Read and gather information. This knowledge and experience will help you make decisions about which techniques you should use in your garden and which plants will grow best there. Chances are you will save yourself a lot of work in the long run. You will also gain an appreciation of why plants respond as they do to your efforts and to the conditions around them.

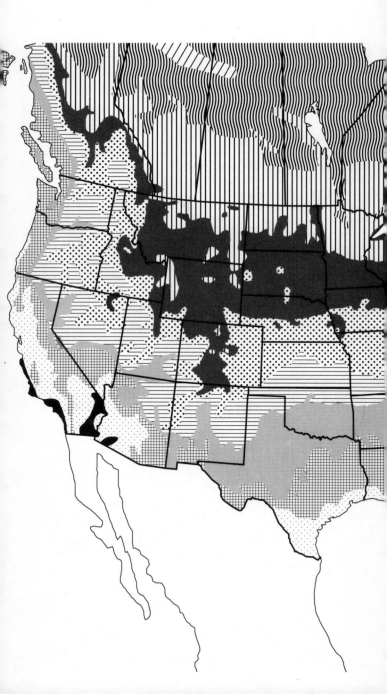

The map below, based on the revised United States Department of Agriculture zone map, provides a broad guideline to temperature extremes in your area.

The key below gives you the average minimum temperatures of the ten zones.

Determine if your area corresponds to its zone allocation by comparing your coldest temperatures with those given in the key.

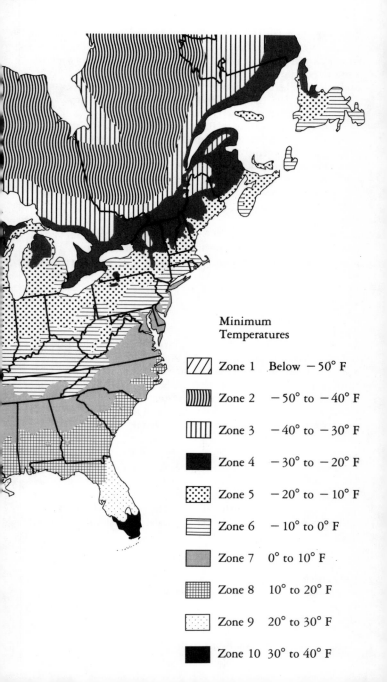

Minimum Temperatures

Zone 1   Below −50° F

Zone 2   −50° to −40° F

Zone 3   −40° to −30° F

Zone 4   −30° to −20° F

Zone 5   −20° to −10° F

Zone 6   −10° to 0° F

Zone 7   0° to 10° F

Zone 8   10° to 20° F

Zone 9   20° to 30° F

Zone 10   30° to 40° F

Preparing the

Soil is the layer of transition between the rock core of the earth and the thin web of life on its surface. It is a very thin layer, measured in inches or feet, but it is the basis for all that stands between life and lifelessness.

Soil is a complex and dynamic mixture of several components: rock and mineral particles, water and dissolved substances, air, living organisms, and decomposed organic matter. An "ideal" soil is said to contain a little less than 50 percent solid particles, about 25 percent liquid, 25 percent air, and less than 5 percent living organisms and organic matter. In actual soils, of course, the relative proportions of these components vary among different regions, and the makeup of any given soil changes with the weather and the seasons.

Soil Texture

Soil is composed primarily of broken-down rocks; mineral particles constitute more than 95 percent of the bulk of most soils. The size of these particles determines the texture of any particular soil. All soil particles are relatively small, but soil scientists categorize them in three groupings. From largest to smallest these are sand, silt, and clay.

Sand

Soil particles ranging in diameter from 0.08 to 0.002 inch are called sand. Sandy soil has a coarse, grainy, gritty texture. If you squeeze a handful and release it, sandy soil falls apart and runs through your fingers. Wet or dry, sandy soil is easy to dig and to till, and easy for plant roots to penetrate. Water and air readily pass through the large pores between sand particles; sandy soil dries out quickly after a rain and doesn't hold a large reservoir of water.

Silt

Particles called silt range in diameter from 0.002 to 0.00008 inch. Silty soil has a slippery texture, like talcum powder. If you squeeze a handful and release it, it slides apart. When silty soil is very dry, water beads and runs off the surface rather than penetrating; but once silty soil is moistened, it absorbs and retains more water than does sandy soil.

Clay

Soil particles termed clay are microscopic—at less than 0.00008 inch in diameter. Clay soil feels sticky when wet and holds its shape when you mold or model it. When dry, clay hardens into dense, bricklike clods. Clay tends to swell when wet, but it shrinks and cracks apart when dry. It is important to time the cultivation of clay soil carefully so that the moisture level is just right—not too wet or too dry.

Soil

Loam

All garden soils are mixtures of particles of different sizes. Loam is
the name for soils comprised of moderate amounts of sand, silt,
and clay. Loam soils contain less than 52 percent sand, between 28
and 50 percent silt, and 7 to 27 percent clay. Loamy soils are
considered ideal for gardening because they are both easy to till
and effective in retaining water and nutrients.

Water and Air in the Soil

The spaces, or pores, between particles of soil can be filled with
water or air. When precipitation or irrigation wets soil, water runs
down through the larger spaces but clings in the smaller ones.
Gravity pulls water down, while adhesion (the tendency of water to
stick to a surface) slows its movement. Water doesn't spread far
laterally through soil, except when it is running down a slope. After
rain or irrigation has ceased, water continues to move through the
soil for hours or days. Excess water drains down through the larger
pore spaces until it reaches the water table, unless its flow is
impeded by a change in soil texture or structure. Draining water
slows down when it reaches a transition zone between finer and
coarser soils—no matter which lies above the other—and "perches"
in the soil immediately above that zone.

Plant roots need water, but they also need oxygen, which they get
from air. If soil is waterlogged, meaning its pores are filled with
water, plants will suffer. Deprived of oxygen, roots—and thereby
whole plants—drown. Unlike animals, plants drown over a period
of days. Worse, bacteria in waterlogged soil give off hydrogen
sulfide, a rotten-egg-smelling gas that is poisonous to roots. And
dead roots are vulnerable to infection by fungal organisms, which
can proceed into living tissue and kill off an already weakened plant.

Organic Matter and Humus

Organic matter is a catchall term for living organisms and plant and
animal residues in various stages of decomposition. As the tiny
animals and microorganisms that live in the soil gradually bite,
chew, and digest dead leaves, stems, roots, and other debris, they
break this material down into unidentifiable crumbs. In the process,
nutrients such as nitrogen, phosphorus, and sulfur are released from
complex molecules as simple ions that can be absorbed by plants. At
the same time, the breakdown of organic matter produces sulfuric,
carbonic, and nitric acids, which help dissolve rocks and release the
minerals needed for plants to grow well.

The volume of residues is greatly reduced until all that is left is
humus, a complex and concentrated molecular stew with a
characteristic dark-brown or black color. (When humus coats or
clings to the surface of mineral particles, it makes soil look dark.)
Humus itself continues to decompose at a rate that depends on

temperature—as slowly as 1 percent a year in very cool climates or as fast as 25 percent a year in the tropics. The value of decomposing humus is that it provides a steady supply of nutrients for plant growth.

Although organic matter and humus furnish nutrients, an even more important benefit is that organic matter changes the physical condition or structure of the soil. Increasing the organic content of a given soil makes it easier to till and easier for roots to penetrate. Water soaks in faster and more deeply.

Soil Structure

The way in which individual soil particles are clustered or arranged into aggregates is called soil structure. The kinds of soil structure range from single-grain soil, where each particle is separate from the others, as in beach sand, to massive soil, where the entire soil mass clings together like modeling clay. Intermediate structures are called granular, platy, blocky, or prismatic, designations that refer to the kind and shape of the aggregates.

A granular, crumblike soil structure is most desirable in the garden. Soil that is well aggregated—that crushes easily but will hold together if pressed—is said to be friable, or to have good tilth. Either term means that the soil is easy to till and ideal for root growth. Adding plenty of organic matter is a good way to improve your soil's structure.

Soil structure can change over time, for better and for worse. Aggregates that form naturally contribute to good soil structure. Alternate cycles of freezing and thawing or of wetting and drying tend to clump particles together. Humus compounds released from organic residues help to cement and bind the mineral particles, thereby stabilizing the aggregates. Also, plant roots push and shape the soil into aggregates. Fine grass roots especially tend to bind soil into little clumps. Aggregates that form naturally contribute to good soil structure.

Aggregates are liable to melt, collapse, or break apart if the soil is disturbed when it is wet. Even a heavy rainfall is enough to destroy the structure of surface soil, forming a puddle that hardens into a crust as it dries. Bare soil is easily damaged, so a covering of plants or mulch protects it from damage. When the aggregates are destroyed, the soil gets compacted and it becomes more difficult for water and air to penetrate. Aggregates of clay soil are particularly vulnerable to disturbance, so it is important not to till or cultivate clay soil when it is wet.

Soil Chemistry

Soil is a reservoir for the water and nutrients that plants need. The water comes from natural precipitation and irrigation. The nutrients come from mineral particles, organic matter, and fertilizers. Only nutrients that are dissolved in the soil water are available for plants to absorb. Water and dissolved nutrients form a thin film that coats the surface of soil particles and adheres to the tiny spaces between them.

Soils differ greatly in their capacity for storing and providing water and nutrients. In general, clay soils and soils high in organic matter can retain more water and nutrients than sandy soils or pure mineral soils. This is because clay particles and organic matter have a greater total surface area and more small pore spaces than sandy soil does.

Soil pH

A molecule of water is made up of two hydrogen atoms and one oxygen atom. Normally these atoms cling together with great tenacity, but substances in the soil can cause water molecules to come apart, or ionize, into two parts—hydrogen ions and hydroxyl ions.

The relative numbers of hydrogen and hydroxyl ions determine the acidity or alkalinity of the soil solution (the soil water and everything that is dissolved in it). If there are more hydrogen ions than hydroxyl ions, the solution is said to be acid. If hydroxyl ions outnumber hydrogen ions, the solution is said to be alkaline (or basic). If the number of hydrogen and hydroxyl ions is the same, the solution is neutral.

Although the effect of hydrogen and hydroxyl ions is great, the actual numbers of ions are very small. Such a tiny fraction of the molecules in water are broken apart at any given time that representing the concentration of ions as a fraction or a percentage would require some awkward numbers. Instead, scientists use a system called the pH scale to rate soil acidity and alkalinity. The pH scale goes from 0 to 14. At pH 7, the midpoint, there are equal numbers of hydrogen and hydroxyl ions. As pH numbers decrease from 7 to 0, the concentration of hydrogen ions increases, meaning the solution is more acid. As the numbers increase from 7 to 14, the concentration of hydroxyl ions increases, meaning the solution is more alkaline. Each number on the scale differs from the preceding one by a factor of 10. That is, pH 5 is 10 times as acid as pH 6 and pH 4 is 100 times as acid.

"Sour" and "sweet" are old-fashioned terms for acid and alkaline soils, and old-time gardeners claimed to be able to determine the pH of a soil by tasting it. Acid substances do taste sour, but you'd be unlikely to detect this in soil. Alkaline substances actually taste bitter, not sweet. A chemical soil test is the only accurate way to measure soil pH.

Soil pH typically varies from about 4 to 8, although it can range lower or higher. Regions of high rainfall tend to have more acid

Preparing the Soil

Below is a list of some of the materials that you can add to your soil to improve its nutrient level, texture, pH, and other important factors.

soil, while regions with dry climates tend to have alkaline soil. This is because alkaline substances such as calcium carbonate (lime or limestone) dissolve and leach or drain out of the soil faster than do acidic substances. Many plants that grow best at a certain pH level may tolerate conditions two or three points on either side of it.

The contemporary issue of acid rain has received considerable publicity. Acid rain can damage plant foliage, and it also makes lake and pond water more acid and damages aquatic life. The effect of acid rain on forest or farm soil is usually minor, particularly since acid-rain-prone regions are likely to have acid soil already. In towns or cities, however, acid rain dissolves calcium from the limestone and concrete that are commonly used in building and paving. As the dissolved calcium accumulates in the soil, it increases alkalinity, causing a net rise in soil pH in urban settings.

Soil Fertility

At least 16 elements are considered necessary for the growth of green plants: carbon, hydrogen, oxygen, nitrogen, phosphorus,

---

Plant Nutrients

Macronutrients: Needed in larger quantities

Nitrogen (N)
Phosphorus (P)
Potassium (K)
Calcium (Ca)
Magnesium (Mg)
Sulfur (S)

Micronutrients: Needed in smaller quantities

Iron (Fe)
Manganese (Mn)
Zinc (Zn)
Copper (Cu)
Molybdenum (Mo)
Boron (B)
Chlorine (Cl)

A measure of the difference between macro- and micronutrients is that nitrogen shows up in plant tissue at 15,000 parts per million, whereas molybdenum appears at 0.1 ppm.

sulfur, potassium, calcium, magnesium, iron, manganese, zinc, copper, molybdenum, boron, and chlorine. Plants obtain the first three—carbon, hydrogen, and oxygen—from carbon dioxide and water. All the rest are absorbed from the soil. These elements are called nutrients, and soil rich in nutrients is called fertile soil. The chart at left indicates which of the soil nutrients are needed in larger quantities (macronutrients), and which are necessary in much smaller amounts (micronutrients).

The sand and silt particles in soil contain most of the plant nutrients as part of their structure, and they release these nutrients very, very slowly as the minerals decompose. Though clay particles contain very few nutrients, dissolved nutrients cling to the particles. Organic matter contains nearly all the nitrogen and much of the phosphorus and sulfur that plants receive.

Soil fertility is a complex subject. Many soils have adequate quantities of some nutrients but insufficient amounts of others. For example, many soils have adequate phosphorus to support healthy plants but are deficient in nitrogen. In cases such as this, providing fertilizer that supplies the missing element can greatly enhance plant performance. (There is much more information on fertilizers in a later chapter of this guide.) Even though a nutrient is present in the soil, it may not be in a form that is available to plants. Plants need iron, for example, but roots can't absorb iron oxide (rust), which is one of the most common forms of iron in the soil. Interactions among the different nutrients can also limit availability. If a soil is high in calcium, for instance, plants may have difficulty absorbing magnesium and potassium. As a further complication, nutrient availability changes at different pH levels.

Fortunately, plants have a remarkable ability to extract nutrients from the soil. They actively pump in nutrients and concentrate them at levels as much as 30,000 times greater inside their root system than in the soil immediately outside. Different plants require different amounts and proportions of the essential nutrients, but many garden plants do fine in soil of average fertility.

As a final note on the topic of fertility, it's worth mentioning soil color. Soil comes in many colors, depending on its origins and history. Aside from basic brown, the most common colors are black, red and yellow, and white. Most gardeners think that the blacker the soil, the more fertile it is. This is not necessarily so. Black soils aren't always fertile, and soils of other colors are sometimes quite fertile. If you're new to a region and the soil color is unusual to you, ask a local gardener, farmer, or extension agent about the soil's fertility before you take any steps to alter its composition.

Life in the Soil

Soil not only supports life, it contains life. A huge and diverse population of organisms, ranging from microscopic bacteria to wriggling worms, are at home in the soil. Their presence is beneficial in many ways, and they should be encouraged in the garden. They recycle nutrients, mix and churn soil particles, and improve soil structure.

Soil Microorganisms

Healthy soil teems with microorganisms. Most numerous are bacteria, so small that they are barely visible by microscope. There can be as many as a billion bacteria in a teaspoonful of soil, but they are so tiny that they constitute only 0.03 percent of the weight of fertile soil. They reproduce and die off at a phenomenal rate, and their populations can double or halve in an hour's time. Most bacteria occur in clumps or colonies in contact with organic residues or plant roots. A few kinds of bacteria perform chemical conversions that are useful to plants. In particular, some bacteria transform atmospheric nitrogen, a gas that plants can't make use of, into nitrates, a nutrient that plants readily absorb and need for growth. Soil fungi produce tangled masses of threadlike filaments called mycelia that interweave among the soil particles and sometimes extend over a distance of several feet. One ounce of soil can contain 1,500 yards of fungal mycelia. Soil fungi are important in the breakdown of plant residues. Fungi can function at lower moisture levels than can bacteria, but they need oxygen and are inactive in waterlogged soil.

Most microorganisms are clustered in the area immediately closest to plant roots and interact with plant growth. Soil organisms give off compounds that either stimulate or inhibit root growth. Some "good guys" act as a shield that defends plants from harmful organisms. Plant roots in turn may leak substances that are beneficial to microorganisms. Specific partnerships between plant roots and soil fungi are called mycorrhizae. The fungal mycelia extend the surface area of the plant roots, reaching many inches farther into the soil and collecting nutrients, particularly phosphorus, which are shared with the plant. In return, the plant provides sugar—an energy source—to the fungus. Mycorrhizal relationships are very common in nature, and are very helpful to plants growing in infertile soil. Current research is exploring the possibility of encouraging or introducing mycorrhizal relationships in garden settings.

Some soil microbes are harmful to plants. Soil-borne diseases cause root rots, and also rots and blights that penetrate stems and affect aboveground plant parts, usually causing wilting or even death. Anthracnose, fusarium, and verticillium are common soil-borne diseases that affect a wide variety of plants. Some plant species and varieties show resistance to these diseases, but there are few treatments to protect or to cure susceptible plants, and it is almost impossible to eradicate these diseases from infected soil. The risk of disease is one reason why federal and state laws restrict the transfer of soil across state lines.

Earthworms and Other Animals in the Soil
Earthworms of many kinds are found in all types of soils, as long as there is moisture and enough organic matter for them to feed on. The more organic matter, the more earthworms. Their populations can reach several hundred thousand per acre. They are most active near the surface, but they can burrow down to six feet deep. Their vertical burrowing carries and mixes material up and down through the soil. Earthworms excrete granular pellets called castings, which are valued as fertilizer in garden folklore, but which in fact aren't especially high in nutrients. Earthworms are better interpreted as an indicator of good soil fertility than as its cause. Their main contribution is an improvement in soil aeration and tilth.

Other small animals in the soil are nematodes, springtails, millipedes, centipedes, pill bugs, snails, slugs, mites, spiders, ants, and many other kinds of insects. Individually these organisms are small, but collectively they have a great effect on the makeup of the soil. They feed on living and dead plant parts, on litter, on bacteria and other soil microorganisms, and on one another. They mix the soil and transport material up and down and laterally. Their tunneling opens passageways that enhance air and water infiltration. A few soil-dwellers, such as nematodes and grubs that damage plant roots, are pests. But the vast majority of soil animals have a beneficial impact in the garden.

Soil Horizons and Soil Profiles
Layers in the upper crust of the earth are generally called soil horizons; the layers at any given point make up what is called a soil profile of that area. Most soil profiles include two or more horizons. The differences between horizons are most easily observed in soils that haven't been disturbed for decades, such as those underneath pastureland or forests. When soil is disturbed by cultivation or construction, the horizons often get mixed up and the distinctions become blurred.

As the drawing on page 46 shows, the O horizon is the layer of undecomposed plant litter that accumulates on the surface of the ground. Where present, this layer serves as a mulch and supplies organic matter and nutrients to the soil. Many soils, however, don't have an O horizon.

The A horizon is the most important layer. This is the topsoil, the layer where most roots grow and where soil organisms thrive. It

Preparing the Soil

Gardeners call the different layers of the earth "soil horizons." These layers differ in texture, structure, color, composition, and fertility. Not all layers are always present.

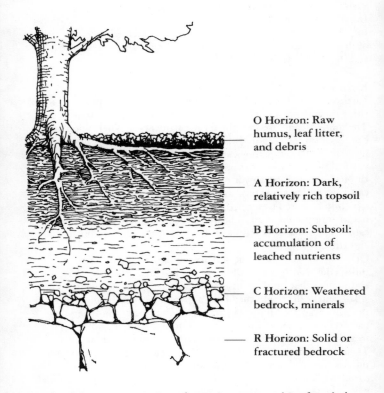

O Horizon: Raw humus, leaf litter, and debris

A Horizon: Dark, relatively rich topsoil

B Horizon: Subsoil: accumulation of leached nutrients

C Horizon: Weathered bedrock, minerals

R Horizon: Solid or fractured bedrock

has the richest concentration of organic matter and is often darker in color than the underlying horizons. The A horizon may be as deep as several feet, particularly in prairie regions; it may be several inches thick; or it may be missing altogether due to such disturbances such as erosion or bulldozing.

The B horizon is the subsoil. It lies immediately beneath the topsoil and usually has a different color and texture. Often the B horizon includes fine clay particles and iron and aluminum compounds that have sifted or leached down from the A horizon. Many plants can root into the B horizon and obtain water and nutrients there, but some soils lack a B horizon.

The C horizon is the parent rock material, broken or cracked into chunks. Some deep-rooted plants penetrate into the C horizon, but few microorganisms live there.

The R horizon is bedrock. You'll know when you've reached it. The composition of the underlying rock and its response to weathering influence the kind of soil that develops. It could take many centuries for rocks to break down into soil particles.

Soil Classification and Soil Maps

There are thousands of different kinds of soils in the United States. Soil scientists have developed a system for classifying soil that compares with the systems biologists use to classify plants and animals. Soil classification takes into account the parent rock, how the soil was developed, its depth, its constituent layers or horizons, its texture, its structure, its organic and nutrient content, and more. The U.S. Department of Agriculture's Soil Survey has produced detailed maps that show soil types on a national, state, or local scale. Your county extension agent or soil conservation service agent has maps of the soil in your area, and can help you identify your soil type and understand its geologic history and special attributes.

How to Evaluate Your Soil

Before beginning a garden, spend some time observing and assessing the soil. You can evaluate the soil's texture, depth, profile, drainage, and exposure, and check for compaction and contamination. Tests of soil acidity and nutrient levels can be done at home, or for more accurate results you can send a representative soil sample to a state or private testing lab.

Soil conditions vary across even a small garden, due to natural factors or as a consequence of human activity. Watch for differences in the soil itself and in how plants grow in different parts of the garden, and note areas that need one form or another of soil improvement.

Testing Soil Texture

One way to assess your soil's texture is to take a handful of earth and feel how it responds when you rub and squeeze it. If it feels gritty, it is high in sand. If it feels sticky, it is high in clay. Here is another way to test soil texture: Take spoonfuls of soil from a few inches below the surface at several spots in your garden. Remove any pebbles, debris, leaves, or roots, and break up any lumps. Mix the samples together, then put a cup of the soil and a cup or two of water into a clear glass jar. Secure the lid and shake vigorously until all the soil is suspended in the water.

Set the jar on a table and get a ruler. After about a minute, the largest soil particles will have settled to the bottom of the jar. Measure and record the depth of that layer, which is the sand. (See the drawing on page 48.) Leave the jar undisturbed for roughly an hour, and the intermediate-size particles will settle out. Measure and record the depth of soil, subtract the amount that was sand, and you have the measurement of the silt layer. Let the jar sit for another 24 hours and take a final measurement. This time, subtract the amounts of sand and silt to obtain the depth of clay particles.

To calculate the percentages of sand, silt, and clay, divide the depth of each layer by the total depth of soil, then multiply by

Preparing the Soil *To evaluate your soil's texture, mix a sample of soil with water in a glass jar. Shake the mixture vigorously and then allow to settle. Measure each layer of particles as it settles, in the time frame indicated; divide the depth of each layer by the total depth of the soil in the jar, and multiply this number by 100. The number you get will be the percentage that each layer occupies.*

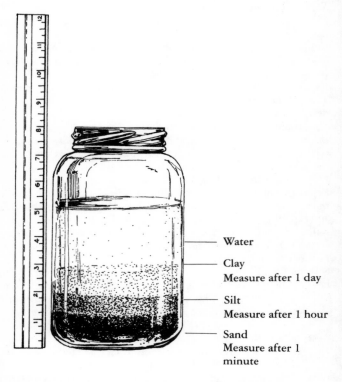

Water

Clay
Measure after 1 day

Silt
Measure after 1 hour

Sand
Measure after 1 minute

100. For example, if the sand layer is 1/2 inch deep and the soil totals 3 inches deep, the proportion of sand is 1/2 divided by 3, or 0.17; multiplying by 100 gives 17 percent sand.

Looking at Your Soil Profile

It is easy to examine the profile of your soil. Just dig a straight-sided hole from one to several feet deep (depending on local conditions) and look at the soil that is exposed. Are there variations in color and texture? How deep are the different layers? What you observe will inform you about the soil's history and about the conditions your plants' roots will encounter. The presence or absence of different horizons and their depths are measures of the soil's potential to supply the support, water, and nutrients that all plants need.

Watch especially for hardpans—dense layers that are particularly difficult to penetrate with a spade or a shovel. These compacted layers form barriers to water movement and root growth. If there is a compacted layer, note how deep it is, and how thick. Check to see if it underlies the entire garden, or if it is limited to certain areas.

Testing Drainage

A simple way to test whether your soil has adequate drainage is to dig one or more test holes about two feet deep. Fill the hole(s) with water and check to see if any water remains in the bottom of the hole after 24 hours. If all the water is gone, the drainage is fine. If just a little water remains, the drainage will be adequate for some plants but not for all. If most of the water remains, drainage is so poor that many plants will suffer.

It is also important to watch the flow of water during and after heavy rainfall. Note the areas where water runs off quickly and the low spots where water collects. You will want to plant them accordingly with plants that tolerate drier or wetter soil.

Checking for Contamination

Soil around houses and other buildings or near roads or driveways is sometimes contaminated with trash and debris, concrete, oil, or lead. Check for buried trash that was abandoned after construction or renovation projects. Remove any chunks of concrete or plaster, since these release alkaline lime into the adjacent soil. Look near driveways or parking areas for oil-stained soil, which must be dug up and removed.

Lead contamination is a possibility in some areas. Lead occurs naturally in all soils, but normally it is found at very low levels. Lead in the soil usually doesn't damage plants, but it may accumulate in their roots and leaves. Lead is poisonous to humans, causing blood and kidney problems in adults and affecting the brain and nervous system in children.

In urban areas, automotive exhaust is the main source of lead pollution, although the rate of contamination has declined considerably since most vehicles have switched to unleaded gas. Lead levels are quite high in the soil adjacent to busy streets and freeways. Another source of lead pollution is the lead-based paints used in years past on many older buildings. Each time the paint flakes or is scraped off, chips land on the ground near the foundation. When the chips break down into dust, lead is released. Before growing food plants in either of these situations—close to a busy street or close to an old painted building—have the soil tested for lead. Contact your county agent or county health department for the address of a testing lab in your area. If your soil sample tests positive for lead, use that site only for ornamental plants, and grow vegetables in a different spot. Never eat vegetables grown in lead-contaminated soil.

Testing Soil pH and Nutrient Levels
An experienced gardener can judge soil pH and fertility by looking
at the plants growing in that soil. Plants show characteristic
symptoms in response to certain soil conditions, and plant
performance is the ultimate test. It takes years of practice to develop
an eye for these symptoms, however, and different plants respond
differently to the same soil. A much more reliable way to identify
pH and fertility is to test the soil at home or send a sample to a lab.
Several brands of home soil-test kits are available at low cost from
garden centers and mail-order catalogs. Most use indicator dyes,
which change color under different conditions, and provide color
charts for reading the results. On a per-test basis, home soil-test
kits cost about the same as most state testing services but less than
most private labs. The home tests are much less accurate than
laboratory results. However, if you test repeatedly, you will soon
become more adept at doing the tests and reading and interpreting
the results.

Testing labs report soil pH and availability of major nutrients, and
recommend how much lime, sulfur, or fertilizer to add to improve
the soil for growing whatever plants you specify. A single test can
serve as a baseline appraisal of your soil. A series of tests repeated
over time will monitor the effect of the treatments you apply. Keep
notes on the test results, the treatments, and on how your plants
look and grow, and you'll develop the eye of an experienced
gardener.

Whether you test at home or at a lab, collecting a representative
soil sample is essential for meaningful results. Dig a few inches
deep (but avoid sampling from the subsoil) and gather small
amounts of soil from 10 or more places around the garden. Then
mix these to make a composite sample. If you want to compare
different parts of the garden—for example, an area that has been
limed and fertilized with one that hasn't—prepare samples for
each area and keep them separate. (Be sure to label which is
which.)

How to Improve Your Soil

Many people move into new homes and discover that their soil is
too sandy, too clayey, too shallow, too infertile, too wet, or too
compacted for plants to grow easily and well. This is discouraging
at first, but with a little work, nearly every type of soil can be
improved.

There are several approaches to soil improvement. One is to buy
organic, inorganic, and chemical materials to mix with your
existing soil. Slower but less expensive approaches are to grow
green manures and to make compost. Adding chemical and
organic amendments can help neutralize overly acid or alkaline
soils. Rototilling, hand digging, and well-timed cultivation can all

help loosen and aerate soil. Installing drains or planting in raised beds improves the movement of water and air through the soil.

Deciding Which Areas to Improve
You don't need to prepare all areas of your garden to the same extent. Focus soil-improvement efforts on those areas where they will have the most effect. Some plants need deeper, looser, richer soil than others. Annual flowers and vegetables benefit the most from soil preparation. These plants have fine roots that are too weak to penetrate hard soil, and they look best and produce most if pampered with optimum conditions.

Perennial beds, lawns, and ground covers also benefit from soil improvement. It is worth spending extra time and effort digging deep, loosening compacted subsoil, and adding plenty of organic matter to the topsoil before installing these plantings, because, once established, they will last for years. Given deep, loose, well-drained and fertile soil, perennials survive much better through winter cold, summer heat, and droughts.

Most trees and shrubs do better if planted into native, unamended soil. Nurserymen used to recommend adding quantities of peat moss or compost to the soil when the hole around the root ball was refilled. In recent years, however, researchers have observed that trees planted in holes filled with fluffed-up soil never root out into the surrounding territory. Such trees are limited to the supply of water and nutrients in the volume of the hole, as if they were growing in containers.

Materials to Improve Your Soil
Topsoil, soil blends, and amendments (materials such as peat moss that are used to improve existing soil) are cheaper in bulk than in bags, although bagged material may be more convenient to transport. If you're buying in quantity, ask at the nursery about truckload delivery. Have the pile unloaded near the driveway, and use a wheelbarrow or a cart to move the material to the garden beds.

You can add as much as 25 percent amendment to the soil in a new bed. Adding 25 percent means spreading a three-inch layer of material on the surface and working the bed 12 inches deep (one-half cubic yard of amendment per 100 square feet of bed). This will make a big difference in how the soil feels and works.

Topsoil
The easiest and fastest way to start a garden on a site with poor soil is to buy large quantities of topsoil or soil blends to fill beds and prepare planting areas. Buying topsoil can be an uncertain business. You may get an unwelcome crop of weeds as well as stones and debris, and the soil itself may be less than "top" quality.

Materials to Improve Soil

•**Topsoil:** upper layer of soil

•**Soil blends (also called improved soil):** topsoil plus composted tree leaves, sawdust or bark chips, manure, or other organic materials

•**Organic materials:** peat moss, reed-sedge peat, composted bark

•**Compost:** homemade or locally produced

•**Agricultural waste:** bedding and manures from cattle, poultry, or horse farms; processing wastes from canneries, hulls and stalks from cotton gins and grain mills

•**Sawdust or bark chips:** add a source of nitrogen, such as ammonium sulfate, to speed breakdown

•**Sand:** coarse, clean, and washed. Add to clay soil only in quantities of at least one-quarter by volume

•**Chemical soil conditioners:** lime (calcium carbonate); gypsum (calcium sulfate)

•**Biological soil conditioners:** may help release nutrients from soil, improve soil structure, and detoxify soil that had been treated with synthetic fertilizers and pesticides

•**Green manures (also called cover crops):** quick-growing plants that produce a large amount of top growth and extensive root systems, which protect the soil

Before buying a truckload, ask where the soil is coming from. You might even want to visit the collection site to see for yourself what you're buying.

Soil blends (frequently called improved soil) are usually more expensive than plain topsoil, but they're a worthwhile investment for small areas such as flower beds. Check your phone book for local nurseries and landscape contractors to ask if they sell truckloads of improved soil. Depending on what part of the country you live in, the soil blend might include composted tree leaves, sawdust, bark chips, manure, and other organic materials. The price will depend on the mixture and the quantity you buy.

Organic Materials

Adding organic material—peat moss, reed-sedge peat, composted bark, or other compost—helps soil in many ways. It increases the microbial activity, which in turn improves the soil structure and makes it easier for water, air, and roots to penetrate. It also increases the soil's water- and nutrient-holding capacity, and it provides a small source of nutrients, particularly of micronutrients. The different forms of organic material all have desirable effects, so choosing among them is a matter of price, availability, and convenience.

Peat is compost that forms naturally in wet areas. Most peat comes from sphagnum moss, a coarse-textured moss that grows in shallow freshwater bogs throughout the northern United States, Canada, and Europe. Old, dark, dead, compressed sphagnum moss is called peat moss, sphagnum peat, or simply peat. Peat moss is sold under several brand names in bags, bales, and in bulk. Reed-sedge peat is also collected from natural deposits of decomposed reeds, sedges, cattails, and similar marsh plants. When relatively young, reed-sedge peat is coarse-textured with lots of visible stems. It breaks down quickly into a fine-textured, dense, humusy muck. Reed-sedge peat generally is much less expensive than sphagnum peat. Keep in mind that all forms of sphagnum moss and peat are acidic and may affect soil pH. Also, it is difficult to moisten dry peat products—water tends to bead up on the surface rather than penetrating—but once wet, peat retains moisture well.

You can make your own compost (see details later in this chapter) or buy locally produced compost as an inexpensive alternative to peat moss. If you buy, look for local sources. Many municipalities, for example, now make and sell compost from lawn clippings, tree leaves, and chipped brush. Some towns sell composted sewage sludge, usually as a dark granular substance that bears little trace of its origins.

Consider recycling agricultural waste, such as bedding and manures from cattle, poultry, or horse farms; processing wastes from canneries; spent mushroom compost; and hulls and stalks from cotton gins and grain mills. You might need to drive a pickup truck to the source, but chances are the price will be low. If you have a choice between fresh and aged material, take the older, darker stuff. It will have a more immediate benefit on the soil structure. If only fresh material is available, use it as a mulch, or layer it in a compost pile for a season before adding it to your garden.

Sawdust and bark chips are cheap and abundant in some parts of the country. Fresh or coarse wood chips need to decompose for several months before they can be worked into the soil. The microorganisms that decompose wood need nitrogen to do the job and can "steal" nitrogen that would otherwise be available to plants. Adding a source of nitrogen speeds up the breakdown of sawdust or bark chips. Use one pound of ammonium sulfate for each one-inch-deep layer of wood chips spread over 100 square feet. Wait until the chips have turned dark, soft, and crumbly before you mix them into the soil. Composted sawdust or bark chips increase soil aeration and improve soil structure, but neither absorbs or retains water or nutrients as well as sphagnum moss. Because clay soil can be difficult to work with, gardeners are often tempted to try improving it by adding some sand. Unfortunately, adding a small percentage of sand to clay soil produces a cementlike mixture. Don't add any sand to clay unless you can add at least one-quarter by volume. Look for coarse, clean, washed sand—the washing removes salt and fine particles.

Chemical Soil Conditioners

Either calcium carbonate (lime) or calcium sulfate (gypsum) can be used to improve the structure of clay soil. Both release calcium ions, which cause tiny clay particles to clump together into crumblike aggregates. This improves water and air penetration, and makes the soil more hospitable for roots to grow in. Adding lime raises the pH of acid soil, which is a useful correction. Gypsum has no effect on pH, so it is recommended for neutral or alkaline soils.

Biological Soil Conditioners

Various kinds of products are manufactured and sold as biological soil conditioners. According to the manufacturers' promotional materials, these contain natural enzymes that release nutrients from the soil, improve soil structure, and detoxify soil previously treated with synthetic fertilizers and pesticides. The value of these products has not been confirmed by long-term trials in actual garden situations, and they may or may not prove to be beneficial.

Green Manures

One way to improve poor soil before starting a garden is to devote a season or two to growing green manures, sometimes called cover crops. These plants cover the soil, protecting it from wind and water erosion, and enrich it by supplying nutrients much as animal manures do. The plants should grow quickly, producing a large amount of top growth and an extensive root system within a few months after seeding. When cut down and turned into the soil, they decompose and provide energy to soil microorganisms, produce acids that dissolve mineral nutrients from the soil, and increase the amount of humus in the soil. Green manures work best in warm, humid climates. In dry climates, they require extra irrigation. In cold climates, it takes a long time for green-manure crops to break down, so permanent planting is postponed while the green manures work their magic.

To plant a green manure, till or hand-dig the soil, then rake the surface smooth. To ensure an even stand, divide the recommended quantity of seeds in half. Sow half as you walk back and forth from north to south, and the other half as you walk from east to west. Then use the flat side of a rake or a wide board to press the seeds into the soil, and water regularly to get the little seedlings off to a good start.

It is usually best to turn under the green-manure crop just before it begins to bloom. The top growth is most tender at that stage and will decompose most quickly. (You may need to mow dense, tall stands.) Then dig or till the bed to mix the plants—tops and roots—with the soil. Allow one or more weeks for the turned-under plants to wilt and begin to decompose before you plant the bed.

Plants to Use as Green Manures

Grain crops make good green manures. Rye, wheat, and barley often are sown in the fall and turned under in the spring. Oats are sown in the spring and turned under in summer. These plants all make a dense stand of grassy foliage aboveground and a soil-binding mass of fine roots underground. Buckwheat, a broad-leaved grain, is one of the fastest-growing green manures, but it requires hot weather to germinate. Sown in early summer, it can grow two to three feet tall and be ready to be turned under within 10 weeks.

Several legumes, including different kinds of clover, alfalfa, sweet clover, cowpeas, and vetch, are useful as green manures. Legume roots are colonized by bacteria that fix nitrogen from the air into a form that can be used by plants. When a legume cover crop is turned into the soil, some of that nitrogen is made available to other plants.

Preparing the Soil

Changing Soil pH

A soil test will indicate the pH of your garden soil. Then you can decide whether to work with the existing condition or change it. Chances are good that plants that are doing well in other gardens in your neighborhood are fairly tolerant of the existing soil pH. Choosing these plants is an easy way to begin, but changing the soil pH somewhat in order to grow less common plants is not too difficult.

Lime is used to treat acid soil and sulfur is used to treat alkaline soil. Both are inexpensive chemicals that can be purchased at local garden centers. The amount of lime or sulfur needed to change soil pH depends on the soil's texture and the amount of organic matter it contains. The finer the soil texture or the greater the amount of organic material, the more lime or sulfur will be needed to raise or lower pH by one point. Check directions on the package to determine how much material to apply per square foot of your type of soil. Also, because a change of one point in pH represents a tenfold change in acidity or alkalinity, it takes a lot more lime or sulfur to change pH by two points than by one. These variables lead to one important conclusion: Test your soil at regular intervals. It is the only way to monitor the effects of the treatments you apply.

Improving Acid Soil—Raising Soil pH

There are several forms of lime appropriate for use in the garden. Fine-ground limestone (calcium carbonate) and dolomitic limestone (which contains both calcium carbonate and magnesium carbonate) are the cheapest, easiest, safest to use, and most readily available. Dolomitic limestone's advantage is that it supplies magnesium, an essential plant nutrient, in addition to reducing soil acidity. Both of these materials are ground-up rocks; the more finely ground, the better, since smaller particles react more quickly than larger ones to neutralize soil acids. (Avoid quick lime and hydrated lime, which are caustic powders that can damage your skin and your plants.)

Lime can be applied to the surface of the soil and watered in, but it is more effective if you spread it and then cultivate to mix it thoroughly with the soil. You can apply lime in any season. If you want to raise the pH of acid soil by more than one point, it is a good idea to apply small doses of lime once or twice a year, retesting the soil pH from time to time to monitor the changes. Lime has a slow and gradual effect on soil pH, but it eventually does its job.

Wood ash can neutralize acid soil as well. Hardwood ashes (from broad-leaved trees) generally are more effective than softwood ashes (from conifers). Wood ash supplies some potassium, an essential plant nutrient, as it reduces acidity.

Improving Alkaline Soil—Lowering Soil pH

Applying sulfur is the fastest way to lower soil pH. Elemental sulfur, often called flowers of sulfur, is a yellow powder that reacts quickly with water to form sulfuric acid, which acidifies the soil. Sulfur can lower soil pH in as little as six to eight weeks, but the treatment isn't long-lasting and must be repeated after six months to a year. Sulfur-containing compounds, such as ammonium sulfate, aluminum sulfate, and iron sulfate, also reduce soil pH. These compounds are sometimes used as fertilizers or recommended as spot treatments for particular plants. They have a rapid but short-term effect, lasting as little as three to four weeks in extremely alkaline soils.

Peat moss, composted sawdust or bark, composted leaves, and pine needles all release carbonic acid as they decompose. Added to alkaline soil as an amendment or mulch, they have a slow but long-term effect on lowering soil pH. Cottonseed meal—the grounds left over after cottonseed oil has been pressed from the seeds—is another organic product that reduces soil pH.

Loosening Compacted Soil

Ideally, garden soil has plenty of openings, or pores, between the particles of mineral or organic matter. Water and air flow through these openings, and plant roots have an easy job penetrating in all directions. Some soils, however, may be compacted so that the pore spaces are closed off. This compaction may occur due to natural forces or to human activity; either way, it has undesirable consequences. If soil is compacted near the surface, rainfall or irrigation water runs off instead of soaking in. Conversely, if drainage is blocked by a subsurface compacted layer, the surface soil is liable to get waterlogged. Tough-rooted trees and shrubs can penetrate these dense layers, but many annual and perennial plants cannot.

It is easier to prevent soil compaction than to cure it. Construction equipment, vehicle traffic, and foot traffic all pack soil down enough to damage it. A house-building crew's pickup trucks can flatten your future garden. If at all possible, prevent such damage by restricting vehicle movement to driveways and designated parking spots, and by restricting foot traffic to clearly marked paths.

The fastest way to treat large areas of compacted soil is to hire tractor-drawn equipment that can break through the compacted zone. This will leave the surface rough, and you will have to follow the tractor with smaller power or hand tools to smooth the area. An alternative, if you have more time and patience, is to plant a crop of a deep-rooted legume such as sweet clover or alfalfa. After a year or two of vigorous growth, the roots of these plants will have penetrated several feet down into the soil. Both the roots and tops

Preparing the Soil

Drainage ditches and pipe systems can be constructed to drain into a dry well. Find the lowest point of the area to be drained; dig a hole 4–5 feet deep and at least 3 feet across. Fill the hole two-thirds of the way with rubble; cover this material with gravel and cover the gravel with topsoil.

contribute organic matter that you can till into the soil before planting a lawn or making beds or borders. For smaller areas, hand digging or rototilling are good ways to loosen compacted soil. (See the following chapter for more information on digging garden beds.)

Adding plenty of organic matter is the best way to improve soil structure and help it stay loose and porous for a period of months or even years. To retain the benefits of tilling, don't walk on the surface of newly worked beds. Designate permanent paths and walkways, and set stepping-stones in key locations. Minimize foot traffic so that the soil will stay loose and the plants will have an easy time sending roots into it. Hard rainstorms can also pack down newly tilled soil. Spreading even a thin layer of mulch over the surface will help protect the soil from the rain's impact.

Improving Water Penetration

Water tends to run off the surface of a sloping garden, unless the soil is so permeable that water soaks in very rapidly. Improving

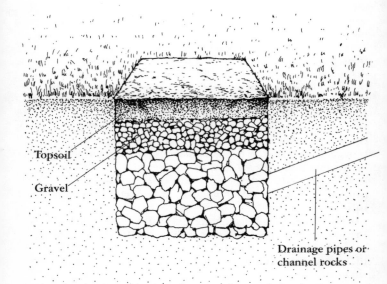

Topsoil

Gravel

Drainage pipes or channel rocks

soil structure and loosening compacted soil help increase water penetration. Keeping the soil covered with growing plants or mulch will slow the movement of water. Keep the soil covered throughout the year (even during the winter) to maximize the amount of precipitation that soaks in and recharges the stored reserves. Making terraces is even more beneficial on sloping sites, as terraces catch runoff and give the water time to soak into the soil.

In arid climates where every drop of rainfall is important, try digging sunken beds 24 to 30 inches deep and filling the beds with a mixture of soil and compost. Make the top of each bed a few inches lower than the original grade. Compact the soil bordering the beds and the paths by walking on it, so that when rain does come, water will run off the surface of these untilled areas and be channeled into the beds.

Improving Water Drainage

Water accumulates in low spots and flat places, and where the soil is compacted, shallow, or underlain by an impermeable layer. Most plants die if their roots are underwater for an extended period of time. To correct major problems with standing water, you may need the services of a landscape architect, who can advise you on how to change the grade and drainage patterns of your property. You can easily solve minor problems by digging drainage ditches, installing drains, or planting in raised beds or on mounds.

Drainage Ditches

Open drainage ditches can be wide, shallow swales leading to an outlet, stream, or reservoir of some kind. If heavy runoff is an intermittent occurrence, the ditches can be planted with turf or low-growing ground covers. During dry spells, the planted ditches will not be objectionable to look at.

Drain Tiles and Dry Wells

If runoff is frequent, open ditches may be muddy and undesirable, making buried clay or plastic drain tiles preferable. Check with a local nursery about the type, size, and layout of the tiles that are best for your site. To install drain tiles, first dig trenches through the area to be drained and fill the bottom of each trench with a layer of coarse gravel. Next set the drain tiles in place. Check to be sure that the tiles slope downhill and that water flows freely. Then cover the drain tiles with more gravel (to prevent soil from washing in and filling them up) and refill the trench. It is best to install drain tiles deeper than the depth to which you dig or cultivate in the area.

If there is no place to direct water downstream and away from your garden site, you can lead the drain tiles into a dry well. Locate the dry well at the lowest point of the area to be drained. Dig a hole at least several feet deep and at least three feet in diameter and fill it with rocks, gravel, or rubble. Top the fill with a layer of gravel and then topsoil. A dry well holds runoff from the surrounding area until the accumulating water can gradually seep down into the water table.

Raised Beds
Planting in beds where the soil level is higher than the surrounding grade solves the problem of wet surface soil. This is especially helpful during cool, wet weather, when soil tends to remain saturated longer. Soil near the top of raised beds drains fast enough so that roots aren't waterlogged. Soil deeper in the beds continues to supply water over a period of time as needed. Depending on the severity of the drainage problem you're trying to overcome, you can raise the beds anywhere from 3 to 12 inches or more. (See the following chapter for more on making raised beds.)

You can plant individual shrubs and trees higher than usual by setting them on shallow mounds of soil and piling more soil over and around the roots. This protects a plant's crown—the junction between roots and stems—from excess moisture, and guarantees that the fine roots near the surface will be in well-drained soil. Deeper roots can reach down for water in the underlying soil.

Potting Soil for Container Plants
If you want to grow plants in containers such as flowerpots, hanging baskets, window boxes, or half-barrels, you need potting soil. Ordinary garden soil doesn't work well in containers because it packs into a dense mass that limits water and air penetration. By contrast, potting soil is crumbly and porous enough for rapid drainage and generous aeration.

You can make your own potting soil or buy it in bags at the local garden center. Either way, there are advantages to using the same mix for as many of your plants as possible. It isn't necessary to have special mixes for different kinds of plants, and standardizing the soil simplifies your watering, fertilizing, and repotting routines. Potting soil is cheap compared with the plants you buy and the time you spend growing and tending them. It's false economy to let valuable plants languish in inferior soil. Mix or buy the best soil you can find, and your plants will respond with superior growth and appearance.

Making Your Own Potting Soil
To mix your own potting soil simply combine equal parts of loamy garden soil, compost or peat moss, and coarse sand. The soil

You can correct very poor drainage with a system of clay or tile pipes. Dig a trench 2–3 feet deep that runs from the highest to the lowest ground. Lay 4-inch pipes end to end on a layer of gravel; cover with a porous layer of rubble or coarse gravel; cover this layer with topsoil. If you install networks of pipes that lead to the main pipe, use smaller (3-inch) pipes.

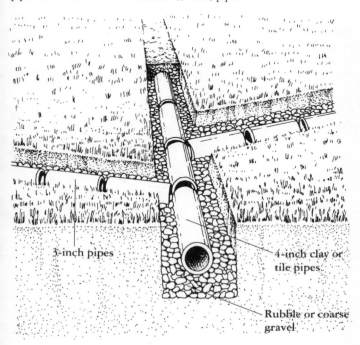

3-inch pipes

4-inch clay or tile pipes

Rubble or coarse gravel

provides nutrients, the compost aids in water retention, and the sand is for drainage.

Start with some of the best soil from your garden, and sift it through a 1/4-inch mesh screen to sort out any sticks and stones. Some gardeners take the extra precaution of pasteurizing the soil to kill any insects, weed seeds, or organisms that might cause disease. Heating damp soil to a temperature of 180° F for 30 minutes will do the job. You can heat it in an oven or microwave, or over the barbecue grill outdoors—hot soil gives off some odors that you might not want in the house. It's a good idea to sift any chunks from the compost or peat moss, but it isn't necessary to pasteurize these ingredients.

For sand, choose the coarsest grit you can get. Anything that passes through the mesh of a window-screen sieve is too fine. Using sand adds considerable weight to a potting soil mix. The added weight is an advantage for tall, top-heavy plants that might otherwise blow or tip over, but it's a disadvantage when you have to carry or move the potted plants. Instead of using sand, you might buy a bag of perlite, a kind of crushed volcanic rock that's very lightweight.

Shopping for Potting Soil
Most bags of ready-mixed potting soil don't contain any real soil
at all. They're "soil-less" mixes, generally composed of peat moss,
ground pine bark, and vermiculite and/or perlite, with lime and
nutrients added. Nearly all modern nurseries use soil-less mixes
because they are of consistent quality, lightweight, and sterile.
Several brands give good results, but it takes practice to learn the
best way to water and fertilize plants growing in these soil-less
mixes.
One approach is to visit your favorite local nursery, ask what kind
of potting soil they use, and ask if they'll sell you some. The
nursery staff can answer your questions on the best way to water
and fertilize plants in that soil mix. Also, plants you buy from that
nursery will have an easy adjustment if you repot them in the same
soil they've been growing in.
Whether or not you buy through a nursery, when you find a mix
you like, buy it in quantity to get the best price. A 40-pound bale
may cost only three or four times as much as a 4-pound bag. Share
the savings by shopping with a gardening friend, or stockpile the
surplus for future use. Kept dry, most soil mixes can be stored
indefinitely.

Compost
Every gardener should consider making compost. This highly
decomposed organic matter has the crumble and feel of fertile
garden soil, and plants grow exceptionally well where it is used. It
is a powerful fertilizer and soil conditioner, and it contains growth
hormones for plants. It often deters pests—bug-free plants have
been seen growing in compost near gardens devastated by insects.
Moreover, compost puts otherwise unwanted material—kitchen
wastes, tough plant stalks, and leaves, for example—to good use,
saving space in the town landfill.
There are two basic approaches to composting: hot and cold. At
their simplest, both involve making large piles of organic matter.
Grass clippings, crop residues, hay, manure, and leaves are just
some of the many materials that can be composted. (See pages
69–71.) In hot composting, the pile is constructed to produce a
high initial level of biological activity that raises the temperature
of the decomposing materials to over $100°$ F. The high temperature
hastens decomposition, and if high enough, it can kill weed seeds
and pathogens.
Hot composting requires a lot of planning, attention, and work.
Most of the difficulties and much of the work are associated with
the necessity of providing adequate moisture and aeration at high
temperatures. Water is one of the by-products of decomposition,
but so much is lost through vaporization that the pile can easily
dry out. Furthermore, the biological activity in the pile is so

intense and the consequent demand for oxygen so high that oxygen is easily depleted—a hot compost pile is like a furnace that sucks up all the oxygen in its vicinity. A pile that lacks oxygen can lose large amounts of nitrogen and humus.

In cold composting, less carefully prepared piles of material decompose more slowly at lower temperatures. Cold composting requires much less work than does hot composting because the demand for moisture and oxygen is less severe. With modest precautions, cold composting should conserve more nitrogen and humus than hot composting. The moderate temperatures also allow for greater biological diversity, and these organisms help control pathogens in the compost as well as in the areas where the compost is applied. Finally, some methods of cold composting can dispose of tough plant stalks that, unshredded, can be a nuisance in a hot-compost pile.

Cold composting takes a long time—a few months to about a year—rather than the few weeks to a few months required for hot composting. A far more serious problem, however, is the likely presence of viable weed seeds in the finished compost. In addition, animals may be attracted to kitchen and certain other wastes before these are adequately decomposed.

Whether you choose hot or cold composting will depend on how quickly you need the finished compost, on whether you need or wish to kill weed seeds and pathogens in the materials being composted, and on how much attention and work you are willing or able to devote to making compost.

Retaining Nitrogen and Humus

Regardless of which method you choose, you will want to minimize the loss of valuable nitrogen and humus that occurs during composting. Nitrogen can be lost from a compost pile in three ways. A pile that is too alkaline will lose nitrogen to the air in the form of gaseous ammonia. A pile exposed to too much rain will leach nitrogen into the ground in the form of ammonium and nitrate. A pile lacking in oxygen will also lose nitrogen to the air as a gas. This "denitrification" is the result of bacteria that, in the absence of other sources, obtain their oxygen from nitrates. The microorganisms that convert raw composting materials to humus require carbon and nitrogen to do so. Lost nitrogen leads to lost humus.

Excessive alkalinity can be a problem with animal manures, but otherwise, with reasonable care, ammonia and leaching losses should be minimal. Minimizing denitrification, however, can require considerable care. The higher the rate of biological activity, the more rapidly free oxygen is depleted. There may be no warning of such depletion. Denitrification can occur at oxygen levels that aren't low enough to produce bad odors. The result is good compost but with lower than optimum nitrogen and organic matter. The most obvious solution to denitrification is to make sure that the pile is adequately aerated. It would also help to minimize nitrate levels by using nitrogenous materials with low levels of soluble nitrogen.

Cold Composting

Cold composting involves little more than making piles of suitable material and letting them sit until they decompose, aided by an occasional turning to put material on the outside of the pile inside. Anything that can be composted hot can be composted cold. Provided with enough oxygen, microbes will eventually break down the material and create compost. Adding soil liberally to the pile usually ensures an adequate supply of oxygen, especially with wet or compactible materials. Even without added soil, a pile of sawdust will break down sufficiently in about a year to be useful as a mulch, although it takes much longer to become earthy compost. Leaves also will rot alone in a pile—probably the best way to compost them—normally in less than a year.

Trench Composting

In addition to composting aboveground, you can dig a trench, fill it with organic matter, and cover it with a layer of soil. Some people trench-compost manure. This is also a good way to break down tough, fibrous, unshredded plant parts.

If you trench-compost between rows of annuals, the following year you can plant over the trenches and dig new trenches in the rows containing the previous year's plants. You can also plant leguminous annuals, such as sweet peas or scarlet runner beans, over newly made trenches. The composting process ties up nitrogen, but legumes can draw nitrogen from the air. You should treat the seeds with an inoculant of nitrogen-fixing bacteria, unless this or a similar legume grew on this spot within the last few years.

Hot Composting

If you have not tried hot composting before, it is best to start with a simple method. It may call for more nitrogen than is necessary as a hedge to ensure that it works. You can think about refinements once you have succeeded with your first pile.

Start with loose hay and fresh animal manure in a ratio of roughly three to one by volume. That's about fives bales of hay per cubic yard of manure. If the hay is succulent and a rich green, you can use less manure. With horse manure, use about half as much hay; in fact, horse manure containing bedding hay may need no additional hay. Avoid manure from caged, egg-laying hens, which is difficult to work with.

Approximately two cubic yards of loose material will settle into a pile about three and a half feet high, tapering from about four and a half feet across at the bottom to three feet across at the top. You can make bigger piles, but don't make them much smaller as they won't heat up properly. One cubic yard usually is considered the minimum size, but this depends on the climate. In general, two cubic yards of material will produce enough finished compost to cover 1,000 square feet of garden with a uniform layer a small fraction of an inch thick. This is enough to maintain soil fertility for plants that aren't too demanding. If you want to improve your soil, compost at least four cubic yards of material for each 1,000 square feet.

Select a level site, avoiding low spots where water can collect. Lay down closely spaced rows of bricks, poles, or timbers to let oxygen into the pile from below. (Brush also works, but can be a nuisance when you are turning or removing the pile.) Spread several inches of hay first, then add manure and hay together. Scatter one forkful of manure for every three of hay. Water periodically unless the hay is succulent and the manure moist. The material should feel like a damp sponge, but if you squeeze it tightly, it shouldn't drip. Be careful with water. If a compost pile does not heat up, the most probable cause is improper watering. If you are unsure about the amount, remember that it is easier to add water later than to remove it.

When all the material is piled up, cover it with a layer of hay to protect it from rain. Then punch numerous vertical holes in the pile with a crowbar to aerate it.

Within a day or two, you should be able to thrust your arm into the pile and feel it warming up. In another few days, the central area should be too hot to insert your arm comfortably. If the pile doesn't heat up, check the moisture. If the pile is is too dry, add water. If it is too wet, you will have to turn it to dry it out; as you do, you can add about one forkful of loamy soil for every ten of compost material. This will help absorb some of the excess moisture.

Check the pile regularly. When it begins to dry out, or the temperature drops, remake it, placing the material that was near the surface of the old pile in the middle of the new one. Water if necessary, and make holes for aeration. The temperature should rise as it did in the first pile. When it falls and the center is just warm, the compost is finished.

The pile will shrink to half or less of its original volume. A certain amount of loss during composting cannot be helped, because the energy consumed by the microorganisms comes from the raw materials. Some of the loss can be avoided, however, by employing one or more of the refinements on pages 66 to 68.

Preparing the Soil

Troubleshooting

The following problems (and suggested solutions) are commonly
encountered in hot composting.

•The pile has an offensive odor: An ammonia-like odor indicates
that the pH is too high, probably due to the natural action of
animal manure (particularly poultry manure), or to overliming if
your compost includes soil that has been limed. Biological activity
should eventually drop the pH and reduce the odor. To speed the
process, you could turn the pile and mix in loamy soil or plant
residues to absorb some of the ammonia. Next time, use less
manure. Other odors indicate that the pile is too wet. Turn it and
add about 10 percent loamy soil.

•Flies and gnats are attracted to the pile in unusual numbers: The
pile is probably too wet and generating odors that attract these
insects. Turn the pile and add about 10 percent loamy soil.

•The pile does not warm up: One cause may be that it is too wet;
add soil as above. Another reason may be that it is too dry; add
water. The materials might also contain significant amounts of
pesticides, which only time will break down.

•The pile warms only a little: The pile is not large enough; add
more material. Alternatively, the ratio of materials supplying
carbon (plant parts) to those supplying nitrogen (manure) may be
too high; turn the pile, adding more manure or other nitrogenous
material.

•The pile heats up properly, but eventually a whitish deposit can
be seen under the surface: The pile is too dry. The whitish deposit
indicates the presence of actinomycetes, which are more tolerant of
dry conditions than are other organisms. Turn the pile and add
water.

Composting Refinements

Once you have succeeded with the method of hot composting
outlined above, you may want to refine your technique. These
suggestions can make composting easier and more efficient.

Compost Bins

Bins make it easier to turn the piles and to compost material that
might get blown away or attract animals. Some people find that
bins are neater and more attractive than exposed piles. On the
other hand, bins cost money and take time to build. Once built,
they can be difficult to move or alter in size. You can make

The simplest compost bin of all is a cylinder, 3 feet or more in diameter, made of chicken wire or fence wire. A lining of cardboard will help to prevent moisture loss.

satisfactory compost with or without a bin, and using one is mostly a matter of personal preference.

You will need at least two bins, one to start the compost and another to turn it into after the first heating. If you turn frequently and make compost continuously, you will need a third bin to store finished compost. Some people also keep a bin for building a pile slowly as materials become available. Each bin should be at least three feet wide, three feet long, and three feet high, to hold enough material to heat up properly. Bins can range from simple wire enclosures to more involved wooden structures, as shown below and on page 68. To reduce moisture loss in very hot weather, line wire bins with cardboard.

Protection from the Environment

Because moisture content is critical to the process, a hot-compost pile should be protected from the rain, if only by a plastic sheet flipped over it during a storm. It should also be protected from the drying effect of wind and excessively hot weather. A roof, like that shown in the drawing, helps protect the pile from rain, wind, and sun. To moderate extreme temperatures, you could also put the pile in a shady spot or, in the deep South, in a pit one to one and a

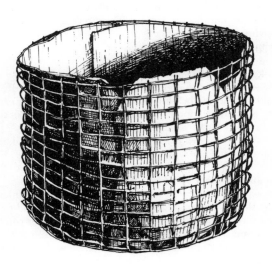

Preparing the Soil   *This sturdy and simple permanent compost bin is made of two-by-fours and 1-by-4-inch slats. The roof protects compost from wind, sun, and rain. The slats are removable; this*   *construction makes it easy to turn the compost or to move it from one compartment to the next.*

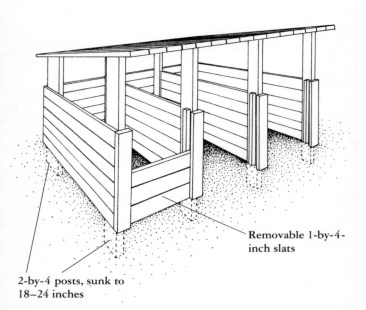

Removable 1-by-4-inch slats

2-by-4 posts, sunk to 18–24 inches

half feet deep. If you locate a relatively permanent pile in the shade of a tree, place it near the trunk and raise it so that there is air between the pile and the ground. This prevents feeder roots from growing into the pile.

Preparing Material for Composting
Plant stalks, leaves, straw, and other large materials compost best when broken into small pieces. Gasoline- or electric-powered shredding machines are helpful, but probably not worth the expense unless you regularly compost a lot of bulky material. You can shred leaves and smaller stalks with a lawn mower, or bruise bulky material with a sharpened garden spade. It also helps to break up material already in a pile with a mattock before you turn it.

Aeration and Internal Temperature
Adequate aeration is essential for providing oxygen to the microbes that digest the raw materials and produce the compost, and for conserving nitrogen and humus during the process. After you have built a pile, you can punch air holes with a crowbar. You can also build a pile around a number of loose poles, then withdraw the poles to create air holes. This works well for larger piles.
The most effective yet labor-intensive aeration technique is to turn the pile frequently. A thermometer that can measure up to

170° F is helpful in determining when to turn the pile. To promote maximum biological activity, turn the pile when the temperature at the center reaches 140° F. To kill weed seeds and pathogens, allow the temperature to climb to 160° to 170° F.

Meeting the Nitrogen Requirement

The two most common sources of nitrogen for composting are animal manures and fresh green-plant cuttings. A rule of thumb for manure is one part by volume of fresh manure to three parts of ordinary vegetable wastes. No such rule is known for green cuttings, although fresh green hay by itself, if in a large enough volume, will heat up.

When Is Compost Ready to Use?

Dark, crumbly, well-decomposed cold compost is ideal, but cold compost can be used as a mulch when it is less decomposed. When hot compost has dropped below 100° F, the hot-temperature phase has ended and the compost can be used. Some people prefer to wait until earthworms have had a chance to work on the material. Adding compost made by the cold method will inoculate a hot-composted pile with beneficial organisms killed by the heat. Composting does continue, however, so the longer you wait to spread it on the garden, the more organic matter it will lose.

Materials for Composting

Virtually any organic material can be composted, though some materials are not suitable. Coal ashes contain sulfur chemicals harmful to the soil and wood ashes are too strong a liming agent. Also, there is no need to compost wood ashes, because the nutrients are already soluble. Here is a list of materials used most often by gardeners.

Animal Manures

These are the most common source of nitrogen for composting. Cow, horse, and poultry manures are the most readily available. Poultry manure from caged, egg-laying hens is hard to work with and is very strong. You need only about one fifth as much cage-layer manure as cow manure. Dog and cat droppings may contain disease organisms that affect humans; they should not be included in compost used for food crops, although they may be satisfactory for ornamentals.

Nitrogen Fertilizer

Soluble nitrogen fertilizers can be used to supplement organic nitrogen sources, but too much fertilizer can promote denitrification.

Minerals
Minerals do not enhance the composting process. They can fortify
the finished compost, but you may want to test the compost to see
if it needs fortification. Rock powders may be rendered more
available to plants as a result of the high biological activity during
composting. One exception is triple phosphate, which is
sometimes used to acidify manure-containing compost and
minimize the loss of ammonia. Never apply lime. The danger of
overliming, and consequently losing nitrogen, is too great. The
pH of acidic compost tends to rise naturally as biological activity
proceeds.

Garden Residues
Dead plants, prunings, leaves, stalks, and similar garden detritus
all make good compost. Fresh, green garden residues are a good
source of nitrogen. Don't compost residues known to contain
diseases unless you are expert enough at attaining the high
temperatures required to destroy them. To be on the safe side,
burn diseased plants. Shred, chop, or cold-compost dense, fibrous
plant residues before putting them in a hot-compost pile.

Grass Clippings
Clippings from the lawn are excellent compost material and
usually rich in nitrogen. Mix them with a bulking agent, such as
hay or straw, before adding them to the pile; otherwise they are
liable to compact.

Hay and Straw
Hay is outstanding for composting. If fresh, green, and undried, it
will compost by itself, without even the addition of water. Straw is
also good for composting, but it is drier than hay and lacks nitrogen.

Human Wastes
Urine from healthy people is sterile, contains nitrogen and
potassium, and is suitable as a compost material. Feces have been
composted for centuries in China, but we in the West do not have
enough experience in protecting ourselves from their hazards.

Kitchen Wastes
Vegetable scraps often are rich in nitrogen and are an excellent
addition to compost. Do not include meat products. They attract
animals, and the fats hinder the composting process. If you cold-
compost kitchen wastes, mix them with a considerable amount of
soil to absorb odors and, if necessary, compost them in a bin to
keep animals away.

Sod

The best way to break down sod removed from a new garden is to cold-compost it with only the soil attached to its roots. The sod will break down within a few months. Turn the pile to put material on the surface into the center and to smother new growth.

Paper

Shredded paper products are good compost ingredients—especially when hot-composted—because cellulose is the principal substance broken down at high temperatures. Depending on the source, some magazine paper contains potentially dangerous heavy metals, but if you combine paper from a variety of sources, the danger is reduced.

Processing Wastes

Many processing wastes, such as feathers, wool wastes, marine products, slaughterhouse tankage, gluten meal, apple pomace, and peanut shells, compost well. Wastes that contain pesticides may interfere with the composting process and affect the finished compost.

Sawdust and Wood Shavings

Wood wastes are reasonably good compost materials, but they are especially low in nitrogen. Hardwoods are generally better for compost than are softwoods, which are much more resistant to attack by microorganisms. Softwood breaks down too slowly to be useful in hot composting, no matter how ample the nitrogen supply. Wood shavings are also slow to break down compared with sawdust, which has a much greater surface area.

Soil

A small amount (about 10 percent by weight) of loamy soil may be beneficial for hot composting. It dilutes the pile and decreases biological activity proportionally, but it does help to aerate the pile, and it absorbs excess water and ammonia. A cold-compost pile can contain any quantity of soil—50 percent soil is reasonable.

Tree Leaves

Deciduous leaves compost well. Evergreen needles decompose very slowly and are better used as a mulch, or turned fresh into a clayey soil to improve the soil structure. Leaves are usually best cold-composted by themselves, unless they are first shredded. Unshredded leaves form a dense, impermeable mat in compost, as well as in the soil, and hinder biological activity. You can compost leaves with succulent materials such as grass clippings, which are moist enough to eliminate the need for watering the pile.

Creating a

Making a garden is a wonderful way to enhance your yard. Whether you decide to plant a small plot of annual flowers or several large perennial borders, you will need to know how to make a garden bed.

There are three basic steps involved. Site selection and evaluation come first. Design and choice of plants are next. Last comes the plain old hard work of making the bed. Skimp on any of these, and you will probably be disappointed with the results. You will wind up spending more time and money in the long run than if you had invested more thought and care at the start. The process is educational and, for the most part, fun.

Selecting a Site

The process of making a bed begins with thinking rather than doing. What effect do you want this garden bed to have in the landscape? Will it serve to show off a particular type of plant—for instance, bearded irises, a collection of succulents, rhododendrons, or roses? If so, you must find or create a site that meets that plant's specific needs. Or would you rather experiment with combinations of various types and adapt plant choices to a site? Do you want the bed to be a private joy, for yourself and your family alone? Or do you want a beautiful public display? How about a combination of both? Think in terms of practicality as well as beauty. Pay attention to traffic patterns, both human and vehicular, around your home. Think about views of the garden. When you are in the yard, where do you spend your time? How do visitors usually approach the house? What is the view from the street? Don't forget the vistas from inside the house. Do you gaze out into the yard from the kitchen, sit by the bay window in the living room, eat by the glass doors of the dining area? Answers to these and similar questions should begin to suggest spots that could really be enhanced by a garden bed.

Finding a Sense of Place

At this point, you are probably beginning to visualize beds in several niches in your yard. But before you grab the shovel, think about the bed in another light. The most wonderful garden beds are not just beautiful, they also seem perfectly suited to their immediate surroundings of yard and home—they seem to belong in the local landscape.

Look around your neighborhood, your town, your region. Look at the gardens, the buildings, the natural landscape. What colors predominate—deep greens, gray-greens, golds, browns, reds? What styles of building are common—white clapboard colonials, brick ranch houses, adobe compounds? What are the characteristic natural shapes—jagged rocks, steep cliffs, serene horizons, calm lake surfaces? What kinds of native plants thrive? Which hybrid

Garden Bed

plants flourish? There has been a tendency for American gardens to be homogeneous, with the same few dozen plants combined in the same ways from sea to shining sea. Home gardeners have recently begun to depart from this limiting approach, recognizing instead the unique beauty of their own regions and choosing landscapes that are inspired by and complement them. Each region has its own history, style, flavor, and natural flora. Let your observations of your environment inspire your garden. It will be not only more beautiful but also healthier than more traditional gardens as a result, because the plants you choose will be at home in the particular conditions your yard provides.

Evaluating a Site

As you consider what type of bed to create and how you would like it to relate to its surroundings, promising sites on your property will come to mind. Now is the time to evaluate the practical qualities of these sites—sun and shade, soil, heat, humidity, and so on. Some people may find this stage less stimulating than the visualization stage and be tempted to skip it—but don't. A perennial bed, in particular, represents a big investment of time and money—it is worth postponing its installation a season to assure yourself that the plants will do well in the location you have chosen.

Sun and Shade

Observe the kind of light your site receives throughout the day and through the seasons. An exposed, north-facing bed near the house may be in full sun all summer, yet be shaded in the winter, early spring, or late fall. A site that lies in the dappled shade of a large deciduous tree during the summer will be much sunnier in the fall, winter, and early spring when the tree is leafless. Ideally, you should observe a site from at least June through December before making a bed. If you just cannot bear waiting, try to extrapolate from what you have observed and from what you know of the changes in the sun's path during the course of the year.

Next, consider the type of sun or shade. Summer, midday, or afternoon sun is much fiercer than fall, winter, or late-afternoon sun. Shade from a tree with a high, airy canopy is much different from that cast by a dense, low-branching evergreen. The former will allow you to grow a rich assortment of plants; the latter will kill off all but a few. Some plants tolerate a range of light conditions, but the majority have special likes and dislikes. Knowing the amount and quality of light your bed will receive will help you select appropriate plants—or a different site.

Microclimates

Plants are as particular about climate as they are about light. Hardiness zones—areas of North America sharing similar average

Creating a Garden Bed

minimum temperatures—have long been used as a guideline by gardeners when choosing plants. (The United States Department of Agriculture issues the most widely used hardiness-zone map, which is shown on page 36.) Books, magazines, catalogs, and nurseries often offer a hardiness-zone designation for a plant, which indicates that it is supposed to survive the lowest temperature listed for that zone. Use these ratings as an aid when selecting plants, but not as a bible. Many gardeners successfully grow plants supposedly too tender for their climate—and lose supposedly hardy ones.

Local variations in climate, often called microclimates, are the main reason why hardiness-zone designations can be unreliable. Microclimates can be as big as a valley or as small as a nook between a house and a fence. Temperature, wind, and humidity can combine to produce conditions in discrete areas that differ considerably from those that generally characterize a region. When you evaluate a site, you need to determine whether it is in a microclimate, and if so, what the characteristics of that microclimate are. Here are some things to look for:

Heat, which is not taken into account when hardiness-zone ratings are assigned, is a limiting factor in a plant's adaptability almost as often as cold is. A plant may survive the winter in an area but not be able to tolerate the heat in the summer. But heat may vary considerably from place to place on your property. South-facing exposures normally are warmer than other exposures. In northern and high-elevation gardens, a south-facing site frequently offers the best gardening possibilities. In warmer climates, a southern exposure can be too hot for most plants. An east-facing site offers gentle morning light and afternoon shade. West is warmer than east, and hot afternoon sun is harsher and hotter than morning light and therefore harder on some plants. A northern exposure is slowest to warm in the spring and quickest to cool in the fall.

In addition to exposure, structures and materials in or near the garden bed can affect the heat and light that reach it. A stone or brick wall, a concrete path, or a dark mulch can all intensify heat. A white wall reflecting light and heat into a shady site can make it suitable for more plants, but a mulch of white river rock in full sun can fry plants growing nearby. A dark mulch will warm the soil beneath it and make plants start growth earlier. A wall of somber gray stone will appear to steal what little light is available in a shady corner.

Microclimates are also caused by wind and slope. Exposure to prevailing winds can lower temperatures and dry out plants. On the plus side, wind helps keep insects and diseases at bay, and promotes strong, bushy growth. If need be, you can temper the wind's impact with fences and rows of sturdy, good-size plants. Gardening on a slope creates dramatic effects, but it has its drawbacks. Frequently, the top of a slope is windy, and the topsoil may be thin due to erosion. The bottom, where cool air and water collect, gets more frost and may have drainage problems, but often it has good soil.

Humidity is a third microclimatic factor. Plants vary remarkably in their reactions to humidity. Entire regions are known for their humid or arid conditions. Microclimates can offer some relief (a shady, sheltered area with trees will be more moist than a windy, sunny spot) or can intensify the condition. But it is difficult to modify humidity enough to satisfy certain plants. Some woodland plants that are comfortable in humid Eastern gardens, for example, just won't grow in the arid West, no matter how much you might change the soil or add water.

Soil

Of all the elements of the site that should be explored, none is more important than the one you find beneath your feet—the soil. Although there are plants that will grow in almost any soil, the vast majority prefer a loose, well-drained soil full of organic matter. Unfortunately, very few of us find this in our yards. But before you rush off in search of bales of peat or tons of rotted manure, spend some time getting to know your soil. Evaluate it as described in the previous chapter, and compare what you discover with what you know of the needs of the plants you wish to grow. Then decide what amendments and improvements are in order. Don't forget to observe and test for drainage—no amount of soil amendment can correct a bad drainage problem.

Existing Trees

Above ground, trees shade, cool, and humidify a site. Below ground, they affect the soil and the availability of water. Some trees, such as silver and Norway maples, horse chestnuts, sycamores, and Siberian elms, are well-known gluttons whose shallow root systems hog the nutrients, water, and space that other plants need to grow. Others, such as oaks and honey locusts, are more benign, their friendly root systems cohabiting with many other plants. Then there is the black walnut, an all-out chemical warrior whose roots secrete a substance that stunts the growth of nearby plants.

Even if you don't know what species a particular tree on your property is, you can tell a lot by just digging in the ground beneath it. If the soil isn't too dry and you still can't dig more than an inch or two before encountering a mass of roots, you've just met up with a glutton. Large surface roots snaking their way over the ground also indicate a suspect tree. If you must make a garden underneath such a tree, you have several options besides removing the tree and its roots. You can dig out the roots in an area, add a

Creating a Garden Bed

great deal of organic matter, and plant. (Be aware, however, that the tree roots eventually will return and out-compete what you plant.) You can cover the soil with a weed-suppressing landscape cloth and build a raised bed aboveground. Just don't cover too much of the tree's root area, or you will suffocate the tree. (The tree roots eventually will penetrate the cloth.) Or you can plant the few extremely tough plants that can get by on such a lean diet, such as periwinkle and sweet woodruff.

The soil beneath all trees, friend or foe, is likely to be dry and infertile, an inhospitable home for young plants. If you are planning a bed under a tree, provide an ample supply of organic matter and fertilizer, and replenish these annually to replace what the tree has taken during the growing season.

Designing the Bed

At this point, the strengths and weaknesses of your site should be familiar enough so that you can make an informed choice of which plants will grow well there. Now you can begin the creative process of combining plants. Here are some guidelines to bear in mind as your design becomes more concrete. (For more on the subject, see *Taylor's Guide to Garden Design*).

Consider all the possible views of your bed. Which ones are the best? Take into account the surroundings, large and small, near and far. Do you want to hide a downspout or a neighbor's garage, or to play up an existing shrub, or a spectacular view of a mountain? Keep in mind the style and ambience of your house and property, and the character of your neighborhood and region.

Deciding on Size and Shape

Always remember that garden beds require ongoing maintenance. The amount of maintenance can vary from the occasional watering and weeding of a well-mulched bed of tough shrubs to the daily deadheading and primping demanded by an elaborate perennial and rose border. Don't commit yourself to a huge, fancy plan if you won't have the time to care for it. A modest, well-tended garden bed is vastly superior to an ambitious, sloppy mess.

A rule of thumb for a bed that will need maintenance at least once a week is that it shouldn't be wider than eight feet unless you provide a path or stepping-stones for inner access. Frequent walking on the bed would compact the soil, starving roots and organisms of much-needed air. The center of an eight-foot-wide bed can be reached (at a stretch) from either edge. If your bed will border a wall or a hedge, leave at least 18 inches between the backdrop and plantings for access.

There are several other general rules for determining the size and shape of a bed. By and large a bed looks well proportioned and balanced when its width is at least twice the height of the tallest plants in it. Also, when viewed from an important vantage point, tall plants should have an expanse of bed in front of them equal to their height. For example, a bed featuring six-foot-tall shrubs will look skimpy if other plants occupy only a couple of feet in front of the shrubs, but will appear nicely filled out if there is at least six feet of garden in front of them. Straight lines and symmetrical layouts create formal, serene moods, while curves and asymmetry appear more dynamic and "natural."

Focal Points

Start your design by identifying existing focal points and placing new ones. Then pick and arrange plants to contrast with or complement them. The form, color, and texture of the plants in the bed, how they interact with one another and with their surroundings, and how they change over the seasons are your raw materials. With them, you can create high contrast and lots of variety, or repetition and simplicity, or unlimited effects between these two extremes.

Remember to select plants that enjoy your site's conditions. Your options are limited only by the factors you have devoted so much time and effort to observing—light, moisture, temperature, soil, and so on.

Putting Your Ideas on Paper

A few gardeners can create beds of great beauty as they work, with spade and plant in hand, but the vast majority need to spend some time with paper and pencil. Of course, gardens are always changing, and some designing is bound to be done by the trowel-and-error method. But the less shifting around plants have to endure, the healthier they will be. Here are two techniques to help you work out your design and make a plan.

Perspective drawings create the illusion of three-dimensionality and give a vivid sense of what something looks like, or will look like. If you don't draw well enough to use this technique, try this shortcut. Begin by taking several black-and-white photographs of the site from likely vantage points. Have them enlarged into 8-by-10-inch prints. Buy several sheets of clear plastic mylar or acetate at a local art-supply store and lay a sheet over each print. Now, with wax pencils or felt-tipped markers, start sketching ideas. If you don't like an idea, wipe the sheet clean with an alcohol-based solvent and try again, or use different overlay sheets to compare different combinations of plants.

A plan view, often called a bird's-eye view, is also helpful. First, go to the site with a measuring tape and some stakes. Locate the bed, roughly, by driving stakes at several points on its perimeter. (If you are unsure of the outline of the bed at this time, just place the stakes at several convenient spots.) Establish the positions of

Creating a Garden Bed

existing structures, plants, and prominent features of the landscape by measuring from one to another and to the stakes, and note these on a rough sketch. Measuring to the nearest foot is accurate enough. Also record any existing features you would like to remove or alter.

Now, using your measurements, plot the bed and its surroundings on gridded paper. Larger squares allow you to work at a larger scale and add more detail. With a plan drawing such as this, you can determine the exact position, shape, and size of the bed, and the locations of the plants in it. You will also be able to calculate how many plants of each type you will need.

Creating the Bed
With the site selected and evaluated, and the design and plant selection complete, you are finally ready to pick up your spade.

When to Dig
If the ground isn't frozen, you can dig a new garden bed any time of year. But if you are adding a lot of organic matter or other amendments, do so at least a few months before you plant. This gives the microbes and bacteria in the soil time to break down the amendments. (See the previous chapter for more on amending the soil.) Before you start digging, squeeze a handful of soil to see how moist it is. If it makes a tight ball that holds together after you open your hand, it is too wet. Wait a couple of hours or a day and check again. If the soil is dust-dry, give the site a good soaking, then test again. Digging dry soil can be back-breaking. Digging wet soil can be back-breaking, too, and if the soil contains a lot of clay, digging can compact it and produce concrete-hard clods.

Laying Out the Perimeter
Before you dig, you need to reproduce on the ground the shape you have drawn on your plan. Measure from existing points of reference (trees, structures, or the stakes you set when measuring to make your plan), and pound in as many stakes as you need to establish the bed's basic position and outline. To lay out a circle, drive a stake at the center point and attach to it a string cut to the radius. Use the string to set stakes at various points on the circumference. If the sides of the bed are straight, connect the stakes with string to establish the outline. If the bed curves, use a garden hose, some powdered limestone, flour, or a can of spray paint to mark smooth curves connecting the stakes. Don't be afraid to change the shape if you are not satisfied.

Eliminating Existing Vegetation
Most new garden sites are already covered with plants, which you will have to get rid of. If you're in luck, there will be only a few

shrubs to dig up. A pick, an ax, or a mattock can help get the more stubborn denizens out. But removing trees that are larger than saplings can be dangerous. If you are inexperienced, call a professional. Many professionals also have equipment for removing the stump of a tree and its main roots.

More than likely, your site will be populated by a ground cover of tenacious perennial weeds, persistent perennial garden plants, or lawn grass—a very determined "weed" when not wanted. No matter which confronts you, do a thorough job of removing it, or it will come back to plague you. Complete eradication is especially important for plants with underground runners, such as Kentucky bluegrass, snow-in-summer, and bindweed. If you attempt to dig these plants out, you are liable to make matters worse. By chopping the running root system to bits, then turning and aerating the soil, you will have propagated rather than eliminated the plant. The little bits will settle happily into their fluffy medium and send out a host of new plantlets in, among, and soon over your new plants. It is far better to smother these unwanted plants or to kill them chemically.

Smothering Unwanted Plants

Although it is cheaper and environmentally safer than killing plants with an herbicide, smothering plants is a slower process, taking months rather than days. Black plastic or thick, overlapping layers of newspaper will do the job. Overlap the sheets of newspaper generously so that there are no places where light can penetrate—the plants will find these gaps in a hurry and grow blissfully through them. Wetting the paper helps make the layers stick together.

Both plastic and newspaper must be anchored to keep the material in place. Stones, bricks, or other heavy objects will work, or you can dig and bury the edges. All this can create an eyesore. A thick layer of wood chips or other organic matter will mask it, and you can reuse the mulch when you remove the plastic, or dig it in with decomposed newspaper. For smothering to be effective, you have to do it while the plants are actively growing. A few fiercely competitive weeds, such as bindweed, should be smothered through two springs and early summers.

Removing Unwanted Plants Chemically

If you decide to use an herbicide, choose the safest, most environmentally friendly product available. Chemicals for gardening have caused a great deal of concern and occasioned a considerable amount of research. At this time, some herbicides on the market appear to leave no toxic residue and cause no harm to soil organisms, insects, and other animals when used exactly as specified. This last point is critical for effectiveness as well as

Creating a Garden Bed

safety. In addition to following instructions to the letter, you should also observe a few precautions. Avoid applying herbicides on days that are breezy or very hot, or when rain is likely within 12 hours of the application. Leave the sprayed plants in place until they have shriveled and turned completely brown. This can take a few days or a few weeks. If after a few weeks the plants are still a bit green, spray once again and wait until they have died off. Then remove any remaining plant parts.

Digging and Pulling Unwanted Plants
The fastest and simplest method of removing most undesirable plants is to pull or dig them out. Make sure you get every bit of taprooted offenders, such as dandelions, which can resprout from small pieces of root. Most annual weeds can be pulled easily or hoed off when young. On a warm, dry, sunny day, the uprooted weeds quickly shrivel and can be dug right back into the soil. Remember that weeds live on in their seeds. If your site has been populated by weeds for more than a year, expect to pull weed seedlings for the next several years. Some seeds can also remain viable for years without germinating. Digging a new bed may be just the disturbance they need to spring to life. If you can make the bed during the warm but not excessively hot part of the growing season, dig the bed and then keep it moist for a couple of weeks. Many of the weed seeds will germinate, and you can then hoe them off while they are small and the bed is still bare. Covering a new bed with mulch while you're waiting for the amendments to break down can help control weeds, too. It also keeps the newly worked soil moist, promoting biological activity and preventing heavy rains from washing the soil away.

Removing Lawn Grass
A lawn may cover better-than-average soil that is a product of the breakdown of grass clippings and dead roots, and of the many insects, worms, and other creatures the grass supports. Be aware, however, that some of these creatures are pests that may make a meal of the tender young plants you will be installing. The large population of cutworms, for example, that can be sustained by a healthy lawn can overwhelm a new perennial garden. The population will drop back into balance in a year or two, but that doesn't help the initial sufferers. Knowledge of the cutworm's life cycle (or that of other pests) might help you time your digging or lead you to plan other procedures to minimize the pest's effects. (See the chapter on pest management.)

If you don't want to smother turf or to kill it chemically, you can strip it with a spade or with a gasoline-powered machine that cuts the sod like a carpet. You can rent one of these machines, which are heavy but simple to run. Sod-stripping is a quick, neat method,

A spring dose of organic soil amendments benefits these hedge-bordered rose beds. New plants should not be fertilized until they are well established—about four weeks after planting.

A damp, shady spot is planted with moss, ferns, rhododendrons, and primulas—plants that thrive in such conditions. Assessing the aspects of a site and choosing plants whose needs it will meet form the most important lesson for beginning gardeners to learn.

Hostas, May apples, and azaleas work well in a shade garden. Coarse organic matter added to the soil assures good drainage, and wood mulch makes an attractive pathway.

In dry climates, it is wise to plan small lawn areas, filling much of the yard with beds of drought-tolerant plants. These beds are heavily mulched to prevent soil from drying out.

Seedlings of summer annuals have been set out in spring in this formal topiary garden. The soil was improved with organic amendments and granular fertilizer before the plants went in.

Once established, the flowers should be fertilized every ten days to two weeks throughout the season.

Informal beds of mixed perennials brighten a backyard (below), while grassy paths invite visitors to view the plants from different aspects.

The steep hillside at right has been terraced and planted with shrubs whose roots do not require deep soil.

A classic double border of perennials, annuals, and herbs flanks a grassy, brick-edged walkway. Achillea, salvia, dahlias, and coreopsis are among the plants chosen with careful thought as to their complementary colors, shapes, and bloom times.

*Bright beds of annuals—
cosmos and zinnias—
add color to more
permanent plantings of
flowering trees and
shrubs. They also serve
as sources of cut flowers
to be enjoyed indoors.*

*Formal rose beds are
edged with stone, which
has been sunk into the
ground. The edging
keeps amended soil in
and grass and weeds out.
It also echoes the stone in
the surrounding wall.*

*The soil next to this
sidewalk has been built
up in a berm that lends
privacy to a small patio
beyond it. Rocks help
hold the soil in place.*

*Rock gardens are
attractive and sensible
solutions for gentle
slopes. They help slow
water drainage while
showing off the plants to
great advantage.*

This formal kitchen garden is planned out in strict geometric patterns and framed with low boxwood hedges. Such a style is a wise choice for level areas of limited space. Once one species has finished blooming, it can be replaced with later-blooming plants.

Terracing turned this slope into a lush bed of light pink geraniums, purple nepeta, blue iris, reddish-pink cheiranthus, and gray-green salvia. The cool colors—blues, purples, and light greens predominating—and the shade provided by the dogwood, have a soothing effect on the eye.

A retaining wall holds this gently sloping garden of cut-leaf maple, 'Noyo Chief' rhododendron, bigroot cranesbill, and cheiranthus. The bed was specially designed to bring plants within reach of an elderly gardener who did not want to do much bending to tend it.

The plants selected for this Western garden need little water. They have been planted in pockets of amended soil and will naturalize easily.

A series of small, easy-care perennial beds has been carved out of this yard. Each bed contains just one type of plant—irises, peonies, or daylilies—chosen for foliage and for blossoms.

The bed of asters, salvia, lobelia, cuphea, and nandina at right was planted in soil piled between rocks to solve a drainage problem.

Native grasses, lavender, and santolina grace an area that receives little precipitation. These tough, drought-resistant plants thrive in dry soils, hot sun, and high winds.

There are almost as many styles of garden edgings as there are gardens. This curved brick edging matches the garden path it flanks, giving a neat, textured look and complementing the greens and deep pinks of the bed. Some skill at brick laying is required to achieve such an effect.

Large cast-cement pavers provide a wide garden border into which plants can spill over, if the gardener so desires. They serve as a path and a work area as well as an edging.

Here impatiens create a
natural edging around
a perennial bed. The
only maintenance
required is careful
trimming of the lawn at
the garden border.

Pockets built into this
brick edging create
small planters for
splashes of annual color.
Plants can be easily dug
up and replaced as their
blossoms fade.

but if your lawn is exceptionally well grown and well maintained, you may miss the deepest runners and roots. Also, a good deal of topsoil comes off with the sod, so be sure to compost the sod rolls, or to use them to patch areas of thin lawn.

Plan to spend half a day or more stripping sod by machine from areas larger than 20 square feet. The soil should be moist but not wet. A helper to remove and shake out the heavy rolls of sod and soil as you move along makes the whole process a lot faster and easier. Make sure you cut deeply—four inches is generally advised for deep-rooted varieties such as Kentucky bluegrass.

Digging a New Bed

When you make a new ornamental garden bed (beds of annuals excepted), your preparations will affect the landscape for years—you don't want to pull up established perennials every year or even every few years to rework the soil. So the way you ready the bed initially—the digging method you use—is important.

There are several methods of digging a bed. Your choice should be determined by the condition of your soil, the condition of your body, and the benefits and drawbacks of each method.

The two most basic methods are single digging and double digging. As the names suggest, the latter method goes twice as deep and requires double the effort. Both aerate the soil; enable you to remove rocks, roots, and debris; and give you a much-needed chance to incorporate amendments and organic matter deeply. For most soils—and for most perennials, annuals, ground covers, and small shrubs—the foot-deep preparation of single digging is ample. (If conditions permit, you may be able to avoid digging and instead prepare the bed with a rototiller.) If your soil is very poor, if you discover a hard, rocky, or clayey layer of subsoil near the surface, or if you are planting many deeper-rooted shrubs in the bed, you should consider double digging. Whichever method you choose, rake the surface of the bed smooth when you are finished.

Single Digging

Turning the soil to the depth of a spade or a shovel is called single digging. Start at one end of the bed, and dig out a trench about a foot deep and wide. Pile the soil in a wheelbarrow or a cart, and dump it at the far end of the bed, onto a tarp. This load will fill your last trench. Add whatever amendments and organic matter you want to the trench, and mix them with the soil at the bottom. Then dig the next trench to the same depth, throwing the soil into the first trench. Continue this way across the bed, filling the final trench with the first load of soil. Because you have loosened the soil and added amendments, the bed will be higher than the surrounding ground, but it will settle back.

Creating a Garden Bed

Dig a trench a foot deep and wide; haul the soil to the far end of the bed. Add soil amendments to the bottom of the first trench. Then turn the soil from *the second trench into the first; repeat the process for the length of the bed, using the soil from the first trench to fill the last one.*

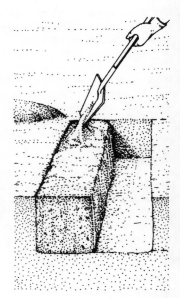

Double Digging

Double digging, sometimes called trenching, starts off the same way as single digging. Dig a spade-deep trench about two feet wide and cart the soil to the far end of the bed, again to be saved to fill the last trench. Now dig the trench down another spade's depth. If this layer of soil is reasonably good, you can work it in place in the trench. Loosen or turn it with a spade or a garden fork to the full depth of the blade or tines, and mix in the amendments thoroughly.

If the soil is compacted, rocky, or very poor, you should remove it from the trench, pick out the rocks or roots, mix in amendments, and then return it to the trench. Loosening the exposed layer of soil at the bottom of the two-spade-deep trench before refilling with additional soil will make life easier for deeply rooted plants. Now, dig the next trench one spade deep and two feet wide and turn this soil into the first trench. This method of working keeps the topsoil on top, whereas inverting the layers would bring poorer subsoil to the surface. You can also combine sod removal with double digging. Just place the pieces of stripped sod at the bottom of the previous deep trench. As with single digging, proceed this way across the bed.

Double digging is a lot of work, but it alleviates potential subsoil problems and gives plant roots a much deeper, healthier area to

Dig a trench 2 feet wide and a foot deep; haul the soil to the far end of the bed. Dig down another spade's depth and loosen the deeper soil. Remove any rocks or old roots, add amendments, and *return the soil to the bottom of the trench. Turn the top layer of soil from the second trench into the first, and repeat the procedure. Fill the final trench with soil removed from the first one.*

push into. It prepares a bed for years of healthy growth, and is particularly valuable for perennial beds, where it is difficult to correct major soil problems after planting.

Rototilling

Machines called rototillers, which are gasoline- or electric-powered, churn the soil with rotary tines. They have long been employed by vegetable gardeners to prepare beds each year and to cultivate during the growing season. Single or double digging is still the best way to adequately prepare soil that needs substantial improvement, but rototilling is an option for ornamental beds if your soil is reasonably fertile and friable, and free of rocks, tree roots, and subsoil problems. In these conditions, six to eight inches of rototilled soil (amended if you wish) will give your plants a good start. Be aware, however, that in some soils rototilling can create a compacted layer of soil at the depth of tine penetration. Also, when rototilling, be sure to protect your eyes from flying bits of soil and stone, and your ears from the roar of the motor. Heavy shoes will safeguard your feet from errant tines.

Raised Beds

A raised bed—a garden created by mounding soil above ground level—can solve a number of gardening problems. With a raised bed you can create a deeper zone of good soil without deep

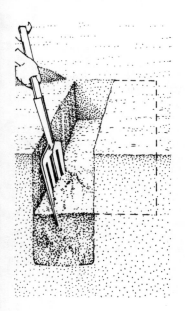
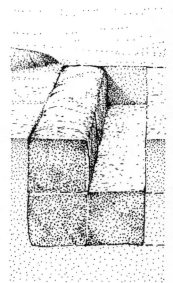

digging, or solve a minor drainage deficiency without putting in drain tiles. If your entire property is laced with greedy, shallow tree roots, or if your prime garden site is afflicted with a drainage problem too difficult or too expensive to fix, building a garden on top of these handicaps may be the only reasonable solution. Raised beds also allow you to extend your gardening horizons and pleasure. You can create a special soil for particular plants, such as a peat bed for acid-lovers or a scree for certain alpine plants.

You can raise a bed six to eight inches above ground level without building a wall to hold the soil in place. Just keep the bed tidy with a rake or a hoe. Containment beds require more initial work but will last a long time. Low walls can be made by simply stacking stone or by anchoring treated planks (two by six inches or wider) with stakes. But a casually built wall won't last as well as one built on a proper base and assembled with some care. The higher the wall, the stronger it must be to withstand the pressure of the soil it contains—and wet soil can exert a great deal of pressure.

Inside the enclosure, prepare the bed as the soil and your plants require. If the existing soil is good, you will just need to add amendments and soil brought from elsewhere to fill the bed; if the underlying soil is problematic, you will have to treat the bed as a huge container and bring everything in. If you are building a raised bed on a site infested with tree roots, lay weed-suppressing cloth, available at garden-supply stores, over the bed and extending under the wall.

Making a No-Dig Bed

If your native soil is in good enough condition, you might want to consider making a garden bed without any digging at all. Although digging allows you to improve the soil in many ways, it has some drawbacks. New beds often are thick with young weeds because long-dormant seeds germinated when the soil was disturbed. Newly turned soil is an inviting site for migrating weed seeds, too. Digging and, in particular, rototilling can also damage the structure of certain soils. And fluffed-up bare earth loses more moisture to the air than does undisturbed soil.

No-dig gardening, also called no-till gardening, leaves the soil largely undisturbed and avoids these problems. Black plastic, weed cloth, or a mulch of organic matter is spread to smother existing vegetation, then is left in place and the garden planted through it after the unwanted plants have died. Acted on by organisms already in the soil, the smothered vegetation enriches the soil. If you use an organic mulch, it too will enrich the soil as it decomposes. As the garden matures, additional amendments can be added as top-dressing. (Plastic or weed cloth can be pulled away eventually to allow top-dressing.) In its simplest form, no-dig gardening relies on the creatures in the soil to do the work rather than the gardener.

Some Disadvantages

There are, however, significant drawbacks to no-dig gardening. Many soils are too poor to support enough organisms to get the process going in the first place. Such soils also need larger infusions of organic matter than that provided by the smothered vegetation. And the benefits of organic matter piled on top of the soil are not as great or as quickly seen as when the material is incorporated more deeply.

If you are making a garden in an old established lawn, meadow, or pasture, and the site is already supporting a variety of healthy plants, consider a no-dig bed. It's fast and easy; from mulching to planting takes only a few months. It's great for large areas that you want to plant quickly. But if you are starting out around a newly built house or a lot dotted with just a few scraggly weeds, digging and amending is probably the best route to a garden.

Tools for Making a Bed

You don't need a lot of tools to make a garden bed. A sharp spade, a digging fork, a flat metal rake, and something to haul material around in are ample. If you have to remove large rocks and roots, a large crowbar, a mattock, and a pick will be a big help. A clawlike tool with four tines, sometimes called a potato hook, works wonders coaxing out small rocks.

Buy good-quality tools and take care of them, and they will last a long time. To prevent rust during the gardening season, clean excess soil off metal parts and wipe them with an oily rag. You can stick blades and tines in a bucket of coarse sand to which a little motor oil has been added. When you store tools for any length of time, give the metal parts a good coating of oil. Stainless-steel tools won't rust, but they are harder to keep sharp and very expensive.

Spades and Shovels

The terms "spade" and "shovel" are often used interchangeably to describe a variety of digging tools. Spades and shovels may be flat or convex, round- or square-bottomed, with short or long handles. For single and double digging, a flat blade cuts straighter and deeper and will make your work a lot easier. A convex blade, however, is better for sandy soil, which just crumbles off the sides of a flat tool.

A sharp spade or shovel is to a gardener what a finely honed knife is to a cook: indispensable. To sharpen a spade, file a shallow bevel on the front side of the blade. Try to make the bevel even all along the edge. You will create a burr of steel on the back of the blade as

Creating a Garden Bed

you file; when you are finished with the bevel, run the file flat on the back to remove the burr. See the illustration on page 105.

Digging Forks
Forks with three or four strong, thick tines are ideal for breaking through compacted layers of soil, for initially breaking ground for a new bed, and for mixing coarse-textured organic matter into the soil. If your soil is rocky, invest in a fork with thick tines that are square in cross section rather than flat. Thin tines quickly bend out of shape.

Tool Handles
When buying a shovel, a spade, or a fork, look for smooth wooden handles with straight grain—these are less prone to splintering and breaking. The tapered wooden handle should fit tightly into a closed socket, or be held by metal straps that extend up the front and back of the handle. The socket or straps should be formed from the same piece of metal as the blade or tines. Cheaper tools are attached by separate pieces of metal, often a tang-and-ferrule arrangement, which is a weaker design. Open-ended sockets let moisture in, which rots the end of the handle.
There are no hard-and-fast rules for choosing handle length. Try to get the feel of a tool before you buy it. Is it too heavy? Improperly balanced? You may find that you want a short-handled tool for some types of work and a long-handled one for others.

Rototillers
Gasoline-powered rototillers are strong tools that make quick work of tearing apart sod, breaking new ground, turning under cover crops, mixing organic material with soil, and loosening and homogenizing the soil in a bed. Most of these jobs are done infrequently enough in an ornamental garden that it may make sense to rent or borrow a tiller rather than buying one. (See the discussion earlier in this chapter.) One day with a tiller is enough to prepare a bed for planting perennials, for example, and that bed won't need reworking for years.
Small, lightweight, gasoline- or electric-powered tillers can be used for some of the same jobs that bigger tillers perform, although they take longer to work the same area to the same depth. But small tillers have advantages that the big ones don't. They fit into narrow or tight spaces between existing plants or next to paths or walls, and they can till a strip as narrow as a spade's blade.
Hand-pushed tillers are simple tools for loosening the surface of the soil. They are good for breaking the crust that forms after a rain, for example, but they don't reach deeper than a few inches.

Here are some of the basic tools you will need when digging your garden bed:
A: *Garden spade;*
B: *Round-pointed shovel (short-handled);*
C: *Half-moon edging knife;*
D: *Digging fork;*
E: *Rake;*
F: *Mattock*

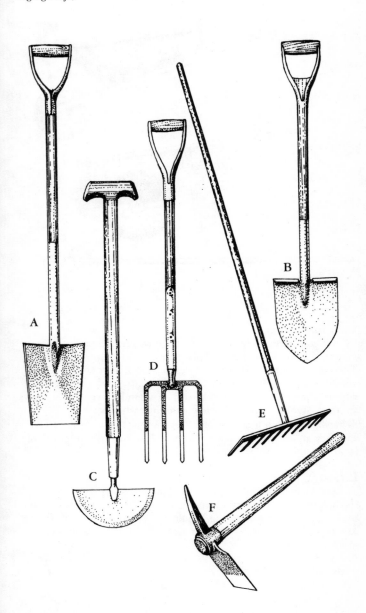

Creating a Garden Bed

A wheelbarrow and a two-wheeled cart are invaluable for hauling away garden debris, bringing out large bags of fertilizer, moving compost, and the like. At bottom is a potato hook— the perfect tool for loosening and removing small to medium-sized rocks from the soil.

Tools for Hauling

Even if you are making a small bed, you will need to move a lot of materials around—soil, rocks, plants, manure, compost, and so on. There are numerous types and styles of garden carts and wheelbarrows on the market. Carts, which have two or more wheels supporting a bin of some sort, can handle large loads. They are more stable but less maneuverable than wheelbarrows. Wheelbarrows can weave gracefully in and out of narrow spaces, and they are a breeze to dump. Carts, unless they have a removable front panel, have to be shoveled out.

Edgings

To keep plants in your bed from creeping out and plants outside the bed from creeping in, you need to consider edging the bed in some way. Besides preventing migrations and invasions, an edging can improve the looks of a bed or make mowing adjacent lawn much easier.

Paths, sidewalks, and driveways made of materials such as brick, stone, asphalt, or concrete can provide ready-made edgings. If you have to install an edging, you can choose from a variety of manufactured edgings or make your own. Most edgings require less effort to install when the bed is freshly dug, fluffy, and empty. There are many methods of edging a bed. The following three will suit most situations.

The spade is perhaps the most important tool for gardeners; when the edge is well sharpened, a good spade can perform a multitude of tasks. To sharpen your spade, make a shallow bevel on the front side with a rasp or file, trying to keep the bevel even all along the length of the edge. When you are finished, run the file over the back of the blade to remove the accumulated burr of steel.

Cut Edges

The cheapest and simplest edging is a cut edge, a vertical or steeply sloped cut in the soil around the perimeter of the bed. Sloping the soil in the bed away from the cut forms a small ditch, which keeps nearby plants from invading.

You can make a cut edge with a flat, square-bottomed spade or with an edging tool, a small, flat, semicircular blade on a long handle. If you haven't dug the bed yet, make your first cuts around the marked outline. Make the cuts vertical if your soil is dense and clayey; angle them toward the bed if your soil tends to be loose. It takes less concentration to maintain a uniform depth of cut with an edging tool—just push the tool full-depth into the ground. Remove a small spadeful of soil from the inside of the bed as you go along. Grade the slope with a rake after you have dug and prepared the rest of the bed. If you have already dug the bed, or if you want to add a cut edge to an older bed, mark straight sides or smooth curves just outside the existing perimeter and make the cuts.

Cut edges demand more maintenance than do many other edgings. They are not terribly durable, and every year or two you will need to recut them. Try not to cut outside the original line, or your bed will keep expanding. When mowing near a cut edge, you may find it tricky to keep the mower wheel out of the bed, so you may need to trim the lawn or ground cover with a weed-eater or hand shears.

Creating a Garden Bed

Strip Edges

Prefabricated barrier strips of steel, aluminum, or plastic require more initial work and expense but less maintenance. As with most things, better-quality products (thicker steel, virgin plastic) usually are more expensive but last longer. Each material has its advantages and disadvantages. Plastic is easy to handle and cut; it bends around curves more readily than does steel or aluminum, but it needs special connectors to form sharp corners. Cheap plastics deteriorate in the sun and look tacky. Steel is heavy and hard to cut, and it rusts. But it is more affordable than some of the other edging materials. Aluminum won't rust and isn't much more difficult to cut than plastic. But it is expensive, and its shininess can be off-putting. None of these materials bends particularly well over a slope, although plastic is more flexible than the other two. Strip edgings should be sunk at least four inches deep, or the plants that spread by running roots will be able to go under them. All strip edgings are installed about the same way. Make a clean, vertical cut along the bed's perimeter, to the depth of the edging, then clear a small trench toward the bed. Set the edging flush against the vertical cut, with its top just barely above the root zone of the lawn, ground cover, or other plants bordering the bed. Be sure the edging doesn't stick up any higher, or it might catch your mower blade. All these edgings are anchored by stakes driven into the undisturbed soil outside the bed.

Edgings often come in heavy and unwieldy lengths, so enlist a helper if you can. Also, wear gloves when installing metal edging to protect your hands from sharp edges.

Mowing Strips

Some gardeners prefer wide edgings of stone, brick, or wood. These flat little paths make mowing easy and give strong visual definition to the bed. A mowing strip keeps out wayward plants, yet it lets the plants inside the bed spill out over the perimeter a bit without making mowing impossible. A neat edge can give a garden a polished, refined look, but some gardeners want to avoid exactly that and allow their plants to meander a bit.

All mowing strips are laid flush to soil level. Dig a trench the depth of the brick, landscape timber, or flagstone, allowing a few inches extra for the layers of gravel and sand you will place beneath the strip to improve drainage and minimize the effects of frost heaving. After putting down each layer of gravel or sand, level and tamp it, then water it in. As you lay the brick, stone, or timber on top of this gravel bed, tamp it in place. Laying bricks end up or on edge, rather than flat, forms a better barrier to invading roots. Flagstones or other materials may not all be the same thickness, so build up the sand where necessary. (Flagstones will also be too thin to prevent plants with running roots from invading the garden.)

After you have laid an area, fill the gaps between pieces with sand. Of the three materials, wood has the most drawbacks. You will need to use landscape timbers or railroad ties that are about five or six inches thick, and these large pieces are difficult, if not impossible, to install around a curved bed. What's more, wood decomposes more rapidly than brick or stone. Pressure-treated landscape timbers or those made of rot-resistant wood, such as cedar, will last longer. Avoid creosote-treated wood. If you choose brick, use brick specifically made for use outdoors in walkways. Secondhand bricks are charming, but most were not made to withstand the elements and will break apart as a result.

Terracing

Gardening on a slope presents many design opportunities, but steep slopes may provide more problems (such as erosion or awkward access) than benefits. Terraces allow you to combine the practical advantages of working on flat or slightly sloped surfaces with the design advantages of a sloping site. Building a series of terraces on a flat yard, even though it requires moving large quantities of earth, can add interest to the site. Terraces also make possible waist-high beds that bring small plants, such as those found in rock gardens, closer to eye level—or fragrant plants closer to nose level. Maintenance can be easier for you and healthier for the plants—you can reach into a high bed without as much bending and without compacting the soil.

The soil in a terrace is held in place by a retaining wall. The higher the wall and the steeper the slope it restrains, the more critical its engineering and construction. Gardeners in areas where the ground freezes and thaws have also to contend with the movement of the earth that freeze-thaw cycles produce.

Stone and timber are the most common materials for retaining walls. Dry-stone walls (assembled without mortar) are ideal for gardens, because they give when the ground moves (frost heaving, for example) and they drain well. Railroad ties and landscape timbers (five- or six-inch-thick planks) can be stacked like blocks and pinned together to build walls. Timber walls rely more on engineering and careful construction than do stone walls, which hold the soil in place through sheer weight. Before you begin building a raised bed or a retaining wall, consult a landscape architect or contractor for help with its construction.

Planting

After your garden bed has been properly prepared, you will be just about ready to do what you have looked forward to all along—purchase and plant your selections. Before you begin, however, there are a few simple principles and techniques you should review.

Choosing and Placing Plants

The first principles deal with laying out the bed, that is, deciding what you are going to plant where. Study other gardens you admire and browse through illustrated books or catalogs to help you define what you like. Note colors, flower and foliage shapes, and overall plant form, and make a list of your plant preferences. Then think about scheduling: During which times of the year do you want the landscape to look its best? Examine your choices again, reading about them in the relevant *Taylor's Guide* or catalog, and limit your list to those whose growth habits meet your desires. Next, consider the cultural requirements of your choices. Does the perennial need well-drained soil and plenty of sun, while your site is damp and shady? Is the tree one that blooms best in the shelter of a windbreak, but your site is an open suburban lot? Be diligent in your research and make adjustments accordingly so that your time and money will be well invested.

You might also ask neighbors who have experience gardening in your area for their tips on choosing and caring for plants. Such people can be an invaluable source of specific information—and of new friends who share your interests. Local nursery personnel are also good sources of advice on choosing plants. Just be aware that, while most nursery employees are experienced and knowledgeable about local conditions, they are also salespeople who may be trying to move what they have on hand. Don't let anyone convince you that you should not grow something you like because it is unpopular this season or disliked by landscape architects. If you like it, and it thrives in conditions you can provide, by all means choose it for your garden. For example, most experts today deplore lilacs because they suffer from powdery mildew toward the end of summer, become leggy, and have no fall foliage color. But if you recall a childhood with hedges of fragrant bouquets every spring, and you want to duplicate that effect, forget the experts and grow lilacs wherever you like. Try training a clematis through them for summer interest, and plant a burning bush beside them for fall color. The dull-green lilac leaves will be the perfect foil.

Considering Colors

While always bearing in mind cultural requirements, check the color combinations of your selections. Make sure that to your eye they do not clash. Using a decorator's color wheel may help you achieve desirable combinations, but when in doubt, think of the flower and foliage colors as if they were choices for interior decorating or a new outfit of clothing. Don't be too timid: Even after you have arranged and planted what you like, you can usually transplant it if the colors disappoint you. You can also change your color scheme with the seasons by coordinating various bloom times.

Planting Along Property Lines
At first glance, your property lines may appear to be a natural place for a shrub border, a tree line, or a perennial bed. If there is a fence, you can use it as a pleasant backdrop or train vines on it. The look of a chain-link fence can be much improved if you lace it with *Clematis montana* and plant a row of peonies and daylilies in front. Or perhaps in order to keep the neighbors' dogs off your property, you may want to install an inexpensive chicken-wire fence and hide it with forsythia or Canadian hemlocks.

A few cautions apply, however. First, do not plant hedges, shrubs, or trees too close to the property line. Whatever grows over onto your neighbor's property is his to do with as he will. Second, be mindful of the fact that weeds growing on your neighbor's side of the property line could invade your planting. A solution is to plan a two-foot-wide "no-plant-land" on the outside edge of your property, laying down a brush and weed killer once a season to destroy all vegetation.

Buying Plants
Once you have done your research and planned a layout (for tips on the latter, see the chapter on creating garden beds), you are ready to purchase plants. Be sure to take the notes from your research along to the local nursery, and keep in mind your analysis of the garden site. If you are ordering your plants through the mail, resist the temptation presented by a glossy photo of something that will not grow in your conditions. If you have established a relationship with an experienced local gardener, take that person shopping with you, or ask him or her to go over your mail-order list. Every gardener loves to help someone else spend money on plants.

Types of Plants to Purchase
All the plants you consider planting in your garden will have one thing in common. They will have been grown from seed under controlled conditions by a nursery or, if you buy seeds, by you. You will be taking these growing things from an artificial situation—a greenhouse or your windowsill—to their permanent home in your garden. Many of the herbaceous plants, annuals, and perennials will be little seedlings with small root systems. Some woody perennials, as well as most trees and shrubs, will have been grown in containers or in nursery beds; others may be shipped to you in a dormant, bare-root state. A few plants that resent movement of any kind may

have to be grown from seed sown directly into the garden. And plants grown from bulbs or corms will require treatment different from any of the above. This makes the planting process look confusing to the beginner, but if you have done your initial research thoroughly, you probably already know (or can find out) about the best way to transplant your choices.

Direct Seeding

The smallest unit that you will plant in your garden is a seed. Anything can be grown from seed, although the length of time it takes for plants larger than annuals and some perennials to mature makes it more expedient for you to purchase seedlings or young plants. Growing plants from seed is certainly the least expensive way to garden, however, and it is the best method to use for plants that will not tolerate any disturbance to their roots whatsoever—even the movement from a container into your garden.

In some cases you may decide to direct-seed plants that would tolerate movement, such as old-fashioned white flowering tobacco, Johnny-jump-ups, white alyssum, or love-in-a-mist, to produce a broad ground cover, perhaps in newly established beds of perennials. You might also sow seeds of bulbs such as guinea-hen fritillarias and Jack-in-the-pulpits where you can wait one to three years for them to flower. Seeds of daylilies, rudbeckias, heliopsis, hollyhocks, Missouri primroses, dianthus, and golden poppies, among others, can be direct-seeded for the same reason.

Sowing the Seeds

If you buy your seeds, you will find specific directions on the packet for how and when to cultivate them. In general, it is best to plant in spring, broadcasting the seeds by mixing them with fine sand and scattering them sparingly. This way, you will not have to thin the seedlings later or discard half of them because of crowding. If you are sowing in spring, watering is not necessary unless it has been unusually dry. If so, water gently with a fine spray. If your soil has already been worked, there is no need to cover the seeds, although most gardeners do recommend providing a thin soil cover by drawing a rake lightly over the bed.

Today, many seeds are marketed in forms that make them very easy for beginners to plant. They may be attached to strips, tapes, sticks, or made into pellets. The seeds on strips or tapes are evenly and correctly spaced so that there will be no need for thinning later on. The sticks are actually labels that have the proper planting depth marked on the side. The pellets have a coating that makes the seeds easier to handle, and they are often dyed to make them more visible. Some contain plant food and fungicides or repellents as well. All of these aids may be beneficial to the beginner, but they are also more expensive than old-fashioned seed packets.

Starting Seeds in Fall
If you want very early blooms on annuals that will tolerate fall
sowing, sow your seeds the previous fall. (Once they are established,
some annuals will drop their own seeds in autumn, in a process
called self-seeding.) Check your seed packets to see if fall planting
will work for the plants you have chosen.

Starting Seeds Indoors
You might also decide to start your seeds early in the season—in
late winter or early spring, following the charts you'll find on the
seed packets. This is quite time-consuming, because you will have
to nurture the seeds in a cold frame or an indoor setting, but it does
give you a head start on the season. You will need starting trays and
flats, a special soil mix, a mister/waterer, lots of light, and the
proper temperatures. Most people's windowsills do not offer
sufficient light or heat, and some plants require what is called
bottom heating, provided by coils or a radiator, to encourage
germination. Artificial "growing" lights, such as those used with
houseplants, will work well with seedlings. Remember to keep the
lights just a few inches above your seed trays. The procedure for
planting seeds in a cold frame or indoors is similar to that for
planting them outside, as described above. (For a more detailed
description of these techniques, turn to the chapter on
propagation.)

Plants From Seedlings
Annuals are sold as seedlings in many nurseries and even grocery
stores each spring. You can also purchase perennial seedlings locally,
or you can order them from several sources. If your research has
shown that the annuals you want would take too long to reach
blooming size if planted from seed, then seedlings are the way to
go. For perennials, choose seedlings of plants that you know will
achieve blooming size in one season. Some popular examples are
rudbeckias, coneflowers, phlox, columbines, daylilies, and
foxgloves.

Buying Seedlings
As you study potential purchases in their flats at the nursery, look
for plants with healthy green leaves all the way down to soil level. If
the seedlings have begun to branch, all the better. Don't be
dismayed by lack of flowers. A well-branched petunia lacking buds
will outshine a scrawny stalk with one flower gasping at its top
within two weeks. If the plants have brown leaves, most likely at
the soil line, they probably were allowed to wilt and dry out. The
browning is compensation for the death of part of the root system.
These plants will take longer to establish in your garden.

Planting

Hardening Off

If you cannot plant your purchases as soon as you get them home, keep them moist and give them as much sun as they will have when they are finally planted out. Sometimes it is best to introduce them to full sun gradually, especially if they have been growing in lower light. Keep them in the sun until their leaves wilt slightly, then move them back to the shade. Gradually increase their time in full sun until they have adapted to their new site. If you have bought annuals before your area is frost free, bring the plants indoors every night.

This process of acclimating seedlings gradually to their permanent place in the garden is called hardening off. It is beneficial for plants acquired even later in the season if they have not yet been acclimatized. If you have grown the seedlings yourself, hardening off is essential as you move them from the controlled conditions of your home, a greenhouse, or a cold frame to the natural environment.

Planting Seedlings

If your plants were grown in a pack designed without divisions between them, gently tap out the entire mass of earth and roots. Some gardeners next carefully pull the plants apart, trying to preserve as many roots as possible for each seedling. Others cut the sections around each plant into equal squares with a knife or a trowel. To plant, dig a hole large enough for the root ball and set the seedling in the ground at the same level at which it grew in the pack. Firm the soil around the plant. Water well with a fine spray, and keep watering once or twice a day until the plants are established. You will know this has happened when they no longer wilt and they begin to send out new shoots. If your plants were leggy when you put them in, you may want to pinch off the tops to encourage new shoots. Simply take off a section at the top just above two leaves.

If your seedlings came in separate little pots or divisions within a flat, shake them out as you plant them. Follow the procedure given above. Because there has been no tearing at their roots, these seedlings probably will establish faster. If they are growing in peat pots, you can plant the whole pot in the soil. If the plant is healthy, roots will have already penetrated the pot sides, but it is a good idea to break the pot open at one or more points to encourage the spread of the roots into your soil.

Container-Grown Plants

Perhaps the best way for a novice gardener to gain an instant garden with the greatest success is to buy container-grown plants. All local nurseries carry these for perennials, shrubs, and trees, and some mail-order suppliers will ship plants in containers as well.

To plant a seedling, gently tease or tap it free of other seedlings. (Just tear a peat pot in several places and plant the whole thing.) Make a hole slightly larger than the root ball, then set the seedling in the soil at the same depth that it was growing in. Tamp the soil around the roots and water well.

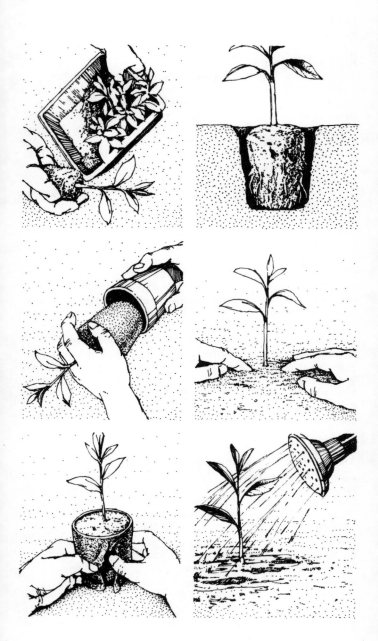

Just be prepared to pay more for your plants than for seeds or seedlings.

Reasons to Purchase
The sizes of container-grown plants will vary, and buying the largest is not always the wisest decision. If your initial plant research has revealed that your choice is difficult to transplant, think about buying it in a small size; it will resent the move less at an early stage of development. This is especially true if your research indicates that the plant will grow rapidly. If you cannot afford a gardenful of these expensive acquisitions, determine which of the plants that you desire are the slowest-growing and purchase these in containers, relying on seeds for other types. It usually pays to buy plants such as coral bells, astilbes, primroses, irises, daylilies, hostas, hibiscus, and ferns in containers.

You may also decide to invest in some container-grown plants in order to get an idea of how your proposed color combinations will work. Purchase a few containers of each type and space these mature plants equally throughout the bed. For example, if you think an early gold daylily would play well against a backdrop of the Exbury hybrid azalea 'Cecile' in a shrub-perennial border, test the combination by planting a few good-size examples of each to view from several perspectives. If you like the effect, fill in with much smaller, almost seedling-size plants.

You should consider container-grown plants for use as garden edgings, too. Not every gardener believes in edging plants, but for close views and along walkways they are a valuable finishing touch. If that initial edge is mature, neat, and full of blooms or beautiful foliage, the eye tends to lull the mind into thinking the rest of the flower bed is equally finished. A few recommendations are coral bells, Jacob's ladder, epimedium, and short daylilies.

Planting
The general rule for planting container-grown plants is to dig a planting hole that is slightly larger than the container. (You can loosen the soil in an even larger area if you like.) Add whatever amendments your soil profile demands, and work them in well. Remove the plant from its container by tapping, pressing, or turning the pot upside down. (Avoid picking up container-grown plants by the stalks or trunks. You can put considerable strain on the roots that way, causing some to separate from the soil and making it more difficult for the entire plant system to remain healthy.) Gently loosen some of the side and bottom roots to encourage their growing out into the new soil. Set the plant in the hole at the same depth at which the soil ball sat in the container. Fill the hole halfway with soil and then fill it to the brim with

water. Watch the soil settle and then tamp it down gently with your foot or hands. Now fill the hole completely with soil. If you are planting during a dry season, or if your climate is particularly dry, build a low wall of soil around the plant, just outside of the original hole. This dike will help hold water close to the plant until it becomes established. Apply a layer of mulch inside this well, using grass clippings, leaves, shredded bark, shredded newspaper, burlap, or whatever else you have on hand that will decompose but hold moisture in the process. Water your new plant conscientiously throughout the first growing season. For most plants, that means a thorough soaking of an inch of water once a week.

Planting Root-Bound Plants
If you take your plant out of its container and notice masses of large, major roots wound tightly around the outside of the root ball, chances are the plant was held in its container too long and is root-bound. This condition is often found in marked-down items, which may have stood in the nursery for a year or more. It is particularly detrimental to trees and most shrubs. No matter how much room you create in the new planting hole, the major root growth will continue in a circular fashion until the plant literally strangles itself.

To rescue a root-bound plant, you must gently tease out the largest of these circular roots, spreading them out into the prepared soil. If the roots are very tightly meshed, spray the soil away with a garden hose set at full force and then separate those major roots. If that doesn't work, it may be necessary to cut off some of them so that you can untangle the rest. Perform this rather drastic surgery in the midst of the growing season only if you can compensate by watering the plant daily for the remainder of that season. If you cannot give the plant such daily care, set it out in its root-bound condition, then dig it up as soon as it has gone dormant and perform the surgery. At either time, make sure the hole you prepare for the new plant is large enough to accommodate the spread-out roots. Don't bother with such surgery for perennials and suckering shrubs, because these are likely to send out new growth even if they are root-bound.

Pruning Container-Grown Plants
Some gardeners will advise you to prune off broken roots, or even the bottom inch of the root ball of container-grown plants, before planting. The fact is that such plants rarely need either root- or top-pruning (which is sometimes recommended to compensate for lost roots). Prune top growth only to remove damaged wood or to suit your taste in shape. Pruning is essential, however, when you are working with bare-root material, as discussed below.

Planting

Remove the plant from the container. Gently loosen some of the side and bottom roots and set the plant in the depth it grew in the container. Fill the hole halfway with soil,

tamp, and add water to the brim. After the water drains away, add the remaining soil, then mulch and water thoroughly.

Special Care for Rhododendrons

The above discussion of root-bound, container-grown plants pertains particularly to rhododendrons and azaleas. In the wild, this group of flowering shrubs grows a huge number of well-entwined, fibrous surface roots. In containers, they tend to become root-bound rather rapidly, requiring some extra work before planting.

Tap the plant out of the container and lay it on its side. Using a sharp trowel, shovel, knife, or edging tool, make deep cuts about four inches apart all the way around the sides of the soil ball, reaching almost to the major stem. (When you are done, you may think that you have killed your plant, but you are actually helping it survive.) Gently lower the root ball into the planting hole and work some of the fresh soil in between the cuts, using your fingers to tamp it firmly into the crevices. This fresh soil aids in the development of new roots, which will literally attach the plant to its new environment and assure it a healthy, long life. Water the plant generously and wait for the water to settle through the roots. Then work more soil into your cuts and water again. Finally, fill the hole with soil so that the plant sits at the same level as it did in the original container.

Make a soil dike around the outermost limit of the roots and mulch well. Since rhododendrons thrive in acid soil, a mulch of pine needles or pine bark is especially good to use. In place of mulch, you could grow a shallow ground cover underneath the shrub to retain moisture for its shallow roots.

Bare-Root Plants

Some plants are sold with no soil surrounding their roots. Such bare-root perennials, shrubs, and trees are purchased during the dormant season, usually very early spring. They are much less expensive than container-grown or balled-and-burlapped plants because they are cheaper for the growers to process and ship. This doesn't mean that they are inferior plants, or that they will grow less rapidly than container-grown types (unless they are species of trees or shrubs that resent the disturbance of their roots). For the most part, even tap-rooted perennials such as Oriental poppies or brittle-rooted shrubs such as tree peonies can be shipped bare-root. The major differences are that you will need to give your transplants more initial care, and that it may take a year or two for them to catch up in size to their container-grown counterparts.

Planting

Study your bare-root purchase carefully before preparing to plant it. If it arrived from a shipper, unpack it immediately and see if the roots are moist. Most growers ship the plants in damp moss, newspaper, or cedar shavings to retain moisture; both the medium and the roots should still feel damp when they get to you. Place the roots in a pail of water and let them soak for 12 to 24 hours before planting. (Although you can skip this step, most plants get an extra boost from the additional water.) Don't let the pail stand outside if it is early spring and the water could freeze. Keep the plant shaded and in a temperate location. Inspect the top growth for any greenery or buds, which should look firm and green, but don't worry if you see nothing.

If your specimen is a perennial, make sure that the roots are firm, not mushy, and check for an odor resembling rotting vegetables, which indicates decay. Even if these tests reveal potential problems, plant the purchase anyway. It may surprise you and grow magnificently. If not, most shippers will replace items without cost if you have followed their enclosed cultural directions and still lose the plant. Just be sure to save all your shipping papers until the plant has established itself.

If you must hold bare-root trees or shrubs more than a day before planting, you will need to heel them in somewhere. Heeling in involves digging a trench deep enough to accommodate the roots when the plant is laid on its side. Place the roots in the trench and cover them with good soil. Keep the whole mass well watered and

Planting

If you can't plant a bare-root plant immediately, lay it in a shallow trench and cover its roots with good soil and a layer of mulch. This process is called heeling in.

Keep the plant moist at all times.

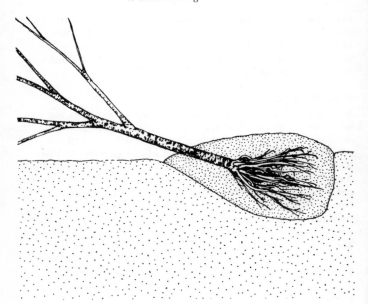

cover it with mulch. Once again, the most important thing to remember in handling bare-root plants is that they will die if their roots dry out.

When you are ready to plant, carefully inspect your purchase for root damage. Trim off any damaged, broken roots and read the cultural-requirement papers that came with the plant. As a rule, shrubs and trees should be planted at the same depth at which they grew in the nursery. Look closely at the base of the major stems or trunks, where the roots begin, and you may see a slight change in color, indicating which portion was growing in the soil. If you cannot determine this, plant the topmost roots three inches below your soil line. Always keep the plant in its pail of water when you are not actively working with it.

The planting hole you dig should be deep enough to accommodate all the roots spread out in their natural directions from the major trunk or stems. If the soil doesn't meet the cultural requirements of your plant, alter it accordingly—with peat to make it acid, sand to make it drain, or humus to make it richer. Place the plant in the hole at the correct depth, refill the hole halfway, and work the soil in among the roots with your fingers. Fill the hole with water, wait for it to drain, and then continue filling with soil and water. Make a dike of soil around the outermost limits of the planting hole and fill the planting area with mulch. (See the drawing on page 120.) If you are planting a long row of shrubs or trees, you can fill one hole halfway, water, move on to digging the next hole, then come back to the first hole and complete it, move on and fill the second hole halfway, go on to the next hole, and so on. You can also dig a trench, as long as you remember to keep your plants' roots damp—even while they lie in the trench awaiting full planting.

Top Pruning

Bare-root trees and shrubs will benefit from top pruning, which means cutting off some top growth to compensate for any lost root growth. This may have been done for you, at the nursery, so study your specimen as you remove it from its soaking in the water pail. The amount of top growth should equal roughly the amount of root growth. If there is more branching on top, trim back until the two balance. (See the chapter on pruning for details of the correct technique.) Be careful in choosing where to trim: On small stock, you are shaping a landscape element that may be around for 100 years. Before planting, make a mental note of how much top growth should be removed, and then wait until the acquisition is in its new hole. Walk around it and decide what silhouette you want to maintain. Proceed carefully with the pruning, stepping back often to gauge the effect.

Balled-and-Burlapped Plants

Another form in which you can buy shrubs and trees is referred to as balled-and-burlapped. The plants are dug out of their growing medium so that a ball of soil surrounds the roots; the ball is wrapped in burlap or other material and tied up for transporting. This usually is the most expensive way to purchase shrubs and trees, but the plants tend to be healthier than container-grown types because they are less liable to become root-bound. (The primary influence on health, however, is the care a plant receives in the nursery.) In general, handle such plants much as you treat container-grown shrubs and trees. If the root ball is allowed to dry out, the roots will suffer and the plant will have difficulty establishing itself. Because much of the roots' surface area is open to the air in balled-and-burlapped specimens, they dry out more rapidly than container-grown plants.

Purchasing

At the nursery, study the top growth of balled-and-burlapped plants. The plant should look as if it was growing in your own garden, rather than in a piece of burlap. Any malformed, stunted, dry, or dead leaves or branches may be a sign that the root ball has dried out or that the plant has a disease. Check the root ball as well; it should be firm, indicating that roots permeate the entire mound. If it does not feel firm inside the burlap, there are probably only one or two major roots and very few lesser, feeder roots still attached to

Planting

To plant a bare-root plant, soak the plant 12–24 hours, then trim damaged or broken roots. Dig a hole large enough to accommodate the roots without bending them. Align the old soil mark on the trunk with the soil surface and spread the roots evenly in the hole. Add half the soil, then water and let drain before adding the remaining soil.

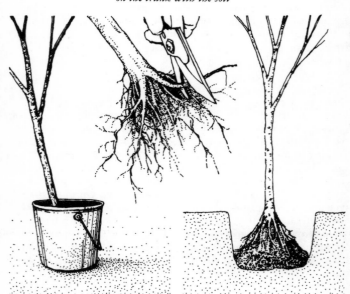

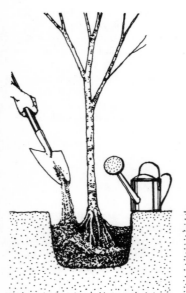
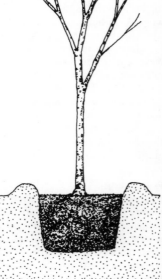

it. As with container-grown plants, do not pick up a balled-and-burlapped shrub or tree by its trunk.

Planting

Some authorities recommend planting a balled-and-burlapped plant just as it comes from the nursery—that is, with the burlap and twine still around it. The theory is that eventually those materials will rot away, and that the roots will push through the loosely woven fabric in the interim. The danger of this method is that, especially if you are a beginning gardener, you may not judge correctly what type of material the "burlap" on your plant is actually made of. Some wraps are actually plastic mesh that will never decompose. Plastic twine is frequently used as well. It is best to take the extra time to unwrap the plant.

If your soil needs amending, dig a hole at least one and a half times the size of the root ball and add the appropriate materials. If your soil is well conditioned, dig a hole that will easily accommodate the root ball. Grasp the balled-and-burlapped plant by its base and move it beside the hole. Unwrap it and gently lower it in by holding onto the base. (You may need a friend or two to help you. The soil used inside the burlap is often clay and therefore heavier than its size would suggest. Nurseries grow balled-and-burlapped plants in heavy soils so that the soil more readily adheres to the roots.) If the shrub or tree is too large for two or three people to handle, make the lifting easier by lowering the plant into the hole with the burlap still in place. Unwrap it there and pull the burlap away from the top of the ball, working it down along the sides. In either case, refill the hole following the directions for container plants. (See page 122.) Because you will not be able to rotate the plant without damaging the unprotected root ball, be sure that its limbs are facing in the directions you prefer before you situate the plant in its new home. You may wish to prune for cosmetic reasons, but it is not absolutely essential to remove a large portion of the top growth.

Transplanting an Established Plant

You can move established perennials, shrubs, and trees to suit your fancy, using variations on the above planting methods. If you are a beginner, it is best to transplant only while plants are dormant—preferably in the early spring, but you can also work in the autumn after leaves have fallen. Any shrub or tree can be transplanted, but some survive the process more readily than others. Check your resource books to determine how a particular type is likely to respond. Those plants that do not transplant easily will suffer more dieback, as will larger-size specimens. Trees usually are more difficult to transplant than shrubs; perennials respond best to the process.

Planting

Dig a hole at least the size of the burlapped root ball. Unwrap small plants before setting in the hole; set the burlapped root ball of large plants in the hole as shown.

Once in the hole, cut all twine, and pull the burlap away from the top of the ball, working it down along the sides of the plant. Continue as for container plants.

First tie up the branches of your plant, making them as tightly upright as possible so that they will be out of the way while you work. Start your initial digging at least two feet from the base of the stems and trunks if you are moving a mature shrub or a young tree. The larger the specimen, the farther out you should begin—most gardeners suggest working at the dripline of the top foliage. Dig down at least two feet all the way around. Some gardeners advise cutting a trench during the season before you make your move, to encourage the growth of a greater number of shorter feeder roots. For a perennial, skip the trench idea altogether and make your initial cuts about six inches from the plant. You probably will need to dig down no more than a foot.

After you have dug down, work your spade inward under the root ball. The plant will not lift immediately; you may have to work around it several times. Each time, try to get farther underneath and rock the root ball toward the opposite side of the hole. You may have some trouble with this at first, but eventually the plant will loosen. If it is a shrub or perennial with many separate stems, you might want to divide the plant at this time. Gently pull its roots apart, using your hands or two spading forks, and replant in a suitably sized hole, much as you would for bare-root plants. Keep the root ball or bare roots damp and well shaded until they are set. Or, better yet, work on an overcast or even a rainy day. (For more information on division, see the propagation chapter.)

Some gardeners wrap the root ball of a plant they wish to move in a sheet of burlap while it is still in its original hole. To do this, rock the plant to one side, slip the material underneath, and then rock the root ball to the other side so that you can pull the material up around it. Tie the burlap to the trunk before trying to lift the plant by its root ball. There is less loss of soil and therefore less damage to the feeder roots this way. (You can skip this step if you are very careful when lifting the root ball.) The plant is undergoing a great deal of stress and needs as many of its roots kept intact as possible. Whatever you do, do not put the root ball in a pail of water, as that would separate the soil from the roots. Instead, keep it covered with a wet cloth in the shade. Transport the plant to its new location, which should be prepared in the same way as for balled-and-burlapped plants. Complete the planting process accordingly and water well.

You can trim away any broken foliage from perennial plants after transplanting, since they will send up new shoots with the coming growing season. Most shrubs will, too, but it will take longer than one season for cut branches to fill in. Any branch removed from a tree will not regenerate; if you do prune trees to compensate for the stress of transplanting, make a careful decision as to which branches to remove.

Transplanting During the Growing Season

Transplanting in the midst of the growing season usually causes considerable dieback. It may help to cut the plant back after moving it so that the extent of its top growth matches that of its roots. Try to avoid moving shrubs and trees until they have gone dormant, but if you must move a plant in the midst of the growing season, try this method of caring for it after it has been moved. Rig a hose above the plant, perhaps by threading it through a ladder. Set the nozzle to deliver a misting spray, and keep the water on constantly for at least a week. If this is impossible, fill the well around the transplanted shrub or tree with water at least twice a day for the remainder of the growing season, and mulch well during the first winter. Take note of what wilted during the week after the move, and be prepared for the possibility that those portions could die the following season.

Staking a Tree, Shrub, or Large Perennial

Regardless of when you transplanted or in what form you purchased them, many trees, shrubs, or large perennials may need to be staked while they establish. Otherwise, at worst, a strong wind may blow them over and expose their roots, thereby killing the plant. At best, the plants may not grow as straight as you would like. If you can determine before planting that your choice will need a stake near its

Planting

When digging up a small tree for transplanting, first tie its branches out of the way. Dig a trench two feet deep around the plant at its dripline. Then work a spade down and under the plant to cut the roots, rocking the root ball away from you as you work. If the root ball is firm, lift it onto a tarp. Or, work the burlap under and around the root ball while it is still in the hole.

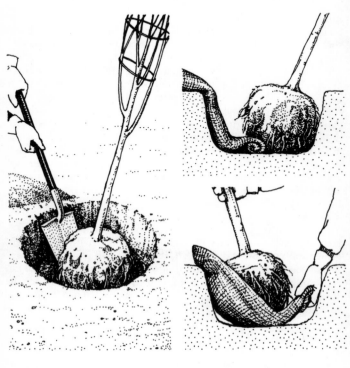

major trunk or stem, place the stake in the planting hole along with your plant. That way, you won't risk pounding it into a major root later on.

Stems of small plants may be tied to one or more metal or bamboo stakes pushed into the ground around the plant. Purchase stakes at any garden center, or create your own from fallen tree branches. A tree five feet tall or more will need the support of stout posts, especially if you have planted it in bare-root form. Pound at least three posts into the soil outside of the planting area, and tie the tree to them using a durable but soft material such as string or even old stockings. If you use wire, be sure that it is covered with something soft, such as a section of an old garden hose, where it comes into contact with the tree. You can also buy plant-supporting kits at a garden center.

If you want to train your tree or shrub in a specific direction, use a stake and ties to pull back on the appropriate branch. Check periodically to see that the ties are not cutting into the bark: If you girdle a tree or shrub stem, it will die above that point.

After a season or two, you can remove all supports from your specimens. Untie them and check to see if they wobble in the

*To protect a newly-
planted shrub or tree from
the wind, wire its trunk
to two or more stakes.
Pad the wires with cut
pieces of an old garden
hose where they contact
the trunk. You*

*can also use the wires to
train branches, pulling
them in the desired
direction, as shown
at right.*

planting holes. If you cannot move them any more than you can
move established plants of similar size, they no longer need their
supports. If there is some movement, something is probably wrong
with the root base; you need to dig up the plant for a look as soon
as it has gone dormant. Something about your site may be
discouraging good root growth, or your plant may have been root-
bound when you planted it. Either problem has the potential for
killing the plant and should be solved as soon as possible.

Training a Young Tree

In addition to keeping a young tree upright, a stake or tie can also
encourage it to grow into a desired mature form. You may use
stakes to train young growth upright, but a more common style
involves the use of stakes or wires to pull some of the branches
down and out (which also serves to help anchor a new tree). Some
gardeners use braces, which they put in the crotches of fruit or
flowering trees, where the branch to be trained outward touches the
main leader. This opening-up process encourages more fruit and
flower production. Use braces if you like, but remember also that
most young trees are naturally upright in growth; they will
eventually grow outward and more open on their own.

Changing the Grade Near a Mature Tree

Homeowners who are starting with empty lots that need grading
often make the mistake of raising or lowering the ground level too
close to an existing tree. The majestic oak or beech that they have

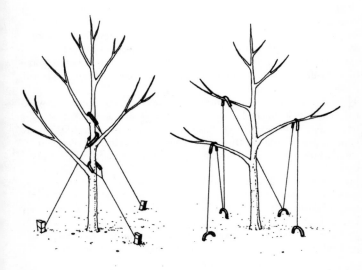

wisely decided to save may then hang on for a few years, but each season it will show more dieback until it is killed completely. This happens because the long-established root system has been disturbed. Nature tends to balance the extent of top growth of any tree with the extent of its root system underground. If part of that underground system is destroyed, then part of the top growth must die as well. (The same reasoning lies behind the idea of top-pruning bare-root plants after planting.)

During the grading process, then, no additional fill should be placed around the base of the tree, or the tree will smother. If you must raise the area near a tree, the best practice is to build a well around the tree so that the original ground level will be preserved in that area. Build the well at least six feet out from the trunk; the closer it is to the dripline, the better for the tree. Have dry-stone walls erected to the projected height of the fill and then let the fill come to meet them. If the tree is not on a self-draining slope, you must ensure drainage away from the tree well by using drain tiles that will run from the open well through the stone wall and out into the fill. If all is properly laid out (ask your contractor for help), your specimen tree should survive.

Saving a tree that is to be left above any new grade is a bit more difficult. You must not disturb the soil within two-thirds of the way out to the dripline when lowering the grade. Have a retaining wall built outside of this area, and fill behind it with improved soil.

Planting Ground Covers

Ground covers are low-growing perennials or shrubs that can save you a great deal of work, while creating an attractive carpet of color in the landscape. They can be a kind of living mulch if you choose the right ones—those that require little maintenance, are controllable, and thrive in the shade of their showier companion plants. Ground covers can choke out weeds and preserve moisture for other plants, thus actually helping to maintain a garden. Some can be invasive, so research the possibilities thoroughly before you make your selection. Then match plants not only to their site but to their purpose as well.

The closer together you plant your initial stock, the quicker it will fill in and look finished. Buying so many ground-cover plants at once can be quite expensive, however. A good compromise is to buy enough plants to space them six inches apart. Within a year, you should have almost total coverage. Multiply the width of your bed by its length (in inches) and divide by six to determine how many plants you need. If you have made friends with experienced gardeners in your neighborhood, they may offer you some of their ground covers—most people have ground covers in excess once they get them going.

It is wise to mulch your larger plants before you set out your ground covers; the mulch will keep the weeds down until the ground cover establishes. Just dig down through the mulch layer to place each ground-cover plant. This relatively easy extra step will save you from weekly weeding for a whole season. Some gardeners lay down a plastic mulch and then plant through that. While plastic is effective in weed control, it prevents moisture from penetrating the soil, does not decompose, is unattractive, and has to be picked up eventually. Small pebbles and gravel look better, but they too do not break down and so add nothing to the soil. It is better to use fallen leaves, grass clippings, straw (not hay, because it has seeds), wood chips, or shredded newspaper as mulch.

Ground Covers as Paths

Ground covers can also be used effectively between paving stones and along paths. The point here is that any area you do not fill with a plant, nature will "plant" for you. Your options, then, are to grow a ground cover, to accept nature's weeds, or to use a strong vegetation killer. Study your gardening books for ground covers or very low perennials and annuals, paying attention to their cultural requirements and speed of covering. Keep your choices low—under four inches—because the higher your ground cover, the higher your path or driveway stones, bricks, or cement blocks will have to be above the ground. With relatively tall ground covers, use larger stones. If your path gets a great deal of traffic, select those plants that will tolerate more abuse.

Moss as a Ground Cover

If you have acid, moist soil, you might wish to try moss as a verdant, velvety ground cover. It probably will grow on its own, but if not, you can pull sheets from a nearby forest floor (being careful not to destroy the natural area) and lay them between your stones. Keep moss moist and it will take hold within two weeks. If you cannot find enough moss, grind what you do find in a blender and add enough buttermilk to create the consistency of gravy. Gently pour this between your stones and keep it moist for two weeks, using the fine-mist setting on your hose—not an overhead sprinkler. If your area is prone to downpours that could wash away the mixture, cover the whole area with cheesecloth until the moss has become established.

Alternative Ground Covers

In a sunny garden, try using prostrate pink baby's-breath, dianthus, creeping phlox, lamb's-ears, or violets as ground covers along step risers. Thyme is a good choice along paths because it is wonderfully fragrant when crushed underfoot. Plants that cannot take much foot traffic should be reserved for risers, edges, and corners. Don't overlook the merits of a ground cover that is generally considered a weed, such as clover. A stone drive or

Planting

Short, steep slopes can be incorporated into your garden by creating small terraces. Retain the soil with large rocks or landscaping timbers, and plant on the narrow, flat ledges in between.

parking area that is completely interplanted with clover can be very appealing.

Planting Ground Covers on Slopes

Ground covers are very effective on slopes or banks, where they help control erosion, forming an anchor for taller-growing, showier plants. Unless the slope is unusually moist due to excess groundwater or a spring, you probably should choose plants that tolerate dry conditions, because slopes drain rapidly. Once again, mulch everything as you plant; this way, you will not have to weed at a 45° angle.

Start planting at the top of the slope and work down. If the angle of the slope is 45° or more, you may need to build a wall of soil on the downhill side of each of your new shrubs or perennials. Otherwise, even with a mulch, the soil may wash away from their roots before they can establish toeholds. Thinking of each construction as a mini-terrace, you can also form a flat surface in which to set the plants by creating a wall on the downhill side out of rocks, bricks, or wood. Then fill in with amended soil behind the wall and set in your plants. Be prepared to water at least weekly for a whole season to be sure the plants become established.

Planting Tools

All the tasks described in this chapter call for the use of gardening tools. You will not need a large number of them, but what you do have should be of the best quality you can find—strong and durable, with sharp edges on all the digging equipment. You can get along

quite well with just a good spade, a hand cart, and a long-handled trowel, but as you become more experienced you will probably want a pair of long-handled lopping shears, pruning shears, a pruning saw, and some battery-operated hedge clippers as well. (See the chapter on pruning for more about shears and clippers.) Some optional but useful tools include a sharp edger and a narrow trowel. As you continue to garden, you will gradually acquire a collection of tools that best suits your strength and your plants' needs. (See the chapter on creating a garden bed for more about tools.)

The Spade
A sharp-edged spade with a strong handle is required for digging deep holes in which to plant shrubs and trees. You can also use it to move rocks, with the handle serving as a lever. A spade will cut through sod, so it is essential when you are preparing a lawn edge around a new bed. You can plant bulbs easily with one plunge of the spade. Some gardeners prefer to use a bulb planter, which looks something like a round cookie cutter, sometimes with a long handle. Others find it difficult to use in sod and among established plantings.

The Hand Cart
A gardener's hand cart follows him or her everywhere—carrying tools, plants to be set out, mulch, or refuse. Some people prefer the two-wheeled variety to a wheelbarrow because double wheels offer more stability and make the cart easier to manipulate. Whatever you choose, be prepared to invest in a high-quality cart that can carry considerable weight. It will be worth every penny.

The Trowel
You will use a trowel to plant everything from seeds to small container-size plants. It will dig out weeds, as well as plants that you wish to move. The most useful type is a long-handled trowel, but this variety is difficult to find. The extra length—two feet as opposed to about eight inches—gives better leverage for digging, and you don't need to bend down as far for most gardening chores. A trowel also works well for planting medium-size bulbs. Whichever style you buy, be sure your choice is sturdy. Test it by placing your palm in the bowl of the trowel and pressing down while using your other hand to push on the back of the handle. If you can bend the trowel at all, move on to a sturdier model. The weaker one will snap with the first rock or woody rootstock you encounter.

The Sprayer
A reliable sprayer is used to apply liquids such as fungicides, insecticides, and even deer repellents to your plants. Sprayers vary considerably in quality, so shop around. Choose one that is lightweight, because the liquids you put in it will be heavy. A

Planting

tough, translucent plastic sprayer is durable and allows you to see the level of liquid that's inside.

The Edger and Narrow Trowel
An edger is really just a blade on a long handle that allows you to cut a straight edge along a predetermined line. It makes for a neater garden, but a spade may be used in its place. Similarly, a long-handled trowel may serve as well as a narrow trowel, but because the latter will create a smaller hole, it is useful for setting in smaller plants and bulbs, and for working in already established borders.

Plant Labels
In addition to tools, many gardeners feel compelled to keep a supply of labels and markers. If you are a beginning gardener, you may feel more secure if you have some way of knowing what should come up next spring in which spot. As you gain experience, you will recognize your plants from their first leaves and no longer require such aids.

There are many different markers available at gardening stores and in catalogs. Some are made of beautiful ceramics, others are metal, and some are simple white plastic or wooden sticks. The prices vary considerably. Choose what you feel most comfortable with, but consider how much you want your markers to show. If one will go next to a prized Japanese-maple seedling by your front door, you may want to spend the money for a good ceramic marker. If it will delineate a row of asters in a cutting garden, then a popsicle stick with the word "aster" written in pencil may suffice. Pencil does seem to last longer than most inks. (If you do use ink, make sure it is waterproof.) Or try the aluminum markers on which you "write" with pressure, actually etching the information into the label.

It is possible to use more natural-looking markers to indicate, for instance, where you have planted some rootstocks that you do not want to disturb inadvertently. Simply lay one small rock on top of another at the site, or stick a twig in the ground.

Plant Supports
Unlike labels, which you may use as a beginner and eschew later on, you will need to rely on plant supports forever. The exact number of supports, as well as the kind you need, will vary with the types of plants you grow. The tree stakes mentioned earlier are one type of support, but there are others—for saplings with tiny circumferences and for perennials with floppy flowers.

Bamboo Canes
If the plant is single-stemmed, such as a lily stalk or a tree of pencil-thin diameter, then a bamboo cane may work as a support.

A long-handled trowel (left) gives extra leverage for digging. The bulb planter (center) is ideal for "naturalizing" bulbs in a lawn—remove a core of soil, drop in the bulb, and replace the soil. A portable sprayer (right) is handy for applying pesticides and watering hard-to-reach transplants.

Loosely tie the plant to the support, using covered wire, gardener's twine, or the like. You may have to tie at more than one point so that the stem does not bow out. For plants that grow up to six feet tall—such as Pacific hybrid delphiniums, bulb lilies, and some trees—bamboo stakes are quite sufficient, relatively inexpensive, and almost invisible.

Rings of Wire or Twine

To support herbaceous perennials that grow in clumps, such as double peonies, you may want to invest in wire rings. The wire ring is connected to metal legs, which you push down into the ground so that the plant grows up in the center of the ring. You can achieve the same effect by pushing several bamboo stakes of the appropriate height into the ground around each perennial, and then tying twine around these stakes. As the plants grow taller, just add another level of twine, hiding it beneath the foliage so that it does not show. The bamboo-and-twine method is a bit more work than the rings, but it is cheaper and allows you to tailor the size of your ring to the size of your plant.

Planting

Small Branches

A more natural-looking way of supporting floppy plants is with small branches. Find branches that still have a large number of twigs on them when cut to the appropriate height. Then simply push them into the soil among the growing vegetation. As the baby's-breath, perennial sunflowers, or asters mature, their branches will rest on these twigs and therefore stay upright. You could even tie a length of green gardener's twine around the entire plant to add more support. In the fall, you can cut the plant and its support down all at once and simply start over in the spring.

Trellises

Some taller-growing perennials and shrubs may look wonderful and benefit from being grown on trellises, as if they were vines. Perhaps the best example is the climbing rose still seen covering the porches of old New England houses. Unless the trellis is freestanding, be sure to place spacers between it and the structure it rests against. The plant stems need room to weave behind the structure as well as in front of it. This is true for both vines and shrubs, though the spacers can be narrower for vines. In both cases, you want to encourage air circulation behind your trellis to discourage diseases and to promote evaporation of moisture (especially from clapboard). If you are covering the whole side of a building, use several small trellises rather than one large one. These will be easier to move at painting or repair time, especially if you have hung them on hooks instead of nailing them to the wall. Then, simply lift them off and hang them, vines and all, over stepladders while you work on the surface behind them.

Investing in fiberglass trellises will likewise save you work. This material will not rot or need repairing. Fiberglass trellises usually come only in white. If your house will accept a weathered look, consider a trellis made out of unpainted redwood or cedar. In some situations, vine supports of fishline or inexpensive wire may be acceptable, particularly if they will be covered by a plant quite rapidly. It's all a matter of aesthetics—study your situation and decide what will look best to you.

Planting at the base of a freestanding trellis is no different from any other type of planting. Near houses, however, you should plant outside the roof's dripline so that your plant will receive rainfall. Do not center the planting hole exactly on the dripline, as water runoff could wash away enough soil to kill the plant. In both cases, watch the new plant growth carefully and train it back to the trellis by bending supple new growth in the proper direction and holding it in place with ties or weights. As growth stiffens, you can remove these. Remove additional branches or vine stems that will not fit into your desired pattern. Once your plant has reached its trellis, continue to monitor growth so that it covers the entire structure evenly. Check your plant's cultural requirements to find out how much old growth should be pruned out annually and how much excess new growth may be removed without damaging the plant's flower production.

It is possible to skip using a trellis altogether, simply putting nails right into wooden house siding and tying the plants to them as they grow. If you are working on a painted house, be sure to use rust-proof nails.

Gardening with Bulbs

Spring-blooming bulbs are best planted in early fall so that they have time to set roots to help them through the winter. Depending on your climate, however, you may be able to plant them well into December, or any time when the ground can still be worked. Check the hardiness zones for your bulb choices before you buy. If your garden is in the far north, you may need to create a warmer microclimate in which to shelter your bulbs. Consider a space close to the house or near a wall that will protect them from icy drafts. (For more detailed information on gardening with bulbs, consult *Taylor's Guide to Bulbs*.)

What to Buy

Plan on planting lots of a few types of bulbs as opposed to a few of many kinds. As is true with your perennial gardens, the overall effect will be more uniform and complete. If you cannot resist trying a little of everything to see what grows best for you, locate your spotty, disjointed arrangement somewhere out of general view. As a rule, the smaller the bulbs, the more of them you will want to plant. For example, three giant imperial fritillarias have an eye-catching effect, but it will take at least 50 of the much smaller guinea-hen fritillarias to create a significant mass.

Since you will be spending time and money on your bulbs, stick with choices known to be hardy in your area. Ask experienced local gardeners about this, check the zones listed in garden guides, and observe what is grown in your town. Every year your plants should naturally double in number, so that in five years you will be able to divide your stock or enjoy huge bouquet-size clumps of your favorites. Always buy quality bulbs that are firm and have little or no green leaf growth.

Planting

The general rule for planting bulbs is to dig a hole two to three times as deep as the bulb is tall. (Many authorities adhere to the two-times-as-deep rule, but bulbs planted three times as deep sometimes prosper longer, especially in cooler sections of the country.) At the base of the hole, you may want to add some bulb fertilizer, following the manufacturer's directions, but if you have good garden soil, this will not be necessary. Cover the bulb food

134

Planting   *Spring bulbs are a*
welcome addition to any
garden. You can plant
them in individual holes
at least two times as deep
as the bulb. Make sure
the pointed end of the
bulb is facing up.

with a thin layer of sand or soil, and then place the bulb in the hole. The flat side, where the roots will grow, should be pointing down, and the pointed end, where the foliage appears, should be pointing up. Don't be unduly worried about correct placement, however. A bulb planted upside down will right itself within a season. Sometimes it is impossible to tell which end is up.

The spacing of bulbs depends on the effect you wish to achieve. If you want a daffodil bed to look ancestral immediately, lift whole shovelfuls of soil and plant half a dozen bulbs in each large hole. If you can wait a few years, plant one bulb per hole and space the holes a foot or two apart. The planting will look sparse that first season, but it will fill in later. Sometimes you may choose to plant your larger bulbs farther apart so that you can plant smaller bulbs in between them. As a rule, larger bulbs should be spaced a foot or two apart, and smaller, thumb-size bulbs should be planted about six inches apart.

Some smaller bulbs will work their way to the surface within a year and flourish right under your mulch level without any soil covering. Indeed, all bulbs somehow reach their desired depth within a few years. If you get your bulbs in early enough, you will not need to water them. If you are late (after about November 1), soak the area well after planting to settle the soil before a hard freeze sets it. Then sit back and wait for the joys of a spring show.

Spring Bulb Choices
Among the first bulbs to bloom in the spring are the appropriately named snowdrops. Try them and marvel at how they bloom while the ground is still frozen solid. In some areas, you may be lucky

enough to find snowdrops naturalized around old abandoned foundations, from which you can dig some up to transplant. In addition, you may want to investigate glories-of-the-snow, eranthis, crocuses, scillas, and squill, among others. All of these flowers will divide rapidly and then reseed; they eventually become invasive. Perhaps the most commonly planted bulbs are daffodils and tulips. If you mix several varieties, you will enjoy blooms for as long as two months. Daffodils tend to be longer-lived than tulips for most people. They also remain disease-free and do not seem to tempt local wildlife. With tulips you may have to use a spray repellent if mice and deer are a problem. It might even pay to plant the tulip bulbs in little wire cages so that the mice cannot get at them.

Naturalizing Spring Bulbs

Some people plant their spring bulbs in prepared beds, while others like to naturalize, or spread them somewhat randomly, in the lawn. Both effects can be quite lovely, but naturalizing calls for letting your lawn grow tall until the bulbs have finished blooming and their foliage has turned yellow. The foliage is storing up strength for next year's blooms, so if you cut it too soon, your bulbs will certainly not bloom the next season and will eventually die. Some people compromise by placing only small bulbs, such as crocuses, in their lawns and then setting their mower blades high until the foliage has ripened. Most bulb foliage is finished ripening by the beginning of June.

A second difficulty with planting bulbs in a lawn involves the planting process itself. It is much harder to cut through sod than through the soil in your perennial border. Some gardeners remove whole sections of sod and plant bulbs in its place in informal, hand-scattered groups. To do this, cut the sod with a shovel or an edger around the outside edge of your planting area. Use your shovel to skim off the sod, and set it aside. Dig down in the remaining soil to the appropriate planting depth. You may either lift all the soil or dig individual holes. Add bulb food at what will be the base of your bulbs, if you desire. Place your bulbs with their flat ends facing downward. Recover with soil and then replace the sod. Tamp everything down by walking on it, and water the sod to help it take hold again.

Bulbs in Wet Areas

While all spring bulbs flourish in sunny well-drained areas, some of the smaller bulbs, as well as daffodils and narcissus, grow equally well in wet soil. Perhaps an area of your yard is often covered by standing water for several days at a time and never seems to dry out completely. You might try planting several small bulbs there as an experiment, following up with more the next season if you have success.

Planting

Managing a Bulb Bed

Some gardeners plant spring bulbs in beds that hold other plant types. Here they can place the bulbs fairly close together, achieving the same effect of profuse blossoms in early spring as you've seen in annual flower borders in late summer. After the bulbs have finished blooming, they can be lifted out and heeled in in an inconspicuous area of the garden, to be replanted in the fall. Meanwhile, their beds can be planted with another selection for the later seasons. Such rotation of plant types does involve quite a bit of work, but it offers one big advantage: magnificent floral displays throughout the growing season.

A bulb bed also allows you to plant spring bulbs in areas where they are not winter-hardy. You can buy bulbs in fall, pot them, and place them outside in a cold frame or inside in a cold cellar until early spring. By that time, they will show growth and can be transplanted into the display bed.

Mixing Bulbs with Perennials and Shrubs

Another way to use bulbs in the garden is to intersperse them throughout your flower and shrub beds. Lower-growing bulbs make delightful ground covers in early spring; as they ripen off, they may be replaced by later-maturing perennials. Taller bulbs are useful as accents in front of shrubs, under shade trees, and throughout all your perennial gardens. Once you have set them in, you need never touch these spring bulbs again. The perennials will grow up between them and hide the foliage as it fades. The wide range of bulb varieties work as flexible additions to your garden.

Ongoing Care of Spring Bulbs

Most authorities advise fertilizing the soil around the bulbs while they are actively growing, following a bulb-food manufacturer's directions. They also recommend deadheading the flowers, which means removing the seedpod that forms in each flower so that all the bulb's strength will remain in the bulb and aid in the production of the following year's flowers. Some gardeners do neither and their bulbs continue to flourish. It is probably best to experiment and see what works for you.

You must not cut off the bulb foliage until it has yellowed, but some gardeners tie the wilting leaves together with rubber bands, twine, or even one of the bulb's straplike leaves. Using this method, the bulb takes up less room in the flower bed and allows other annuals or perennials to receive more light and air. Other gardeners believe that such a strangled appearance is unsightly and that it limits the amount of exposed leaf surface, thus lessening the bulb's ability to store its strength for the following season. Again, your own decision should be based on your inclinations, and reevaluated after you have had some experience.

Spring Bulbs and Frost

There is no need to run outdoors with each late-spring frost to cover your early tulips, crocuses, and daffodils. In severe cold, their stems will wilt to the ground, but they will perk back up with the first warmth. If they do remain wilted, it will be because they became so weighted under ice or snow that the stems were permanently bent. This is a rare occurrence, however, and you should not feel you must brush off each snowfall. A cold spell (near 0° F) may turn the first green top growth brown, and these tips will stay brown during the growing season. But no harm will be done to the flower or the later green leaves.

Transplanting Bulbs

As is true with most plants, it is best to transplant bulbs while they are dormant. Mark the spot where your favorite clump grew so that you can find and separate the bulbs sometime between midsummer and late fall. Begin digging out far enough from the patch so that you do not risk slicing into a bulb. (If you do slice one, plant it anyhow. It will suffer a setback but will eventually mature.) You can also move all bulbs easily in very early spring, as soon as the soil has thawed and just as the green top growth appears.

Start digging at least the distance of the bulb's diameter away from the visible growth. Work slowly, and use your fingers often to feel for the bulbs in the soil. Dig deeper than the base of the bulbs, because you want to keep as many roots as possible. In very early spring, these will already be as long as the bulb is high. Therefore, for a three-inch-high daffodil bulb, you will be digging down at least six inches, plus the depth of the soil over the top of the bulb. Your total excavation could easily be a foot deep. Gently pull the bulb clump from the soil. If there are more than three or four bulbs together, you may want to pull the clump apart. Do this slowly, trying not to break the roots or top growth. Reset the bulbs in new holes at the same depth they grew originally and water the transplants immediately.

If you transplant bulbs when they are in flower, the result will be less flower production for a year or two. Improve the odds by continuing to water every week until dormancy, and by adding some bulb fertilizer to the hole under each transplant. Very small bulbs, such as snowdrops and grape hyacinths, will show no setback if they are moved in bloom, and they are easier to find and work with while they still have their green top growth. Again, water them well after transplanting—or work with them just before it rains, or even in the rain.

If you need to lift your bulbs for storage, dig them as described for transplanting. You must do this if you are growing bulbs that need a winter season in a warm climate, or if you are growing tender bulbs in a cold climate. In both cases, your task is simpler

if you can wait until the foliage has ripened off. If not, you must
heel in your bulbs, which means replanting them in some other
spot until the ripening off is completed. If you fail to do this, your
bulbs will not rebloom and they will eventually die. After the
foliage has yellowed, remove it from each bulb by giving it a sharp
yank or by cutting it. Shake excess dirt from the bulbs. Some
people remove the outermost brown "skin" from their bulbs, but
this is not necessary. All roots should have shriveled as the bulb
ripened off, but if there are a few remaining, you may want to
remove these, too. Spread the bulbs in single layers on something
that allows good air circulation—an old window screen or slatted
wood works well. Place them in a cool, dry, shaded location until
you are ready to replant. Never store your bulbs in a refrigerator;
it will dry them out too much.

Lilies

Perhaps the queen of all bulbs is the bulb lily. It comes in endless
varieties of color (except blue), shape, and height—from about one
to eight feet—and some are exotically fragrant. If you plant a mix
of varieties, you can enjoy lily flowers from spring until frost.
Consult *Taylor's Guide to Bulbs* or other plant resources for specific
information, and then make choices that please you and suit your
climate. You can plant lilies in beds of their own, mix them into
borders, or place some varieties in the shade under trees. Plant
them in groups of at least three, and consider setting at least one
fragrant clump near your most-used door or under your bedroom
window. Like spring daffodils and narcissus, lilies will turn their
flowers toward the sun, so plant accordingly; if there is a flower
border south of your house, you will see the backs of any lilies
planted in it.

Planting

Lilies never really go dormant, but the best time to buy them (from
a reputable grower) is as soon as they are dug up in the fall. The
bulbs and roots should be firm, and both the bulbs and any packing
material should be moist. A small amount of bluish mold on some
of the outer scales, or sections, of the bulbs is nothing to worry
about. Replant your lily bulbs immediately. If you must store them
for a short period of time, keep them in a cool place that is moist
but not wet, as they will rot easily. Do not put them in the drying
cold of your refrigerator.

Because some of the taller-growing lilies may have bulbs larger than
your fist, you will need to dig some deep holes, following the two-
to-three-times-the-depth-of-the-bulb rule outlined above. If you are
planting Oriental hybrids, which mature late in the season, dig
your holes as soon as you have ordered the bulbs, so that you will
not have to struggle to do so after the ground has frozen in

December. Simply fill the hole with mulch until you are ready to plant in it. Place some bulb food at the base of the hole, and cover it with a thin layer of sand or good soil. If it is late in the season, water well after planting so that the bulbs will set roots before the ground freezes.

With a few native exceptions, lilies must have very good drainage. They are perfect to use in a raised bed or on a slope, but they thrive equally well in any good garden soil where water does not stand. Some gardeners plant their bulbs in a bed that slopes at a 45° angle to achieve this drainage. The bulbs also do well with a ground cover or a mulch around their base to keep them cool. The taller varieties of lilies (over three feet) definitely need staking. Every year, your lilies will increase in number, each bulb forming its own colorful clump. You can divide them as you did your spring bulbs, if you choose. (For further information on dividing lilies, consult the chapter on propagation.)

With the exception of some native species and the stunning Oriental varieties, most lilies do not suffer from any diseases. The bulbs are a favorite food of deer and mice, however, so you may want to take the same precautions as you do for tulips (see above). Planting the bulbs near the roots or stumps of trees can discourage the mice.

Creating a Hedge

In addition to specimen shrubs, trees, and flower borders, you may want to plant a hedge somewhere on your property. Perhaps you need a privacy screen or a windbreak, or you want a rich backdrop for a border. Different plants can serve different functions as hedges, so your first task is to determine what purpose you want your hedge to serve. Next, decide what time of year the hedge will be most needed. If you want a screen between your front porch and the neighbor's mainly during the summer months, when you use the porch most often, a vine grown on a loosely woven trellis or a row of tall-growing, perennial hibiscus will do nicely. If you need to block the view of a neighbor's compost pile year-round, then you should probably choose evergreens, planted two rows thick. If your space is limited, you can skip the two rows of white pines and settle for a tightly trimmed single row of cedars.

Once again, consult *Taylor's Guide to Shrubs, Taylor's Guide to Trees,* and other reliable gardening books for suggestions of potential hedging material. Then remember that you can use just about anything, so dare to venture beyond the authorities' suggestions to consider shrubs and trees that you especially like. Ask about them at local nurseries and among local gardeners, and, as always, be sure to take into account your site and the plant's cultural requirements.

Mixed Hedging Material

Many gardeners create informal hedges of mixed plantings, even combining evergreens with deciduous shrubs. They consider the plants' textures, colors, heights, and flowers in designing compatible mixes. Such a hedge can also solve the problem presented by a site that stretches from an area of, say, wet shade to one of dry sun, because you can choose plants that thrive in each condition. Experiment with a selection of your favorites and create a living tapestry in your yard.

Planting

One way to plant a hedge is to dig a long trench, set the plants in it, and then backfill all at once. Dig the trench down a bit below the depth of the plant roots so that you can loosen the soil at the bottom, and add whatever fertilizer may be suggested for the particular plant. Another planting method is to set plants in individually, in one of the manners described earlier in this section under a tree or shrub planting. Place the plants in a straight line, or stagger them to create two closely spaced lines for maximum coverage. In either case, water your hedge well the entire first season. If the hedge plants grow tall, they may need to be individually staked, or you could erect a fence nearby and anchor the plants to it until they have developed a good root base.

Spacing of Hedge Plants

The spacing of hedge plants depends on how dense you want your hedge to be and how quickly you want it to be effective. If you have strength and money enough, you can create a full-size cedar hedge in a day's time. A plant such as deciduous tallhedge buckthorn may go in at one foot tall and grow two feet per year. Read descriptions of the plants you like to see how wide they become at maturity, as well as how fast they grow annually. As a rule, place the plants a bit closer than their mature width; when they are young, you will be looking at a lot of open space, but the plants will not choke each other as they grow.

If you have chosen a particularly slow-growing plant for your hedge but are not willing to pay for mature plants or wait for young plants to fill in, consider planting a faster-growing, less expensive plant in amongst the desired species. Keep the interloper pruned away from your first choice, and cut it down eventually as the other one matures.

Formal vs. Informal Hedges

Informal hedges are usually unsheared, pleasantly disheveled rows of deciduous shrubs. They are pruned to fit their space, but an attempt is made to keep the branches at various lengths. In contrast, formal hedges are generally sheared and often evergreen.

Maintaining them is a never-ending responsibility, but the neat effect is worth it to many gardeners. Sometimes broad-leaved evergreens such as rhododendrons are used in formal hedges. They are not pruned smooth, but they are shaped so that the effect is much the same.

Formal pruning must be done correctly or the hedge can be killed. (Correct hedge pruning is described in the pruning chapter of this book.) If you neglect your hedge for a few years, it can be difficult or impossible to bring it back to size. You must be careful to shape the growth so that the base of the hedge remains full and green. This means making the top of the hedge somewhat narrower than its base so that the lower branches will receive sufficient sunlight.

Protecting Plants from the Weather

All newly set plants—in a hedge or a perennial border, or standing alone—benefit from some protection from the harsher elements. Many books discuss the dangers of winter weather, but most plants also need sheltering from late spring and early fall frosts as well as summer heat. While many plants thrive in direct sun, too much of it in summer—especially with too little rain—may be harmful. Newly transplanted specimens are especially threatened by dry heat. Some gardeners cover these tender plants with small lath structures, broken bushel baskets, cloches, or anything else that offers partial shade. How often this treatment is necessary depends on the size and variety of the plants and the temperature and dryness of the air. As you become more experienced, you will know when to offer protection in your garden. As a beginner, listen to weather reports to track frosts in spring and fall, and watch for the first sign of leaf wilt in summer. If you make all your protective coverings the same, they will be more aesthetically tolerable to your eye than if you use a variety of structures.

Cloches

Structures called cloches, made of a strong frame covered with burlap, cardboard, or plastic, are available at garden centers in a variety of sizes. Some people make their own cloches out of metal or wood covered with whatever protective material they have on hand. Sheets of plastic are perhaps the most durable and successful covers, but they do not allow water to reach tiny seedlings directly. If you do make your own cloches, be sure to anchor them to the ground with stakes or rocks so that the wind will not blow them away.

Winter Shelters

Cloches can also be used to give winter protection to tender, recently transplanted plants. Alternatively, you can use burlapped frames, hollow plastic collars, wire or netting, or woven evergreen branches. The aim is to create a frame around your plants. During the winter, fill the inside of the structure with straw, wood chips, or oak leaves to offer further insulation.

Some gardeners tie the branches of their less hardy plants together and cover them with burlap in winter. The purpose is to minimize cold damage by letting each branch in the bundle act as an insulator for the others. While effective, this method looks unattractive for a large part of the year. The lath houses that some people place over their foundation evergreens to prevent cold and snow damage look a bit better. An invisible solution to the cold-weather problem is to spray more delicate plants with anti-transpirants, chemical mixtures that prevent excessive moisture loss, which is the major destructive effect of harsh winter winds. If you choose to try an anti-transpirant, get specific information on frequency and manner of use from experts at your garden center or by reading the labels on the products.

Perhaps the most successful way to protect tender winter plants is to place them in a cold frame. With this method, you actually dig the plants out and heel them in inside this structure. A large plant such as a climbing hybrid tea rose can be half dug out and bent to the ground so that a cold frame can be built over it. You then fill the interior of the cold frame with an insulating material to cover the entire plant.

A cold frame is simply a bottomless box with a movable top. The top can be fashioned of glass or clear plastic if you want plants to grow inside the box, or it can be opaque if the box is merely offering winter protection to dormant plants. The movable top allows ventilation as you harden off the cold frame's contents for the harsher, outside climate. This top usually is slanted so that water and melting snow will not stand there and add additional weight. There is no artificial heat inside a cold frame—only natural solar heat. If your cold frame is protecting plants in a very cold climate, such as climbing hybrid tea roses in zone 3 (see the Plant Hardiness Zone Map on pages 36–37), then you should bank the outside of the frame with bales of hay or straw, additional soil, compost, leaves, or some other material besides the insulating material inside the frame. Some gardeners build a second frame or box about a foot out from the original frame and fill this with insulating material, too. Some cover this space with tar paper or plastic for waterproofing. On very sunny winter days, you may have to prop open the cold frame to prevent excessive heat buildup, and at night, you may need to put additional protection over the glass, such as wood shutters, blankets, or mats. It all depends on the delicacy of your plants and the severity of your climate.

Although all of these protective devices can extend the growing season and allow you to grow a larger variety of plants, they do add considerably to the time and effort you need to spend caring for your garden. Remember to weigh this time against the effect and decide how much effort you are willing to make. If the extra work puts you off, you can always limit yourself to plant choices that are bone-hardy in your climate zone.

Wind Protection

If you live in an area buffeted by strong winds, and especially if many of your plants have lanky top growth, you should consider using windbreaks. Strong winds can shred leaves, speed the destruction of individual blossoms, and even stunt growth. At the very least, they can force plants to lean awkwardly in one direction. A windbreak can be a living hedge of sturdy plants, a garden wall, or some slatted lath work. A bonus is that in the winter, your windbreak will create microclimates that are at least one climate zone warmer than surrounding areas.

A windbreak is effective for a distance of about 20 times that of the height of the plants it shelters. Therefore, if you plant tall Douglas firs as opposed to shorter red cedars, your windbreak can be located farther from your house or garden. In either case, the planting should be at least 100 feet from the area to be protected and on the side from which the winds blow.

On windy, open locations such as the Great Plains, you will need more than one row of hedge plants to create an effective windbreak. There, you should plant the first row about 100 feet away, using a comparatively short material such as lilacs, which grow to 15 feet. Space a second row of the same height 10 feet farther away. Going back another 10 feet, plant something quite tall, such as Douglas firs. With about 10-foot separations, you can plant as many as five additional rows, each somewhat shorter than the previous one as you move farther away, until you have stepped back down to the 15-foot lilac height. Then, to really finish it off, leave a wider corridor of as much as 30 to 40 feet and plant one more double row of 15-to-20-foot plants. In most parts of the country, such an undertaking is not necessary, and two double rows approximately 100 feet away will be sufficient. Most people prefer to use an evergreen for the center rows and plant a light-colored, flowering tree in front of that. The evergreens create a perfect backdrop for the blooms of dogwoods, magnolias, hydrangeas, and lilacs.

Using Mulch

A final way to protect your plants is to cover their root zones with mulch. Some plants, such as rhododendrons and azaleas, must be mulched continuously to conserve moisture for their shallow roots. All other plants benefit from similar treatment, especially those that are newly transplanted. Most mulches also serve to keep the

Planting

To protect a plant from wind and snow, cover its crown with a thick mulch (top); wrap large plants with burlap (center left); or construct a lath frame (bottom left). Spray with anti-transpirant (center right) to retard damaging moisture loss. A portable cloche (bottom right) protects tender plants from wind and cold.

These seedlings have been densely planted to provide a mass of blossoms later in the season, but not so closely together as to compete with each other for space and nutrients.

Geranium seedlings were transplanted into this formal garden according to a specific pattern of spacing that both creates a design and allows room for growth.

Beds of woodland
wildflowers, such as the
phlox and honesty
shown here, will seed
themselves each fall and
reappear in spring.

The tight spacing
within classic perennial
borders calls for frequent
dividing of some plants
so that they do not
overgrow others. The
extra divisions can be
planted elsewhere.

The sweet woodruff shown here propagates itself quickly through underground runners and self-seeding. The result is an attractive, healthy, fragrant ground cover that needs some grooming to prevent its becoming weedy. Sweet woodruff does best in moist, well-drained, shady sites in which the soil is slightly acid.

This private greenhouse shelters both nursery-grown stock and seedlings started by the owner. They will be held here until the weather is warm enough for planting out.

The outdoor display area of this perennial nursery offers plants that are perfectly adapted to the local climate. Asking questions of nursery personnel is a good way to get specific hints as to regional variations in widely grown species.

This cold frame is being used for propagation during the summer. In winter or early spring, the glass will be substituted for the screen so that seedlings can be sheltered in the frame.

Perennials grown in containers should be set outdoors for several days before planting in order to become acclimated to the conditions in their permanent locations.

Peonies, lilies, and irises are easy to propagate by division, which involves digging out the rootstock and pulling or cutting it apart to form two separate plants.

The heavy stalks of delphinium (left) usually require staking and protection from the wind, but this extra care is amply rewarded in profuse early summer blossoms.

Iris hybrids (below) respond particularly well to dividing, which is best done in summer. They grow best in moist, acid soil but are adaptable to less than ideal conditions.

Bedding begonias are best bought as seedlings, as they are difficult to grow from seeds. Shown here are wax begonia hybrids 'Rio White' and 'Vodka'.

Plants in containers add bright accents to these garden steps. Container gardening is especially well suited to small spaces; it allows for great variety and easy rearrangement of plants. Special soil mixes, good drainage, and frequent watering and feeding are keys to success.

These raised beds are filled with improved soil to support plants that would not otherwise thrive in the surrounding dry soil. Using raised beds also helps save water.

Raised beds keep this
townhouse garden
looking neat. They also
create visual interest by
presenting plants at
various levels within the
enclosed space.

Extra water and care
can be concentrated on
the marigolds in this
raised bed while the rest
of the garden survives on
normal rainfall. The
height of the bed also
makes it easy to tend.

soil comparatively cool and to prevent weeds from growing. In addition, mulch makes an attractive path through a vegetable or woodland garden.

There is a huge variety of mulching materials from which to choose; your task is to decide which is most appropriate for your needs. (See the chart on pages 162–163.) Many gardeners use natural mulches—such as bark, grass clippings, or compost—because they eventually decompose, enriching the soil. These materials also tend to be more attractive than the synthetics, which include products such as foil or plastic. What you are really doing in using organic mulches is spreading a shallow layer of compost material over everything, eventually creating a rich soil.

If you think of the leaves that fall from your trees in the autumn as mulch and allow them to remain in your garden, you will save yourself much raking and benefit your plants at the same time. You can also mulch with waste from tree and lawn trimming, if you are careful not to pile the clippings too thickly, which can smother the plants. Some people use shredded newspapers and cardboard as mulch, placing it under a natural mulch for aesthetic reasons. Perhaps more gardeners will find this useful as the call to recycle paper wastes becomes stronger. Whatever material you choose, don't underestimate the labor-saving and soil-building value of a good mulch.

Final Advice

The best way to begin a garden—after you have read a basic text such as this one—is to go out and buy a plant that you like (and that is recommended for your area), come home, and plant it immediately. It's important to remember that you can grow what suits you, and that it is neither as complicated nor as long a process as this chapter may make it appear. You will have some failures, but you will have many more successes. As each plant survives year after year, you will experience the special satisfaction that has lured people to gardening for centuries. Daily troubles tend to fall into proper perspective as you spend more and more time in your garden.

Mulching Materials

MATERIAL	ADVANTAGES
Bark chips, ground bark	Attractive and easy to apply. Size of pieces varies.
Compost	Excellent organic mulch material. Adds nutrients to soil. Attractive, natural appearance.
Ground corncobs	Easy to apply. Natural appearance.
Cottonseed hulls	Add some nutrients to soil. Easy to apply and lightweight.
Grass clippings	Easily available. Decompose quickly to add organic matter and nutrients to soil.
Hay and straw	Easy to apply and easily available. Attractive, natural appearance. Add nutrients to soil.
Leaf mold	The best organic mulching material. Natural appearance. Adds nutrients to soil.
Newspapers	Readily available. Decompose quickly.
Peat moss	Adds organic matter to soil. Natural appearance.
Pine needles	Natural appearance. Readily available. Add organic matter to soil.
Leaves	Excellent mulch if leaves are ground up and come from several different types of trees.

DISADVANTAGES	THICKNESS
Some bark may be acidic. Expensive for large areas. Harbors some insects.	2–3 inches
May harbor weed seeds.	3–4 inches
Take nitrogen from soil as they decompose. Compensate with high-nitrogen fertilizer.	3–4 inches
May blow away in windy areas. Possible contamination from chemical sprays.	3–4 inches
Sometimes contain weed seeds. Thick layers will mat and burn plant crowns. Tie up nitrogen.	2 inches
May contain seeds. Susceptible to fire and wind.	6–8 inches
Requires much time and large quantities of leaves to make. Turns soil acid, but can be corrected with lime.	3–4 inches
Unattractive, but can be covered with more attractive mulch.	1/4 inch
Expensive. Not recommended because it repels water when it dries.	2–3 inches
Slightly acidic unless lime is added.	3–4 inches
May smother delicate plants if leaves mat or are too large.	6 inches in fall

Propagation

Many gardeners consider propagation, or the multiplication of plants, to be the most challenging and the most rewarding aspect of gardening. With simple techniques and a minimum of tools, propagation gives you access to a much broader range of plants than is ordinarily found in garden centers. Suddenly, nearly every plant you see—fruits and vegetables, herbs, bedding plants, bulbs, ground covers, flowering perennials, shrubs, and trees—becomes a candidate for your landscape. In addition, propagation allows you to multiply the plants you already have. Propagation lets you freely share plants with your friends and fellow gardeners.

All propagation methods and techniques fall into one of two categories: growing plants from seeds, or sexual propagation, and growing plants from other plant parts, called vegetative or asexual propagation.

Plants from Seeds

Growing plants from seeds is probably the first gardening experience most of us have—what child doesn't plant a bean or radish seed and marvel at the magic of its emergence from the soil? For adults, planting seeds is a simple, easy, and inexpensive way to grow a great many different garden plants. Not all the plants you will want can be grown from seeds, but there is enough variety and merit among those that can to keep even the most ardent seed-starter busy for years.

In nature, propagation by seeds is by far the most common means of plant reproduction. It is also the most efficient and widely used method for propagating cultivated plants. Seeds range in size from the dust-fine grains produced by orchid, campanula, and begonia, to the double coconut seed, which weighs in at several pounds. Seed shapes run the gamut from the nearly two-dimensional seeds of desert willow and catalpa through a multitude of irregular and geometric shapes to the nearly perfect spheres produced by prickly poppy, radish, and golden-rain tree.

Because seeds contain a mix of genes from male and female parts, a seedling frequently is different from its parent or parents and different from its siblings. For centuries, plant breeders have taken advantage of this variation to develop plants, often called hybrids or cultivars, with desirable traits. Very special development programs and fertilization techniques have succeeded in producing identical seedlings for certain bedding plants and vegetables. But for the majority of specially bred plants, propagation by asexual means is the only way to exactly reproduce in subsequent generations the traits bred into the parents.

Although you can grow plants from seeds without knowing anything about the biology of seeds, it can be useful and interesting to know something about how seeds are made, what they contain, and how they germinate.

How Seeds Are Formed

Sexual reproduction in plants, as in animals, involves the union of female sex cells (the egg) and male sex cells (the sperm). Unlike animals, plants often contain both male and female reproductive organs, which are located in the flowers, as shown on page 167. The female sexual organs are the calyx and corolla, which are collective terms for the sepals and petals, respectively; and the pistil, comprising a stigma, a style, and an ovary. The male parts include the stamen, each with a filament and an anther.

Carried by insects, wind, humans, or other agents, pollen from the anthers lands on the often sticky surface of the stigma. In some species, a flower will accept its own pollen or pollen from another flower on the same plant; other species require pollen from a different plant or even a different cultivar. Compatible pollen soon germinates and grows a pollen tube through the stigma and the style into the ovary, where it fertilizes an ovule, or egg. The fertilized egg, called a zygote, develops into a seed.

The Seed

All seeds include an embryonic plant, or embryo; food-storage tissues; and one or more protective coverings. At each end of the embryo is a growing point, one of which will form a shoot, the other a root. Attached to the growing points are one, two, or more cotyledons, or seed leaves. Food sufficient to allow the seed to germinate and the embryo to grow is stored in the cotyledons or in surrounding tissue. Protecting the contents of the seed are seed coats, leftover food-storage materials, and often parts of the flower or fruit. These coverings may have a dramatic effect on the germination of the seed. (Some "seeds" are actually structures containing several true seeds; the burr sold as buffalograss seed, for example, usually contains from three to five true seeds.)

How Seeds Germinate

Germination, which for non-dormant seeds usually occurs within one to three weeks of sowing, is a three-step process. In the first step, the seed imbibes water, which swells its tissues and softens, or sometimes breaks, its coverings. Stored enzymes are reactivated and new enzymes are manufactured. Within a few hours or days, the radicle, or embryonic root, emerges.

During the second step, the chemical constituents of the cells activate cell systems, and products necessary to growth are moved to the embryo's two growing points. During the final step, the cotyledons expand. Cell division increases the size of the radicle and forms the plumule at the other growing point. The seedling stem is now divided into two sections. Below the cotyledons is the hypocotyl, containing the radicle; above the cotyledons is the epicotyl, which contains the plumule.

Propagation

Soils for Starting Seeds

Probably no other topic outside plants themselves garners more interest among gardeners than soil mixes. The considerable attention paid to soil mixes is directly proportional to the variation between one gardener's soil mix and another's.

A perfect soil mix does not exist. But all good soil mixes share certain characteristics. They must retain moisture, while draining and aerating well. (These qualities are interrelated, and depend both on the nature of the individual components of the mix and on how those components behave in combination with each other.) They must be low in soluble salts and provide some nutrients for the seedlings' initial growth, and their pH must fall within a small range of neutral (pH 7).

Garden soil, even the best, generally is unsuitable for starting seeds in containers. Watered and allowed to settle in the container, it often resembles a relative of concrete. And it may be contaminated with weed seeds and disease organisms, which can devastate seedlings. Gardeners have long made their own mixes from equal amounts of sand, soil, and peat moss, but these homemade mixes have been largely supplanted by commercially made mixes. Relatively cheap and readily available, commercial mixes commonly contain no soil at all, instead combining two or more of the following non-soil ingredients: peat moss, perlite, ground bark, sawdust, and vermiculite. (Despite the absence of true soil, these mixes are customarily referred to as soil mixes.) In addition to appropriate moisture retention, aeration, drainage, and pH, most mixes provide at least a modicum of nutrients. Commercial mixes are highly uniform, lightweight, and easy to store. And they contain few, if any, insects, disease organisms, or weed seeds.

Almost any reputable seed-starting mix will do the job. But mixes do differ. Particle sizes vary, some mixes take up water or drain more readily than others, some form a firmer root ball than others, and so on. Some differences are more subjective—one mix will "feel" better in your hands than another, for example. So if you are just starting out, experiment with various mixes to find the one that suits you, as well as your seeds, best.

Containers

Just about any container that can hold soil and drain excess water from its base can be used for germinating seeds. The width of the container is not important; you can use a small pot to sow a few seeds, or large flats to sow hundreds. The container's depth, however, affects the aeration and water-holding capacity of the mix in it. The reasons for this are somewhat complex, but, simply put, soil at the bottom of a container will hold more water and less air than the soil above it. Roots don't grow well in poorly aerated soil, so this layer may hamper the root development of the seedlings.

The flowers of many plants contain both female and male sexual organs. Pollen from the anthers lands on the stigma, where it germinates. A pollen tube grows through the stigma to the ovary and fertilizes an egg, which forms a seed.

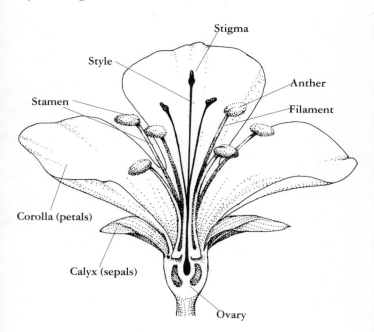

Although most commercial seed-starting mixes have been formulated for use in containers only one and a half to two inches deep, you might try deeper ones. To test the effect, sow the same kind of seeds in shallow and in deep containers, and compare the root development.

If you recycle your containers, they must be cleaned and sterilized to control diseases. Plastic, glass, ceramic, and metal containers are easier to clean than are those made of wood, fiberglass, or Styrofoam, which often have hard-to-get-at cracks and crevices. Scrub the containers with a soapy solution and a stiff brush to loosen and remove larger soil particles. Then sterilize them by soaking them for 30 minutes in a 10 percent solution of sodium hypochlorite (add nine parts water to one part laundry bleach).

Containers should be filled with already moistened soil. Pour some mix in a bucket or a pan (cleaned and sterilized if it has previously contained soil) and mix with water. To check the moisture content, firmly squeeze a handful. If the soil does not fall apart when you release your fingers, but does fall apart when you shake your hand, it is ready for the containers.

Fill each container to overflowing; be sure to work the soil into the corners. Then draw a ruler or other straight edge across the top of the container to remove the excess. Lightly tamp to firm the

Propagation

Cover a container of newly sown and watered seeds with a piece of glass or plastic to cut down on evaporation and keep the soil moist. Remove the cover once the *seeds have germinated. To minimize fluctuations in temperature, place a sheet of dark paper over the glass, as shown here.*

seedbed to within a quarter to a half inch of the container's rim. Do not put a layer of gravel or other "drainage" material in the bottom of the container—it will just lessen drainage, moisture retention, and aeration. (Layering several different mixes also has the same unwanted effect.) Place a few small pebbles or similar objects over drainage holes if you are worried about mix washing through them.

Sowing the Seeds

You can sprinkle, or broadcast, seeds evenly across the surface of the mix, or sow them in parallel rows that are approximately one inch apart. Sowing in rows has two advantages. Seedling diseases, which can spread quickly through a container of broadcast seeds, are often contained in a row, sparing seedlings in other rows. Row-sown seedlings are also easier to transplant.

After sowing, cover the seeds with mix to a depth two to three times the thickness of the seeds. Spread the mix by hand or through a screen over the entire surface. Very small seeds (such as begonia, eucalyptus, petunia, paintbrush, and campanula) should not be covered.

The number of seeds you sow depends on how many plants you want, the germination rates, and the anticipated mortality rate of the seedlings. Many suppliers indicate germination rates on the

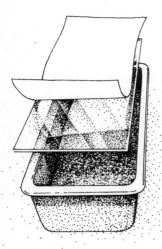

packets. Seeds generally are inexpensive, so you can sow more than you need and choose the healthiest seedlings for growing on. In general, give seeds more rather than less room in a container. Crowded seedlings are weaker, not uniform in size, more susceptible to disease, and more difficult to separate and transplant. If you want to produce large numbers of seedlings, the following rule of thumb can serve as an upper limit: On average, a standard 11- by 22-inch flat can accommodate 1,000 to 1,200 small seeds, and between 750 and 1,000 larger seeds. Normally, it is a good idea to sow only one species or cultivar to a container unless you are combining seeds that will germinate and grow at the same rate.

Watering

Sown in properly moistened mix, many seeds will germinate before additional water is required. You can cut down on evaporation by covering your containers with sheets of plastic or glass, or by placing them inside plastic bags. Don't put covered containers in direct sunlight; temperatures inside the covering can quickly reach levels lethal to seeds or emerging seedlings. Remove the coverings once seedlings have emerged.

Check the mix in uncovered containers several times a day. Never let it dry out. When you need to water, set the container in a pan containing an inch or so of water; capillary action will draw the water up through the soil. Or, gently wet the surface with a fine overhead spray. Bottom watering is best for very fine seed, which is easily washed away by even the finest spray. Use water that is room temperature or warmer. Cold water applied to seeds or seedlings can retard germination and growth. After watering, let the container drain completely.

After germination, water so that the seedlings, but not the soil, are dry by nightfall. Nighttime temperatures normally are lower and air movement is stilled, conditions that are conducive to the start and spread of disease. You can judge the soil's moisture content by its color (wetter is darker) and by the weight of the container (wetter is heavier). Both bottom watering and spraying will work for seedlings, but if you spray, be careful not to wash the seedlings out. Allow all excess water to drain completely away rather than catching it in a saucer or pan beneath the container. As seedlings grow, water them less frequently, allowing the soil surface to dry slightly between waterings. This will aid in the control of water-borne diseases.

Temperature

Different plants respond to different germination temperatures, but in general, plants fall into one of two groups. Those whose seeds and seedlings require warm temperatures include tropical and subtropical plants, summer vegetables, the bean and nightshade

Propagation

families, gaillardia, and lobelia. Those requiring cool temperatures include cosmos, delphinium, penstemon, perennial baby's-breath, freesia, and cyclamen. Seed packets may specify optimum temperatures; if not, you will have to rely on experience.

For optimum results, warm-temperature seeds should be germinated at temperatures above 68° F. Seeds of many of these species have been found to germinate best when temperatures are kept at 86° F for eight hours and then dropped to 68° F for the remainder of the day. Cool-temperature seeds should be germinated below 68° F.

If you must start warm-temperature seedlings in a cool spot, you can place the containers on heating elements to raise the soil temperature. A number of heating strips and blankets designed for this purpose are available from garden centers or mail-order suppliers.

Many seeds will germinate even if subjected to a wide range of temperatures; they will just take longer to do so. Optimum temperatures for seedlings usually differ from those for germination, and a 10° F reduction is often recommended.

Light

As with other conditions, the reaction of seeds and seedlings to light varies by species, cultivar, temperature, and the age of the seeds. Most grasses, herbaceous vegetables and flowers, conifers, and species with small seeds germinate best in the presence of light. The germination of other species, including tree-of-heaven, delphinium, English ivy, phlox, allium, amaranthus, and phacelia, is inhibited by light. Seeds kept in dry storage for several weeks to several months often lose their need for light during germination. The length of the exposure to light each day may also affect germination. The seed packet will probably tell you whether light is needed for germination.

Light falling naturally on a windowsill or a cold frame should be sufficient to germinate seeds that need light. You can also place sown containers approximately six inches beneath 40-watt fluorescent lamps that are on eight hours a day. (If you have a footcandle meter, strive for levels of at least 75 to 125 footcandles.) Operating the lamps continuously may speed germination.

The intensity and duration of light needed by seedlings also varies. Some, such as petunias and buckwheats, thrive when subjected to continuous light, while others, such as some members of the buttercup family, benefit from a daily period of darkness. If you are not aware of a species' light needs, place the seedlings several inches beneath fluorescent lamps for 16 hours or more per day. (If you can meter the light, strive for 500 to 1,200 footcandles of either artificial or natural light.) Then watch the seedlings themselves closely. Spindly, weak seedlings are probably suffering from too little light.

Fluorescent lights allow you to start and grow seedlings in dimly lit places. Place the lights several inches above the container during germination. As the seedlings grow, *raise the lights so they're always about two to six inches above the tops of the plants.*

Those with "burned" or discolored leaves may be receiving too much.

Seedling Nutrition

The small amount of nutrients in soilless mixes will soon be used up by the seedlings or washed out by watering, and will need to be replaced. (Not all mixes contain nutrients, and those that do may not say so on the package, due to curious legal regulations regarding labeling.)

You can use almost any general houseplant fertilizer containing approximately equal amounts of nitrogen, phosphorus, and potassium on seedlings. There are no hard-and-fast rules for timing fertilization. Some gardeners prefer to fertilize once a week, others do so each time they water. Beyond these recommendations, observe your plants. Weak, spindly growth often accompanied by yellowing of the leaves and increased susceptibility to disease can indicate nutrient deficiency. Too much fertilizer causes the leaf edges to "burn" and the stems to collapse. Too much fertilizer can also cause a white, salty substance to form on the surface of the soil or container. You can wash this out of the mix by watering several times in quick succession with clear water and allowing the excess to drain completely away from the bottom of the container.

Propagation

To transplant seedlings, gently lift a clump of them from the flat (top left). Grasping a leaf—never the stem—tease them apart (top right). With your finger or a pencil, poke a hole in the transplant mix and insert the seedling to its previous depth (bottom left). Water the transplanted seedlings immediately (bottom right).

If the label does not provide recommendations for diluting the fertilizer for seedlings, halve or quarter the ordinary rate for once-a-week fertilizing. If you fertilize with each watering, you will need to dilute even more, perhaps as much as one-tenth of the recommended rate.

Transplanting

Seedlings usually are transplanted after they have grown a set of "true" leaves. These leaves, which resemble those of the mature plant, follow the expanded cotyledons, often called "seed" leaves, that typically appear first. True leaves can appear within days, as with marigolds and zinnias, or weeks, as with begonias and rhododendrons. Temperature, heat, and light levels can also hasten or delay the appearance of the true leaves.

Although a growing medium of coarser ingredients can be used for transplanting than for germinating, most gardeners use the same kind of mix for both. Again, almost any container that will drain can be used. (To guard against disease, wash and sterilize containers, and don't reuse mix.) Choose a container size adequate for the plant's habit and rate of growth. You can transplant bedding

plants into cell-packs (usually containing four or six cells), or into flats, spacing the plants to avoid crowding as they grow. Plants that will grow larger before they are set out into the garden can be put in individual pots two, three, or four inches wide. Fill the containers with moistened soil and tamp just as you did when preparing seedbeds.

Seedlings of the woody plants and the few herbaceous species that produce a strong, deep taproot may benefit from being transplanted in special containers designed to prevent roots from spiraling around the bottom of the container. Spiraled and massed roots can seriously affect these plants' future growth. Trees that depend on the formation of a strong, well-spaced root system have been known to perform poorly or even fall over during high winds merely because the seedling root system was poorly formed in the transplant container.

Some special containers have ribbed sides, which direct roots that contact them down rather than in spirals around the pot. In addition, some containers expose root tips entering the bottom zone to air. This exposure kills the tips, forcing the root behind to grow additional tips, which are in turn killed when they grow and contact the air. This phenomenon, called "air pruning," not only prevents root spiraling, it also creates a root ball with more roots and root tips, increasing the plant's ability to absorb nutrients and water. Plants grown in these containers often grow faster than those grown in typical containers.

How to Transplant a Seedling

Several hours before transplanting, water the seedlings well. This helps limit the shock of transplanting and ensures that the seedlings are turgid. Moist, well-drained mix also separates easier than dry or overly moist mix.

With your finger, a pencil, or a similarly shaped stick (called a dibble), gently remove seedlings individually or in clumps, lifting as much of the root system and its attached soil as possible. Place the plant or clump in the palm of your hand or on a flat surface. Holding only the leaves (never the stem or the roots), pull individual seedlings free of a clump. Disturb the soil adhering to the roots as little as possible. Many taprooted species benefit if you pinch off the tip of the taproot before transplanting; this forces new root tips to develop.

Poke a hole in the soil in the transplant container. Then, aided by a finger or a dibble, guide the roots into the hole so that all are buried and the seedling is neither deeper nor shallower than it was in the germination container. A simple flick of the dibble or finger replaces and settles the remaining soil into the transplant hole. Don't press the soil around the seedling; this can reduce the soil's aeration and water-holding characteristics. The soil will settle enough the first time you water. Water the seedlings soon after transplanting. Delaying this first watering can cause the seedlings to dry out, resulting in poor future performance.

Care After Transplanting
After transplanting, many species grow better at temperatures lower than those for germination or for initial seedling growth. It often helps to reduce light levels for recent transplants for several days, giving them time to recover from transplant shock. Once they have recovered, you can give them even stronger levels of light. Most seedlings need transplanting only once before they reach their final destination in the garden. As they approach a size suitable for setting out, you will need to harden them off, gradually subjecting them to conditions similar to those in the garden. Place seedlings that were grown indoors or in a cold frame in increasingly more exposed conditions outdoors. Remember that small containers heat up rapidly in direct sunlight, and may reach temperatures lethal to tender young roots.

Seedling Diseases
The warm, humid conditions that promote germination and seedling growth are also ideal for the growth of fungal disease, called "damping-off." Found in soil and infected plant tissues, and on seeds, containers, and tools, these fungi can prevent seeds from germinating, or wipe out a batch of new seedlings in a matter of hours. Infected seedlings collapse suddenly due to restricted movement of water and nutrients through either the roots or the stems. If you inspect the seedlings closely, you will find dark, rotted roots or dark, shrunken stems that appear to be girdled, usually at the soil surface.

Damping-off can occur when seedlings are over-watered, crowded, or poorly ventilated; when the soil mix drains or aerates poorly; when temperatures are cold; or when equipment, soil, hands, or seeds are contaminated with fungal spores or vegetative matter. Since there is no cure for affected seedlings, prevention is essential. Use only clean soil mix, containers, and tools. Never combine clean mix with old or previously used mix. Avoid overcrowding seedlings or watering with cold or dirty water, and ensure that seedlings have good air circulation.

As an added precaution, you can treat soil and seeds with a fungicide. Drop a pinch of powdered fungicide (Captan or Benlate, for example) into the seed packet and shake the packet to coat the seeds. Treat soil with liquid preparations mixed according to label directions; you can soak the mix before or after sowing seeds. Watering seedlings weekly with a fungicide solution can also help prevent disease. (As seedlings grow, light levels increase, and air temperatures decrease, seedlings become less susceptible, but not

Some seeds require special techniques to overcome defenses that protect them from harsh conditions. Seeds with hard or water-impermeable coatings can be scarified by *puncturing the coating with a knife or melting it with hot water. Seeds that require a cool, moist period before germination can be placed in a moist medium and refrigerated (top right).*

immune, to damping-off. Remember that fungicides are supplements to providing proper conditions, not substitutes.

Starting Difficult Seeds

Some seeds need more than just warm, moist conditions to germinate. Many of the more unusual plant species and species from temperate or desert climates have evolved seeds that are protected from harsh conditions or that will germinate only after passing through a certain sequence of conditions. Growing these plants from seed can be challenging, but rewarding. If you don't already know them, discovering the seeds' germination requirements takes a little detective work. It helps to know something of the climate and conditions of the plant's native habitat. And it is important to understand dormancy.

Dormancy

Seeds that are alive but do not readily germinate under generally conducive conditions are said to be dormant. Breeding has

Propagation

eliminated dormancy (if it was ever present) from vegetable and common bedding plants, but the seeds of many other plants exhibit one or more of these types of dormancy: physical, mechanical, chemical, rudimentary embryo, undeveloped embryo, physiological embryo, epicotyl, and double.

Seeds with physical dormancy have a water-impermeable seed coat, which conserves moisture and enables the seeds to survive long periods of dry weather. All or some members of the bean, nightshade, mallow, morning-glory, and goosefoot families exhibit physical dormancy.

A seed coat that does not allow the interior embryo to expand even after it has absorbed water imparts mechanical dormancy. Examples include seeds of a few nut and stone-fruit species.

Seeds containing chemical germination inhibitors exhibit chemical dormancy. In nature, these chemicals disappear with time, or are diluted or washed away from the seeds by rains. Examples are scattered throughout the plant kingdom, and include seeds of apples, pears, grapes, melons, bitterbrush, and barberry.

In some species, seeds ripen and fall from the plant even though the seed embryo has barely formed. Before a seed with this rudimentary embryo dormancy can germinate, the embryo must continue to develop. Seeds in the magnolia, poppy, and buttercup families continue this development at temperatures below 59° F, or at alternating temperatures, high during the day and low during the night.

Seeds with undeveloped embryo dormancy are shed from the parent plant with a more highly developed embryo than those of the rudimentary type. But they must still undergo further development to germinate. Seeds of carrots, rhododendrons, cyclamen, and some gentians will continue development during a prolonged period of warm, moist conditions. Cyclamen, for example, requires three to four weeks at 68° F, while some palm species need three months at temperatures between 100° and 104° F. Some species also require a subsequent period of cool temperatures before they can germinate.

Physiological dormancy is controlled within the living tissues of the seed, and includes sensitivities to warm or cold temperatures and to light. These dormancies are easily overcome if you know the precise germination temperature or the seed's requirements for light or darkness. Some physiological dormancies, such as those common in grasses, vegetables, and flowers, tend to disappear with time in dry storage.

Seeds with embryo dormancy need a period in cool, moist conditions before they will germinate. The seeds of many plants native to the temperate zones exhibit embryo dormancy.

Epicotyl dormancy is a somewhat complicated type in which the radicle, hypocotyl, and epicotyl each require different temperatures in sequence before germination. Some species of lilies, viburnums, and peonies, for example, require a warm, moist period of one to three months for root and hypocotyl growth, followed by one to three months of cool, moist conditions for the epicotyl. Subsequent warmth produces normal seedling development. Trilliums and other native perennials of the temperate zone need first a cool, moist period for continued development of the embryo; then a warm, moist period for root growth; finally, a cool, moist period for shoot growth. In nature, two full years may pass before the seedling emerges from the ground.

It is not uncommon for a seed to possess more than one type of dormancy, each type needing to be overcome before germination can occur. Probably the most common of these double dormancies combines a water-impermeable seed coat and a dormant embryo.

Overcoming Seed Dormancy

Even though the factors involved in seed dormancy can be complicated, overcoming the vast majority of them is relatively easy. Seeds that exhibit several kinds of dormancy may have to be subjected to several kinds of treatment before germination is possible.

Scarification

The scarring, puncturing, scraping, abrasion, or softening of the seed coat to allow water and air to enter the seed is called scarification. In nature, wind and water scarify seeds. You can do it with sandpaper, files, or knives. Take care not to cut or abrade deep enough to damage the embryo or cotyledons inside. Plant scarified seeds immediately, before they lose valuable moisture.

To soften hard seed coats or to melt water-impermeable ones, cover the seeds with hot water (170° to 212° F) equal to four to five times their own volume, then allow the water to cool for 12 to 24 hours. Plant swollen seeds right away, before they dehydrate. Try the same treatment again for those that haven't swollen. (Scarifying seeds by freezing is sometimes recommended, but the benefits are unproven.)

In nature, seed coats often are broken down by microbes. You can encourage microbial activity by subjecting seeds to non-sterile, moist, and warm conditions for several months. Seeds that require scarification followed by a period of cool, moist conditions can be planted outdoors in summer or early fall. Keep them moist to promote microbial activity, and leave them in the ground for germination in the spring.

Stratification, or Moist-Chilling

Seeds that need a cool, moist period before germination usually get it in nature by spending time on the ground during the cold winter months. To simulate these conditions, foresters used to place layers of seeds in a moist medium inside a large container. Maintaining the temperature around the container between 34° and 41° F for the required length of time broke dormancy. Because the seeds were put in layers, or strata, the technique became known as stratification.

Even though the strict layering process is no longer practiced, the term "stratification" is still used for the technique of subjecting seeds to cool, moist conditions. The term is used so frequently, however, that it has lost some of its meaning. So instead of "stratification," we'll use a more descriptive term, "moist-chilling," to specify moist conditions between 34° and 41° F.

Prepare seeds that require moist-chilling by first soaking them in warm water for 24 hours to ensure that they have fully imbibed. Thoroughly moisten some peat moss, vermiculite, or sand, and squeeze out excess water. Mix the seeds with two or three times their own volume of moist medium. Put the seed/medium mix into a box, jar, can, or other container with a perforated lid. Polyethylene bags work well because they hold moisture but allow for some gas exchange. Put the container in a refrigerator that can be maintained at 34° to 41° F. If you are treating only a few seeds, sow them normally in a small pot containing pre-moistened soil. Label the pot, enclose it in a polyethylene bag, and place it in a refrigerator. Regularly check the moisture content of the refrigerated medium, and renew it if necessary. Cool, dry conditions will not break dormancy.

The amount of moist-chilling time required varies by species and occasionally by seed lot. Recommendations generally are between one and four months, but your results may vary. Check the refrigerated seeds regularly for germination. If some have germinated, even before the prescribed time, it is likely the other seeds in that container are ready to germinate, so remove and sow them. If seeds are refrigerated too long after germination, they will form roots that can be easily damaged when the seeds are subsequently sown or transplanted. You may want to schedule moist-chilling treatments so that the seeds will be ready to germinate when you are ready to grow seedlings.

You can also meet moist-chilling requirements by merely sowing the seeds outdoors in the fall and letting normal winter temperatures do the job. (Temperatures only a few degrees below freezing or much above 41° F will not satisfy the chilling requirement.) Take care to keep the seeds moist at all times during the winter.

Leaching

You can leach out water-soluble germination inhibitors by placing seeds in continuously running water for 12 to 24 hours. Alternatively, you can soak the seeds in large volumes of water that are periodically drained and replaced. After treatment, sow the seeds in a normal fashion.

Collecting and Saving Seeds

In addition to being fun, challenging, and inexpensive, collecting and saving seeds may be the only way you can obtain certain plants. Remember, however, that many plants grown from seed will differ from the parent plant, and that this difference may be the absence of an endearing quality or the acquisition of an undesirable one.

In preparation for seed collecting, learn about the plant's usual flowering and fruiting periods. Dates seldom can be exact because of the great influence of weather on these periods. Some plants also bloom and ripen seeds sporadically throughout the season. Learn to recognize the seeds and the plant's mechanisms for dispersing them. Some species quickly and forcibly expel seeds a short time after the seeds have ripened. Some seeds are easily knocked off by hail, wind, or rain, while others may remain on the plant for months. Many seeds are collected and consumed by animals before the seeds are ripe. You can prevent seed dispersal and protect seeds from animals by enclosing the fruiting head or branch in a paper or cloth bag. The ability to judge the ripeness of seeds is gained with experience. Here are a few pointers: As early as a week before the flesh of pulpy fruits becomes soft and juicy, the seeds inside usually will be ripe enough for collection. Ripe seeds of most other plants will be firm, full, and dark, although a few ripen light or white in color.

Collecting and Cleaning Seeds

Most of the time, you can remove ripe seeds from a plant with a bare or gloved hand. You may want to remove only the fruiting body or seedhead, or it may be easier to clip stems and separate the seeds later. Place seeds or fruits in paper or cloth sacks. Green leaves, stems, and the fleshy portions of fruits collected with some seeds will quickly deteriorate and possibly destroy the seeds if kept in moisture-retentive containers. Put the collected seeds in a warm, sheltered location for further drying. You can leave small quantities of seeds in the paper or cloth bags and stir them occasionally. But it is best to spread the seeds over sheets of newspaper for quick and thorough drying.

Separating dried seeds from leaves, stems, seed appendages, and other plant trash requires experience, ingenuity, and creativity. One popular method is to place seeds and trash on a wooden board covered with a ribbed rubber floor mat. Rub with a block of wood (which may also be covered with rubber matting) to separate the seeds from the trash. Experience will teach you how much pressure to apply without crushing the seeds. You can separate seeds from chaff using a stack of homemade or commercial screens, each of a

Propagation

different mesh size, with the largest mesh on top and the smallest on the bottom. Place the seeds and trash on the top screen and shake the stack. The screens will filter out particles of different sizes, and with any luck, one screen will contain pure seed. To separate heavy seeds from lighter trash, drop small portions in front of a fan. With some experimentation, you can learn at what distance from the fan to drop the portions so that only the seeds fall and the trash is blown away.

Seeds in fleshy fruits must be cleaned immediately after collection to avoid molds and fermentation. Methods include crushing the fruit with a rolling pin, forcing the fruit through screens, or crushing the fruit by hand in water. You can put the macerated fruit in a bucket of water and skim debris and pulp off the top, leaving the heavier seeds to sink to the bottom. After draining the water, screen the seeds and spread them to dry for storage or immediate planting. You may not need to remove the thin fruit coverings of some seeds, such as those of sumacs and silk-tassel, before pre-sowing treatments or sowing.

Storing Seeds

Not all seeds can be stored. So-called "recalcitrant" seeds quickly lose viability if they dry appreciably, so these should be sown or treated for dormancy immediately. Examples include seeds of the oak, willow, poplar, and oily nut families, as well as seeds of many tropical and aquatic plants.

The length of time that other seeds can be stored depends on the moisture content of the seeds and the temperature at which they are stored. In general, the seeds of most temperate-zone plants store best when dried to between four and six percent moisture content and stored at temperatures of 35° to 40° F.

It is easy enough to control the temperature with a common refrigerator, but measuring the seeds' moisture content is difficult unless you are working with a large quantity of seeds or a precise weighing device. Dry seeds exposed to several days of relative humidity in the range of 20 to 25 percent usually can be counted on to have moisture levels acceptable for storage. Seal them inside a closed, airtight and moisture-proof can, jar, or other container, and store them in the refrigerator until you are ready to sow them. It is always a good idea to label the stored seeds with the collection date and the location where they were collected.

Many seeds with hard seed coats can be expected to store for long periods without refrigeration. No seed, however, will remain viable long in the hot or humid conditions found in kitchens, attics, damp cellars, or greenhouses. Seeds stored under less than ideal conditions may fail to germinate, or may germinate more slowly and with less vigor than properly stored seeds.

Growing Ferns from Spores

Growing ferns from spores is not an entirely different process than growing other plants from seed, but it does demand more patience, more attention to cleanliness, and an understanding of fern biology, which differs from that of seed-producing plants in several regards. The full growth cycle of ferns involves two separate generations of organisms. The familiar plant with fronds, roots, and stems is the sporophyte generation, which is produced asexually. Spores form on the underside of fronds in special bodies called sporangia. When ripe, the tiny spores are released and are often carried far from the parent plant. Upon germination, these spores begin the sexual, or gametophyte, generation of the fern's life cycle.

Over a period of many days to several months, each germinated spore forms a small, green body called a prothallium. On the underside of the prothallium are areas that produce male and female sex cells. In favorable conditions, sperm cells are released from the male area and migrate through free water across the prothallium to the female area, where they unite with the eggs. Each fertilized egg develops into a fern plant, and the cycle begins again.

The first step in growing ferns from spores is to inspect the underside of the fern fronds with a magnifying glass to see if the groups of sporangia (called sori) contain any spores. Collect fronds containing spores in a paper envelope and dry them for at least a week at 70° F. Then, with a very fine screen, separate the dustlike spores from the remaining chaff. Store collected spores in an airtight and moisture-proof container in a cool place until you are ready to sow them.

Spores must be sown on a medium that is scrupulously clean of disease, weed seeds, and other pests. A popular mix consists of two parts peat moss and one part perlite. Perlite from an unopened bag should be sterile. Although peat moss generally is not treated for pathogens or pests, that from an unopened bag should be clean enough. Moisten the medium and fill a sterilized container (a four-inch plastic pot will do) to within an inch of the top. To avoid contamination, use distilled water when wetting the medium.

Sow the spores thinly and evenly, and cover the container with a pane of glass or other clear material. (You will keep the cover on from now until the new plants have formed their first leaves.) Place the sown container in moderate light and 65° to 75° F temperatures. Keep the spores and medium moist at all times; replace lost moisture by gently spraying or misting.

Upon germination, a mosslike growth of prothallia, about one-eighth inch thick, will form on the surface of the medium. It will take three to six months—depending on temperature, light, and the species of fern—for the eggs to be fertilized. Before this happens, however, you will need to transplant the prothallia to

Propagation

You can make a simple cold frame by nailing together a box of one- or two-inch-thick lumber. (Reinforce the corners of large frames with posts.) Set it on top of the ground or bury it partially, orienting the top toward the south. Old storm windows make good covers; you should be able to prop them open at different heights for ventilation.

give them more room. Separate small sections of the prothallia with tweezers, move them to another similarly prepared container, and press them to the surface at a wider spacing. After this, the prothallia should expand to approximately one-half inch in diameter, and begin producing small sporophyte plants with primary leaves and roots.

Prior to the emergence of the primary leaves, you can start fertilizing with a very weak solution of an all-purpose houseplant fertilizer. Continue fertilizing regularly. When leaves appear, begin lifting the cover gradually. Remove it when the plants are somewhat established. As the plants grow, transplant them to larger containers or to the garden as you would any other plant.

Growing Succulents from Seed

Succulents share the ability to store water in leaves, stems, or roots, thus giving them a fleshy appearance. Contrary to popular belief, succulents are not exclusively desert plants, and are found from the tropics to the tundra.

Although most texts treat succulents separately from other plants, they can be propagated from seed in the same manner as other plants, though it is prudent to pay extra attention to soil aeration. Most, if not all, succulents can be grown hydroponically, with their roots constantly moist or immersed in water, so it is too little

oxygen in the soil, rather than too much water, that causes problems with their growth.

You can make a simple and economical sowing mix by combining any commercial mix with perlite. A combination that is one-third to one-half perlite will provide the necessary moisture retention and aeration. Some succulents are particularly susceptible to damping-off disease, so pay special attention to sanitation at all times. Do not place a layer of gravel in the bottom of the container—this will just reduce the aeration of the mix on top of it.

Sow the seeds as you would for other plants—use pre-moistened soil, do not cover very small seeds and so on. Cactus germination is slow and erratic; have patience. To avoid damping-off, remove container covers gradually to reduce the humidity around emerging seedlings; water from the bottom to keep the seedlings dry and the soil wet. Many desert succulents germinate and grow in nature only in the shade of the parent or other larger plants, where light and moisture conditions typically are more conducive for survival. Not unlike other plants, succulent seedlings should not be exposed to full sunlight until they have become firmly established.

Transplant the seedlings once they have developed their first set of true leaves. At this time, cactus seedlings will be one-eighth to one-quarter inch in diameter and consist of a set of short, fat cotyledons and some vertical growth showing some spines. Many succulents have a fine, delicate root system at this stage, so take care not to damage it when transplanting. Transplant into the same kind of amended mix. The plants' capacity to withstand extreme drought and even poorer soils does not indicate a need for these conditions, just a tolerance of them. With properly aerated soil, succulents of all types can withstand heavy applications of water and moderate amounts of fertilizer applied regularly.

Cold Frames and Hotbeds

These miniature greenhouses provide well-lighted, protective environments for propagating seedlings and cuttings, and for extending the growing season in the spring and the fall. By providing your plants with year-round shelter from battering rains, rapid temperature fluctuations, and damaging winds, you can relieve some of the difficulties of growing delicate plants or practicing special procedures. A hotbed is just a cold frame that generates its own heat. In the old days, decomposing manure and vegetable matter beneath the frame provided the heat; today, gardeners generally rely on electrical heating elements.

Building a Cold Frame

Choose a location that gets full sun during the day and is well protected from winds. Frames typically are low and built entirely or partially in the ground. Orient the roof, or cover, so that it slopes

Propagation

from north to south. If you specialize in growing shade plants or plants whose seedlings demand shade (such as azaleas and rhododendrons), you may want to orient the cover so that it slopes from south to north. Drainage is critical, whether the frame is built into the ground or on top of it; avoid poorly drained sites. If you are growing directly in the frame (rather than placing containers in it), you can prepare the soil inside as you would for a bed.

You can use old window sash or storm windows for covers, and size the frame accordingly. Rigid fiberglass sheets or plastic film stretched over homemade wooden frames also makes good covers. Films, fiberglass, or other coverings specially manufactured for greenhouses contain ultraviolet-light inhibitors, which prolong the life of the material. These often are available at garden centers or from mail-order suppliers.

You can construct the frame of wood, bricks, cinder blocks, or any other rigid material. Boards one or two inches thick nailed to four-inch-square sunken corner posts make a simple, sturdy frame. Cedar, redwood, or cypress will last longer than pine or fir, but not as long as woods that have been pressure-treated with preservatives. Creosote fumes are toxic to plants, so don't use creosote-treated railroad ties.

Insulation will help retain heat during cold months, but be sure to use only moisture-proof insulation. The earth surrounding below-grade frames is, of course, insulation. You can also insulate the frame covers during the night or extremely cold days with blankets, foam insulation, straw mats, or other materials. Remember that small-volume frames will respond quicker to outside changes in temperature or light than will larger ones.

If your frame will house plants in containers, remove any vegetation that somehow survived the building process, and spread a layer of sand or gravel, about two inches deep, for drainage.

Building a Hotbed

The basic structure and siting of a hotbed are the same as those of a cold frame. Since you are adding heat during cold periods, it makes sense to insulate the frame effectively. If you buy thermostatically controlled electric heating cables, strips, or mats, place them on top of a bed of vermiculite, perlite, or sand, two inches or more thick. Then cover them with a one-inch-thick layer of soil or sand to help diffuse the heat. Place wire screen with quarter- to half-inch mesh over this layer to protect the heating devices from puncture. If the hotbed is for plants in containers, cover the screen with a thin layer of sand. If you want to root cuttings directly, cover the screen with four to six inches of propagation medium.

You can also heat a frame with incandescent light bulbs, although these aren't as effective and don't supply heat to the roots as uniformly as do devices designed for the purpose. Incandescent

By insulating and providing bottom heat to a cold frame, you can start and grow a wide range of plants in colder conditions. Set the hotbed into the ground; place a heat

mat or cables on two inches of sand, perlite or vermiculite. Cover it with an inch of soil or sand and a wire screen for protection.

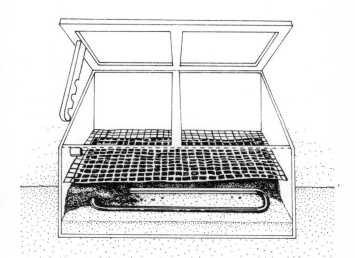

bulbs can generate a lot of heat, so it is prudent to wire them to a thermostat.

Remember that electricity and water are a dangerous combination. If you are not certain of wiring requirements for outdoor outlets and fixtures, ask a professional for help.

Operating Cold Frames and Hotbeds

Regulating the temperature inside the frame is the most important, and time-consuming, part of using a cold frame or a hotbed. A frame or a bed can quickly accumulate levels of heat that are debilitating or fatal to plants. Place a simple thermometer in the frame, in shade at the same level as the plant leaves, to check the temperature. Although each plant species and cultivar will react differently to different temperatures, most are seriously affected by temperatures of 90° to 95° F or more. To reduce the temperature, you can prop the cover open, or shade the frame with lath, cloth, newspapers, or other materials, or both. Some gardeners fit their frames and beds with automatic vent arms, which can be calibrated to open and close according to the temperature.

Humidity is more difficult to measure and control than temperature. High humidity and poor air circulation can create conditions conducive to the germination and spread of fungal diseases among seedlings. You will learn from observation and experience when and how high to raise the covers to avoid heat and humidity problems.

Vegetative Propagation

Plants have the wondrous ability to produce a new individual from
a part of an old one. Under certain conditions, a portion of a leaf,
stem, shoot, or root can generate a completely new plant, which is
identical, or nearly so, to its parent. Over centuries, gardeners and
horticulturists have developed techniques to initiate or enhance this
natural phenomenon in order to increase their stock of plants.
Almost all the vegetative parts of a plant (virtually everything but
the seeds and associated sexual parts) are candidates for this asexual
type of propagation. Cuttings commonly are taken from the
terminal, internodal, or basal portions of a stem at different times
in its growth cycle, from youth to dormancy. Crowns are divided, as
well as roots and rhizomes and the plants arising from them.
Specialized plant structures such as bulbs and corms can be divided
or forced into growth that can later be divided and multiplied.
Many of the techniques of vegetative propagation merely take
advantage of work that nature has already done. Bulblets, bulbils,
and cormlets are naturally formed on bulbs and corms, respectively,
and gardeners need only harvest, plant, and tend them. The suckers
that arise from the roots of sumacs, poplars, lilacs, and other plants;
the runners on plants such as strawberries and bugleweed; the
stolons on Bermudagrass, mint, redtwig dogwood, and others—all
are capable of producing new, independent plants without human
intervention. Agaves, yuccas, and aloes frequently form offsets
that can grow into new plants. Stems that come in contact with
the ground often form roots where they touch the ground or are
covered by it.

Division

Perhaps the easiest and most successful vegetative-propagation
technique is division. In nature, plants frequently grow and divide
themselves over the years into two or more independent plants.
Gardeners can duplicate this process by lifting an entire plant and
dividing it into pieces, each piece a small plant complete with
leaves or buds, stems, and roots.
When dividing plants, often you need to be able to identify leaves,
stems, shoots, and roots that may not at first glance appear to be
these parts. The leaves of a lily, for example, are easily recognized
on the flowering stem, but they also occur in a modified form in
the bulb, from which they can be separated to produce new plants.
Unfortunately, the terminology used to describe plant parts can
vary from source to source. We have tried to be consistent and use
widely recognized terms here, but you may find the same plant
part called different things in different books.
Normally plants are divided in the early spring or in the fall. Spring
weather promotes good shoot and root growth in the newly
separated plants, which have a full growing season to become

established. In northern regions, plants divided in the fall, after deciduous plants have lost their leaves but before the ground freezes, have some opportunity to continue growing roots before very cold weather prevails. In southern regions, where excellent root-growing temperatures occur throughout the winter, gardeners may prefer to divide in the fall rather than in the spring.

Dividing Plants That Form Crowns

Any plant that forms a crown at its base is a candidate for division. A crown is a collection of living and many times dead stems; it forms over a period of years, and increases the diameter of the plant. Chrysanthemums and daisies, for example, form crowns that often consist of a ring of living stems surrounding a few stems that grow or flower poorly. Dividing plants with crowded crowns or those that are flowering less abundantly can restore their vigor. You can also divide healthy, flourishing plants to increase your stock.

As a rule, most species are best divided in early spring before growth begins. Some plants, however, will do best if divided at specific times of year according to their growth cycle. Plants that normally bloom in the spring can be divided in the late spring and early summer, or even in fall. Plants that bloom in late spring and go dormant shortly thereafter, such as Oriental poppies, can be divided in the summer. Wait until they have bloomed and the foliage has begun to discolor before dividing. Many herbaceous species can be divided at any time of year, so successful are they at reestablishing themselves. Gardeners commonly refer to this practice as taking "slips."

Before you lift and divide a plant, thoroughly water the surrounding ground and allow it to drain, and prepare the soil in which you will plant the divisions. If possible, divide plants on cloudy days; the lower temperature and higher humidity will reduce moisture stress. Dig around and under the plant with a shovel or a garden fork to create a generous root ball. Then lift the plant with as many roots as possible, and place it onto a firm surface.

Although it is best to leave as much soil as possible on the roots, you may have to shake off or wash away some soil so that you can locate the growing points—each division must contain structures capable of producing new roots and shoots. A number of plants— rhubarb and peony, for example—do not reestablish quickly from divisions, so you should try to disturb their roots as little as possible.

Some plants can be separated easily with your fingers or a hand fork. Others may need to be cut apart with a sharp shovel or a sturdy knife. You can force apart large plants with tough, compact, or tangled roots, such as daylilies, by thrusting two garden forks back to back into the center of the crown and levering one against the other. Some plants may be too large to comfortably lift. If so,

Propagation

You can divide crown-forming plants to restore their health or increase your stock. Lift the plant with a generous root ball. Shake off loose soil to locate the growing points. Some plants separate easily with your fingers; others you'll need to cut with a knife or pry apart with garden forks. Transplant and water new divisions as soon as possible.

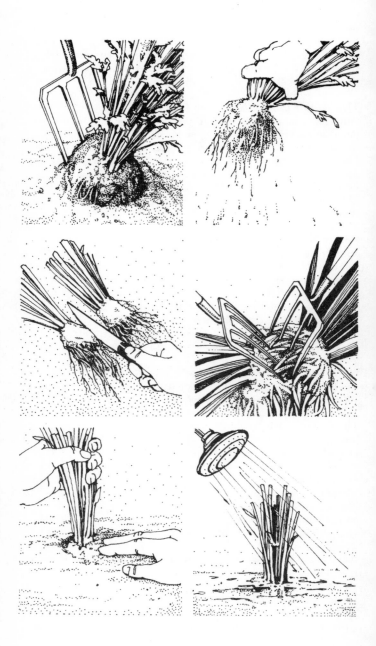

you can divide them in the ground by slicing off portions from the edges of the crown.

After it has been separated from its parent, a new division should be treated like any other new plant. Put it in the ground as soon as possible. Don't let the roots dry out. Water it immediately and thoroughly. Keep it watered and protected from intense sunlight, heat, and wind until it is well established. (See the chapter on planting.) If you have the space, you can plant small divisions in a nursery bed where they can grow to a decent size before being transplanted to their final location. If you plant small divisions in the fall, mulch the soil around them to prevent subsequent freezing and thawing from pushing them out of the ground.

Flowering Herbaceous Perennials

Plants in this category whose crowns consist of numerous, annually renewed shoots often lose overall vigor or develop dead centers over the years. Depending on species and cultivar, you can divide these plants every three to five years to renew their health.

Lift and divide the plant as described above. Take a generous root ball, and be sure that each division contains structures necessary for forming a new plant, usually at least one shoot with healthy roots. Candidates for this type of division include coreopsis, bleeding-heart, foxglove, aster, campanula, anemone, butterfly flower, daisy, primrose, herbaceous peonies, sedum, veronica, viola, and rudbeckia.

Woody Plants

Any of these plants that form crowns are divided in exactly the same manner and at the same times as herbaceous plants. Because of their size, however, a bit more brute strength and sturdier tools may be necessary.

Gardeners frequently are told to prune back the tops of woody plants before division. Theoretically, this brings the plant's top growth into balance with the smaller root system that results from division. Recent research, however, indicates that it is better to leave the top growth alone when dividing, and to prune only those portions of the top that die back after replanting. Leaving the top intact allows the plant to develop as many leaves as possible, each of which aids in the recovery by manufacturing foods necessary for root survival and growth. Large, unwieldy plants may still need to be pruned so that they can be maneuvered during the operation. Candidates include barberry, heath, spirea, clematis roots, leadwort, potentilla, and coralberry.

Dividing Plants with Runners and Stolons

Many gardeners confuse runners and stolons with other plant structures. For our purposes, a runner is a specialized stem that

Propagation

Some plants form special stems called runners or stolons that grow horizontally along the ground. To propagate from them, pin a runner or stolon to the ground at a node and keep the surrounding soil moist. When roots and shoots form, you can cut the new plant free of the parent and transplant it.

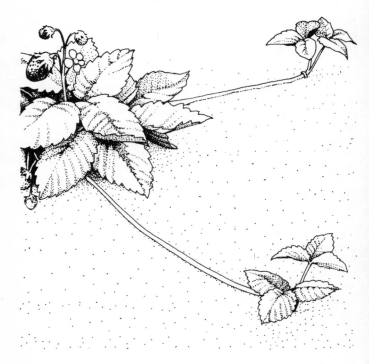

develops from the axil of a leaf in the crown of the plant. The stem grows horizontally along the top of the ground and usually has long internodes. Where conditions permit, the nodes can develop roots and shoots and become independent of the parent plant. Plants producing runners often grow as a rosette or a crown. A large number of ground covers are included in this group of plants. Stolons are modified aerial stems that grow along the ground, often rooting at the nodes. They, too, may form shoots at the nodes and over time become independent of the parent plant. Plants that produce stolons include redtwig dogwood, Bermudagrass, bugleweed, mint, and stachys.

Gardeners can propagate plants with runners or stolons merely by enhancing the plant's natural tendencies. Pin or peg a runner or a stolon to the ground at one or more nodes. Keep the soil around the pinned nodes moist to allow any roots that are formed to become established. When roots and shoots have formed (tug gently at the roots to see how well established they are) cut the new plant free of its parent and transplant it. Some plants, such as strawberries, are ready to be separated in a few weeks, others, like redtwig dogwood, can take as long as a year. Water the new plants well, and protect them from sun and wind.

Some plants produce offspring on short, thick stems originating at the plant's base. When these offsets have developed their own roots (tug on them to find out), you can sever *them from the parent and transplant them.*

Candidates include many ground covers, strawberry, bugleweed, strawberry geranium, false strawberry, Bermudagrass, redtwig dogwood, mint, and stachys.

Dividing Plants with Offsets

The term "offset" is probably more scrambled than either runner or stolon. Technically, an offset is a type of lateral shoot or branch that develops from the base of the main stem of certain plants. It usually is a shortened, thickened stem resembling a rosette. The term occasionally is also applied to certain bulblets, and to certain lateral branches of palms, bromeliads, agaves, yuccas, and aloes.

In nature, offsets often become independent of the parent plant by establishing their own root systems. This is most apparent in agaves, where, in most species, the parent plant dies after blooming. You can take advantage of this natural means of asexual propagation by separating and transplanting offsets that have formed their own roots. Offsets that have not yet formed a root system can be propagated like a leafy cutting.

Candidates include aloe, yucca, datepalm, pineapple, banana, and century plant.

Propagation

Suckers, new plants growing from stem tissue or roots, can often be divided from the parent and transplanted. To evaluate a candidate, *dig down and inspect its roots; if they're prolific and healthy, sever the sucker, taking as many of its roots as possible, and transplant.*

Dividing Plants with Suckers

A sucker is a shoot that arises from root tissues below ground, but the term commonly is also used for shoots arising from stem tissue near the crown of the plant. Suckers may appear at any distance from the parent plant.

Divide and transplant suckers during the dormant season, in the spring or, second best, the fall. To determine if a sucker has enough roots to support itself, dig down and make an educated guess based on the quantity and quality of the roots you find. If the sucker's roots are healthy and prolific, cut the root connecting the sucker to the parent plant with pruners. Lift the sucker with as many remaining roots and as much soil as possible, and transplant it. As for other woody divisions, don't prune healthy roots or top growth if you can help it.

Candidates include lilac, sumac, raspberry, blackberry, hazel, plum, serviceberry, filbert, poplar, black locust, chokeberry, sand cherry, jasmine, mock orange, heavenly bamboo, flowering quince, rugosa rose, and coralberry.

Dividing Plants with Rhizomes

Rhizomes are storage structures that grow horizontally at or just beneath the surface of the soil. These segmented stems have nodes and internodes from which roots grow and lateral branching occurs. Leaves, flowering stems called culms, and upright, aboveground shoots also develop from the rhizome or its lateral branches. Most rhizome-bearing plants are monocots, and they include lily-of-the-

A number of plants, including irises, have subsurface stems called rhizomes that can be divided to produce new plants. Lift the rhizomes with a fork and sever their branching parts where they join. (Each iris branch should contain one or two leaf fans.) Remove dead leaves and cut back the remainder to conserve water. Replant at the same depth.

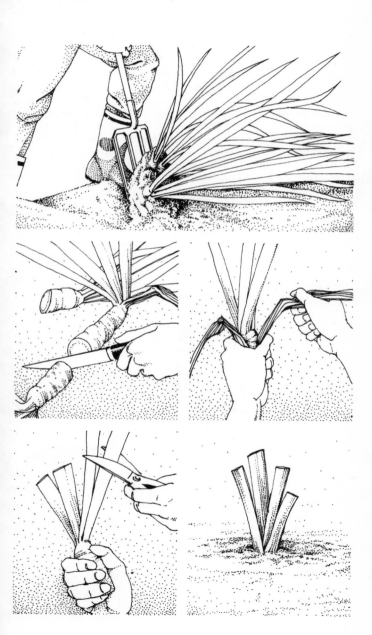

Propagation *Dig up the tuberous roots of dahlias, and cut each cluster so that each piece contains a bud. Dust the cut surface with a fungicidal powder; then plant the cuttings in soil.*

valley, Japanese spurge, rhizomatous iris, many grasses including bamboo and sugar cane, and some ferns.

There are two major types of rhizomes of interest to gardeners. Bearded irises are the best-known example of plants with determinate rhizomes, which terminate in a flowering stalk. Their growth cycle starts with the formation of a lateral branch on a section of the rhizome that has produced a flowering culm. When the culm dies, the lateral branch produces leaves that grow and store food, and by the end of the season, it produces a flower bud of its own. The bud forms a flowering culm the following season, and the process repeats. Over time, these plants form clumps of rhizomes, which should be divided before they become overcrowded. Dividing rhizomes helps prevent weakened plants and declining flower production.

Determinate rhizomes can be divided when growth begins in early spring or when it ends in late summer to early fall. Don't disturb the plants during the period following flowering, which is crucial to the formation of new leaves and flowers. Lift the rhizomes and cut lateral branches from a rhizome at their point of attachment. Iris branches will contain one or two leaf fans. Cut the top growth back to reduce water loss before the new roots get established and replant at the same depth. Discard older sections of the rhizome.

Lily-of-the-valley exemplifies the plants with indeterminate rhizomes, which grow continuously in length from the apex and from lateral branches. Although each node contains a lateral bud, these usually remain dormant, so the plant spreads widely over a large area. These plants generally begin the growth period vegetatively and bloom later in the same period.

Indeterminate rhizomes are propagated in much the same fashion as determinate types. Cut off and transplant the lateral rhizomes (called "offshoots" in lily-of-the-valley) along with their roots. Apical or terminal rhizomes containing flower buds will bloom the following year, but some transplanted lateral branches might not. You can divide lily-of-the-valley nearly any time of the year, but the dormant season is preferred.

Other candidates for this type of propagation include bamboo, Solomon's Seal, false Solomon's Seal, and bulrushes.

Dividing Tubers

Like a rhizome, a tuber is a specialized, underground stem that stores food. Spread uniformly over the outside surface are eyes, which consist of one or more buds (the stem's nodes, each with a leaf scar from previous season's growth). Tubers are connected to the parent plant by stolons. Tubers are produced annually, remain dormant over the winter, and begin growth during the following season.

Tubers are simple to propagate. Dig up the tubers and slice them into several pieces, each with at least one eye or bud and enough tuber to sustain initial growth. Dust the pieces immediately with a protective fungicide and leave them for several days where it is warm (70° F) and humid so that they will form a protective layer of cells over the cut surfaces. This process, called suberization, helps prevent the tuber from further drying and decay. Finally, plant the pieces in your garden at a depth appropriate for the species. Candidates include potatoes, caladium, and Jerusalem artichoke.

Dividing Tuberous Roots

These swollen secondary storage roots have no eyes. Instead, buds are found only on the crown of the root, and the fibrous roots are only at the opposite end. Tuberous roots require two full growing seasons to form and mature, and they go dormant when the herbaceous stems go dormant. During the second spring, buds from the crown produce new shoots, nourished by food stored in the the old root. During the season, the old root is depleted and new tuberous roots are produced.

Dahlias provide a good example of this propagation technique. Typically, dahlias are dug in the fall, dried for a few days, and then stored over the winter at 40° to 50° F in sawdust or vermiculite. In late winter or just before planting in the spring, separate the root

Propagation

Many of our favorite spring flowers are produced by bulbs, which are really compact underground stems. Specialized leaves or leaf bases called scales protect and provide food for the emerging plant.

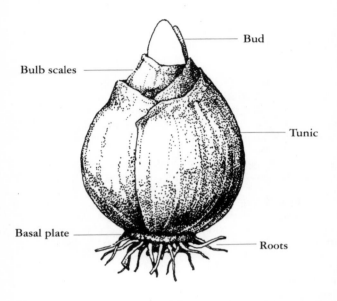

Bud

Bulb scales

Tunic

Basal plate

Roots

clusters with a knife. Include at least one bud on the crown end of the root for shoot growth. Dust the cut surfaces with a fungicide and plant the separated roots with the buds located at the soil surface. Small roots may produce only foliage the first year, but will flower if replanted the following year.

Candidates include dahlia, sweet potato, and Persian Ranunculus.

Dividing Tuberous Stems

A tuberous stem is a storage structure that begins to form when a portion of the primary root swells shortly after a seed germinates. As the plant matures, the upper end of the crown contains the buds and the lower end produces fibrous roots. Tuberous stems enlarge laterally every year.

You can divide tuberous stems, such as tuberous begonias, after growth begins in the spring. Cut vertically through the swollen stem, making sure that each section contains at least one strong shoot. Dust the cut surfaces with a fungicide and replant each section with the crown at or just above the soil surface. Be careful to avoid damaging any fibrous roots that tuberous begonias may have developed. If you are dividing unplanted tuberous begonias that have begun growth, let the divisions dry for several days before planting so that the cut surfaces can suberize. The success rate for dividing cyclamens is low, so they are usually grown from seed.

Dividing Bulbs

Bulbs are underground stems. Short and normally globose, they bear at their tips either a growing point or tissue containing the yet undeveloped flowers. Providing protection and food storage to the growing point or embryonic flowers are specialized leaves or leaf bases called bulb scales. The outer layers of bulb scales usually appear fleshy, while the interior layers appear more leaflike.

There are two general types of bulbs. Onions, daffodils, and tulips are examples of bulbs whose outer scales are dry and papery, and provide protection against moisture loss. These outer scales resemble tunics, so these bulbs are referred to as tunicate bulbs. Inside these protective layers, the bulb scales are tightly held together.

Bulbs such as lilies and fritillarias lack protective coverings, and are referred to as non-tunicate or naked bulbs. Their bulb scales are held together only loosely, and can easily come apart, so they are easy to divide, but they must be handled carefully and protected from moisture loss.

Candidates include allium, onion, Sego lily, camas, and crocus. Although bulbs can be and are propagated by seed, especially by breeders, the process is slow, often taking six to seven years before the plant flowers. Gardeners can increase their stock of bulbs much more quickly by separating naturally occurring offspring, called bulblets and bulbils, from the parent bulb.

The term "bulblets" describes the small bulbs that often form in the leaf or scale axils at the base of tunicate and non-tunicate bulbs. After the aboveground foliage has died down, you can dig the parents up and easily pull off these bulblets, also referred to as offsets. Plant them just as you would a full-size bulb, but at a depth only twice their own diameter. You can plant the bulblets immediately, or store them for a later date. Bulblets may take several years to grow to flowering size, so you may want to plant them in a nursery bed.

Small bulbs that form on other portions of the parent plant are called bulbils. Certain lilies (*Lilium tigrinum, L. bulbiferum, L. sargentiae,* and *L. sulphureum,* for example) form bulbils in the leaf axils of the flowering stem, both above and below the soil surface. Bulbils generally are smaller than bulblets. You can plant them at the same time and in the same manner as bulblets, or you can store them over the winter in dry peat moss in a cool, dry place and plant them in the spring. Alternatively, you can plant them half an inch deep in flats or other containers, and grow them indoors before transplanting them outside the following spring or fall.

Some bulbs that do not naturally form bulbils in leaf axils can be encouraged to do so. Simply remove the flowers as they form, then a week later cut off the upper half of the flowering stem. (*Lilium candidum, L. × testaceum, L. chalcedonicum, L. × hollandicum,* and

Propagation

You can increase your stock of bulbs by dividing the small bulbs, called bulblets, that often form in the leaf axils at the bulb's base. Divide them after the parent's foliage has died back. Store and plant them as you would a full-size bulb, but only twice as deep as their diameter.

L. × *maculatum* respond well to this procedure.) To coax the Easter lily, *L. longiflorum,* to form bulbils, you can pull the stem from the parent bulb right before it blooms and bury its entire length one inch deep until bulbils form in the leaf axils. (You can also cut and bury pieces of the stem, each containing a leaf.) Plant the bulbils four inches deep in October, then replant them six inches deep the following September.

Bulb Scaling

Non-tunicate bulbs such as lilies can be propagated using a technique known as bulb scaling. During the dormant season, carefully lift the bulbs and wash them free of clinging soil. Snap individual bulb scales from the base of each bulb, dust each with a fungicide, and put them in damp peat moss or vermiculite inside a polyethylene bag. After several weeks of storage in a warm, dark place, the scales will grow roots. Remove rooting scales from the bag and plant them a quarter to a half inch deep in trays or pots filled with moistened potting soil. Water the containers thoroughly

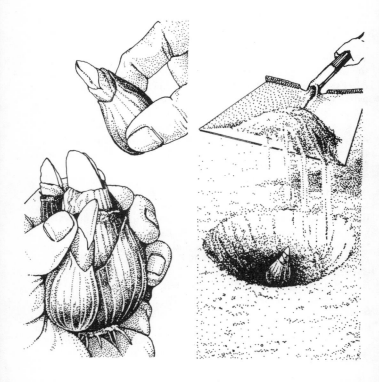

Some lilies form small bulbs in the leaf axils of the flowering stem. You can collect and plant these bulbils outdoors just like you do bulblets. Or you can plant them indoors in a flat and transplant the young plants in the spring.

and place them in a spot at 65° to 70° F with light. (Some plants require a period of cold dormancy, so to be on the safe side, you could refrigerate the bag containing the scales with well-formed roots for eight weeks at 35° to 40° F before planting them.) Soon, green, grasslike sprouts will appear, only to gradually disappear as one or more very small bulbs form at the base of the old bulb scale. After about six weeks, separate these tiny new bulbs from the scale and either plant them in a protected location in the garden if weather permits, store them for planting in the spring, or grow them in a container for an additional year.

Lilies can be scaled soon after blooming in summer, in the fall, or even in midwinter. Since plants grown from scales may take several years to bloom, you may wish to remove only the outer two layers of scales for propagation—if replanted immediately, the parent bulb should continue to bloom.

Dividing Corms and Cormels

Corms, like bulbs, are swollen underground stems that store food for the new plant, and they are often confused with bulbs. If you dig them during their dormant period, typically you will find a new corm growing on top of the previous season's shriveled and depleted corm. Enclosed by dry leaflike scales, the new corm will have a growing point at the top, lateral buds along the side, and offspring called cormels attached to it. If large, cormels are known as offsets; if small, they are called spawn.

In cold climates, gladiolus corms are lifted each fall, and the new corms are separated from the old and stored in a cool, dry place until they are replanted in the spring. When you lift the corms, remove the cormels and store them along with the corms. In the spring, plant offsets and spawn in a nursery bed for a year or two to allow them to attain blooming size. Some cormels may become very hard with dry storage and not resprout quickly in the spring. If this has occurred, store them in moist peat moss at 40° F, or soak them in cool running water for a day or two, then keep them in moist conditions. At the first sign of root development, plant them immediately. Small cormels replanted only an inch or two deep will increase in size faster than if they are planted at the same depth as the parent corm. Cormels of any size will form only grasslike leaves during their first growing season.

The lateral buds of corms are capable of producing an adult plant, so you can divide a corm by cutting it vertically into three or four pieces, each with a lateral bud. Dust the pieces with a protective fungicide and plant them outdoors, sprout side up, when you plant whole corms. You can increase the production of cormels by planting a corm only a few inches deep.

Candidates include gladiolus, crocus, colchicum, tritoma, and freesia.

Cuttings

Propagation by cuttings is the method most often used to produce ornamental shrubs and many greenhouse plants, as well as several fruiting species and cultivars. It is the easiest method available for propagating a large quantity of plants in a small space from just a few stock plants. And almost all plants arising from cuttings will be genetically identical to the parents.

Unlike divisions, which contain the necessary growing points for both shoots and roots, cuttings have to regenerate either the shoots or the roots, or both. Every plant cell contains all the genetic information necessary to reconstitute the entire plant, so you should take cuttings from those parts of the plant in which cells will most readily regenerate, and provide the levels of moisture, temperature, and light conducive to their doing so.

Selecting Cuttings

It can be difficult to determine which part of the plant is best for cutting. Differences between terminal and lateral stems, between sections of the same stem, and between flowering and nonflowering stems can affect rooting. Results may be dependent on the seedling

Cut a corm into several pieces, each containing at least one bud. Dust the cut surface with a fungicide; plant corm a few inches deep in the soil, with sprout side up.

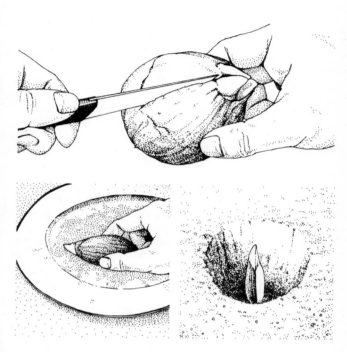

selected, even though all are from the same parents, or on the time of year the cutting is taken. Fortunately, by using a variety of propagation techniques you can propagate many plants from a variety of cutting types. Turn to page 208 for a discussion of these categories (softwood cuttings, semi-hardwood cuttings, etc.) and the species for which they are recommended.

Here are some general rules of thumb that apply to all cutting types. Take cuttings only when they are fully turgid (full of water). Turgid cuttings are stiff or firm and break with a decided snap when bent. (Don't confuse turgid cuttings with over-mature cuttings, which have become thickened due to age alone.) Cuttings taken in the early morning from well-watered plants are most likely to be turgid. Take cuttings from moderately vigorous, disease-free plants. Avoid overly vigorous plants, or those damaged by disease, frost, insects, or drought.

Cuttings taken from immature plants almost always form new root systems more readily than those taken from more mature plants. Conversely, however, aerial and root cuttings taken from near the base of a plant—that is, from the older part of the plant—may root and produce shoots more readily than those taken a greater distance from the base. Although cuttings from some species readily root regardless of their original position on the stock plant, cuttings

Propagation

from other species may not root at all if taken from positions high on the bush or tree. The classic example of this is English ivy. Cuttings taken from the juvenile English-ivy foliage root very easily, but those taken from stems with mature foliage are sometimes extremely reticent to root.

Light has been shown to be an important factor not only for rooting the cuttings, but in the selection of plants from which to take cuttings. Cuttings from rhododendrons, dahlias, hibiscus, English ivies, and some pines, for example, root best when taken from stock plants grown under low light levels.

Taking a Cutting

If you can do it cleanly, without tearing, you can snap a cutting off the stock plant with your fingers. Otherwise, cut it off with a very sharp, disinfected knife or pruners just below a node or slightly lower; provide enough length to allow you to make an additional cut just before you dip the cutting into the rooting compound. (See the sections on different types of cuttings for specifics on where and how long to cut.)

It is best to prepare and stick cuttings immediately. (Sticking is simply inserting the cuttings into the rooting medium.) But if you cannot, cuttings of many species can be held in a polyethylene bag and stored refrigerated for several hours or, occasionally, for several days. Chrysanthemum cuttings, for example, typically are shipped throughout the world without a serious loss of the rooting ability. Before sticking, remove from the base of each cutting any leaves that might be inserted in the rooting medium (the leaves will rot if covered with the rooting medium). Strip them by hand if you can do so without damaging the cutting, or cut them off with a sharp knife. As a precaution against contamination during the propagation process, dip cuttings in a liquid fungicide, such as benomyl, before applying rooting hormone. Be sure to mix the fungicide according to the instructions on the label.

Rooting Hormones

One of the greatest advances made in the propagation of plants from cuttings was the discovery of natural and artificial root-promoting substances. When produced naturally within the plant, these substances are called hormones. Synthetic root-promoting substances are not, technically, hormones, but they are so often referred to as such that we will do so here. Synthetic rooting hormones do not, contrary to common belief, promote the development of roots on cuttings that otherwise would not root under the best of circumstances. They can hasten the initiation of roots; increase the percentage of cuttings that do root; and increase the number, quality, and overall uniformity of the roots formed.

Two of the most commonly used synthetic rooting hormones are indolebutyric acid (IBA), and naphthaleneacetic acid (NAA). The more important of the two is IBA, which has proven effective for a large number of plant species and is nontoxic over a wide range of concentrations. Occasionally, combinations of IBA and NAA are recommended. Both IBA and NAA are available in powder form, which is used straight out of the container, or as liquid, which can be diluted in water to the desired concentration. Most beginners find that the powders are easier to acquire and use, while professionals generally prefer the liquid formulations. Most commercial preparations arrive complete with instructions for use and recommended concentration levels for a number of species. Concentrations usually are given either in parts per million (ppm) or as a percentage.

Do not use more hormone than recommended. High concentrations can kill tissue at the base of the cutting, which can in turn kill the cutting. If you cannot find a recommendation for a species or cultivar, try using a 0.2 percent (2,000 ppm) formulation of IBA.

Applying Rooting Hormone

Just before dipping the cuttings into either IBA or NAA, make a fresh cut at the base of each cutting. The moist surface allows talc preparations to adhere and gives liquid formulations a better opportunity to be absorbed.

Cuttings dipped directly into the stock preparation of talc or liquid could contaminate the stock, so separate only enough talc or liquid to treat the cuttings at hand. When you are finished, discard any that is left over. Keep a tight lid on the stock preparation at all times.

To apply talc, pour a small quantity onto a piece of creased paper. Insert only the basal portion of each cutting into the talc, rolling it to ensure that the entire circumference is covered. Tap the cutting against something solid to remove excess talc, which could harm the cutting. If the talc doesn't stick, moisten the base by lightly spraying it with water or by pressing it against a damp sponge before dipping it in the talc.

To apply liquid rooting hormone, prepare a dilute solution of the recommended concentration and dip the base of each cutting in it. Some professional propagators use a simpler technique, called quick dipping, with undiluted hormone in concentrations of one percent to two percent (10,000 to 20,000 ppm). Pour a thin layer of concentrated liquid into a small, shallow container. Dip only one fifth to two fifths of an inch of the base of a cutting, or a bundle of cuttings, into the preparation for five seconds. Then allow the cuttings to dry for a short period or stick them immediately into the propagation medium.

Wounding

Cuttings from certain species, including juniper, rhododendron, arborvitae, manzanita, maple, magnolia, and holly, are difficult to root or form root systems that are difficult to transplant. These cuttings, and others involving old wood, may respond to a technique known as wounding, which exploits the tendency of internal stem tissues that have been exposed by a wound to form roots.

To wound a cutting, you make a one-inch-long vertical slice through the bark and into the wood on one or both sides of the basal end with a disinfected knife or razor blade. Alternatively, you can remove a thin slice of bark from the same area, making sure not to cut too deeply into the wood. (Stripping the lower leaves sometimes wounds the cutting sufficiently.) After wounding, treat the cutting with talc or liquid rooting hormone as usual.

Wounded cuttings are able to absorb more water and rooting hormone, and generally produce a larger, better-balanced root system from all cuts, including the cut initially made to take the cutting. Some practice and experience are necessary to gain confidence with the method. You can make a handy wounding tool by taping a number of single-edge razor blades back to back with tape, or pinning them into grooves cut in a block of wood.

Selecting a Rooting Medium

The composition of rooting mediums can differ dramatically from one propagator to the next. But as different as these compositions can be, they all share certain characteristics. They must support the whole cutting, and provide moisture and aeration to its base. Sand, peat moss, vermiculite, perlite, and pumice are the most common ingredients.

Sand, often mixed with peat moss, is a good medium for juniper, yew, and arborvitae cuttings. Sharp sand is most often recommended, but a uniform grade of spherical sand is probably better.

Peat moss usually retains too much moisture when used alone. Frequently it is mixed with perlite, the peat moss comprising one quarter to two thirds of the mix. Many propagators combine shredded peat moss with sand.

Vermiculite is often mixed with an equal volume of perlite. It compresses with reuse, and may then hold too much water and too little air. Use only horticultural grades.

Pumice, which varies widely in particle sizes, is frequently combined with peat moss or perlite.

Perlite, alone or in combination with vermiculite or peat moss, is increasingly favored by propagators because it can provide the moisture and aeration needed to root a wide variety of species. Perlite is also sterile, readily available, uniform in size from one bag to the next, and relatively cheap. And it can be reused in potting mixes for larger plants. (Don't reuse it to root more cuttings, however.) Buy an intermediate horticultural grade.

The rooting medium can determine the type of roots formed on the cutting. Rooted in sand alone, cuttings may form long, coarse, non-branched, and brittle roots, which may be difficult to remove from the medium and to plant. Roots formed in mixtures of sand and peat moss, or perlite and peat moss, are generally well branched, slender, and flexible, and are much easier to move and to plant. Though the roots of difficult-to-root species may be greatly influenced by the rooting medium, many species can be successfully rooted in a variety of mediums. If you cannot find specific recommendations for the plant you wish to root, experiment by sticking cuttings in several different types.

Provide at least two inches of medium for cuttings. If the medium is any shallower, the cuttings' basal end will be too close to the bottom of the container, where moisture levels are at their highest and aeration levels are at their lowest.

Sticking Cuttings

Before inserting the cuttings into the rooting medium, or sticking, water the medium well and allow it to drain for a few minutes. With a clean finger or a sterilized implement, make individual holes in the medium the same diameter as or larger than the diameter of each cutting's basal end. Sticking the cutting straight into the medium might brush off rooting hormone or damage the cutting. If you are sticking a lot of cuttings in a tray, you can make deep grooves to accept them.

Insert a typical three- to five-inch cutting up to half its length and gently push the surrounding medium into the hole. If you press the medium firmly around the cutting, you risk inhibiting aeration. Stick shorter cuttings proportionally shallower. When all the cuttings are stuck, water them thoroughly.

Caring for Cuttings

Professional propagators many times have controlled, often automated, environments to maintain the correct moisture, temperature, and light conditions for rooting cuttings. But you needn't spend a fortune to provide the right conditions for rooting cuttings of many species.

Moisture is critical to successful propagation. Some species can maintain sufficient water levels while rooting in a glass of water, but most require additional measures. Mist propagators, as described on page 207, offer the most control. Glass- or polyethylene-covered cold frames, hotbeds, terrariums, aquariums, or individual containers enclosed within a clear polyethylene bag commonly are used to enhance moisture retention. Even covering an outdoor bed of cuttings with a simple layer of polyethylene

Propagation

tucked in at the edges can be successful. All these structures retain moisture and keep the interior levels of humidity high. But they all must be checked periodically. Cuttings left for just a few minutes without proper moisture during daylight hours may die.

Ideally, cuttings should be kept at an air temperature of 70° to 80° F during the day and 60° F at night. The rooting medium should be 70° to 75° F day and night, if possible. But don't despair if you can't control temperatures precisely. Temperatures higher or lower than the optimum may only delay root or shoot formation. Temperatures as high as 90° to 95° F, however, can be fatal. A plastic-bag propagating tent, for example, can quickly become an oven in direct sunlight.

The amount of light required to root cuttings varies from species to species. Cuttings of blueberries, forsythias, viburnums, hibiscus, and weigelas, for instance, root better under low levels of light than under high. Unfortunately, there are no clear-cut ways of determining the best light level for cuttings. You will have to rely on your own experiences and those of others.

In addition to controlling and monitoring moisture, temperature, and light levels, keep the propagating area clean at all times. Fallen leaves and dead cuttings can spread disease rapidly. If fungal diseases have been a problem for you, periodically drench the cuttings and rooting medium with a fungicide.

Transplanting Rooted Cuttings

Depending on a host of factors, cuttings can take weeks or months to root. After a reasonable period of time (which will vary according to species and your conditions), test for roots by lightly tugging on each cutting. Any resistance usually indicates that the cutting has rooted. To see if the roots are sufficient for transplanting, carefully dig the cutting out of the rooting medium and inspect it.

Rooted cuttings, like other seedlings, must be hardened off before they are transplanted. Gradually alter the conditions to approximate those in the next phase of growing. Decrease misting intervals in a mist propagator (discussed below); lift hotbed and cold-frame covers or open plastic bags for longer periods each day. When the cuttings are thoroughly rooted and hardened off, lift them gently from the rooting medium, being careful not to damage the root system or to remove any adhering medium. Pull apart the entangled root systems of adjoining cuttings as gently as possible. Transplant the cuttings immediately in a good potting mix. Make sure that the surface of the potting soil comes up to the same place on the cuttings as did the rooting medium. Water the transplants thoroughly, place them in a sheltered location, and mist them occasionally to aid in their recovery and establishment. Gradually wean the cuttings from shelter and misting, and treat them as you would any new plant.

Mist Propagation

Arguably the greatest advance in propagation has been the development of mist systems, which periodically spray a fine mist over the tops of cuttings, providing moisture and high humidity. Mist evaporating from the leaves also cools a plant, which reduces its rate of transpiration and respiration, and allows it to use its stores of food and energy for root production. These systems apply mist intermittently, so are called intermittent-mist systems. Intermittent mist has made it possible to stick larger cuttings, and cuttings taken earlier in the season, which are too soft and succulent to survive other propagation methods. Mist systems also keep difficult-to-root cuttings alive longer, thus enhancing their chances of rooting. Although mist is most commonly used, water delivered periodically by sprinklers of all types has proven successful. Likewise, devices that create fog-size particles have extended even further the range of species and the size of cuttings that can be rooted.

In addition to the spray heads and piping, a mist system typically contains two simple timing clocks. One turns the system on during daylight hours and off during the night. The other controls the duration of each misting and the interval between mistings during the day. You can monitor conditions inside and outside the greenhouse, frame, or bed, and change the mist settings as needed to maintain a film of moisture on the leaves at all times. Maintaining the right amount of moisture is important. Too much mist can leach nutrients from the leaves of the cuttings; and too little mist will cause the cuttings to dry out. Some systems automaticaly monitor evaporation or light levels and adjust the mist setting accordingly.

Mist systems for commercial propagation can be extensive and expensive, but a few smaller, less expensive systems, some no bigger than an aquarium, are made for home use, or you can assemble your own system from parts. Combined with bottom heat, mist systems can be used year-round in a greenhouse. If you don't have a greenhouse, you can set up a mist system outside during the warmer months in a lath house or in full sun.

Not all species do well propagated in mist. Cuttings of certain succulents and plants whose leaves yellow under mist are sometimes better suited for rooting in a closed-frame propagation bed. Species whose leaves are heavily covered with fine hairs, as is characteristic of many desert species, may also respond better in a closed, high-humidity propagation bed.

Types of Cuttings

Experience has shown that certain types of cuttings root best for certain species. The following are some different methods of propagation and the species they work best with.

Softwood Cuttings

Sometimes called green cuttings, softwood cuttings usually are made from soft, succulent spring growth of deciduous or evergreen woody plants and herbaceous perennials or annuals. (The terms "softwood cutting," "green cutting," and "herbaceous cutting" often are interchanged, depending on the plants being propagated.) The period for taking softwood cuttings from woody plants and from herbaceous perennials can generally last from two to eight weeks. Take cuttings from the tips of terminal or side branches whose growth is neither too soft, tender, or fast-growing, nor too woody, as is found in older stems. The cuttings should retain some flexibility but be stiff enough to break when sharply bent. The tips should be of average growth and growing in full sunlight. Collect them in the early morning, when temperatures are cooler and growth is more likely to be turgid. Protect them from the sun, and keep them cool before sticking, if necessary, by periodically misting them. Process and stick them as soon as possible; they can be temporarily kept in a plastic bag or immersed in a bucket of water for short periods only. To collect your sample, cut just below a node and take a cutting three to five inches long, including at least two nodes. Just before treating it with rooting hormone, remove the lower leaves. Concentrations of rooting hormone generally are lower for softwood than for other cuttings, and typically range between 1,000 and 3,000 ppm IBA. Many of the more common herbaceous plants root easily without rooting hormone, though a low concentration promotes uniform development.

Softwood cuttings lose water faster and are more susceptible to drying than are more mature cuttings. You can limit water loss by cutting away one quarter to one half of each of the leaves remaining on the cutting, and by removing all flowers and flower buds. After sticking the cuttings, pay extra attention to moisture and humidity levels.

Candidates for this type of propagation are numerous, and include manzanita, dutchman's-pipe vine, saltbush, butterfly bush, blue-mist spirea, plumbago, euonymus, fuchsia, hydrangea, St.-John's-wort, jasmine, honeysuckle, mock orange, potentilla, willow, salvia, elderberry, spirea, yew, vinca, geranium, carnation, pink chrysanthemum, four-o'clock, coleus, tomato, petunia, marigold, dayflower, phlox, snapdragon, goldentuft, begonia, cactus, pocketbook plant, snow-in-summer, dahlia, sun rose, heliotrope, candytuft, impatiens, and lavender.

Semi-Hardwood Cuttings

Also called semi-ripe cuttings, semi-hardwood cuttings have partially matured after a flush of growth. Depending on latitude, they may be found anytime from mid-July to early September. Take cuttings from terminal shoots, or occasionally the lower

Rhododendrons and
azaleas require acid soil
in order to thrive and
bloom profusely. Soil
acidity can be increased
through the use of
sulfur and other
amendments.

Plants in containers,
such as these petunias,
salvia, sweet alyssum,
and linaria, require
frequent applications of
fertilizer to prolong
their bloom times.

Fertilizer and water requirements vary greatly with the type of plant and soil conditions. Most of the herbs in this kitchen garden thrive on fertilizer high in nitrogen, which encourages foliage growth over that of flowers.

Low-nitrogen fertilizer benefits these geraniums by boosting flower production. Geraniums do especially well in containers because they do not seem to suffer from crowding.

This cool-season lawn grass is fed in spring and fall with high-nitrogen, slow-acting fertilizer, which causes quick, green growth and helps roots store needed carbohydrates.

Lawn fertilizer can be applied in liquid or granular form, by hand or through a spreader.

The roses at left do well if fertilized monthly during the summer, after the first flush of blooms. Feedings stop in early fall to allow the stems and buds to harden for winter.

A light application of fertilizer in late summer helps many flowering shrubs, such as the viburnum shown below, set buds for the next growing season.

Spring bulbs benefit from an application of bonemeal or superphosphate at planting and again as the blooms begin to fade. Sources of nitrogen applied when leaves emerge and again after flowers fade will keep leaves healthy and help bulbs store food for the winter.

Well-fertilized lawns
like the one below thrive
because their roots are
able to store adequate
supplies of carbohydrates
to fuel growth.

Lime and
superphosphate mixed
into the soil of container
plants, such as the
basket-of-gold and
lobelia seen at right, gets
them off to a healthy
start.

Nitrogen is the most
important element in
lawn fertilizers, but
phosphorus aids in root
growth, and potassium
increases resistance to
disease, drought, and
heat. Here, a lawn in

the Pacific Northwest
shows the benefits of
correct feeding.

A deliberately small lawn area, surrounded by native trees and drought-tolerant perennials, results in significant savings on water and maintenance time in this backyard.

The plants were chosen so that their needs would be met by local conditions, and those with similar water needs were grouped together.

The small lawn area in the New Mexican garden below is set close to the house—for easy watering and to provide an oasis of cool green.

No water beyond natural precipitation is required to keep the garden at right healthy. The plants include lavender, santolina, euphorbia, and feather reed grass.

A decorative water basin surrounds a tree to prevent runoff and to hold water where it is needed most.

222

Roses receive a morning watering. The directed spray cuts down on waste by reaching only those plants that need it. It should not be used during periods of high wind, however, when much water will be lost to evaporation and scattering.

The spray from impulse sprinklers clears the tops of plants and can be set to cover areas from 90 to 360 degrees around them.

A pop-up sprinkler placed near a garden path falls back to ground level when not in use. Such in-ground irrigation systems are ideal for well-traveled areas.

The best time to water most gardens is in early morning, when the air is still and the moisture can soak into the ground before warmer air causes it to evaporate.

sections of these shoots, by cutting just below a node. Strip the lower leaves, dip in rooting hormone, and stick as described in the general section on cuttings.

Candidates include camellia, rhododendron, euonymus, evergreen azalea, holly, citrus, olive, chokeberry, saltbush, butterfly bush, broom, clematis, redtwig dogwood, cotoneaster, daphne, heath, forsythia, kalmia, mahonia, mulberry, heavenly bamboo, passionflower, photinia, pyracantha, willow, coralberry, veronica, and viburnum.

Hardwood Cuttings of Deciduous Plants

One of the easiest and least expensive methods of multiplying deciduous woody plants is with hardwood cuttings taken from mature, dormant stems.

In late fall or early winter, cut dormant stems of one- to two-year-old wood from healthy, moderately vigorous stock that has been growing in full sun. (Some easy-to-root species can be cut just before planting in the spring.) Select stems of moderate size, approximately one-quarter to one-half inch in diameter and free of long internodes. Cut off and discard the top inch or two of the tip portion, and cut the remainder of the stem to lengths between 4 and 30 inches, each containing at least two nodes. The length of the stem depends on the plant species and how large of a plant you want. For lengths with only a few nodes, cut just below the bottom node and one-half to one inch above the top node. Don't worry about the position of the cuts for stems with many nodes. Make the top cut at a slant to remind you which end is the top of the cutting.

If your winters are mild, you can plant the cuttings outdoors immediately. Stick them vertically in good, moistened soil, leaving only one or two nodes aboveground. Some species, such as willows and some poplars, root easily without rooting hormone; others should be dipped before planting. Keep the planting moist at all times.

Where winters are cold, cuttings taken in late fall or early winter must be stored for planting in the spring. The following storage procedure also enhances a cutting's chances of rooting by promoting a growth of protective callus tissue at the basal end. After taking the cuttings, treat them with rooting hormone and tie them into bundles with their top ends pointing in one direction. To keep the cuttings cool and moist over the winter, bury them outdoors in sandy soil, sand, or sawdust. You can place them horizontally, six to eight inches deep, or vertically in a well-drained pit, with their tops down and their basal ends several inches below the soil surface. This treatment can also benefit cuttings planted in mild regions. Instead of burying the cuttings, you can store them aboveground in boxes filled with moist sand, sawdust, or peat moss. Or you can pack them in one of these moist materials and refrigerate them at

Propagation

40° F for the duration of the winter. In the spring, plant the stored cuttings deep enough to cover all but the top one or two nodes with moist, well-prepared soil.

Candidates include privet, forsythia, wisteria, honeysuckle, crape myrtle, spirea, fig, quince, olive, mulberry, grape, gooseberry, pomegranate, some plums, currant, redtwig dogwood, and tamarisk.

Hardwood Cuttings of Narrow-Leaved Evergreen Plants

As a group, these plants are difficult to root; you will have most success with cuttings taken from young plants. During late fall or early winter, after a number of frosts, take terminal cuttings, four to eight inches long, from the previous season's growth and strip the lower one to two inches of leaves. If stripping does not wound the cuttings of upright junipers, spruces, firs, hemlocks, and pines, make artificial wounds. Then treat the cuttings with 2,000 to 5,000 ppm of IBA rooting hormone.

Stick the treated cuttings in sand or a one-to-one mixture of peat moss and perlite in a well-protected and well-lighted cold frame, or a hotbed equipped to provide bottom heat of 75° to 80° F. Keep the medium moist throughout the rooting process. Have patience—some species or cultivars may take up to a year to root. Candidates include false cypress, juniper, yew, spruce, pine, hemlock, and fir.

Leaf-Bud Cuttings

Cuttings consisting of a leaf blade, a short piece of stem, and the attached axillary bud are useful when stock plants are in short supply.

Leaf-bud cuttings are best made from plants with well-developed axillary buds and actively growing, healthy leaves. Cut the stem into short sections, each containing a node and attached leaf. (You can vertically split a stem containing two opposite leaves to make two cuttings if you are really short of stock. Treat all cut surfaces with rooting hormone and insert in the rooting medium to a depth of one-half to one inch. It is important that these cuttings root quickly, so provide high humidity and bottom heat if you can. When the new shoots (which arise from the axillary buds) and roots are sufficiently developed, lift and transplant.

Candidates include black raspberry, boysenberry, lemon, camellia, rhododendron, geranium, English ivy, clematis, passionflower, mahonia, and many indoor plants.

Root Cuttings

New plants can be produced from sections of roots as well as from aboveground plant parts. These cuttings first produce shoots and then roots, which often form at the base of the new shoot rather than on the original root cutting.

Take root cuttings from young, dormant plants. Most plants are dormant from fall to spring, though some, such as Oriental poppy, go dormant in summer.

For small, finely rooted plants, cut the roots into sections one to two inches long and scatter them over the surface of a flat filled with sand. Cover the cuttings with an additional one inch of sand and water them well. Then cover the flat with a pane of glass or a piece of plastic film and place the flat in a shaded spot. Remove the covering when the new plants begin to grow. This process is probably best suited for greenhouses and hotbeds.

For plants with fleshy roots, cut the roots two to three inches long, making a slanting cut on the end nearest the parent. Stick them vertically in the medium, making sure that the slanting end is pointing up.

Cut large roots two to six inches long, making a slanting cut on the end nearest the parent. If you make a lot of cuttings, tie them in bundles. Before planting, pack the cuttings in damp sand, peat moss, or sawdust and refrigerate them at 40° F for three weeks to allow them to form callus and get a head start on rooting. Then plant the cuttings vertically, the slanted end on top, at or just below the surface of the soil. You can also plant them horizontally, one to two inches deep.

Candidates include smooth-leaf elm, lilac, Japanese pagoda tree, sassafras, blackberry, raspberry, sumac, callery pear, flowering almond, European aspen, poplar, leadwort, phlox, Oriental poppy, apple, flowering crabapple, fig, golden-rain tree, California poppy, daphne, sweet fern, flowering quince, bittersweet, trumpet vine, mulberry, silk tree, tree-of-heaven, catalpa, locust, and yucca.

Layering

In nature, it is possible for aerial stems that come to rest on top of the ground or become buried underground to take root and, with time, become separate plants. Gardeners can mimic this process, called layering, to propagate new plants. The technique typically is used for plants that naturally layer, or for plants whose cuttings have proven difficult to root. Although layering yields a relatively small number of plants, it requires no specialized equipment and produces large plants with good root systems. Since virtually little or no harm comes to the parent plant during layering, the method can be used for multiple layerings.

Simple Layering

During early spring, before growth commences, select a plant with low, flexible, one-year-old shoots that can be bent to the ground. A short distance from the tip of a shoot, strip the leaves off a portion of the stem where it will fall on the ground. Then bend and bury it three to five inches deep in soil that you have loosened and

Propagation

amended to provide a fertile, friable medium for new root growth. Depending on the stiffness of the stem, you may have to pin the stem in place with sticks, wires, or a rock.

You can enhance rooting on many species by wounding the stem before burying it. You twist the stem to wound it, or with a sharp knife you can girdle, notch, or slice halfway through it. If necessary, keep the wound open by inserting a small stem or a toothpick. Dust the wound with rooting hormone, then bury it and water thoroughly.

The long, flexible stems of some plants can be layered at several points along their length. Grapes, wisteria, clematis, honeysuckle, jasmine, rambling roses, and most other vines and ground covers are good candidates for this technique, called serpentine or compound layering.

Keep layered stems well watered while roots form. Depending on the species, climate, and other variables, the layer may root sufficiently within the same growing season, or it may take up to two full growing seasons. If the stem resists gently tugging, it has developed roots. To determine whether they are sufficient to support the plant, you will have to dig down carefully and examine them. If they are, sever the stem from the parent, then transplant and care for it as you would any new plant.

Candidates include serviceberry, magnolia, rhododendron, lilac, silk-tassel, photinia, ground cover and other horizontally growing conifers, daphne, mahonia, flowering quince, dogwood, and almost any plant whose stems can be bent to the ground.

Tip Layering

Tip layering occurs naturally with a number of plants that bear berries on canes. The tip of a bent cane that comes in contact with the soil often roots if conditions are appropriate, sending up shoots and forming a new plant.

In late summer, examine the current season's canes, noting those that have arched and whose tips have come in contact with the ground. Shortly after making contact, the terminal bud on each tip will curve upward, producing a sharp bend. Bury the tip end in a hole four to six inches deep. Shape the hole so that the side away from the plant is perpendicular and the opposite side slants toward the plant. Place the cane on the slanted surface and the upward curving tip against the perpendicular wall, then fill the hole, pressing soil firmly against the shoot. Water immediately, and keep moist throughout the rooting period.

The tip often roots sufficiently in the same season to allow you to cut it free of the parent and transplant it. A rooted tip may not have emerged from the ground when you are ready to transplant it, so leave a length of the old cane attached above ground to help mark the new plant's location. You can also leave rooted canes in the

ground over the winter and move them the following spring.
You can encourage the production of arched canes suitable for tip layering by pinching off the tip of new canes when they have reached 18 to 30 inches. You can also cut off the terminal buds of first-year canes and bury them in pots to root.
Candidates include black and purple raspberries, vine blackberries, dewberry, boysenberry, and loganberry.

Air Layering
With air layering, instead of taking the stem to the soil, you take the soil to the stem. The technique normally is applied during the spring on stems of the previous year's growth, although older stems can also be selected.
Some distance back from the terminal bud, but within the previous season's growth, girdle the stem with a sharp knife, removing a section of the bark one-half to one inch wide. Scrape if necessary to ensure that all the bark is removed. Alternatively, you can make a two-inch-long, upward-slanting cut through the bark on one or both sides of the stem. (Insert a toothpick or some peat moss to keep the cuts from growing back together.) With a small paintbrush, dust all girdled or cut surfaces with rooting hormone.
Soak some peat moss with water, squeeze two handfuls to remove all excess water, and pack the peat moss around the wounded stem. Completely enclose the moist peat moss with plastic or polyethylene, using several wraps if necessary to prevent moisture loss from overlapping edges. (This is the most difficult part of the procedure, usually requiring the aid of a third hand.) Tie or tape the ends of the plastic to ensure that moisture does not escape or enter the peat moss during rooting.
If you use clear wrapping, you will be able to see when roots have formed. Frequent unwrapping of opaque coverings to check for roots will entail some moisture loss, so moisten the peat moss with water from a spray bottle before rewrapping.
Sufficiently rooted air layers on indoor plants can be cut free of the parent and transplanted at any time. Outdoor air layers should not be cut from the parent until the dormant season, when demands on the new plant will be lessened. Air layers of hollies, lilacs, azaleas, and magnolias may have to be left on the parent plant for two full growing seasons before the roots are substantial enough to support the new plant. (Unfortunately for northern gardeners, the roots formed during the first season of the air layer may not survive cold winter temperatures to grow the second year.)
When the air-layered stem has developed adequate roots, cut it from the parent and remove the covering but not the peat moss. Then plant, protect, and treat the rooted cutting just like a new plant.
Candidates typically include tropical and subtropical trees and shrubs, but all woody plants can be propagated by this technique.

Fertilizing

Plants draw the nutrients they need to live and to grow from air, water, and soil. Although gardeners may be concerned about the effects of air pollution on their plants, we need not worry yet about the air's ability to deliver sufficient quantities of carbon dioxide and oxygen to plants. The supply of nutrients in the soil, however, is a constant concern. Fortunately, there is much that we can do about soil. We can improve its structure, texture, aeration, and drainage, as outlined in the chapter on soil. And we can fertilize.

Some soils have inherently low fertility. Sandy soils and certain clay soils, for example, are incapable of holding adequate nutrients and releasing them gradually to plants. Some soils contain all the nutrients plants need, but in forms they cannot use. More common are soils whose nutrients have been depleted by plants, by leaching, or by erosion. Natural processes in soils act to replenish the supply of nutrients. In nature, some nutrients are returned to the soil as leaves, stems, and branches decompose. In the garden, regular applications of compost and other organic matter can accomplish the same thing. But these processes are relatively slow and may not be able to keep up with plant needs.

Fertilizer provides nutrients that are unavailable in the soil and replaces nutrients that plants have used. With fertilizer, you can speed the growth and increase the size of young plants, and you can maintain the quality and healthy growth of older ones. But you should not look to fertilizers to satisfy all your plants' needs or to solve all their problems. Remember that temperature, moisture, wind, sunlight, insects, disease, and soil pH all affect plants as well. Indeed, fertilizer can sometimes compound a problem. To use fertilizer effectively you should know your plants, your soil, and your climate, and you should know some background about plant nutrients and how fertilizers supply them.

Plant Nutrients

Fertilizers come from many different sources. They may be organic or inorganic, natural or manufactured compounds. Whatever their origin, however, we use them because they contain one or more of the 16 chemical elements that scientists currently identify as essential for plant growth.

It is useful to distinguish here between plant foods and plant nutrients, terms commonly treated as synonyms. Foods are ready-made sources of energy and chemical compounds. Green plants are unique in their ability to manufacture their own food. The raw materials from which plants make food are light and nutrients—the nutrients being the 16 essential elements. (The terms "nutrient" and "element" are interchangeable in this context.)

The role that essential elements play in plant growth is complex. Some are incorporated into plant tissues; others are involved in processes inside the cells without becoming part of the cells. For our purposes, it is enough to know that if any one of the essential elements is missing or deficient, a plant will grow, reproduce, and develop abnormally. In addition, an essential element cannot be replaced by another element. Sodium, for example, can substitute for potassium, but not completely. Thus, potassium is an essential element; sodium is not.

The essential elements are classified in two groups. The major elements, or macronutrients, are carbon, oxygen, hydrogen, nitrogen, phosphorus, potassium, sulfur, calcium, and magnesium. The second group, called trace elements, or micronutrients, includes iron, manganese, boron, copper, zinc, molybdenum, and chlorine. All of the essential elements are equally important for normal plant growth.

Although carbon, oxygen, and hydrogen play many important roles in plant growth, some classification systems separate them from the major nutrients because plants obtain them from air and from water rather than from the soil. For the same reason, we normally do not take these elements into account when considering fertilizers.

The Major Nutrients

Before we examine the elements individually, it is worth noting that any discussion of them involves a certain amount of talk about their chemistry. If your grasp of chemistry has slipped since high school or college, or was never very firm, do not be alarmed. You need not be a chemist to grasp what nutrients are and what they do for plants. Providing your plants with the right types and amounts of fertilizer is not as difficult as the following discussion of nutrients might make it seem.

Nitrogen

Of all the nutrients absorbed from the soil, nitrogen (chemical symbol N) is the one that plants require in the largest quantities. Given proper light conditions, moderate amounts of nitrogen promote strong, sturdy growth and plentiful flowers and fruit. A lack of nitrogen drastically reduces plant height, leaf size, and the production of leaves and branches. Plants may flower sparsely and develop smaller than normal fruits, if they fruit at all. Nitrogen is an important component of the green pigment, chlorophyll, so a nitrogen-deficient plant will be pale green to yellow, with its older leaves affected before the younger. (The chart on page 232 outlines other symptoms of deficiency; in addition, it provides a handy reference to plant nutrients in general.) Too much nitrogen can also be detrimental, promoting soft, weak growth. Flowering and fruiting plants that receive an excessive amount of nitrogen may produce lush, succulent, vegetative growth at the expense of flowers and fruit.

Correcting Nutrient Deficiencies

Element	Natural Source	Role in Plant Growth
Nitrogen (N)	Soil, legumes, organic matter.	Formation of amino acids that make proteins. Component of chlorophyll.
Phosphorus (P)	Soil, organic matter.	Role in photosynthesis, respiration, transfer of energy within cells. Stimulates root branching and production of root hairs.
Potassium (K)	Soil.	Cell metabolism. Water retention. Protein synthesis.
Sulfur (S)	Soil minerals, rain.	Protein synthesis.
Calcium (Ca)	Limestone, clay soil, organic matter.	Cell division, hydration, and expansion. Chromosome stability.
Magnesium (Mg)	Soil minerals, dolomitic limestone.	Central atom in chlorophyll molecule.
Iron (Fe)	Soil minerals.	Chlorophyll production. Respiratory enzymes.

The chart on the following pages will help you detect and repair deficiencies of important plant nutrients in the soil. Elements are listed at

the far left; the next column shows their natural source. The center column describes the element's role in plant growth. On the facing page,

symptoms of that element's deficiency are described; and the last column outlines steps you can take to correct the deficiency.

Deficiency Symptoms	To Correct Deficiency
Entire plant has a pale-green or yellow cast. Older leaves lose chlorophyll first. Growth reduced. Smaller and fewer leaves, branches, fruits, and flowers. Fall color shows early.	Use complete fertilizer, slow-release fertilizer, urea, or organic fertilizers.
Leaves become very dark green; red to bronze color develops on underside. Red pigmentation may show in veins and petioles, especially on younger plants. Shoots normal until deficiency is severe.	Use complete fertilizer, bone meal, or super-phosphate.
Lower leaves show marginal and interveinal chlorosis. Scorching of margins of lower leaves severe, starting on oldest leaves. Leaves may crinkle and roll upward. Weak stems. Wilting. Lower disease resistance. Reduction in yield and quality of flowers and fruit.	Use complete fertilizer or wood ash.
Entire plant has a yellow cast. All leaves lose chlorophyll at the same time. Growth reduced. Symptoms very similar to nitrogen deficiency.	Use gypsum, superphosphate, or animal manure.
Shoot tips stunted; terminal dieback may occur. Young leaves may be small, distorted, with tips hooked back. Roots may show symptoms before shoots; black, stunted, root-tip dieback. Flower petals may wilt even with adequate soil moisture.	Use ground limestone.
Lower leaves show primarily interveinal chlorosis and some marginal chlorosis (red color develops along the margins first). Scorching of leaf margins normally not present. Shoot growth relatively normal until deficiency is severe.	Use dolomitic limestone or magnesium sulfate.
Symptoms sharply limited to young leaves; no stunting or dieback initially. Young leaves and shoots lose most of their chlorophyll; turn yellow to almost white when deficiency is severe; very narrow band of chlorophyll shows along veins. Older leaves remain green. Tip and marginal scorching of young leaves eventually develops. Shoot length normal; diameter reduced.	Lower soil pH; use iron sulfate or iron chelate.

Correcting Nutrient Deficiencies

Element	Natural Source	Role in Plant Growth
Manganese (Mn)	Soil, organic matter.	Synthesis of chlorophyll.
Boron (B)	Soil minerals, water in Plains states, organic matter in South.	Not definitely known. Translocation of sugars and carbohydrates.
Copper (Cu)	Soil minerals.	Component of enzymes.
Zinc (Zn)	Soil minerals.	Synthesis of growth regulators. Component of enzymes involved in protein synthesis.
Molybdenum (Mo)	Soil minerals.	Essential for nitrogen fixation. Protein synthesis.
Chlorine (Cl)	Soil, water, atmosphere, road salt.	May be involved in photosynthesis.

Deficiency Symptoms	*To Correct Deficiency*
Dieback primarily in younger leaves; some in older leaves when deficiency is severe. Young leaves become yellow; spots of dead tissue develop between veins; relatively wide band of chlorophyll along veins. Shoot growth reduced.	Lower pH. If pH is too low (below 5), manganese toxicity can occur; raise pH with lime to correct excess.
Some discoloration of leaves; bronzing, scorching. Young leaves affected first. Leaves smaller, distorted. Shoot tips stop growing, form rosettes; lateral shoots near tip tend to grow, creating witches'-broom effect. Shoot tips die back when deficiency is severe.	Use Borax.
Necrosis of tips of young leaves. Young leaves smaller. Shoots form rosettes near tip; dieback may follow.	Use copper sulfate or fungicides.
Young leaves uniformly yellow; some interveinal chlorosis, and necrotic spots when deficiency is severe. Young leaves small, very pointed (little-leaf syndrome). Older leaves drop. Shoots stunted, with tufts of small leaves at tip; may die back.	Use zinc sulfate.
Yellowing of young leaves first. Marginal scorching and rolling. Pronounced reduction in leaf width (strap leaf or whiptail). Shoots short when deficiency is severe.	Use sodium molybdate applied with phosphate; raise soil pH.
Deficiency not a problem. Toxicity is: Small, yellow leaves. Leaf scorch at tips and margins; complete browning and early leaf drop. Affects evergreens especially.	To correct toxicity, reduce levels through leaching.

Fertilizing

Although the atmosphere is about 78 percent nitrogen, this inert gas is unavailable to plants. In nature, soil bacteria "fix" nitrogen drawn from the air by combining it with other elements to form organic compounds. These compounds are in turn broken down by other bacteria into soluble forms that plants can absorb. The chemical industry accomplishes similar transformations of atmospheric nitrogen by combining it with hydrogen and large amounts of energy, both drawn from natural gas.

The amount of nitrogen added to the soil by bacteria is quite limited, particularly in ornamental gardens. Farmers and vegetable gardeners plant as cover crops or green manures legumes that host nitrogen-fixing bacteria. You could do the same when preparing a new ornamental bed, but it is impossible to plant cover crops once perennials are planted. Members of the legume family grown as ornamentals, such as wisteria, honey locust, broom, redbud, and lupines, also fix nitrogen, but only enough to meet their own needs.

Since such natural processes as nitrogen fixation and weathering cannot furnish plants with enough of this crucial element, it is necessary for you to supply it. Unfortunately, nitrogen in the soil is very transient. Plants absorb nitrogen in two forms. The principal form is nitrate ions (NO_3^-), which leach rapidly from the soil. A smaller amount is absorbed as ammonium ions (NH_4^+), which do not leach, but which are continually converted into nitrates. Maintaining adequate amounts of nitrogen throughout the growing season is the gardener's challenge.

There are very few forms of nitrogen that will remain in the soil, available to plants, for an extended period of time. The closest thing to a permanent source is organic matter that contains about 10 to 12 times as much carbon as nitrogen. (This ratio is often abbreviated as C:N.) Because microorganisms in the soil use nitrogen when breaking down carbon compounds, materials with a higher C:N ratio (such as straw and sawdust, which can have a ratio as high as 90:1) will tie up much of the free nitrogen in the soil and prevent plants from obtaining adequate amounts for growth. Organic matter must also be constantly replenished, which is more difficult to do in a perennial garden than in a vegetable garden.

The easiest way to maintain nitrogen levels in your garden is to apply a nitrogen fertilizer throughout the growing season. Organic forms of nitrogen stay in the soil considerably longer than do most inorganic forms. But the nitrogen in organic fertilizers, such as manures, fish meal, sewage sludge, and cottonseed meal, must be acted on by soil bacteria before it can be used by plants, whereas nitrogen in inorganic fertilizers is immediately available. (See the section on fertilizer choices later in this chapter for further discussion of organic and inorganic fertilizers.)

Phosphorus

Although it is found in relatively small amounts in plants in comparison to nitrogen, phosphorus (P) plays a key role in photosynthesis, respiration, and the transfer of energy within cells and tissues. It stimulates root branching and the production of root hairs, and it helps plants mature more rapidly, which can be critical in areas with early frosts. Seedlings and new transplants need phosphorus, and starter fertilizers are formulated with a high phosphorus content. Leaves of plants suffering from phosphorus deficiency turn a dark green on top and red to bronze underneath.

Plants take up phosphate ions from several sources. Some of these ions are gradually released from organic matter by soil microorganisms, others come from relatively insoluble phosphate compounds present in soil, and still others from fertilizers containing phosphorus. In soils that are more acid or more alkaline, phosphorus reacts with other elements to form insoluble compounds that are unavailable to plants. In soils containing 20 percent or more organic matter (those prepared for container-grown plants, for instance), phosphorus is available at pH levels as low as 5. When applied to the soil in a fertilizer, phosphorus forms relatively insoluble compounds; consequently, it does not leach from the soil. But it forms these compounds so quickly that it seldom moves far from where it was applied. The phosphorus in liquid fertilizers does not penetrate more than an inch or so into the soil before it is completely tied up. That in solid fertilizers is largely found right around the granules. To make sure that phosphorus reaches plant roots, you should mix granular fertilizers into the soil down to the root depth.

Potassium

Potassium (K) has several important functions in cell metabolism and it plays a major role in regulating the opening and closing of leaf stomata. It is also involved in protein synthesis, water retention, and the movement of carbohydrates from one part of the plant to another. Symptoms of potassium deficiency include weak stems, a tendency to wilt, a lower level of disease resistance, and a reduction in yield and quality of flowers and fruit. A highly mobile element within plants, potassium moves from the lower leaves to the upper when a deficiency occurs; thus, deficiency symptoms show up in the lower leaves first.

Potassium is considerably more mobile in the soil than is phosphorus, but less mobile than nitrogen. The materials used in fertilizers to supply potassium are quite soluble, but once in the soil, potassium is held in a variety of forms. Some of these are more readily available than others, but even tightly held potassium is gradually released to the soil solution. Potassium leaches most readily from light, sandy soils.

Sulfur

Besides being an important constituent of critical amino acids, sulfur (S) gives onions, garlic, mustard, horseradish, and cabbage their characteristic odors and flavors. Sulfur is plentiful in fertilizers; gypsum, which makes up about half the total content of superphosphate, is 12 percent sulfur. In nature, a substantial amount of sulfur comes from rain containing dissolved sulfurous gases released by the burning of fossil fuels. If it is not recycled or absorbed by plants, sulfur may be leached from the root zone by heavy watering or rainfall. The symptoms of sulfur deficiency are similar to those of nitrogen deficiency, except that young and old leaves of sulfur-deficient plants turn yellow at the same time.

Calcium

Required for cell division, chromosome stability, cell hydration, and cell expansion, calcium (C) is also the principal component of the layer between cells that sticks one cell to another. When calcium is deficient, the plant's growing points do not develop normally, young leaves are badly distorted, and in severe cases shoot and root tips die. Although calcium usually is plentiful in heavy silt and clay loams, it tends to leach from sandy, acid soils.

Most gardeners apply calcium (in the form of lime) to the garden not to meet plant-nutrient requirements, but for the more important objective of raising soil pH and to promote the formation of soil aggregates. (See the chapter on soil for more on this.) If a soil test indicates that the pH is correct but calcium is deficient, add gypsum (calcium sulfate), which supplies calcium without changing the soil pH.

Magnesium

As the central atom in the chlorophyll molecule, magnesium (Mg) is essential not just to plant growth but to all life. It may be deficient in sandy, acid soils; it is depleted primarily by plant uptake rather than by leaching. Good sources of magnesium are dolomitic limestone, which raises soil pH, and magnesium sulfate, which does not alter pH. Deficiency symptoms appear first in the older leaves as a chlorosis, or yellowing, between the veins. As the deficiency becomes acute, younger leaves higher on the plant also become chlorotic.

The Trace Elements

Iron, manganese, boron, copper, zinc, molybdenum, and chlorine—the trace elements, or micronutrients—are required in very small quantities in comparison to the macronutrients, but a deficiency of any of them affects plant growth and development just as severely as does a macronutrient deficiency. Conversely, too much of a trace element can prove toxic to plants. The margin between too little and too much is relatively narrow for trace elements, so you must take great care when fertilizing plants with them. It is best to apply a trace element only if you are sure that a symptom is due to a deficiency of that element (laboratory plant analysis can confirm this), or if the soil in a particular area of your garden is chronically deficient. Apply only the deficient element; blanket applications of trace elements may result in toxic levels of one or more of them. Nevertheless, many fertilizers formulated for ornamentals include small amounts of trace elements as insurance against deficiencies.

Iron

The trace element found in most abundance in plants is iron (Fe). It is a catalyst for the production of chlorophyll and it plays a role in respiration. The iron content of most soils is very high, but in soils with a pH above 7, the iron is tied up in a variety of insoluble compounds and unavailable to plants. The most obvious symptom of iron deficiency is the yellowing of young leaves and shoots. Acidifying the soil is the first step in correcting an iron deficiency. Lowering the pH usually makes the iron normally present in the soil available in sufficient quantities. If that doesn't work, spray the foliage or amend the soil with an iron chelate. Interference with normal root activity—caused by poor drainage and aeration, high levels of soluble salts, or diseases and insects that injure roots—can reduce iron uptake. In these cases, treat the problem (improve the soil, for example) before trying to treat the symptom.

Manganese

In conjunction with iron, manganese (Mn) aids the synthesis of chlorophyll. Manganese deficiencies, like those of iron, appear first as a yellowing in young leaves. Deficiencies frequently occur in poorly drained soils, because the manganese is converted into unavailable forms in the absence of oxygen, and in sandy soils, which are low in natural manganese and are prone to heavy leaching. Manganese is not readily available to plants above a soil pH of 6.5. Conversely, at pH levels below 5.0, manganese toxicity can be a problem. (You can correct an excess of manganese by applying lime to raise the pH.)

Boron

Although the importance of boron (B) to plants is certain, its precise role has yet to be established. Found in soil minerals and in organic matter, boron is gradually released to the soil solution by soil microorganisms. Because boron is very soluble once it has been liberated, it tends to leach out of the soil and needs to be replenished to meet plant requirements. Among the signs of boron deficiency are small, distorted leaves and a cessation of shoot-tip growth. Borax is commonly sprayed on leaves or applied to the soil to supply boron. In some plant species, the difference between a deficient and a toxic level is very small. (Borax is used as an herbicide, too.) Soils on the eastern seaboard generally are lower in boron than are soils in the Midwest; in the Plains states, soils and water normally contain large amounts of boron.

Copper
A component of several important plant enzymes, copper (Cu) may also be involved in photosynthesis and the formation of chlorophyll. Weathering of soil minerals releases copper to the soil solution. Solubility is greater in acid soils than in alkaline soils. Copper deficiency affects young leaves, which are smaller and die at the tips as a result. Clay and silt loams ordinarily contain enough copper to meet plant requirements, whereas deficiencies may occur in sandy soils because of leaching, and in peat and muck soils because the copper is tightly bound in complex organic compounds. Copper sulfate is the most common copper fertilizer, although copper-based fungicides can sometimes supply enough. Heavy applications of copper fungicides, however, or of fertilizers containing copper supplements can build up toxic levels.

Zinc
Zinc (Zn) is a key element in the synthesis of auxin, one of the most important natural-growth regulators in plants. This relationship is evident in symptoms of zinc deficiency. Auxins regulate cell expansion, and as the deficiency becomes severe, young leaves and the internodes of the shoot tip fail to expand. Found in the surface layers of the soil, zinc can be removed by erosion or by land clearing. In soils above pH 6, zinc forms insoluble compounds and becomes unavailable to plants. For this reason, zinc deficiencies are especially severe on calcareous (limestone) soils despite their large concentrations of zinc. And, because of complicated chemistry also related to pH, zinc is not readily available in soils to which large amounts of phosphorus have been applied. The most common form of zinc fertilizer is zinc sulfate.

Molybdenum
Essential for nitrogen fixation by microorganisms, molybdenum (Mo) also plays an important part in the use of nitrogen by plants. When molybdenum is deficient, protein synthesis is blocked and plant growth stops. Symptoms first appear in young leaves, which turn yellow, show marginal scorching and rolling, and fail to develop their full width. Very small amounts (two ounces per acre) of sodium molybdate applied to the soil in conjunction with phosphorus or sprayed on the leaves will correct a deficiency. Adding lime to raise the soil pH above 5.5 may do the trick in acid soils.

Chlorine

Another essential element whose role in plant life is undisputed but not fully understood, chlorine (Cl) is found everywhere—in soils, in water, in fertilizers, and in the atmosphere. Thus, chlorine deficiency is rare. Chlorine toxicity is more likely, especially in irrigated arid regions, near the seacoast, and along highways treated with salt during the winter for ice removal. The salt thrown up by automobiles can severely affect evergreens, even those located some distance from the roadway. Toxicity symptoms include small, yellow leaves; leaf scorch at the tips and along the margins; complete browning; and early leaf drop. Leaching is the most effective way to reduce the levels of chlorine in the soil.

Nutrients and Soil pH

The availability of nutrients to plants is directly correlated to the pH of the soil. Most of the essential elements are available in adequate quantities at pH levels ranging from 5.8 to 7.0, with the optimum at 6.5 to 6.8. In soils with large amounts of organic matter (more than 20 percent), certain elements will be more readily available to plants than those elements would be in poorer soils (containing one to five percent organic matter).

Soil pH also has a significant effect on the activity of soil microorganisms. The bacteria that convert the nitrogen in organic materials to forms that plants can use work more effectively between pH 5.8 and 7.0 than they do in extremely acid or alkaline conditions. Don't guess when it comes to pH; have your soil tested and follow the recommendations of the specialist who interprets your test results.

Fertilizer Choices

You only have to visit your local garden center to discover how many different products you can use to provide your plants with essential nutrients. An understanding of the basic fertilizer types will help you make choices between all these alternatives.

Fertilizers can be characterized by the selection of nutrients they contain, by the compounds or forms in which the nutrients are provided, by the origin of the materials used (organic or inorganic, natural or manufactured compounds), and by the form of the fertilizer (liquid, powder, granules, and so on).

Nutrient Selection

A complete fertilizer contains nitrogen, phosphorus, and potassium. The percentages of these elements are represented by the numbers on the front of the package; nitrogen is listed first, followed by phosphorus, then potassium. A fertilizer with a 5-10-5 ratio, for example, contains 5 percent by weight of nitrogen, 10 percent phosphate, and 5 percent potash.

Some fertilizers have only one or two of the primary elements. Superphosphate (0-20-0) is 20 percent phosphate; the balance is primarily gypsum. Diammonium phosphate (21-53-0) contains 21 percent nitrogen, 53 percent phosphate, and no potassium. A number of fertilizers may contain other macronutrients.

Organic vs. Inorganic

Fertilizers are formulated from organic materials and from natural or manufactured inorganic compounds, but plants absorb *all* of their nutrients in the form of inorganic ions. Whether these ions originate from an organic source, such as cow manure or fish meal, or from an inorganic one, such as rock phosphate or lime, makes no difference to their effect on the plant. Likewise, nutrients in fertilizers formulated from natural sources and those in fertilizers synthesized in a chemical factory are absorbed by the plant in exactly the same form.

You may have concerns about the energy consumed and the pollution entailed in the creation of synthetic fertilizers, but remember that plants, and the environment in general, cannot distinguish between a synthetic fertilizer and a natural one—too much manure can pollute a stream just as too much granular fertilizer can.

Organic and inorganic fertilizers perform differently in the garden. In certain circumstances, these differences can be important enough to influence your choice of fertilizer.

Organic Fertilizers

Manures, composts, and other plant and animal residues contain varying amounts of plant nutrients, as shown in the chart on page 244. Most gardeners, however, use them primarily to improve the physical structure of the soil, valuing their organic matter more than their nutrient content. (See the chapter on soil for more on this subject.) Manures and composts are quite coarse and bulky, and are difficult to spread uniformly. As with other organic fertilizers, the nutrients in manures are not available until soil microorganisms have broken the material down. To reduce nitrogen loss during this process, turn the manure into the soil, or in established plantings, work as much as possible into the top layer of soil.

Other organic materials, including bone meal, blood meal, dried sewage sludge, cottonseed meal, and fish emulsion, are dried, pulverized, or processed before they are packaged as fertilizers. (Some animal manures are treated this way as well.) These materials do not condition the soil; their purpose is to supply nutrients. The only manufactured organic fertilizer is urea, but it acts like an inorganic fertilizer once it is added to the soil.

Organic fertilizers have several advantages over inorganic compounds. Because they must first be processed by microorganisms, they are more slowly available to plants. They are safer to use because they do not burn plants as readily, and they are less likely to leach from the soil. They also have disadvantages. They cost more per unit of nutrient, and many of them are not a balanced source of nutrients. In addition, the release of nutrients by the microorganisms is unpredictable, due to the influence of soil temperature, moisture level, and pH on the organisms' activity.

Inorganic Fertilizers

Most inorganic fertilizers are manufactured from a variety of chemical salts, but several are found in natural deposits. Rock phosphate, limestone, sodium nitrate, green sand, and granite meal are used in the same chemical form in which they are mined, although they must be ground into a very fine powder to serve as fertilizer.

In contrast to organic fertilizers, inorganic fertilizers provide maximum control over nutrient levels. The nutrients are in a soluble form, and they dissolve into ions that are immediately available to plants. Since they usually are more concentrated, inorganic fertilizers are more economical per unit of nutrient. But because it takes a smaller amount of inorganic fertilizer to supply a specific quantity of nutrients, you must be careful not to apply too much and burn your plants. (The chart on page 246 gives rates of application for various inorganic fertilizers.)

Inorganic fertilizers are also available in several specialized forms, such as starter solutions and slow-release compounds. Starter solutions are fertilizers high in phosphorus and readily available nitrates. They help plants recover more rapidly from the shock of transplanting, when damage to the root system limits its capacity to absorb water and nutrients.

Slow-Release Fertilizers

Some inorganic fertilizer compounds release nutrients at a relatively slow rate. There are several different types. Urea-form and sulfur-coated urea fertilizers contain urea particles coated with sulfur or reacted with formaldehyde. These urea compounds, commonly found in lawn fertilizers, make it possible to apply relatively large amounts of nitrogen without burning the grass. Some of the nitrogen is water-soluble and immediately available, but the release of most of the nitrogen depends on temperature, moisture, and the activity of soil microorganisms.

Magnesium ammonium phosphate is a slowly available source of nitrogen, phosphorus, and magnesium that is slightly soluble in water. To a large degree, particle size determines the rate at which the nitrogen is released, but temperature and moisture levels also play a role. Soil microorganisms are not involved. Fertilizers containing magnesium ammonium phosphate are formulated with a potassium compound to produce a complete fertilizer.

Organic Fertilizers

Fertilizer	Nitrogen	Phosphorus
Activated Sewage Sludge	4–6%	2–4%
Animal Tankage	5–10%	2–4%
Bone Meal, Steamed	2%	25–30%
Castor Pomace	5%	2%
Cottonseed Meal	6–7%	2–3%
Cow Manure, Dried	2%	1.8%
Dried Blood	9–14%	1.6%
Fish Emulsion	12%	0%
Fish Meal	4–9%	7%
Guano	10–12%	11–25%
Poultry Manure, Dried	6%	4%
Seaweed Extract (Kelp)	2%	1%
Soybean Meal	6%	1%
Urea	42–46%	0%
Wood Ash	0%	trace

This select list of organic fertilizers gives the amounts of the three primary elements each contains, the suggested application rates, and any special comments or instructions.

Potassium	Application Rate	Comments
trace	4–6 lb./100 sq. ft.	Acid pH. May contain heavy metal; do not use in vegetable plot.
1–2%	3 lb./100 sq. ft.	Acid pH.
0%	4 lb./100 sq. ft.	Alkaline pH. Is 20–30% calcium.
1%	5 lb./100 sq. ft.	Acid pH. Contains deadly poison; keep away from animals.
1–2%	5 lb./100 sq. ft.	Very acid pH.
2.2%	6–8 lb./100 sq. ft.	
0.84%	2 lb./100 sq. ft.	Acid pH.
1%	1 tbsp./gal. 25 gals./100 sq. ft.	Contains many trace elements. Offensive odor.
trace	2–4 lb./100 sq. ft.	Acid pH. Offensive odor.
2%	2–4 lb./100 sq. ft.	
3%	2 lb./100 sq. ft.	Can cause plant injury if too much is used.
4–13%	2–3 lb./100 sq. ft.	Neutral pH. Good source of trace elements.
2%	4–5 lb./100 sq. ft.	
0%	1/2 lb./100 sq. ft.	Very soluble; leaches rapidly.
5–10%	5 lb./100 sq. ft.	Alkaline pH. Do not store in rain.

Inorganic Fertilizers

Material	Percent Nutrients		
	N	P_2O_5	K_2O
NITROGEN			
Ammonium Sulfate	20	0	0
Ammonium Nitrate	33.5	0	0
Sodium Nitrate (Nitrate of Soda)	16	0	0
Calcium Nitrate	15.5	0	0
Potassium Nitrate	12–14	0	44–46
PHOSPHORUS			
Superphosphate	0	20	0
Treble Superphosphate	0	45–48	0
Monoammonium Phosphate	11	48	0
Diammonium Phosphate	21	54	0
POTASSIUM			
Potassium Chloride (Muriate of Potash)	0	0	62
Potassium Sulfate	0	0	48–53
MAGNESIUM			
Magnesium Sulfate	0	0	0
CALCIUM			
Calcium Sulfate	0	0	0
BORON			
Borax	0	0	0

This chart shows some common inorganic-fertilizer materials and the percentage of the essential nutrients they supply to the soil. The rates of application listed are for average soil conditions, per 100 square feet.

Amount per 100 Sq. Ft.	Other Nutrients
1 lb.	24% S
10.5 oz.	
1 lb.	27% Na
1 lb.	17% Ca
1/2 lb.	
3–5 lb.	18% Ca, 12% S
21–40 oz.	12% Ca
21 oz.	1.4% Ca, 2.6% S
1 lb.	
1/2 lb.	
1/2 lb.	18% S
2 lb.	10% Mg, 13% S
2–10 lb.	23% Ca, 19% S
1/4 lb.	11% B

Fertilizing

Currently, the most promising slow-release inorganic fertilizers are coated compounds—individual granules coated with a plastic membrane. Water passes through the membrane and dissolves the fertilizer, which then diffuses out through the membrane at a constant rate. The process is not affected by soil pH or soluble-salt levels, and the activity of soil microorganisms is not required. The release rate increases, however, as temperatures rise. Coated fertilizers are complete fertilizers formulated to release nutrients for either three to four months, for eight to nine months, or for 12 to 14 months.

A slow-release fertilizer that delivers trace elements is produced by dissolving inorganic salts of iron, boron, manganese, copper, zinc, and molybdenum in molten glass. When dropped into water, the glass congeals and shatters (this process is called fritting). The fritted glass is then ground into a very fine powder. The rate at which the elements are released to the soil solution depends on the solubility of the glass used to make the frit. Fritted trace elements are very effective as insurance against trace-element deficiencies. They do not, however, release any of the trace elements fast enough to correct a problem if they are applied after deficiency symptoms appear.

In their normal state, ground limestone and superphosphates are, in effect, slow-release fertilizers. A single application can supply all of the calcium, phosphorus, and sulfur that most ornamentals will need for a growing season, and may be adequate for several seasons, depending on soil composition and growing conditions.

Reading a Fertilizer Label

The label on a fertilizer container provides important information, and can help you choose the fertilizer appropriate to your needs. Prominently displayed is the fertilizer analysis or the percentages by weight of nitrogen, phosphorus, and potassium, always in that order. The nitrogen is measured in its elemental form, whereas phosphorus is measured as phosphoric acid and potassium as potash. The balance of the material in the fertilizer consists of the other elements in the compounds with nitrogen, phosphorus, or potassium, or fillers. The nitrogen in ammonium sulfate, for instance, is 21 percent of the fertilizer's weight; the sulfates and other chemical impurities account for the remaining 79 percent. Fillers prevent the chemical salts from caking and provide bulk for easier spreading. Gypsum and ground limestone are the most common fillers, but sand and ground corncobs are also used. The concentrations of macronutrients and trace elements listed on the label are guaranteed by law. The percentages represent the minimum concentration of an element; the fertilizer usually contains a small amount more. (Fillers do not change the guaranteed N-P-K analysis.) The label also provides information about the compounds used to supply the essential elements that are guaranteed to be in the fertilizer.

Fertilizers can acidify soil, and most labels indicate the fertilizer's potential effect on acidity. Typically this is expressed as the amount of calcium carbonate (ground limestone) that would be necessary to neutralize the change in pH that a ton of the fertilizer could cause. The higher this amount is, the more acid the soil will become when you apply the fertilizer. In many soils, the changes in pH induced by fertilizer will not cause problems. But when fertilizer is applied to soils with an already low pH, the increased acidity can seriously affect the availability of nutrients. Likewise, repeated applications of large amounts of fertilizer with a high acid residue (on container-grown ornamentals, for example) can alter nutrient availability.

Comparing Fertilizer Prices

If the nutrients in a fertilizer total less than 30 percent of its weight, it is classified as a low-analysis fertilizer; if more than 30 percent, it is called a high-analysis fertilizer. The greater weight and extra packaging required for low-analysis fertilizers make the nutrients more expensive per unit.

Equal weights of two different brands of fertilizer with the same nutrient percentages provide equal quantities of nutrients and should be priced competitively. A higher price per unit of nutrient may be justified if the nitrogen is supplied in an organic form or as a slow-release compound, which are more expensive than ordinary inorganic compounds. Fertilizers containing fillers may also be more expensive. For a rough comparison of the cost of one brand of fertilizer with another, add up the N-P-K numbers and divide the total into the cost of the fertilizer. If the bags are of equal weight, and the two fertilizers seem otherwise the same, then the one with the lower figure is the better buy.

Applying Fertilizers

Fertilizers come in a variety of physical forms. Inorganic fertilizers may be loose, dry granules; solid tablets or spikes; soluble powders; liquids; or slow-release compounds. Organic fertilizers are mainly powders and granules. Some forms are better suited to certain plants or garden conditions than are others.

Granular Fertilizers

Loose, dry, granular fertilizers can be spread over small areas by hand, or over large ones, such as a lawn, with a mechanical spreader. Distribute the fertilizer on the surface as uniformly as you can, then mix it into the soil. This is the most effective way to apply lime and superphosphate, and to get the nutrients in a complete fertilizer (especially phosphorus) down near plant roots. In a bed of established plants, you can use a technique called side-dressing.

Fertilizing

Sprinkle the granules on the soil surface in narrow bands along one or both sides of a row of plants, or in a circle around individual plants. Leave the fertilizer on the surface or scratch it into the soil (not too deeply, to avoid damaging roots). Be careful not to get granules of fertilizer on plant leaves; it can burn them.

Solid Tablets
Solid tablets of fertilizer, buried in the soil less than halfway to the root zone, are most often used for container plants. Long-lasting types are available for treating clumps of perennials and small shrubs. Solid spikes, which are driven into the soil, are made for large shrubs and trees. Space the tablets or spikes carefully to avoid concentrating the fertilizer in a few spots, and use enough of them to obtain uniform distribution of nutrients. Fertilizers in this form are expensive in relation to the nutrients they supply.

Soluble Powders and Liquids
Effective and easy to use, soluble-powder and liquid fertilizers provide immediately available nutrients to plants. They are both used in the same way, though liquids usually are more expensive per unit of nutrient. Dissolve the specified amount of powder or liquid in a container of water and drench the soil. Apply enough solution to wet the soil down to root depth; more just wastes fertilizer.
If you have a very large garden, you can apply the fertilizer with a garden hose. A hose-end sprayer, which mixes concentrated fertilizer with the spray of water, is simplest. Attaching a metered siphoning device between the faucet and the hose gives more control over the concentration of fertilizer delivered. (You can use a similar device with more extensive irrigation systems.) Go over the same plants several times and direct the spray carefully to ensure even distribution. The nutrients that land on the leaves will be absorbed quickly, but most of the solution will end up on the soil. Therefore, water after you have finished spraying to push the fertilizer on the soil down to the roots. Plan to make several applications during the growing season, rather than supplying all the nutrients at one time. Too high a concentration at one time will damage leaves and stems.

Foliar Fertilization
Although spraying plants with a fertilizer solution as described above is a form of foliar fertilization, it is inefficient. The water droplets are large, and much of the fertilizer solution ends up on the soil surface. It is much better to apply the nutrients with a fine-mist sprayer and just enough water to wet the leaves. This method is used most often to supply trace elements, especially when conditions prevent the uptake of trace elements applied to the soil.

Absorption through the leaves is normally very rapid, and symptoms frequently can be alleviated in a few days. Chelated forms of trace elements work best, because of their higher rates of penetration and use in plant tissues. But you can use other forms of trace elements; some elements, such as boron, cannot be chelated. Generally, one or two applications are enough to correct a trace-element deficiency.

Foliar fertilization is not recommended for supplying the major elements. It is not possible to apply enough of any of these elements at one time to meet plant requirements without burning the leaves—it might take five or more foliar applications to supply the same amount of nitrogen, for example, as can be applied in a single soil drench. Urea is relatively safe if you must apply nitrogen this way, and it is absorbed into the leaves very quickly. To prevent the urea from burning the foliage, mix it with sugar, which also improves urea absorption.

Fertilizing a New Bed

When you make a new bed or replant an old one, you may wish to incorporate fertilizer. If you plan to grow perennials in the bed, this may be your only opportunity for quite a while to add large quantities of bulky organic matter, such as manure or compost. Once the plants are in place, it is not easy to incorporate these amendments deeply into the soil. (See the chapters on soil and planting for more on preparing soil and making a new bed.)

Before fertilizing, it is advisable to have your soil tested. A good soil test will indicate what, if anything, you need to do about the soil's pH and nutrient levels. If the test shows a lack of calcium or phosphorus, add those elements as you prepare the bed. Since phosphorus does not move much in the soil, work in a high-phosphorus fertilizer, such as superphosphate, as thoroughly and as deeply as you can with a spading fork or a small garden tiller. (Dig it in at least six to nine inches and up to 15 inches deep if you can.) Because other macronutrients are more transient, wait until you plant to incorporate them. Remember that the organic matter you added will provide a steady source of nutrients, including trace elements, as it breaks down. If the soil test indicated a need for nitrogen and potassium, and the organic matter you added will not supply enough, mix in some organic nitrogen or a slow-release fertilizer containing nitrogen and potassium. At most, apply two to three pounds of a complete inorganic fertilizer per 100 square feet, and mix it into the soil well. You want to apply enough to meet the needs of your plants as they start to grow, but not so much that you raise soluble salts to a level at which they interfere with water absorption by new roots. Once the plants are in the ground (given a boost by a shot of starter fertilizer), you can fertilize them on a regular basis.

Fertilizing Programs for Specific Plants

Most ornamental plants benefit from a basic program of fertilizer application to maintain their health and to promote vigorous growth.

Fertilizing Flowering Annuals

Flowering annuals provide color all summer and into the fall. Whether you purchase them from a garden center or grow them from seed in flats, give them some starter fertilizer when you transplant them to the garden. As soon as they show signs of new growth, begin fertilizing regularly, once a week in sandy soils and every 10 days to two weeks in heavier soils. Use a soluble powder, such as a 20-20-20 or a 15-30-15, at the rate of one tablespoon per gallon of water. Apply about one quart of solution per square foot to wet the soil thoroughly. (If the soil is dry, water it before you apply the fertilizer solution.) If fertilized plants show lots of lush green growth but few or no flowers, they may be getting too much nitrogen. Stop fertilizing for a while; when you resume, use a lower-nitrogen fertilizer.

Fertilizing Spring Bulbs

Most spring-flowering bulbs need more fertilizer than gardeners usually provide. Some recent research indicates that the reason tulips, for example, fade out after a few years is lack of nutrients. At the time of planting, apply four to five pounds of bone meal or superphosphate per 100 square feet, and mix it in as deep as you expect to plant the bulbs. Then in early spring, as soon as leaves begin to emerge, apply about one pound of a 5-10-10 per 100 square feet. Try to keep the granules from getting in among the leaves. When flowers begin to fade, repeat the application of bone meal or superphosphate and apply an organic source of nitrogen, or make a second application of the 5-10-10 to keep the leaves green longer. This allows the bulbs to store more food, which is so important for the formation of flowers the following year. An alternative program is to apply a four-month-duration slow-release fertilizer in place of the 5-10-10 early in the spring. Use the equivalent of two pounds of 5-10-10, but apply the coated fertilizer only once.

Fertilizing Herbaceous Perennials

For new perennials, follow the fertilizing schedule for flowering annuals. Stop applying fertilizer toward the end of July in cool regions, in mid-August in moderate areas, and later in warmer sections to allow plants to slow down soft vegetative growth and harden off tissues in preparation for winter dormancy. If you use organic or slow-release fertilizers, apply amounts that will be depleted before the end of the summer. Plants that are fertilized too late in the season can be damaged, even killed, by cold weather.

Fertilizing Roses

Prepare the soil well for new roses. Add large amounts of organic matter, adjust the pH to 6.5 to 6.8, and mix in three to four pounds of superphosphate or three to six pounds of bone meal per 100 square feet. After planting, do not fertilize new plants until they have become established, which usually takes three to four weeks. Then begin a program of regular fertilizing, using soil tests as a guide to which formulations of fertilizer will be best.

For mature plants, make the first application of fertilizer just as growth starts in the spring, using one-quarter pound of a 5-10-10 or its equivalent per plant. After the first flush of flowers, repeat about once a month until midsummer to late summer, no later than mid-August in the North, into the fall in the South. Stop fertilizing about four to six weeks before the first frost in order to give stems and buds time to harden off sufficiently for winter dormancy.

Fertilizing Shrubs and Trees

For young shrubs and trees, follow the fertilizing program for roses. As shrubs and trees approach full size, plan to apply nitrogen annually, and phosphorus and potassium every three to five years, more often in light, sandy soils. Apply six pounds of actual nitrogen per 1,000 square feet. If you are applying nitrogen alone, you can spread it on the surface with a lawn spreader and soak the soil so that the nitrogen penetrates down to the roots. (Acid-loving shrubs, such as azaleas and rhododendrons, prefer nitrogen in the ammonium form over the nitrate form.)

If the fertilizer you are using contains phosphorus and potassium (a 10-10-10, for example), do not spread it on the surface. An amount sufficient to supply the nitrogen would contain enough phosphorus and potassium to severely damage grass or a ground cover. To apply a complete fertilizer, punch or drill holes roughly 12 to 15 inches deep at two-foot intervals in an area that begins about two and a half feet from the trunk and extends to slightly beyond the dripline. (Just punching holes in a circle around the dripline does not distribute the fertilizer properly and can injure the shrub or tree, because too much fertilizer is placed in too few holes.) Pour half a cup of a 10-10-10 or its equivalent into each hole. If you are applying phosphorus and potassium without nitrogen, put two level tablespoons of superphosphate (0-20-0) and one tablespoon of muriate of potash (0-0-60) into each hole. Refill the holes with sand or soil.

Another method of applying a complete fertilizer is to inject a solution of 20-20-20 at the rate of 15 pounds per 100 square feet into the soil using a soil needle powered by a hydraulic pump. Inject the solution to a depth of 18 inches in holes spaced approximately two and a half feet apart.

Fertilizing Ornamentals in Containers
The small volume of soil in containers holds a limited supply of water and nutrients, and both must be replenished at frequent intervals. Since containers may need watering once a day, and sometimes more often as plants get larger, nutrients are subject to leaching.

Before you plant, mix lime and superphosphate into the soil, adding about four ounces of dolomitic limestone and two ounces of superphosphate per bushel of loose, well-drained soil mixture. Then each time you water, apply a fertilizer solution containing roughly one and a half ounces of a 20-20-20 or its equivalent per 10 gallons of water. (If you apply fertilizer only once a week, use five ounces per 10 gallons.) As a substitute for applying fertilizer solutions all summer, mix a slow-release fertilizer into the soil before you plant. Add about four pounds of a 14-14-14 formulated to release over three to four months per bushel of soil. Water the plants as needed.

Recognizing Nutrient Deficiencies
Well-prepared soil and a regular program of fertilizing go a long way toward keeping your plants healthy. But at times plants develop problems due to a deficiency or an excess of nutrients. You can diagnose nutrient problems by noting visual symptoms, by soil testing, and by leaf analysis. Try first to determine the cause from the plant's visual symptoms. If you are still stumped, have the soil tested; if that is inconclusive, consider leaf analysis. Keep in mind that nutrients are only one of many potential causes of plant problems. As you search for the answer, think about the possible role of temperature, moisture, insects, disease, and so on.

Visual Symptoms
You should regularly look at your plants with a critical eye. In doing so, you will gain a sense of how plants grow when they are healthy and how they grow when they are not. With experience, you will be able to spot problems before they get out of hand. When an essential element is deficient, plants typically develop characteristic symptoms, but the cause of the symptoms is not always clear-cut. Certain symptoms can have any of several causes. Severe wilting and leaf damage, for example, might be caused by severe desiccation or by several nutrient deficiencies. Early diagnosis is critical. By the time deficiency symptoms become very distinct, plant growth probably has been drastically reduced. Even with treatment, the plant may not be able to gain back all of the growth and quality that it has lost. New leaves and shoots will grow normally and be free of symptoms, but older shoots will be shorter and thinner than normal. Old leaves may regain their usual color but not their size, and any shoots or leaves that were distorted, misshapen, or severely damaged will remain so. (The chart on

Calculating How Much Fertilizer to Apply

Once you have had your soil tested, you will need to figure out how much packaged fertilizer it will take to meet the lab's recommendations. This is relatively simple and requires only basic arithmetic. The easiest way to explain the calculations is with the following examples.

Problem #1

The soil-test report recommends two pounds of actual nitrogen per 1,000 square feet. You are fertilizing 100 square feet with a 5-10-10 fertilizer. How much should you apply?

Start by asking how much 5 percent fertilizer it takes to supply two pounds of nitrogen. Set up a simple equation, using x as the unknown amount of fertilizer:

$.05x = 2$ lb.

$x = \dfrac{2}{.05}$

$x = 40$ lb.

It will take 40 pounds of a 5-10-10 per 1,000 square feet to supply two pounds of nitrogen. Since you are fertilizing one tenth as much area, you need to spread only four pounds of 5-10-10 fertilizer to meet the lab's nitrogen recomendation.

Problem #2

The lab recommends that you apply five pounds of phosphorus per 100 square feet. You have 20 percent superphosphate on hand. How many pounds should you apply to your 100-square-foot plot?

$.20x = 5$ lb.

$x = \dfrac{5}{.20}$

$x = 25$ lb.

What if the only phosphate fertilizer you can buy is treble superphosphate? The bag is labeled 0-48-0.

$.48x = 2$ lb.

$x = \dfrac{5}{.48}$

$x = 10.42$ lb.

To make it easier to measure, apply 10-1/2 pounds per 100 square feet. The extra amount will not be a problem.

Fertilizer recommendations are sometimes expressed as a ratio instead of in percentages. A 10-10-10 fertilizer has a ratio of 1:1:1; so does a 20-20-20. Although they both have a 1:1:1 ratio, it takes twice as much 10-10-10 as 20-20-20 to supply the same amount of nutrients.

Fertilizing

page 232 outlines the visual symptoms caused by deficiencies of the specific nutrients.)

Soil Tests
Considerable knowledge and experience are needed to accurately identify a nutrient deficiency from plant symptoms. Most specialists rely on soil-test results to confirm their diagnosis. Soil tests can also detect problems before they become visible. Soil low in available potassium, for example, may not be deficient enough to cause symptomatic yellowing of a plant's lower leaves, but it may be lacking enough to reduce growth. Treating a deficiency before the more obvious symptoms develop is much better for the plant.
If you are testing to confirm a diagnosis, send the sample to a soil-testing laboratory such as those operated by State Agricultural Experiment Stations, by commercial laboratories, or by fertilizer companies. At these laboratories, trained, experienced personnel conduct the tests using specialized equipment for chemical analysis. These specialists are experienced in interpreting the soil-test values and are familiar with the soils and growing conditions of your area.
When you take the soil sample, make sure it is from the soil in which the plant roots are growing, and carefully follow the directions provided with the test. Be sure to fill out questionnaires thoroughly. The more information you provide, the better equipped the specialist will be to make recommendations. When you get the results, make a mental note of the soil-test values and any comments the specialist has made. Correlating these with the appearance of your plants will help you develop your own diagnostic skills. Even if you get pretty adept at identifying plant problems, it is a good idea to continue testing your soil, if for no other reason than to confirm your opinion.

Leaf Analysis
As helpful as soil tests are, they tell us only what nutrients are available in the soil, not whether those nutrients are being taken up by the plant. Many factors, including soil compaction, poor drainage and aeration, root injury, cold soil temperatures, and low or high pH, can interfere with nutrient uptake. Leaf analysis shows the quantities of nutrients that have actually been absorbed by a plant, and makes early diagnosis possible. It can confirm the existence of a nutritional problem, indicate if nutrients are in balance, and tell which elements are deficient or present in excess within the plant.
Leaf analysis also tests for more nutrients than do soil tests. The latter generally are limited to determining the levels of available

phosphorus, potassium, calcium, magnesium, pH, and soluble salts. A routine leaf analysis provides information about nitrogen, phosphorus, potassium, calcium, magnesium, iron, manganese, boron, copper, zinc, sodium, and aluminum. (A more complicated test for sulfur can also be done upon special request.) The information leaf analysis furnishes about trace elements is particularly valuable. Labs do not analyze soil for trace elements because the tests are difficult, time-consuming, and subject to inconsistencies due to complex and antagonistic interactions among soil elements.

A leaf analysis is more expensive than a soil test, however, and because many extra steps are required, you have to wait longer for the results. Most experts don't recommend using leaf analysis routinely as a guide to fertilizing during the growing season. It is best used for diagnostic purposes in problem areas, and might be used to check the nutritional status of valuable plants once a year. How you collect the sample of leaves for analysis is crucial. Leaf position, stage of growth, cultivar type, date of last fertilization, and even time of day may affect the nutrient content of leaves. Follow the instructions for sampling specific plants if they are provided. If they are not, collect the youngest, fully expanded leaves from the middle to upper third of new shoots. Unless you have explicit directions to do otherwise, do not sample leaves that are dead, diseased, or damaged by insects or mechanical equipment.

The levels of nutrient elements in leaves are classified in four groups or ranges. (The standard values differ for each plant species.) In the deficiency range, plants show deficiency symptoms and a reduction in growth and quality. Plants in the hidden-hunger range are normal in appearance, but will show a striking response when fertilized with the deficient element. The upper limit of this range is the critical nutrient value, that is, the lowest nutrient level at which the plants will thrive. In the normal range, plants are normal in appearance, and their growth and quality can reach the maximum. The upper levels of this range are known as luxury levels—concentrations of nutrients in excess of what are needed for maximum growth but not in toxic amounts. Finally, plants in the excess, or toxic, range either show clearly visible symptoms of a nutritional disorder or have a normal appearance but significantly reduced growth. Obviously, your objective in fertilizing your plants is to keep levels of nutrients in the normal range, above the critical value and up to the luxury level.

Watering Your

Water is critical to plants. Some plants are made up of about 90 percent water, and all plants process a great deal of water during the course of their lives—it can take several hundred pounds of water to produce one pound of dry plant material. Water is essential for seeds to germinate and for plants to grow, flower, and set fruit. How well they do these things depends on when and how much water is available. Yet of all the gardening techniques, watering is the most elusive. To understand how to water your plants, it is useful first to learn about how plants use water and how water behaves in the soil.

How Plants Use Water
Water plays a role in every plant process from germination to seed production. The following is a brief description of the important ones.

Photosynthesis and Translocation
Water is a critical raw material for photosynthesis. With water, sunlight, and carbon dioxide, plants manufacture the sugars they need to grow and develop. In the process, they also produce the oxygen that we breathe and, directly or indirectly, almost all the food that we and many other creatures eat. (Fragrances are also affected by water, because plant oils and nectars are derived from plant sugars.)
Dissolved in water, the sugars formed by photosynthesis and the minerals taken up through the roots are moved through the plant via specialized tissues called the xylem and the phloem. This process is called translocation.

Pigment Formation
Plants use water to form chlorophyll, the common green pigment that absorbs the sun's energy and makes it available for photosynthesis. Water also helps form other pigments that make up the colors of foliage, fruit, and flowers.

Growth Regulation
Cells, the basic building blocks of plant life, are inflated by water, a condition called turgor. If cells lose turgor, the plant wilts and cell processes suffer. In this way, water acts as a growth regulator. Without sufficient water, the rate of cell division and enlargement is retarded. Plants may be dwarfed; have shortened stems, small leaves, and weak foliage and flower color; and produce small flowers and fruits, or none at all.

Transpiration
As important as water is to plants, only one to five percent of the water absorbed by the roots is actually used by the plant. The rest

Plants

is transpired, passing back to the atmosphere as water vapor. Transpiration cools plants in much the same way that perspiration cools humans.

Plants transpire through stomata. Located mainly on the bottom surfaces of leaves, stomata are pores flanked by a pair of specialized cells called guard cells. When the guard cells are turgid, the pores are open and the plant transpires. When the guard cells lack water, they collapse and close. The rate of transpiration is determined primarily by the difference between the amount of water vapor in the atmosphere (humidity) and the amount of water vapor in the leaf. The leaf's internal water vapor is usually close to 100 percent, so the drier the air is outside, the more rapid the transpiration will be.

Transpiration is affected by light, temperature, relative humidity, wind, and leaf structure. Stomata generally are closed in darkness and open in the light, so most transpiration occurs during daylight hours. As sunlight raises the temperature inside a leaf, the amount of water vapor the leaf can hold increases, as does the rate of transpiration. Likewise, a breeze or even a slight movement of the air can increase the rate of transpiration by blowing away water vapor surrounding the leaf surface. Although the number, size, and position of stomata differ from species to species, 80 percent of the water lost by any plant is lost through its stomata.

Seed Germination

Water is critical in initiating germination by swelling the cell walls inside the seed, a process called imbibation.

Water and Soil

Most plants in the garden extract their moisture from the soil. The ease or difficulty with which they do so depends on the soil's texture and structure. The texture of a soil is determined by the size of the particles—sand, silt, or clay—making up the soil. A soil's structure is determined by the way the particles group together to form aggregates. (For more on soil texture and structure, see the chapter on preparing the soil.) Air and water reside and move in the spaces between the particles and between aggregates. The larger the particles and aggregates, the larger the pore spaces. Water moves rapidly and drains freely through the large pore spaces of sandy soils; its movement is more restricted in denser clayey soils.

Plants need air as well as water to grow and develop, but because air and water move in the same pore spaces, they may displace each other. If the soil is over-watered and kept too wet, water displaces air and the plant roots, starved of oxygen, "drown." Waterlogged soil also supports certain disease organisms that survive without oxygen, which can affect the health and vigor of the plant. In general, you can improve water drainage by adding organic matter to the soil. (See pages 59–60 for more on drainage problems and solutions.) The term "field capacity" is often used to describe the amount of water that remains in the soil after any surplus has drained away. When soil is wet to field capacity, plants easily obtain all the water they need. Plants actively pump water from the soil, and it takes more and more energy to extract water as the soil dries out. When the amount of water left in the soil is so small that plants wilt and fail to recover, the condition is called the "permanent wilting point." The field capacity of different soils varies considerably depending on their makeup, as does the permanent wilting point for different plants.

Movement of water through the soil is largely vertical. When the horizontal layers of soil are of different textures, water will not move through to the second layer until the first layer has become saturated. For example, if the top layer is a clayey soil and the lower layer sandy, water will not move through to the sand until the clay has become saturated. For the same reason, placing gravel or stones at the bottom of a planting hole or a pot does not necessarily improve drainage.

Water continues to move through different layers of soil until it reaches a saturated zone, called the water table. In semiarid and arid climates, there is usually a dry zone between the top layers of soil and the water table. A layer of compacted soil, or hardpan, can create an artificial or "perched" water table. As water builds up there, its capillary action moves it back up through the soil profile. The rising water carries salts upward, and when the water evaporates, the salts are deposited as a white crust on the soil surface. (Soil in a container develops the same deposits if the container sits in a dish of water.) To get rid of the salts, water thoroughly so that they are leached out of the soil.

Plants' Water Needs and Adaptations

By taking on various forms and structures, plants have adapted to a range of environments. Classified by their water needs, plants fall into three broad categories: water plants (hydrophytes), moist-soil plants (mesophytes), and dry-soil plants (xerophytes). Because their water needs are specific, you should grow plants of the same group together, rather than trying to mix them.

Hydrophytes

Plants adapted to growing in water are called hydrophytes. Some, such as duckweed, float in or on the water. Others, such as water lilies, are rooted in the mud. Water plants normally have thin leaves and rot-resistant roots and stems. The stems and leaves often contain large air chambers, which provide buoyancy and store carbon dioxide. To survive, these plants need to secure oxygen.

Mesophytes

The plants traditionally grown in gardens fall into this group. They generally have broad, thin leaves of varying textures and color, and prefer moist soil and high relative humidity.

Xerophytes

Plants in this category are native to semiarid to arid climates where the relative humidity is often as low as 5 to 35 percent and the evaporation rate is high. Xerophytes have evolved many features that allow them to survive on limited amounts of water. To reduce transpiration, leaves may be small, firm, and leathery, or have a thick, waxy coating. They may have hairs or fuzz, an apparatus that traps moisture and raises the relative humidity around the leaf surface. Some xerophytes roll or fold their leaves inward to reduce water loss during periods of drought. Some, such as cacti, may be leafless, but have green stems. Although most plants open their stomata in the daytime, some xerophytes open theirs at night and absorb carbon dioxide when temperatures are low and relative humidity is high. The stored carbon dioxide is available for photosynthesis during the day, while the stomata are closed, reducing water loss. The adaptations that limit transpiration also slow growth.

The root systems of some xerophytes are far more extensive than their aboveground parts. Roots may be limited to the top few inches of soil to capture as much precipitation as possible, or they may grow down to the depth of the water table. Some plants remove and store large quantities of water from the soil when it is available, while others go dormant during dry periods and recover when water is again obtainable.

When to Water

Knowing when to water requires careful observation of your garden's microclimates, soil, weather, and plants. Become familiar with the microclimates created by structures, landforms, and large plants in your garden. Moisture levels and humidity, like light and temperature, vary in these small environments. Get to know the characteristics of the soil in your garden. Determine its composition and test how well it drains. (See the chapter on preparing the soil for more on analyzing soil drainage.) Remember that the soil can vary from place to place on your property.

Wind and temperature affect the timing of watering. High winds remove moisture surrounding the leaves, and can quickly desiccate plants, especially young transplants or seedlings. High temperatures increase rates of transpiration from leaves and evaporation from the soil. When temperatures are above 90°F, monitor soil moisture and plants carefully.

Finally, know your plants. Learn to recognize signs of water stress.

Watering Your Plants

Besides the obvious signs of wilting, plants give off other signals of distress. Dull or droopy foilage, premature dropping of leaves, poor flower production, or small or undeveloped fruits may indicate stress from either too much or too little water. Certain types of plants have characteristic stress signals. For example, when the leaves of a xerophytic plant curl inward, it probably needs water.

Also, learn what sorts of development to expect under different growing conditions. If you are growing a plant with succulent roots in water-holding clay soil, monitor rainfall and irrigation closely so that you don't over-water it and cause root rot. A plant that prefers full sun may not flower if grown in the shade, so watering may not improve its flower production even if it is water-stressed.

And lastly, learn the water requirements of your plants at different stages of development. Small or new transplants need lighter, more frequent waterings, while more mature and established plants prefer deeper, less frequent waterings. Water stress during certain developmental stages can also inhibit flower or fruit production.

How Much Water?

Plant roots absorb water most readily when the surrounding soil is at or near field capacity—in simple terms, when the soil is moist but drains freely. One approach to watering is to strive to keep the soil in this optimum condition, continually replacing the water that the plants absorb and that evaporates from the soil. Another approach is to water thoroughly and deeply, and then allow the soil to dry out until the plants begin to show signs of mild water stress before watering deeply again. The first approach undoubtedly produces healthy plants, but it may require a lot of water and, unless you spend hours each day in the garden, an expensive automatic delivery system. The second system is a little harder on the plants, but it may use less water and demands less vigilance.

Gauging Soil Moisture

Regardless of which watering method you choose, it is helpful to learn how to gauge the amount of water in the soil. You can conduct a "feel test" by taking a handful of soil and squeezing it firmly. In general, good garden loam at field capacity will form a ball, and, if you roll the ball between your fingers, a little damp soil will stick to them and leave an outline of the ball. Different soils, however, have different "feels." For example, at less than 25 percent moisture content (too little water), a sandy loam will be loose and flow through your fingers; a silty loam will be powdery and crumble easily; and a silty, clay loam will be hard and won't readily break into powder. At 75 to 100 percent moisture content (the preferred condition, given good aeration), a sandy loam will

Water penetrates some soils faster than others. This drawing shows how far one inch of water penetrates in three general soil types after about 24 hours.

Soil depth

4"

8"

12"

Clay soil   Loam   Sandy soil

form a weak ball even though it may break up easily, while a clay loam will form a ball, stick readily to your fingers, and smoothly ribbon out when rolled.

When you water, it is important to moisten the root zone to its full depth. This encourages deep rooting, and the deeper the roots are, the longer plants can go between irrigations. Some books note rooting depths for specific plants—shallow, deep, taprooted, for example. You can also learn a lot by taking note of the roots when you divide or transplant. In general, with the exception of shallow-rooted plants, most plants grow roots between 6 and 18 inches deep.

To estimate how much water is needed to reach roots at various depths, you can use the following rule of thumb: On the average, one inch of water will penetrate approximately 12 inches deep in a sandy soil, 7 inches in a loam soil, and 4 to 5 inches in a clay soil. Use this rule to get you started, then check to see how water actually behaves in your soil. About 24 hours after watering, dig into the soil with a trowel or a shovel to see how far the water has penetrated. To keep from wasting water through runoff, water less-absorbent soils with small amounts of water applied over longer periods of time.

Depending on its composition, soil loses moisture at different rates. Coarse, porous soils dry out rapidly. Plants growing in them can appear healthy, then suddenly wilt overnight. And the time between wilt and permanent damage can be very short, especially in extremely hot weather. Clay soils, on the other hand, dry out more slowly, and plants grown in them will have a gradual curve of drought stress. Some soil types have peculiarities that affect watering. Clay, for example, shrinks and cracks when dry and expands when wet. Water runs through the cracks without wetting plant roots. If your soil is cracked, try watering twice, first to seal the cracks and then to provide moisture for the plants. Learn about your soil's idiosyncrasies by paying attention to how it behaves in a variety of conditions.

If you want a more precise method of determining how much to water, you can make use of evapo-transpiration (ET) rates. The ET rate is the amount of water, calculated in inches per day or per month, that evaporates from a specified area of soil surface and transpires from the plants growing there. ET rates are influenced by temperature, relative humidity, wind, and day length. They are measured for specific plants, often agricultural crops, but they can serve as a guide for gardeners. In some cities, ET rates are announced during weather reports or are available from the local county extension service.

Ways to Apply Water

Portable and in-ground systems alike make use of a number of watering devices and strategies. The pros and cons of using some of the most common are discussed in the chart on pages 266–269. More general information is given below.

Hand Watering

Years ago, most gardeners simply hauled water to their plants in a sprinkling can or a bucket. Hand watering is still one of the most therapeutic and valuable gardening activities. As you stand with hose or watering can in hand, you can really observe the individual plants. Unfortunately, hand watering can be very time-consuming, prohibitively so if you are deep watering. It is also haphazard—gauging the amount of water you have applied is tricky, and the amounts vary from one watering to the next.

Choosing Other Methods

Despite the pleasures of hand watering, most gardeners soon find themselves employing one or more of the many mechanical watering devices available today. These can be as simple as a portable sprinkler or soaker hose connected to a hose bibb—you put it where it is needed, turn it on, and go do something else. Or they can involve a complex system of in-ground pipes that feed permanently located sprinklers, soaker hoses, drip tapes, or subsurface irrigation lines. Fitted with a programmable timer and automatic valves, such a system can keep your plants happy for days or weeks while you're away.

Given the variety of watering devices and systems available, it can be mind-boggling to choose which best suits you. Ask yourself some basic questions: During how much of the growing season will you have a need for supplemental water? How large is your garden or landscape? What kinds of plants will you be growing? What is your source of water? How much money can you afford to spend?

The simpler alternatives are easy enough to evaluate by trial and error. If one doesn't work out, you haven't lost a lot of money or time. But the more complex systems warrant thought and planning. If you are planning a new landscape or garden, don't do so without considering irrigation. Intricate landscape designs incorporating tapering and odd-shaped beds, slopes, or combinations of plants that require different amounts of water can make water-system plans more complicated. Design the system for the maximum demand, so you won't come up dry at a critical moment. If you are short on experience, consult a landscape architect or contractor. A modest amount of money spent on professional help upfront may save you a great deal at a later time.

Sprinklers

These setups emit fine sheets, fans, or pulsating streams of water. They vary greatly in size and coverage, from tiny microsprinklers that emit a cone of spray several feet in diameter to large rotary units that can cover an area 200 feet in diameter. Depending on size and coverage, sprinklers can deliver between one-quarter and two inches of water per hour. Small fixed-head sprinklers are good for low-growing, closely spaced plants. Rotary or oscillating sprinklers are best for lawns and large areas of ground cover, especially where there is foot traffic.

On the plus side, some sprinkler systems offer uniform coverage and allow you to control how much water is applied. On the minus, only 65 to 75 percent of the water they emit ends up in the soil, where you want it. The rest evaporates, is intercepted by foliage, or is blown away by the wind. Moreover, sprinklers are not selective—everything in their path gets watered, whether it needs it or not. Sprinklers attached permanently to in-ground systems are usually mounted on risers. Attached to the underground line, these vertical lengths of pipe position the sprinkler head above interfering foliage to provide the best coverage.

To find out how long it takes a sprinkler to apply an inch of water in a specific area, place several flat-bottomed cans on the ground—within its reach. Turn on the water and record the time it takes for

Portable, Hose-End Systems	Description
Hand-held spray nozzle 	Screw on to ordinary garden hose and squeeze trigger to spray. A variety of types are available, some of which provide high-pressure water streams or have spring-loaded shut-off handles.
Perforated hose 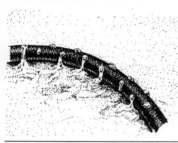	A garden hose with small holes that emit water in a trickle or a fine spray, depending on the water pressure. (A similar system, the soaker hose, is made of porous material through which water seeps.)
Oscillating sprinkler 	Device with sprinkler bar that tips back and forth, delivering a fine spray across a large area.
Fan sprinkler 	A simple spray device that sends a fine half-circle of water in one direction.

Advantages	Disadvantages
Offers good control over amount and direction of water flow. Especially helpful in giving newly planted trees and shrubs a good soaking. Can save water because operation requires the user's close attention.	Does not work unattended. User may apply water with too much or too little force, thus injuring or over- or under-watering plants. Users tend to under-water.
Excellent to soak newly seeded areas. Flexible enough to serve areas of different shapes and sizes. Slow discharge rate reduces runoff waste. Inexpensive and can be left unattended for a period of time. Works in a way similar to drip irrigation (see next page).	Wears out quickly. Fine spray evaporates easily or is blown by wind. Irrigation pattern can be uneven. Pressure may need regulating by keeping hose length less than about 50 feet.
Covers large square or rectangular area. Useful for watering trees, shrubs, turf, or ground covers. Allows for slow penetration of water into soil.	Throws water high into the air, where it can be lost through evaporation or carried away by winds. Less expensive models may be unreliable and give uneven spray patterns.
Soft spray makes it especially useful for watering delicate flowers and ground covers. Single direction allows for fairly accurate aim. Device has a long life.	If used with high water pressure, misting and evaporation occur. High-volume output can cause runoff. Does not cover large area.

Fixed, In-Ground Systems	Description
Pop-up spray head 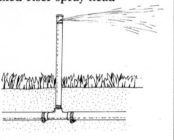	A high-volume system in which water pressure forces a riser out of its buried housing. Then water is distributed through a spray head on the riser. Discharges 1–3 gallons per minute.
Fixed-riser spray head 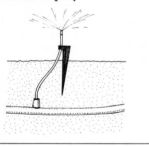	High-volume system similar to pop-up spray heads, with fixed heads that remain above ground.
Low-volume spray 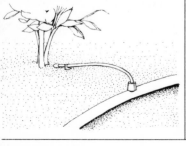	Narrow plastic tubing connected to supply lines and topped with a small spray cap rises above ground to distribute a fine spray 4–15 feet in radius. Discharge rates are $\frac{1}{10}$–$\frac{3}{4}$ gallon per minute.
Drip irrigation	Narrow tubing runs from supply line directly to base of plant and discharges water very slowly.

Advantages	Disadvantages
Excellent for areas of turf or ground cover because the risers (available in various heights) clear the tops of plants. Buried risers do not obstruct lawn mowers and are unobtrusive. Offer low trajectory so little water is lost through evaporation.	May discharge water faster than soil can absorb it. One head every 10 feet is required. (Similar devices called pop-up impact heads and gear-driven stream rotors require fewer heads.) Makes it fairly difficult to rearrange planting area once installed.
Less expensive than high-rise pop-up head but offers similar advantages. Requires lighter digging to install.	Risers are always in view, make mowing difficult, and can be tripped over. Other disadvantages similar to those of pop-up head, above.
Slow application rate is excellent for ground covers, shrubs, and trees and for small areas. Permits deep penetration of water. Various spray heads offer different coverage patterns; system may use pop-up or fixed risers. Easy to install and unobtrusive.	Pressure-reducing device is required. Narrow tubing may become clogged. Fixed risers are easily damaged.
Subject to little evaporation and minimal runoff; excellent for use on slopes and for establishing new plantings. Emitters can be buried under mulch to keep them out of sight. Very inexpensive and easily changed.	Requires use of pressure-reducer and strainer between supply line and emitter. Difficult to verify operation if tubes are out of sight.

Watering Your Plants

one inch to accumulate in each can. The water pattern will be irregular, so some cans will fill faster than others. You can average the time between the first and last to fill if you want to be precise. Then compare this figure to the amount of water your plants need and adjust the sprinkler accordingly.

Drip Irrigation

These systems apply water slowly and evenly close to the soil. They may be laid on the ground or dug into it. Water flows through flexible plastic tubing and drips out of emitters. Drip tape is tubing with regularly spaced emitters installed at the factory. Drip tubing with plug-in emitters lets you determine your own spacing. Emitters are, in effect, tiny water meters, and they are rated by gallons of water delivered per hour.

Because drip systems apply water only where the plants need it and not on walks, streets, or weeds, they can save a lot of water. They wet the ground, not the foliage, so they can reduce foliar diseases. And they are unlikely to cause erosion even on steep slopes. If you wish to keep the soil moisture in your garden at field capacity, a drip system or a subsurface system is the most effective way to do so. There are disadvantages to drip, however. Although a simple drip system can be run off a hose bibb, an extensive system can be expensive. Beyond a certain length, drip tubing can lose pressure and flow. And emitters can clog.

All drip systems, however simple or complex, require water pressure lower than that usually found in most communities (8 to 15 pounds per square inch rather than 40 to 60 psi). Some drip emitters are designed to step down the pressure themselves. For those that aren't, you will need a pressure regulator. Every system should have a filter to help keep debris from clogging emitters. Where you place emitters depends on your soil and the root structures of the plants. Ordinarily, emitters are spaced wider for clay soils than for sandy soils, and closer for shallow-rooted plants than for deep-rooted ones.

Drip-irrigation apparatus that is buried four to six inches underground is often called subsurface irrigation. Water seeps through porous plastic tubing or special emitters fitted in plastic tubing in ways similar to the drip systems described above. These systems supply water directly to the root zone, with no waste from overspray or evaporation. You also don't have to be concerned with trimming around sprinkler heads.

But there are drawbacks to subsurface systems. Because they are invisible and silent, you don't know if they are working properly until the plants show signs of stress. The initial cost is up to 20 percent higher than for standard aboveground systems. Subsurface systems aren't suitable for use on rocky or extremely porous soils. (Effective positioning in other soils depends on a knowledge of the

You can water large trees and shrubs by building a soil dike near the plant's dripline and slowly filling the basin with water. The basin irrigation technique *also works well for small planting beds.*

soil type and profile.) And, once installed, they are troublesome to modify.

Flood Irrigation
The flood-irrigation watering strategy includes several low-tech methods that have advantages for certain types of terrain and plants. If the site is fairly level, and a large enough volume of water is available, you can flood the entire garden with enough water to wet the root zone.

Basin irrigation involves flooding on a smaller scale, and is an effective way of watering large and deeply rooted trees and shrubs. Around each plant, build a soil dike up to six inches high, extending a short distance beyond the spread of the plant's branches, as shown in the drawing below. Slowly fill the basin with water, which will then percolate through the soil profile to the root zone.

Basin irrigation can also be used for small beds (about four by five feet) of vegetables, annuals, or perennials. Surround each bed with a dike (which can also serve as a walkway), and inside make the

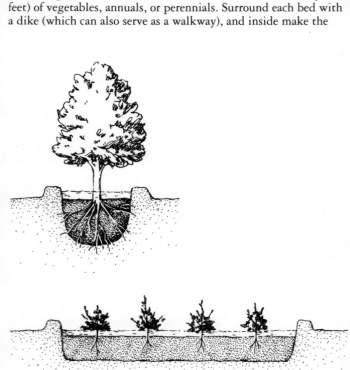

surface of the bed slightly below ground level. Good drainage is critical, so amend the soil to a depth of 18 to 24 inches if necessary. Basin irrigation is useful in arid climates, where it offers protection from drying winds that increase evaporation. In areas of abundant rainfall, basin irrigation can lead to over-watering. Furrow irrigation, wherein troughs between rows of plants are flooded, is used mainly in growing food plants. It is best suited to gently sloping land, and will work in most types of soils except very coarse ones. Because cultivating the furrows keeps the soil loose, erosion is a danger. Water must flow slowly enough to be absorbed and not create erosion.

In-Ground Irrigation Systems

Whether you are watering your garden by hand, or hauling portable sprinklers or drip hoses from one bed to another, you may soon find that watering has become your main gardening activity. If your garden is large and your climate dry, you may also find that you can't keep up and you are beginning to lose some of your favorite plants. An in-ground irrigation system may be what you need to save your plants, water, and time.

The following discussion won't tell you how to install a system, but it will familiarize you with the workings of in-ground systems and their components. You should have little trouble installing a simple system guided by the brochures available from suppliers and manufacturers of irrigation equipment. Even if you are a confident do-it-yourselfer, it is prudent to consult with a knowledgeable landscape architect or contractor before installing an extensive system.

In an in-ground system, buried pipe replaces aboveground hoses. The pipe connects the water supply to one or more valves that control the flow of water through additional buried pipe to sprinklers, drip- or subsurface-irrigation lines, or hose bibbs. A simple system can be run from a single, existing hose bibb. Larger systems connect the water main or well directly to a number of valves, each valve controlling one or more lines that serve a portion of the landscape. The valves can be distributed individually throughout the garden, or ganged together in one or more manifolds for convenience. You can open and close the valves manually, or install automatic controls and a timer.

An irrigation system must deliver water to the sprinklers or irrigation lines at an adequate flow and pressure. Pipe, pipe fittings, valves, and other components all reduce water pressure and flow. The more extensive the system, the greater these reductions can be. The smaller the pipe, the larger the loss of pressure. So in general, use the largest-diameter pipe and fittings you can. To determine the size of the pipe, fittings, and valves best for your system, you will need to know the flow and pressure at the

In small areas, an espalier, which is the result of creative pruning and training, can provide much-wanted "acreage" of favorite plants.

These pansies, like many other annuals, will produce prolific blooms if they are dead-headed and pinched back judiciously during their blooming season.

An espalier can be
trained and pruned to
ascend a fence or to cover
a wall. Here, ceanothus
provides a lush backdrop
for smaller shrubs.

Some vines, such as the
clematis shown below,
produce flowers only on
new wood. They must be
pruned each winter to
encourage blossoming in
spring.

276

A knot garden such as
the one seen here is the
result of many years
of careful pruning.
Sheared back hard every
year, these low-growing
santolinas and
barberries produce even
new growth that gives
the garden hedges their
neat and controlled
appeal.

The Exbury hybrid
azalea at left has been
carefully shaped by
pinching of terminal
buds to encourage lateral
growth and stronger
forked branches.

This formal-looking
parterre, with tulips
growing from the center,
is formed of carefully
trimmed and pruned
boxwood.

Roses can form
beautiful, fragrant
hedges when properly
pruned. The prolific
bloom gives way to cool
green later in the season,
and the thorns serve to
deter unwanted visitors.

In pruning trees, the style and extent of the pruning are determined by the kind of tree. The fig tree below has been pruned to open up the branches, preventing cross-growth and enhancing the tree's strength. Mature garden trees are often "limbed up" to give high shade while providing light to garden plants below.

The best time to prune deciduous trees is during the winter. While woody growth has stopped for the period of dormancy, a tree is somewhat protected from the shock of pruning. What is more, a tree's true shape is easier to see and sculpt in the winter, when the leaves are gone.

A trellis or a fence provides a suitable support for many climbing plants, such as the morning glories below. A well-trained vine will also mask an unsightly wire fence.

When properly pruned and trained, a trellis plant (right) creates a shady bower or an inviting portal. Roses, honeysuckle, and wisteria are ideal for such use.

Climbing roses, such as the one seen here, do not actually climb. Instead, their long, supple canes must be tied to a trellis, arbor, or other support.

Garden clean-up is more than an aesthetic matter—it is an important part of keeping your plants healthy. Leaf litter, fallen branches, and other garden debris create a perfect environment in which diseases and pests thrive.

It is vital to clean rose gardens of debris after pruning to prevent the spread of disease. It is also a good idea to spray with fungicide at this point.

A layer of mulch, laid at planting time or during winter clean-up, will further efforts to keep down weeds and hold pests and diseases at bay. Mulches also provide insulation during the cooler months, help the soil retain moisture, and lend a neat appearance to the garden bed.

Early-blooming plants—especially weedy or naturalized annuals—should be cleaned up and removed to make room for flowers that bloom later. The forget-me-nots below have provided a cheery early display of color, but now they are being dug out of the ground, to give the rest of the garden a chance to come into its own.

This no-frills irrigation set-up would allow you to run one or more sprinklers or several driplines (depending on water flow and sprinkler size).

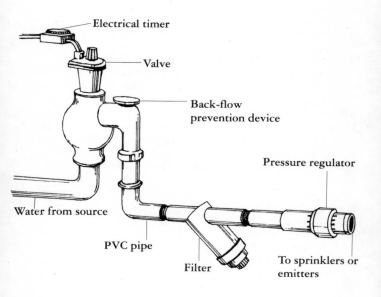

Electrical timer

Valve

Back-flow prevention device

Pressure regulator

Water from source

PVC pipe

Filter

To sprinklers or emitters

water main, and the pressure loss for various diameters and lengths of pipe and for various fittings. Charts covering these items are available from suppliers of irrigation equipment. The calculations aren't difficult to make, although they can become involved for large systems.

Components of In-Ground Systems

All in-ground systems, whether simple or elaborate, are comprised of pipe and a range of pipe fittings and valves. (An example is shown in the drawing above.) The building codes of most cities and towns dictate some form of backflow prevention, to keep water in the irrigation lines from being sucked back into the municipal water system. As a rule, drip lines will require a filter and pressure regulator.

Pipe

Plastic pipe is durable, inexpensive, and easy to install, and it offers the least resistance to water flow of any piping material. Polyvinyl chloride (PVC) pipe can be cut with a hacksaw, and assembled with slip fittings and solvent and with threaded fittings. Polyethylene (PE) pipe is also used for in-ground irrigation, but it must be assembled with fittings rather than solvent, and its low pressure ratings make it unsuitable for pressurized main-line runs. Galvanized-steel and copper pipe are more durable than plastic in exposed locations, but they are much more expensive and difficult to install.

Pipe is often buried about six inches deep; you will need to go deeper in cultivated beds to avoid damage from hand tools or rototillers. Burying beneath the frost line isn't necessary in cold climates as long as you drain the system before freezing weather.

Valves
In a simple system, a hose bibb may be the only valve you need. A variety of valves specially designed for irrigation systems are available. In general, they differ from one another by size, material, and mode of operation (manual or automatic). Some valves are fitted with backflow-prevention devices. Larger valves cause less pressure drop. Ultraviolet light can degrade exposed plastic valves.

Backflow Preventers
Code requirements for backflow prevention vary, so be sure to check your town's regulations. Some codes allow simple, anti-siphon backflow preventers (built into some plastic valves) if these are installed more than six inches higher than all the lines they service. You can also install a single, large anti-siphon device on the main service line, placed higher than the rest of the system.

Filters and Pressure Regulators
Dirty water clogs drip emitters. A 150-mesh screen filter will trap algae and dirt. And unless you are using pressure-compensating emitters, you will also need a pressure regulator. Buy good-quality filters and regulators; the reliability is worth the extra expense.

Timers
Automatic timers typically allow you to control four to six watering zones (a zone consists of one or two valves). Electronic timers are more expensive than mechanical ones, but they offer more flexibility in programming. Timers vary, but the good ones let you program what days and times the zones will be watered and the duration of each watering session. The wires that connect the valves to the timer can be buried alongside the pipe.

Conserving Water
Recent droughts have heightened concern about the availability and quality of water throughout North America. In some areas, water conservation may cease to be a choice and become a necessity. New beds and landscapes should be designed from the beginning with water consumption in mind. Older gardens and

landscapes developed without thought to water use can be made more efficient.

You don't need to tear out your existing landscape to achieve significant water savings. Just changing old practices and habits can save about 10 percent of the water you use. Here are some things you can do:

Water only if the plants need it. Pay attention to the different water needs of various plants and to how they change with the seasons. If it rains, adjust or shut off automatic systems. Check the soil's moisture level before and after watering, and make sure that water has penetrated the root zone. (Don't water beyond the root zone—it won't benefit the plants and can deposit excess fertilizer or other contaminants there.)

Water deep-rooted plants infrequently but deeply. Be aware that water may be more efficiently applied to some soils in several short sessions rather than in one long one. Consider installing underground sensors to monitor moisture levels. Remember that mature trees and shrubs require less water less often than do newly planted ones. Position, adjust, and monitor sprinklers and irrigation lines to minimize overspray and runoff.

Group together plants with similar needs. Reduce the area planted with high-water-demand plants, such as Kentucky bluegrass. Water during the cooler part of the day, when evaporation and winds are at a minimum. Mulch to reduce evaporation from the soil. Weeds compete for water, so remove them when they are small. Consider growing plants native to your area, which are more likely to survive with less (or no) supplemental watering. Don't waste water cleaning rocks, driveways, and so on. For more tips on conserving water in the garden, consult *Taylor's Guide to Water-Saving Gardening.*

Pruning

The various procedures that collectively are called pruning include some of the most important, most commonly practiced, and yet most universally misunderstood techniques of ornamental horticulture. Pruning is the purposeful removal of a limb from a tree or a branch from a shrub. But it is also the plucking of spent flowers to conserve plant energy or to induce reblooming; the pinching of selected buds or growing tips to direct new growth in a specified pattern; and the amputation of circling roots to prevent girdling. In fact, the term "pruning" is applied to the intentional removal of any plant part, except perhaps cut flowers or ripe fruit and vegetables.

Pruning can be done with fingernails, or a chain saw, or anything in between, depending upon the specific plant part being excised. By learning the particular pruning techniques that will work for your own plants, you will be able to enhance the health and beauty of your landscape. The secret is to learn what works and why, so that you will understand the processes involved and be able to adapt to the constant growth and change in your garden. You don't need to be an expert; learning the rudiments of pruning will help you to improve the health, beauty, and usefulness of your plants.

Why Prune?
There are many important reasons to prune plants—some routine, some specialized. You will probably have to do some or all of the following to keep your landscape looking its best:

•Remove dead and diseased portions of plants for aesthetic and sanitary reasons

•Repair structural damage from ice, wind, or impact

•Correct or thin misdirected or overly dense growth

•Reduce the size of overgrown plants

•Pluck spent flowers on ornamentals to conserve plant energy reserves, to induce reblooming, or to prevent the establishment of inferior volunteer seedlings

•Remove weak wood to improve structural strength, to enhance disease resistance, or to intensify subsequent floral display

You may take on some other pruning techniques strictly for artistic reasons: the creation and maintenance of topiary, espalier, hedges, bonsai, penjing, and other forms that entail the manipulation or restraint of a plant's natural growth patterns. The common thread in all these procedures is that, done properly, they can enhance the health, appearance, and lifespan of your plants.

Plant growth is regulated by hormones, called auxins, that are synthesized in the growing tips (apexes) of the plant. If left unpruned, a growing tip will continue to grow straight out (a tendency called apical dominance); if a plant is pruned, however, other branches—with new growing tips, producing more growth hormones—will form.

Pruning entails risks, but you shouldn't be afraid to prune; the performance of your plants depends upon it. Most gardeners expect their "tame" plants to exhibit branching patterns and floral displays that are not possible in the wild. In fact, many of today's popular and promising plant cultivars and hybrids do not even exist in nature. Moreover, most yards—no matter how well tended—are less than perfect, environmentally. Most of us live in areas with heavily compacted subsoil, pavement, air pollution, road-salt runoff, turf-root competition, and the absence of beneficial soil microorganisms. So don't let nature take its course and assume that you will have a picture-perfect yard. Learn the pruning methods that are proper and necessary for your particular landscape and learn to avoid those procedures that might have disappointing results, then proceed with confidence.

How Pruning Works: Plant Physiology

Almost every pruning decision you make will result in a growth reaction of some sort, for better or worse, in the plant you are treating. Before you get out your shears, therefore, take a moment for a brief discussion of plant physiology. Understanding the forces of plant growth will make pruning easier, more efficient, and more effective.

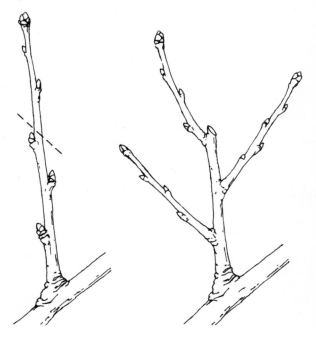

Pruning

In conifers, if the central leader is damaged, it may fail to reestablish itself. You can train one of the horizontal branches to grow up, thus keeping several buds from opening at once —an event that can lead to the establishment of weak crotches.

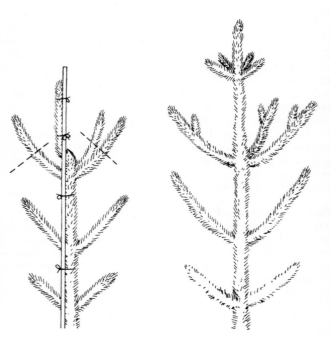

A plant's growth takes place primarily in an area called the cambial meristem—the layer in the stem where interior cells become wood and exterior cells become bark—and in the apical meristem, the growing tips where leaves and shoots are formed. ("Apical" is from apex—tip, point, summit.) External factors, such as sunlight, nutrients, water, temperature, and pathogens, react with internal factors, such as genetic limitations and plant hormones, to direct the specific responses of a plant to a pruning cut.

Apical Dominance
Plants synthesize growth hormones—called auxins—continuously in the growing tips, or apical meristem. Once generated, these hormones move downward in the plant, exerting a significant influence on its development. Auxins promote wood development and regulate response to light (phototropism). They also inhibit the growth of lateral buds and keep dormant (or latent) buds from opening.

If left unpruned, the terminal bud of a shoot (i.e., the one at the apex) will continue to grow straight up and produce auxins that inhibit other buds, not at a growing tip, from branching out. This process of growth regulation by a shoot tip, or a root tip, is called apical dominance. If you cut off or pinch back this terminal bud (thereby cutting off the production of auxins), the lateral or latent buds will develop into side shoots, making a shorter and bushier plant. Thus you can change the entire shape of a plant with a simple pruning cut.

Because it is tied to the production of auxins, apical dominance lessens with age. Thus a young conifer, for example, typically has a "Christmas-tree" shape, with a dominant central leader; but when the tree matures, there is a change in the auxin balance, and the top flattens out. Significant amounts of auxins can be synthesized only by a young, vertical shoot; thus apical dominance can also be lost in young plants if a vertical shoot is tilted permanently to one side, either by accident or design.

When a plant's root tips encounter favorable pockets of soil, moisture, and nutrients, they branch out to exploit these—a result that also reduces apical dominance. Roots absorb soil nutrients only near their tips; therefore more branching means that more tips are created, resulting in more efficient absorption. This is why, when you transplant, the number of roots remaining attached and their degrees of branching are more important than their length.

Likewise, if the entire central leader of a tree breaks or is removed, the existing lateral branches sometimes continue growing horizontally. If no vertical leader reestablishes itself, you can train one of the lateral branches to grow upright. Training a single lateral branch will keep several buds from opening simultaneously and forming multiple vertical leaders, resulting in weak crotches.

The ratio of carbohydrates to nutrients in a plant regulates the formation of growth hormones. A plant's leaves manufacture carbohydrates, while its roots absorb and supply nutrients; this ratio, therefore, can be adjusted temporarily by pruning. Top pruning (of buds and branches) decreases carbohydrate production and creates a surplus of nutrients—especially nitrogen—that stimulate vegetative regrowth. Pruning a plant's roots, on the other hand, lowers the nitrogen supply and creates a surplus of carbohydrates, stimulating root regrowth and reproduction. By keeping roots and tops in balance, you will encourage healthy plants to maintain normal growth.

Pruning and Disease Resistance

A plant that has been pruned gains additional resistance to disease, for pruning stimulates certain responses similar to those a plant exhibits when wounded—responses that help to inhibit the spread of decay. At the same time, the cambial meristem forms woundwood to cover the cut and seal it from further infection. Thus, although pruning wounds never heal—the tissues do not regenerate—careful pruning will not debilitate a healthy plant.

Pruning

Heavily overgrown shrubs sometimes need drastic pruning. In the technique called rejuvenation, all excess branches and sucker growth are cleared away, and the remaining branches are headed back nearly to the ground. The plant therefore starts again as if from scratch—but in the long run it will be healthier.

Successful recovery from pruning depends upon the procedures you use in making the cut, as well as upon the availability of nutrients and water, and climatic factors—particularly temperature. If recovery is too slow, your tree or shrub could be in trouble. The plant may also be at risk if it experiences too much shock from radical pruning; or if the pruning coincides with the immediate presence of large quantities of decay-producing fungal spores, egg-laying adults of wood-boring insects, or disease vectors that are attracted by the aromatic sap exposed by the pruning wounds. Pruning may stimulate the development of unwanted branching—water sprouts and feather growth—and intense sunlight can easily scald newly exposed bark.

Basic Pruning Techniques

A number of basic pruning techniques are used in different ways on different types of plants. You can, for the most part, predict what effects these procedures will have on the plants in your garden.

Rejuvenation

Gardeners use a technique called rejuvenation to promote new growth and restore vigor to overgrown or neglected shrubs. Not

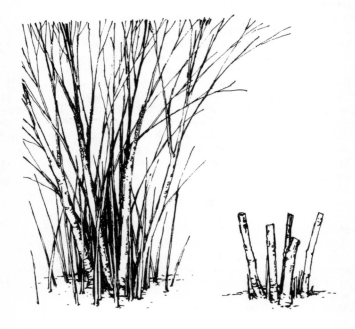

every shrub will survive rejuvenation, however; it is a radical technique that involves paring away all but the most basic plant parts. Only plants with abundant latent buds, and those that can form new adventitious buds, are capable of initiating new growth after a radical pruning. If you aren't sure whether a given plant will withstand rejuvenation, look among the older stems for suckers. If, for example, you have an old neglected lilac, it may look like a cloud of suckers surrounding a maze of old, diseased, and dead stems. Such a plant is an excellent candidate for rejuvenation. In late winter or early spring, cut the entire shrub within a few inches of the ground, using clippers for small stems, a saw for larger ones. In clump-forming plants, it is often a good idea to reduce the diameter of the plant clump by severing its peripheral suckers underground. To do this, use a sharp spade to cut a circle around the perimeter of the core of the plant; hold the spade nearly horizontal as you slice downward, so that you will cut the suckers, and not merely push them farther underground.

If a shrub is healthy and has adequate energy reserves, it will respond to rejuvenation with vigorous juvenile growth that can be worked into a shapely, manageable specimen. But if you are concerned that the total removal of all growth may be too much of a shock (for the plant or for yourself), prune gradually by removing the oldest stems to the ground each year over two or three years. Carefully dispose of the old wood and suckers that were removed so that any diseases or pests they bear will be less likely to infect new growth. Once the shrub has begun to thrive again, thin it out annually to keep it growing and looking its best.

Heading Back

In the technique called heading back, you remove the growing tip of a branch or a stem partway along its length. You may use your fingernails, clippers, or a saw, depending on the size of the branch. Almost every plant needs some form of heading back at some point its life cycle. To induce branching, gardeners pinch the growing tips of annuals and some perennials; chrysanthemums and certain other perennials will grow tall and limp and produce relatively few flowers unless they are cut back repeatedly in mid-growth. The purpose of heading back in these situations is to force branching of vegetative growth and encourage a dense, stocky plant with heavy bloom. Do not head back plants with basal leaves and leafless flower stalks, such as daylilies and irises. Doing so will destroy the flowers but will never make the plant dense or bushy. After the plants bloom, however, you should deadhead the spent flowers (pluck them from the stalk or remove the stalks down to the leaves), to prevent seed formation. You should also head back most perennials by removing the top half of their foliage when you transplant them (after blooming).

Pruning

You want to use basic pruning techniques to enhance the vigor and beauty of your shrubs. Before you begin to cut, step back and look at your shrub and visualize the shape you would like it to have (1). Use a combination of heading back and thinning (2) to achieve the look you want.

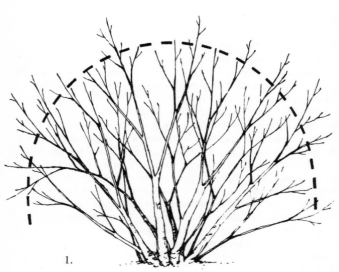

1.

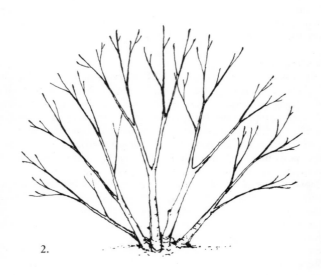

2.

*Remove unwanted
growth of your tree or
shrub by clipping
back feather growths
(B) and water sprouts
(A), and by pulling
up suckers (C).*

Head back woody plants, with special care, as a follow-up to
rejuvenation or after planting. Head back older wood by drop-
crotch pruning, not stubbing; refer to the sections on pruning
shrubs and trees later in this chapter.

Thinning

The removal of the weakest, most crowded portions of a tree or a
shrub is called thinning. The object is to dispose of dead or diseased
wood, eliminate crossing or crowded branches, admit more light,
and reduce structural stress from weight or wind while leaving
behind a well-balanced and vigorous plant. Use clippers (or a saw, if
the branches are thick) to thin your shrubs at the same time that
you head them back; it is also a good idea to thin plants as they
grow back after rejuvenation. Established plants often need no
pruning other than the elimination of a few unwanted branches.
Heavy thinning is sometimes called renewal pruning.

When thinning cane-forming shrubs, such as roses and raspberries,
remove the oldest canes to the ground. Thin trees and treelike
woody shrubs by removing the unwanted branches back to a crotch.
Regularly remove unwanted growth, particularly the water sprouts
(vertical shoots) and feather growth (slow-growing, spreading
branches) that form from latent or adventitious buds on many trees
and shrubs, unless one of the sprouts is needed to replace a broken

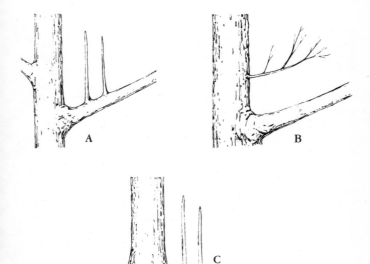

Pruning

When you shear a hedge or a shrub, be sure to leave the base wider than the top. If the top is wider than the base, the plant will develop spindly, sparse growth.

Wrong   **Correct**

top. Thinning too heavily, though, will stimulate more suckers and water sprouts, so thin in moderation unless you are performing what will amount to a phased rejuvenation.

Sucker Removal

Some trees and shrubs persist in generating suckers—vigorous vertical shoots—from their base or roots. Sometimes suckers sprout from grafted plants. Other plants that have evolved in unstable environments or in habitats in which seedling establishment is difficult often clone themselves through suckers. Sumacs, sassafras, plum trees, and aspens generate suckers when their stems are destroyed by fire. Paper birches, basswood, willows, and alders respond slightly differently, by developing new stems from stump sprouts. Such trees grow in clumps, which results from basal sprouting, while species that survive by root suckering, such as aspen, form groves.

Removing these suckers regularly will help keep your garden tidy—although gardeners who enjoy a less tame-looking landscape may prefer to let the suckers grow. Suckers are less likely to grow back if you pull them, rather than cut them, preferably during their first growing season. No matter what you do, some plants that survive by root suckering will send up an occasional sprout—regardless of the growing environment you provide. After cutting older, woody suckers at their base, you may treat the wound with a growth retardant. To discourage the production of unwanted suckers, use mulch and shade and protect the roots.

Watch out for erratic or girdling root growth, which may cut off the free flow of nutrients to a tree. Remedy this situation by slicing the girdling root where it crosses other roots, as shown at left. If a root causes pavement to heave, cut it off with a spade. Insert a metal growth barrier below ground to direct the root's growth downward.

Shearing

In the pruning technique called shearing, all of a plant's branches are cut and trained to a specific outline or shape. This type of pruning is usually done on hedges, with hedge shears or an electric hedge trimmer. When properly sheared, a plant will remain vigorous through periods of controlled, almost unnoticeable growth. If you wish to shape your plants in this way, select a plant variety that tolerates shearing and accustom the plant to being trimmed while it is still small. Some plants, such as privet and boxwood, will recover from even the most radical shearing and form a respectable hedge. Other, more open shrubs, such as forsythias and azaleas, are best left to grow naturally in a shrub border rather than in a formal hedge. Shearing is also used on pines to develop the characteristic Christmas-tree shape. Once you start shearing pines, you must cut them annually, within a three- to four-week period in early summer, removing only a specific percentage of each current growth candle. After hedges and Christmas trees, shearing is most commonly used to maintain topiary, the shaping of shrubbery into animals and architectural forms, such as cubes, globes, and pyramids.

Shearing is a relatively drastic form of pruning and can prove disastrous if performed on the wrong plants. It is not an acceptable

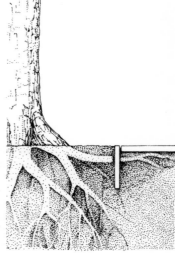

substitute for other standard pruning practices on any plant. In fact, inappropriate shearing probably does more harm to the landscape than does any other pruning technique, except perhaps tree topping.

Root Pruning

Pruning the roots of a plant is a somewhat risky procedure that reduces water uptake, upsets the balance of carbohydrates to nutrients, and retards growth. What is more, unless you are in the process of planting a bare-root plant, you will usually have to do root pruning blind. Despite such drawbacks, root pruning is essential to save trees that have developed girdling-root syndrome and it is advisable under certain other circumstances as well. Girdling roots are generally the result of improper container practices at the nursery or of careless transplanting; unfortunately, the problem may be concealed for years before you notice that one or more of your tree's lateral roots is encircling the base of the tree instead of growing outward like a wheel spoke. As the tree expands with new growth each year, the circling root becomes a tightening noose that, left intact, will eventually strangle the tree. Proper root pruning with a mallet and a chisel in such circumstances is a necessity—the sooner, the better. Of course, the ideal time to prune girdling roots is when you are planting a new pot-bound plant and can easily clip all circling roots.

You may prune the roots of a tree or shrub to prepare for future transplanting—root pruning condenses the root spread, making transplanting easier. If you undercut taproots and slice lateral roots, the roots will branch close to the trunk and remain near the surface. When you dig the tree for transplanting, you will extract a dense root system with it. Once you replant it in its permanent location, it will resume normal root growth. Root pruning thus spreads the shock of transplanting over an extended period, reducing its final impact.

If you decide to prune roots for this purpose, do so in late spring, slicing through the roots at the drip line. Make sure to provide extra water and care all summer long to compensate for the tree's reduced root capacity; then, transplant in the fall.

You may sometimes need to root-prune to keep trees from heaving sidewalks, buckling foundations, or clogging septic systems. If you do prune roots for such a reason, it is a good idea to install a growth barrier afterward, so that the plant does not send out new roots and cause the same problem repeatedly.

Division is a form of root pruning most commonly employed to check the growth of overgrown perennials and to prevent transmission of vascular diseases by cutting root grafts between trees. If you plan to use a systemic herbicide to curtail the unwanted expansion of a shrub, ground cover, or turf plant, first

Below are some basic tools that you will need when pruning. At the top is a pruning knife, with a curved blade and a short handle. The shears at left are *excellent for clipping hedges; at right are two long-handled, serrated knives.*

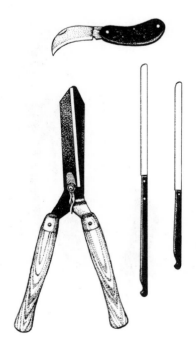

divide the clump, severing all connections between the area to be treated and the remainder, to control herbicide damage.

You can also use root pruning to control the growth spread by runners or underground stolons; and root pruning can also slow the growth rate of plants. The potted miniature trees of China (penjing) and Japan (bonsai), some of which are centuries old and only inches tall, are dramatic examples of the very precise growth control accomplished in part by root pruning.

Root pruning may stimulate the roots of certain plants to send up suckers. Using a sharp spade to slice vertically down through the shallow surface roots of a clump of sumac will cause each severed root to sprout suckers at the end closest to the original stem, rapidly converting a scattered planting of shrubs into a dense mass of autumn brilliance. The same technique will work to form groves or masses of certain other shallow-rooted plants, such as plum, aspen, sassafras, aralia, and several locust species that are easily propagated by root cuttings.

Pruning Tools

Before you rush out to purchase one of every type of cutting instrument in your local hardware store, spend a moment or two considering the respective uses, and relative merits, of each. The

Pruning

Hand-held pruning clippers may be of the bypass type (A) or anvil type (C). Long-handled loppers (B) require two-handed operation; they are efficient where an extended reach is needed, but they are also good for closer work. A long-reach pruner (D) will help with light pruning tasks at a distance of up to six feet.

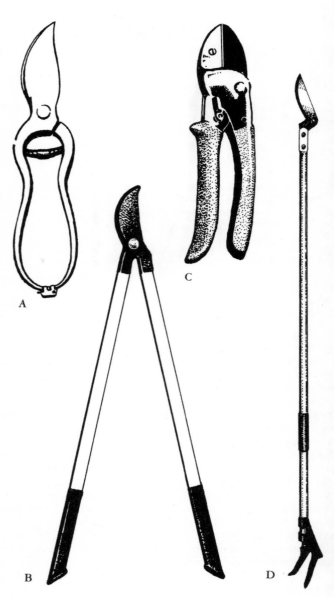

A

B

C

D

general categories that you will need to consider are knives, shears, clippers, saws, and perhaps power tools, as well as such optional accessories as ropes, ladders, and growth-retardant dressings.

Knives

Many of the old masters of horticulture were known for their skill with a pruning knife. A good folding knife with a curved blade is valuable for the selective removal of buds and young shoots; for deadheading fibrous flower stalks; and for fine, intricate pruning in tight quarters where clippers and saws can be cumbersome. Some gardeners graduate to the pruning knife once they have mastered other pruning tools, since it requires more advanced knowledge of plant growth characteristics and the ability to envision the eventual results of small cuts. A folding knife is handier and safer to carry around than any other pruning tool—and if you are more likely to carry it, then you are more likely to use it when it is needed.

Even in the hands of an expert, however, the knife is not the answer to all pruning problems. Shearing knives, scythes, and sickles are technically knives, but functionally they have little in common with the pruning knife. Modern, lightweight shearing knives are used almost exclusively by tree farmers for Christmas-tree shaping. They are lighter and easier to use than hedge shears, and a lifesaver for the marathon sessions required to shape the thousands of pines in a Christmas-tree plantation during the few weeks in early summer when this work must be completed. Be forewarned that these tools can be very dangerous to use; you should not try them without some expert, hands-on training.

The scythe and the sickle are two antiques that really were traditional mowing and harvesting instruments. They do have limited value today for some pruning situations, such as cutting back half-hardy ground covers like hypericum, or touching up secondary growth on a sheared hedge. These tools are hazardous unless used carefully and with common sense.

The wood chisel has some value for touching up large pruning wounds or mechanical injuries to tree bark, and it is the tool of choice for cutting girdling roots. The big advantage of a chisel is that its tip is a blade, so it can make heavy-duty cuts in places that saws and other tools cannot reach.

All knives cut in one of two ways: by pressing through or by slicing. You can sever tender new growth, buds, and other easily cut plant tissue with the pruning knife by pressing straight through. Handle girdling roots similarly with the chisel, using a mallet to provide the impact. When cutting woody twigs or using a sickle or a scythe, slice into plant material with the blade at an angle.

Pruning

Shears

In the garden, shears have largely been supplanted by electric devices—string grass trimmers and electric hedge trimmers. Nonetheless, a well-made pair of shock-absorbing hedge shears is a good tool for a beginner to use. Hedge clippers also come in handy for some specialized aspects of topiary and Christmas-tree shaping. There are other kinds of shears for specialized jobs, such as florist shears with jaws that clip and hold flowers; kitchen shears for harvesting or cutting back herbs and other tender shoots; and grape shears for harvesting grapes.

Clippers

The pruning tool you will probably use the most often is a pair of clippers. These modified scissors are fairly safe to use, but like any cutting instrument, they still must be handled with respect. Clippers come in two basic designs, bypass and anvil; and in two size classes, hand clippers and loppers.

Bypass clippers feature a convex cutting blade that cuts by sliding past a concave hook blade. Anvil clippers use a cutting-board action, with a straight blade cutting against a soft metal opposing surface, the anvil. Each method has its loyal followers, and you will undoubtedly come to favor one or the other based upon your own preferences.

Hand clippers come in a huge range of models and prices. Among the options available are Teflon blades, rotating handles, impulse-hardened steel, rustproofing, graphite and alloy construction, fixed pivot bolts, nylon bushings, thumb or finger latches, replaceable blades, chrome plating, molded grips, ratchet mechanisms, double fulcrums, sap grooves, shock absorbers, sliding actions, holsters, wire-cutting notches, and hollow-ground blades. There are even designs for large and small hands and left-handed operators. Choose your clippers on the basis of your individual needs—what you will prune, how often, for how long, and so on. Inexpensive basic clippers are very serviceable for weekend gardeners if the blades are kept sharp and properly adjusted to make a clean cut without tearing or crushing the branch. You should have at least two pairs; use one for pruning buried roots, cutting dead wood, and doing other knock-around work that might damage the blades; save the other pair for more delicate or exacting jobs.

Loppers are heavy-duty clippers that work like hedge shears—they require two-handed operation, but they are relatively easy to use. In fact, gardeners with small hands or stiff joints may find loppers easier to use than clippers. They offer many of the same options as hand clippers, but they bridge the size gap between hand clippers and saws; some loppers can handle branches up to two inches in diameter. Loppers cost more than hand clippers or saws, and there is nothing they do that can't be

Three types of saws are seen here. At left is a pull saw, with teeth designed to cut on the draw stroke. At center is a heavy-duty lance-tooth push saw. The bow saw, right, has a thin blade and delicate teeth; many gardeners find it efficient and easy to use.

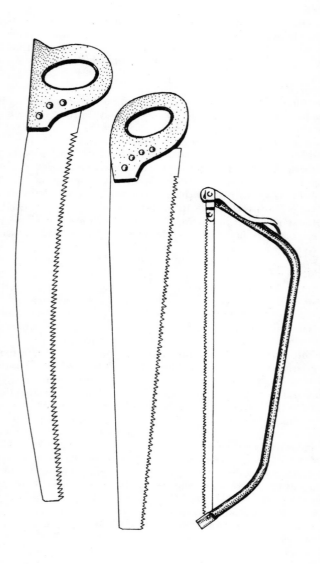

done with either a hand clipper or a saw. But if you need to prune an orchard, vineyard, or other area with medium-sized woody growth, a good pair of loppers will save you time and work. The long handles of loppers will extend your pruning reach slightly, but the handles are intended more for leverage than for overhead use. If you try to use loppers at arm's length, the leverage is lost.

Pruners
For distant work, the right tool is the long-reach pruner (for light one-handed pruning up to about six feet away) or the telescoping pole pruner (for two-handed pruning of growth up to 12 feet off the ground). Some long-reach pruners have detachable gripper jaws for picking apples (or anything else) and are very handy for plucking stray weeds from the back of a flower bed as well. Many pole pruners come with a detachable saw blade for cutting branches larger than about three-quarters of an inch in diameter. These versatile tools can be difficult to use with precision when fully extended, but they reduce the need for gardeners to climb trees or ladders. Like loppers, pole pruners with saw blades provide a transition between hand clippers and pruning saws.

Saws
Pruning saws are designed for live wood rather than dry lumber. Most such saws, including those mounted on pole pruners, are toothed to cut on the draw stroke; their concave blades maintain contact with the surface during the pull stroke, and they are sometimes called "pull saws." Smaller saws normally have unidirectional lance teeth, but larger saws often have coarser, more aggressive tooth patterns that help to clean the sawdust out of the kerf, or groove, being cut. A handy compromise combines the universal tooth pattern with fine teeth at the end of the blade (for starting the cut) and coarse teeth along the remainder. Always select the right size saw for the job. Use a saw with a finer tooth pattern for pruning hardwood trees and a coarse-pattern saw for resinous trees and softwoods.

Along with tooth pattern and direction, the set of a saw influences its cutting capabilities. If you examine the cutting teeth closely, you will see that they are bent, or set, alternately to the right and left. The wider the set, the wider the kerf (groove) and the less the saw is likely to bind in green, gummy, or compressed wood. Wide sets and wide kerfs require more energy per cut, though, because more wood is being converted to sawdust.

Bow saws were designed with this problem in mind. If used in the right situations, bow saws cut faster than any other hand saw. Because the blade is anchored at both ends to the bow frame, it can be made from narrower, thinner, more flexible steel than the blades of other saws. These thin, narrow blades have light sets that form narrow kerfs, saving energy for the pruner. They also cut on both the push and pull strokes. The disadvantage of bow saws is that they are too bulky to fit into many of the nooks and crannies where pruning is needed. Bow saws are most useful for cutting fallen or pruned limbs into firewood.

Many heavy-duty tree-surgery saws are designed to cut larger limbs on the push stroke, like carpenters' saws, or on both the push and pull strokes, like bow saws. One type that is particularly handy if you are climbing a tree or up a ladder to prune is the duplex model, which has teeth on both edges—coarse on one side, fine on the other. This makes climbing a little safer, since you have to carry only one saw to do two jobs. On the other hand, the duplex may be a little more hazardous for the tree, because the top edge of the saw will almost invariably cut into one branch while you are trying to use the bottom edge to cut another.

Some pruning saws have coated blades that do not gum up as easily as uncoated blades, and these are particularly good for pruning resinous conifers. Whether or not your saw is coated, it is a good practice to clean it often with a 70-percent solution of isopropyl alcohol.

Power Tools

The most important thing to keep in mind when using any kind of power tool is safety. Power tools are noisy, energy-consuming engines of destruction—effective in the garden precisely because they are so lethal. So before you purchase a power tool, be sure that it is really necessary.

If you do decide that your gardening needs call for power tools, you will ordinarily consider just a few—brush cutters, hedge trimmers, and chain saws.

Brush cutters are heavy-duty, straight-shafted, gasoline-powered cousins of the string trimmers used to edge and trim lawns. To make them effective in a variety of situations, they can be fitted with interchangeable heads, including brush blades, string heads, and saw blades of various types. Brush cutters are helpful in reaching awkward places, such as thorny thickets, and they ease back strain when you are rejuvenating masses of old shrubs or bramble beds. They also come in handy for other yard-maintenance jobs normally handled by the smaller string trimmers. Never use brush cutters to trim a hedge—a job for which they are unsuited and dangerous—nor above waist height, nor for any pruning task other than rejuvenation. Always wear appropriate clothing, including eye protection, gloves, and heavy, steel-toed boots.

Hedge trimmers are hand-held reciprocating sickle-bar mowers powered by electric motors or by two-cycle engines. Some of the light-duty electric models are cordless, which makes them much

Pruning

safer and more convenient to use. Their only function is to clip hedges, but they are very good at it. Hedge clippers work fast, so before you start be sure to lay out the trimming pattern properly with lines of string or other guides so that the finished job will have a uniform, professional look. Always wear eye protection, gloves, and heavy shoes. If you are using hedge trimmers with an electrical cord attached, be extremely careful not to cut through the cord. You might want to practice your skills with the trimmers on a small, hidden section of your hedge.

Chain saws suitable for pruning are miniature versions of the logging tools used to fell, limb, and cut commercial timber. A small saw, either electric or gasoline-powered, with a cutting bar of 12 inches or less, is the best for amateur use. Such a saw will handle your firewood chores as well as rough pruning, and a skillful operator can even cut down trees that are twice as thick as the length of the bar.

The average homeowner with a few trees on a suburban lot has no need of a chain saw. These tools are expensive, require frequent maintenance, and are the most dangerous garden tool you can own. However, if you have a wood-burning stove or a country estate, the chain saw can be quite indispensable, and you might as well use it for rough pruning as well as for cutting firewood or forest management. Just remember, however, that chain saws are designed to sever woody limbs—which are much tougher than your own limbs. If you don't know how to handle a chain saw, ask an experienced person for instruction. Practice using it on fallen limbs or trunks until you gain confidence and experience—this may take 100 hours or so. Of course you should read very carefully the owner's manual and any other safety information provided. But the best teacher will be experience. Once you have emerged unscathed from your first near-miss, you will begin to understand how dangerous this tool is.

If you do decide to use a chain saw for heavy pruning, do not use the saw overhead, or with your arms fully extended, or while leaning to one side, or in any other unstable or awkward position. Always keep the top end of the bar nose clear to avoid kickback, and always remember the amount of damage that the saw can do to anything it touches, including parts of the tree that you might not intend to cut as well as your own body. You should use a hand saw in congested areas, as well as for the final cut—unless you are confident in your ability to make a smooth, precise finish with a chain saw.

Always clean, lubricate, sharpen, and store your power tools properly. With careful use and correct maintenance, they make short work of certain pruning tasks. But they cannot substitute entirely for the skillful use of hand tools for precision work.

Basic Tool Care

Both hand tools and power tools require maintenance. By learning to care for your equipment, you will make your yard work easier and more effective. Some tools require special care, so be sure to read the instructions carefully.

Keep all pruning tools clean, and if you are working with diseased plants, disinfect the tools between jobs with a solution of 50 percent bleach or 70 percent alcohol. If your tools are not rustproof, administer a light protective coating of oil before storing them. Tools with moving parts, such as clippers, need lubrication and occasional tightening and adjustment. Keep all cutting edges properly sharpened; different blades require different kinds of edges, so unless you learn to sharpen your own tools and acquire the necessary jigs, have someone do it for you. Watch how it is done and ask questions; then you can decide which tools you might be able to sharpen yourself in the future. Learn which face of the blade to sharpen, at what angle, and how to remove the burr and to prevent loss of tempering.

Some tools and tool parts are easier to replace than to repair or sharpen. This includes bargain-basement hand clippers and the disposable blades of bow saws and brush cutters. Most other tools are worth sharpening until the cutting blades become cracked or so worn that they are dangerous or ineffective. At that point, you can either replace the blade or purchase a new tool.

Remember that even the most well-meaning friends and neighbors may not be as careful with your tools as you are. You can guard against damage by making it a policy not to lend your tools, but if you feel that such a stance is harsh, be prepared to repair your equipment once it is returned to you.

Accessories

Along with your pruning tools, you may need a few auxiliary devices, especially for tree work. The list that follows is not comprehensive but it covers most do-it-yourself situations.

•Sturdy and stable ladder of the proper height (you can tie it to the tree if it cannot be placed securely). Three-legged orchard ladders are especially useful.

•Gloves, goggles, hard hat, sturdy work boots, and, for chain-saw work, earplugs.

•Felling wedge, which is a plastic or hardwood wedge for opening the kerf behind a saw on large, binding cuts.

•Rope for lowering cut limbs around buildings or above other plants.

•Sharpening stones and files, for tool touch-up.

Pruning

After a plant blooms, take off the spent flowers—if only to keep your garden tidy. On hostas (left) and other plants with basal leaves and single-bloom flower stalks, cut back to the basal leaves. On plants with multiple blooms per stalk, such as daylilies (right), remove spent blooms; do not cut back the stalk until bloom is ended.

•Spade for root pruning and cutting suckers.

•Growth-retardant sprays for controlling sucker and water-sprout regrowth.

•Facilities or equipment for the proper and legal cleanup and disposal of your pruning debris.

•Cleaning solvent (alcohol) and oil for tool maintenance.

•A disinfectant (70 percent alcohol or 50 percent diluted bleach) for working with diseased plants.

Pruning Tips
Improper or inefficient handling of tools can produce fatigue and injury. Conversely, economy of motion and using the right tool for the right job in the most effective position to perform the work will minimize problems and maximize work output. Ten basic tips are listed below to help you get started.

•Work close to your body, at a bent arm's length. Don't try to apply force to hand tools, to control power tools with your arms at full length, or to lift with your back arched or extended.

•Wear the proper protective gear, including safety goggles, strong shoes, clothing that is comfortable but not baggy, and a hat.

•Select a tool that fits you physically—right-handed or left-handed clippers, for example—with handle sizes and shapes that feel right. You will frequently have to prune with gloves on for

protection against blisters, winter cold, thorns, and other hazards, so wear the gloves when you try out a new hand clipper. Be sure your hand is large enough to fully and easily open and close the tool and that the handles don't pinch your hand or glove.

•To reduce the chance or severity of elbow and wrist ailments, always try to operate hand clippers with your wrist straight and your elbow flexed, especially if you are pruning tough wood for extended periods.

•Flex the branch slightly away from the cutting edge, using your free hand or the weight of the part of the branch being removed, to thus open the kerf (groove), making a smoother and easier cut. Open the kerf when using clippers as well as saws—especially anvil clippers, which can crush tender shoots.

•When using hand clippers or loppers, always position the blade so that it cuts at about a 45-degree angle. Always cut live branches; make your cut just above an outward-facing shoot or bud, and never force or twist the blades when cutting.

•When using extension tools such as pole pruners, space your hands at least two feet apart on the handle. Doing so will increase your control of the tool and lessen strain.

•Plan your work for economy of motion, minimizing position shifts and tool changing. But try not to stay so long in one position that your muscles become stiff.

•If you are using several tools in one pruning session for any significant length of time, purchase or devise a system of holsters, belt hooks, and slings that will keep the tools accessible but safe.

•Know your limitations. Don't overestimate your stamina, tolerance of sun or heat, or skill; once you reach your personal threshold for any of these limitations, stop. Avoid working at dusk, when the fading light can make work much more dangerous. No amount of pruning experience qualifies you to work high up in a tree or ladder without proper safety equipment and a helper. Never work anywhere near power lines.

Pruning Herbaceous Plants

Since herbaceous plants by definition do not develop woody growth, pruning them is a simple task with the chief goal of manipulating the way a plant produces flowers or fruit. Except for the harvesting of materials such as fruits, cut flowers, culinary and medicinal herbs, and dry-bouquet materials, most herbaceous-plant pruning can be classified as pinching, thinning, deadheading, and removal of damaged or senescent parts.

To induce branching and make plants more compact, pinch them— that is, clip them or use your thumbnail to prune growing tips.

Pruning

Annuals and perennials that develop leafy stems with terminal flower clusters, such as asters and chrysanthemums, will have denser growth and more flowers if you induce branching by pinching the stems prior to bud set. Doing so will also make tall plants sturdier and less floppy, reducing the need for staking. With foliage plants such as coleus and basil, the purpose of pinching is to prevent blooming and encourage vegetative growth; you must pinch whenever a new terminal flower bud forms.

If, however, your objective is to produce a few prize-winning specimen flowers, you can concentrate your plant's energy wonderfully by removing surplus shoots and secondary flower buds. Many gardeners do so with phlox (by thinning shoots) and peonies (by disbudding). The disadvantage is that often a very large flower is achieved at the expense of the overall attractiveness of the plant. Many people maintain their special cut-flower plantations behind the garage or in the vegetable garden.

The removal of spent flower heads is called deadheading. Spent flowers that remain on a plant will begin to form seeds and usurp energy that the plant could otherwise use to produce more flowers. You should deadhead about once a week or as needed during the blooming period. Cut back to the topmost healthy leaf on plants that bloom on leaf-bearing stems, such as phlox. On plants with basal leaves and bare single-bloom flower stalks, such as redhot poker, prune to the basal rosette; if the stalks have multiple, sequential blooms, like daylilies, pluck each spent flower until the entire stalk has finished blooming, then cut the stalk. Do not deadhead plants such as solidago, yarrow, and autumn joy sedum that have decorative seedheads or pods later in the season. Sterile plants do not need to be deadheaded, but you may wish to do so for appearance reasons.

Most bulbs, such as daffodils, tulips, and crocuses, need their green foliage to store up carbohydrates for future growth and bloom. Once the foliage turns brown, you may remove it for aesthetic reasons.

Some perennials, such as a few of the salvias and artemisias, are slightly woody, but their shoots are not hardy through a cold winter. Treat these, as well as some butterfly bushes (*Buddleia*), vitexes, Russian sage (*Perovskia*), and other root-hardy shrubs that bloom on the current year's growth, like herbaceous perennials; cut them back each fall or spring to the ground (if they sprout freely) or to woody tissue.

Some perennials become overgrown and lose their vigor in time. When it becomes apparent that a plant is too large or its foliage or flowers have deteriorated in size or vitality, you should divide it. Division is a root-pruning procedure that leads to the propagation of additional plants; it is discussed in detail in the chapter on propagation. A few plants—peonies and poppies, for example—recover slowly from division and should not be disturbed frequently.

Pruning Woody Plants: Shrubs, Vines, and Trees

Unlike herbaceous plants, which live only one year or die back to the ground in winter, woody plants have the capability of initiating new growth each spring at the point where the previous year's growth stopped. Woody plants that grow where winters are not too severe continue to build upon the previous growth year after year. Proper pruning of trees and non-suckering shrubs thus becomes increasingly important, since you cannot start from scratch the following year if you make a mistake, as you can with herbaceous perennials.

The somewhat arbitrary classifications of "shrub," "vine," and "tree" are based solely upon the vegetative growth forms of the plants. Many plants are not easily defined and are called large shrubs by some people and small trees by others. Certain plants may be shrubby in harsh climates or soils yet grow as trees in more favorable situations. A few polymorphic species, such as poison ivy, can appear as a shrub, vine, ground cover, and small tree—all on a single acre of land.

For the most part, however, the distinction is fairly clear. Vines generally grow very fast, producing somewhat limp stems that need external support or a surface on which to cling. Shrubs are erect, self-supporting, multiple-stemmed woody plants that never grow taller than a specified height (usually about 12 feet). Trees tend to exceed shrubs in height under normal conditions and generally develop a single stem. Since these classifications are imposed by humans upon a natural continuum of growth forms, gray areas do exist; but the classifications allow for an organized discussion of pruning practices.

While young, all woody plants should be pruned gradually and sequentially over several years to help them develop the growth form best suited to the style of pruning you will use over the long term. This early training will pay dividends in attractive, healthy plants that respond well to minimal future maintenance. If you are not sure how to approach the pruning of a particular plant, study other examples of the same species grown by arboreta or master gardeners. Ask questions about the life cycle of the plant so that you can learn to predict its response to different pruning options.

Pruning Shrubs

The standard techniques of pruning—rejuvenation, heading back, thinning, sucker removal, shearing, root pruning—are effective on different shrubs at various stages of their growth. Remember that even the most definitive recommendations presented here are only general guidelines, and must be interpreted and adapted for your

Pruning

Some shrubs, such as the hybiscus, bloom on the current year's growth. In the early spring of the first year, remove surplus or weak growth; head back main shoots to strong outward-facing bud (A). During late summer (B) strong shoots will produce flowers. The next spring, (C) head back last season's growth by half.

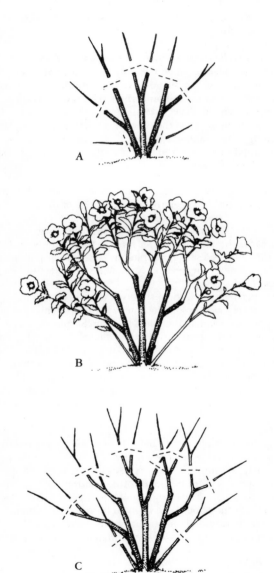

Prune shrubs that bloom on old wood right after they flower. In the first year, remove weak growth and head back to outward-facing buds (A); strong basal and lateral shoots will develop (B). In later years (C), head back flowering stems; these (D) will produce laterals that will bear the next year's flowers.

individual plants and your specific objectives. You must take into account not just the kind of plant but also its age, growth habit, and other factors.

Pruning Deciduous Shrubs

Your objective in pruning deciduous shrubs is to make the most of each plant in its landscape situation. Bear in mind that there may be more than one way to prune a given plant but once you have chosen a method, learn it well and use it correctly. You may wish to use a combination of techniques—rejuvenation and thinning, for example. Remember, too, that overly exuberant shrubs are often easier to replace than to control. Good landscape

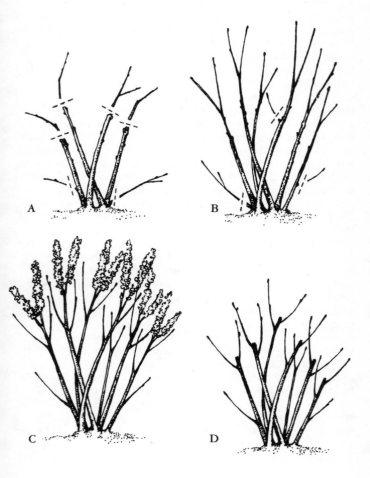

Pruning

design and proper planting will reduce the need for continued pruning.

The best time to prune flowering shrubs depends mainly on whether they bloom on new wood—that is, the current year's growth—or on old wood. Unfortunately, there is no foolproof way to tell if a shrub blooms on old or new wood. In general, plants that bloom before the first of June do so on old wood, and those that flower later bloom on new wood. There are notable exceptions, so it is best to ask about the correct pruning time when you buy a shrub. Prune flowering shrubs that bloom on the current year's growth (such as amorpha, the beauty berries, potentilla, oakleaf hydrangea, *Hibiscus syriacus*, clethra, caryopteris, and hypericum) in fall or early spring. Spring-blooming shrubs that bloom from buds or spur growth on the previous year's wood should be pruned after they have finished flowering; this group includes azaleas, lilac, spicebush, flowering quince, forsythia, plum, and others.

If you want your shrubs to keep their natural shapes and growth forms, all you have to do with most of them is remove dead or damaged stems, control unwanted suckers, and lightly thin misplaced, wayward, and weak growth as needed throughout the year. Occasionally head back lightly after blooming, if necessary. Regular, minimal attention will keep your shrubs healthy and attractive, and maintain their natural look. With all deciduous shrubs, the branch structure is easiest to see before the plant is in full leaf, but dead and diseased branches are easiest to find after the plant starts to leaf out, so time your pruning accordingly.

Deadheading, usually recommended for herbaceous plants, can also be beneficial for flowering shrubs. It improves the appearance of the plant and prevents the energy drain that accompanies seed set. Remove only the spent flowers, after the bloom is over, taking care not to cut the buds at the base. For most shrubs, however, deadheading will not stimulate reblooming as it does with annuals. And deadheading is not practical for shrubs that do not bear their flowers in large clusters or that bear decorative fruits.

Handle shrubs that sprout readily from old wood, such as forsythia, weigela, kolkwitzia, willow, and spirea, by annual post-bloom rejuvenation or by more subtle combinations of thinning and heading back; your choice will depend on the effect you desire and ornamental value of the stems, juvenile bark, and flowers. Some free-sprouting shrubs die back each winter but bear attractive flowers or bark on current growth; these include caryopteris, butterfly bush, and vitex. Rejuvenate them by cutting them to the ground each fall or in early spring prior to bud break.

Some shrubs, such as witch hazel, magnolia, fothergilla, and some viburnums, do not sprout routinely from the base and cannot withstand rejuvenation. To give them a strong limb structure and

If you have never pruned roses, you should seek the advice of an expert. Remove weak and diseased canes, or any that cross through the bush (A); leave three to five strong, sturdy, healthy canes. When heading back, always cut to an outward-facing bud eye— whether you cut the canes back slightly (B) or severely (C).

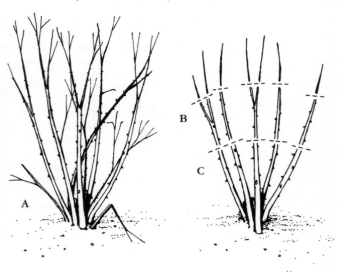

to achieve the effect you desire, prune these shrubs while they are still young. Pagoda dogwood, hawthorns, dwarf Japanese maples, and similar kinds of miniature trees that are cultivated for their interesting branching structure may need very little pruning once their limb framework has been trained. Shearing hedges or topiary requires some advance planning, starting when the shrubs are installed. When you plant hedges of euonymus, privet, barberry, honeysuckle, and similar plants, head them back to four or five inches tall; do the same with existing overgrown plants to rejuvenate them. Then shear the new growth back to a somewhat shortened, undersized version of the desired shape. Be careful to establish a full base that is broader than the top. Allow the hedge to increase in size very slightly each year for several years, until a dense peripheral branch structure has been developed. Touch up the new growth periodically throughout the spring and midsummer; if you live in a cold climate, allow subsequent growth to harden off before winter. To minimize sunscald on leaves and twigs, avoid heavy shearing during extremely hot, sunny periods. Be careful not to shear or head back fruit-bearing plants such as some viburnums, callicarpa, snowberry, and deciduous holly after bloom, or the fruit will be lost.

Pruning Roses
Roses are a specialty; if you have never pruned roses before, it is a good idea to consult an expert or refer to a dedicated source book. A

few general guidelines, however, may be helpful. With newly planted rose bushes, pruning should be kept to a minimum. Many rosarians remove the first blooms, allowing only the second cycle of bloom to develop to maturity. Doing this gives the bush more canes and stronger growth for the summer as well as for the remainder of the year. When pruning roses, do not use anvil shears, which can crush the cane.

A new cane, called a basal break, may form on the bud union or crown. This can occur throughout the year, but generally happens in the spring when the bush breaks dormancy. Then the question is how to treat the new basal breaks. On some bushes the basal breaks may only grow two feet tall, while on others they may grow to four feet. (The tall ones may break off in a wind storm, so it is not a bad idea to tie them to a stake.) You may prefer to pinch the top out when the cane has reached a certain height—roughly speaking, about 12 inches in the North and 15 to 18 inches in the South. This procedure should make the cane stouter and encourage it to put out two or three new canes.

When a leaf drops off or is removed from a cane, it leaves a crescent-shaped scar. The area above the scar will produce a swelling, from which a new cane will form; such a swelling is known as an "eye" or "bud eye." Cutting to an outward-facing eye gives the bush a better shape. Depending on a bush's vigor and the number of healthy canes, you will want to retain from three to six young canes.

As you prune the cane, be sure to examine the color of the center, or pith. If the pith is white, you have a good live cane. However, if the cane has a brown pith, cut a little more off the top, continuing to snip off a little at a time until you have located the white center. After a particularly severe winter, some rosarians cut back to a bud eye where the center is slightly colored or is a very light tan.

It is advisable to seal all cut canes; use fingernail polish, Elmer's Glue, carbolated vaseline, or a tree-wound compound to protect against borers and disease.

Pruning Evergreen Shrubs

For the most part, you should prune your evergreens in much the same way that you prune deciduous shrubs. There are, however, some specific guidelines to remember when pruning different types of evergreens.

Yews will form adventitious buds and can be cut back to old wood if necessary. When trimming yews, spruces, or firs, clip back to a pair of lateral buds to induce branching the next growing season. Junipers, arborvitae, hemlocks, and certain other evergreens will not sprout dependably from old wood, so you should not head them back or shear them beyond the peripheral green zone of live foliage. Most pines will not sprout from hardened wood. Shape them, if

When trimming a yew (A), spruce, or fir, cut just beyond lateral buds; they will form branches the next season. Prune scale-leaf conifers, such as junipers, anywhere in the green zone of live foliage (C). In pines, remove part of the new candle (B) in late spring for smaller, denser trees.

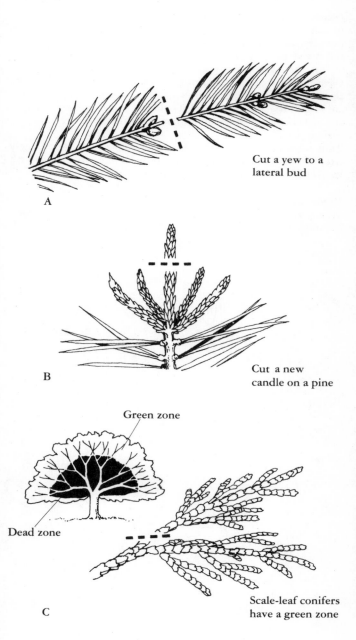

Cut a yew to a lateral bud

A

Cut a new candle on a pine

B

Green zone

Dead zone

C

Scale-leaf conifers have a green zone

Pruning

Rhododendrons have two kinds of buds: terminal leaf and flower buds (A). To encourage branching, snap off the leaf bud (B). Deadhead the spent blossoms, which contain seed capsules (C). A new shoot will produce several new branches; pinch it back and multiple buds will develop, making blooms and growth more dense (D).

necessary, by pinching the tender new growth candles in late May or early June.

Some broad-leaved evergreens, such as bayberry and boxwood, will tolerate almost any pruning style. Prune rhododendrons and azaleas to enhance flowering as well as foliage by deadheading spent flowers (without damaging the adjacent buds) and pinching the tips of young new growth to increase bud set. Rhododendrons are subject to root diseases and should not be root-pruned, but the suckers should be removed from below the bud union on grafted plants.

Thin old stems of pyracantha plants, but do not head back severely after blooming, or the fruit—which is much more striking and long-lasting than the blossoms—will not develop.

Pruning Vines

Woody vines can be classified as clingers, twiners, tendril-formers, or ramblers. The clingers, such as winter creeper, Boston ivy, and

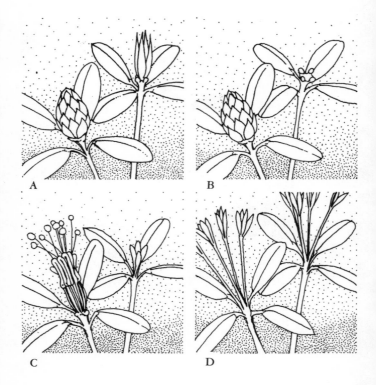

woodbine, attach to their support by developing permanent specialized aerial roots. Twiners, such as morning glory, bittersweet, wisteria, and honeysuckle, grow in a helical pattern (always in the same direction) and wrap their stems around the support. Some tendril-formers, such as grapes, use twin leaf bracts; others, such as clematis, use twining leaf petioles to hold onto their support. Ramblers, including brambles and climbing roses, simply grow fast, covering the ground or anything else they can lean upon or become entangled in. When pruning ornamental vines, keep these different growth styles in mind.

To control the rampant growth of many vines and contain them within their allotted space, use top pruning as well as root pruning, if necessary. Vines used as ground covers need only to be kept within their beds and off of any shrubs or trees that share the same area. Species grown for their attractive flowers, such as clematis and trumpet vine, often require severe pruning after flowering to stimulate regrowth and future blooming.

Some vines can be very picturesque if you allow them to develop massive stem growth on an arbor or a large tree. Although some flowering may be sacrificed, pruning may enhance the year-round appeal of the vine; envision, for example, the pleasing naturalistic beauty of an ancient wisteria. Remember to contain a vine's ultimate reach, however, for the sake of the arbor or tree involved, and to train the primary stems early. You will also have to train and anchor the limbs of those species that develop a permanent woody structure, such as Boston ivy and grapes.

Regardless of the pruning pattern you select, be sure to remove all dead and diseased branches of vines.

Pruning Trees

Trees should be pruned for many of the same reasons as shrubs, using many of the same techniques. You will want to prune your trees to remove dead and diseased wood, to improve the structure, and to ensure good flowering, fruiting, and appearance. Most mature trees, however, are tall enough to make safety a factor when pruning. Conscientious gardeners will safeguard both the immediate and long-term welfare of the tree, as well as themselves and the other plants or objects nearby. All of the following recommendations are offered with the admonition that you must recognize your limitations and seek professional help with large trees when necessary.

Training Young Trees

Every tree is governed by genetic and environmental forces that encourage it to develop a characteristic shape. When you anticipate that the future shape of a young tree will have some inherent disadvantage, you should correct it early. Your objective

Pruning

When making a pruning cut, always work at a 45-degree angle just above an outward-facing bud eye. The twig at left shows two possible cuts; at center is a cut with too steep an angle, which will inhibit bud growth; at right, the cut has been made too shallowly and too far from the bud.

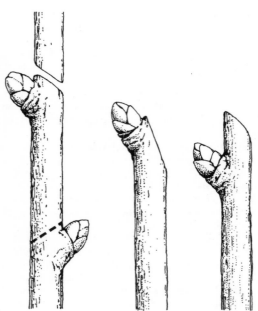

may be a structural one, such as eliminating a narrow or multiple crotch, removing a crossing branch, or heading back one side of a balanced fork to redirect dominance to the other. Or it could be purely aesthetic; many trees that have attractive bark, flowers, fruit, or branching patterns display these features to the best advantage at eye level if they are trained to a multiple-stem clump form, like a shrub, or to a multiple-leader open form, like an orchard tree. Some conifers, especially pines and Douglas-fir, will become much denser if they are sheared. In a lawn or along a boulevard, establishing adequate physical or visual headroom might be the primary goal. It is critical that trees do not grow too close to your house and that you maintain adequate clearance for wind-flexing.

To accomplish these and other objectives, and to ensure a sound limb structure, it is important to begin training your trees very early. When you transplant new trees, a moderate amount of thinning or heading back may be helpful to reestablish the balance of carbohydrates and nutrients. Be cautious, however; the removal of too much of the crown will inhibit root regrowth, and many experts discourage this treatment until the second season after planting or transplanting.

A fork that is evenly balanced by two limbs of equal size and weight will be likely to trap included bark as the tree grows (top), resulting in a weak crotch. In young trees you can correct this problem by heading back one side of a balanced fork to an outward-facing limb (bottom).

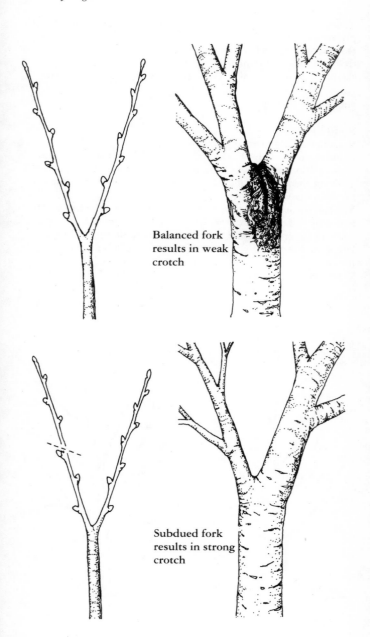

Balanced fork results in weak crotch

Subdued fork results in strong crotch

Pruning

Three chief techniques are used in pruning young trees: heading back (A), to encourage well-placed, vigorous limbs; (B) thinning weak or adventitious growth; and (C)

drop-crotch pruning. These techniques will help to develop a picturesque, strong, low scaffold of limbs and a low crown in a flowering tree or a treelike shrub.

Young trees can benefit immensely from the thoughtful use of the pruning knife and the fingernail. Select buds and young shoots that are well spaced and oriented in the pattern that you want the tree to follow and remove others that would compete with or establish dominance over them. In this way, you can train the young tree with a minimum of heavy cutting. Be sure to make your cuts correctly.

Scaffold Limbs
Branches should form a spoke pattern on the trunk, with about five branches to each wheel or tier of branches; the branches should grow at about a 45-degree angle from the trunk. For a large-growing shade or ornamental tree, the optimum vertical distance between branches is three to four feet.

You can stimulate the formation of an even scaffold of limbs. The first year, remove part of the new wood of the central leader; place a collar of paper or masking tape around the topmost remaining lateral bud to help direct its growth vertically and prevent the formation of a new crook, which would weaken the central trunk. When working with young maples, ashes, and other trees with

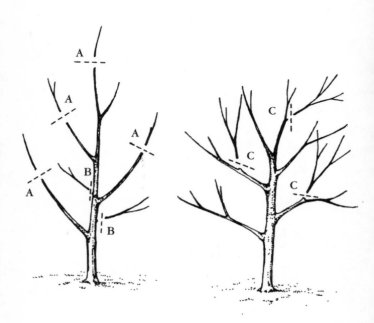

To reduce the height of
a tree, or the weight
of its crown, use the
technique called
"drop-crotch" pruning.
Cut back the branch
to where it meets
another, smaller

branch no less than
about one-third
its size.

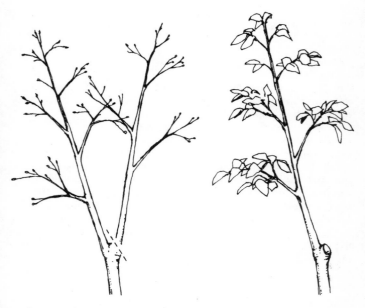

opposite or whorled buds, remove all but one before you install
the collar.

The amount of wood—or, more precisely, the number of
buds—that you remove in any one year should be limited. When
you limb up a young tree for headroom, for example, do not
completely remove the lower branches very early, or the trunk will
become spindly and weak. Remove the branches from the ground
up at a rate no faster than the rate that new branches are being
formed at the tree's top. Work up from the bottom, thinning out
whorls of branches over a two-year or three-year period. A good
plan is to cut back the lowest side branches by about one-third
(to a point where a smaller side branch joins it) the first year; the
next year, remove those pruned branches entirely and head back
the next tier of branches by one-third. Continue this process
for several years until the lowest branches are growing at the
desired height.

Whorled Branches

Young oaks, pines, flowering dogwoods, and some maples have a
tendency to whorled branching, which means that multiple
crotches develop where three or more limbs join. When removing
such groups of limbs, some of which can be nearly as large as the
central leader, don't cut adjacent limbs at the same time. Cut every
second or third limb and temporarily head back the others, then
wait a year or two before removing the remainder. Doing this will

Pruning

allow the leader to recover dominance and will minimize the girdling effect that sometimes results from cutting the whole whorl at once.

Using Braces
Another pruning technique that is possible only with young trees is to redirect the growth of a valuable but wayward branch, or a tilted leader, with a temporary brace or bamboo splint. Tie the splint in place with twist-ties, soft yarn, plastic flagging, or multiple wraps of fresh blades of prairie grass. The grass will deteriorate before the next growing season, but you must remove the other types of ties before they girdle the growing plant. You can use braces to spread branches that otherwise would develop narrow, weak crotches. Cut a light stick or wood lath to size, notch each end, and insert the brace between the branch being spread and the collar of a higher branch. The brace should be just long enough to spread the branch to the desired position without splitting it, and you should leave it in place only during the growing season to minimize abrasions on the bark.

Pruning Mature Trees
When pruning large trees, you must consider safety first. Do not attempt the job yourself if the pruning is beyond the safe reach of your ladder; if you need to climb more than 10 feet into the tree and don't know how to rig a safety harness; if your tree is decayed or otherwise hazardous; or if you will be working around power lines or over traffic. Ask an arborist to show you his or her insurance certificate and copies of the National Arborist Association's Pruning Standards for Shade Trees and the ANSI Standard for Tree Care Operations. Ask for references, and don't be shy about having a look at his or her previous pruning jobs. Finally, if everything seems to be in order, stand back and let the expert do the job.

As with all plants, there are some basic rules of thumb to follow when you prune your trees. These guidelines are general, and you will have to adapt them to your specific circumstances.

A narrow crotch with included bark will become ever weaker and more subject to splitting as the tree grows. If you have not pruned or trained a tree when it was young to remove and to prevent narrow crotches, have a professional arborist brace or cable weak crotches that develop in older trees.

To remove lateral limbs, begin by heading them back, which will retard the diameter growth of the limb and increase the ratio of the diameter size of the parent stem to the limb. The rate at which a pruning wound heals or closes is governed by this ratio. As long as the size and rate of growth of the stem significantly exceed the size and rate of growth of the limb, the eventual final pruning cut should close quickly.

If you must reduce the height or crown weight of a tree, do so by heading back to a crotch, a process sometimes called drop-crotch pruning. Cut back the branch to where it meets a smaller branch no less than about one-third its size. Some trees, such as grafted globe locusts, require severe annual pruning, known as pollarding. Remember when pollarding to limit your cuts to the removal of most, but not quite all, of the new wood. Never, for any reason, dehorn or decapitate any tree.

Certain diseases require fast pruning action. When you discover a localized infection of oak wilt disease in a white oak or a flag of Dutch elm disease in an elm, you must act swiftly before the fungus spreads. Make your final cut with a sterilized saw at least 10 feet toward the roots from the last sign of leaf wilt or phloem or sapwood discoloration. If the infection is systemic, pruning will not help, but you might be able to isolate the disease from susceptible trees nearby by removing the infected tree and then root-pruning to a depth of at least three feet, midway between the trees. Be sure to burn or dispose of all infected trimmings.

Pruning Coniferous Trees

Coniferous trees generally require very little pruning, unless you decide to shear them. The spire-shaped, "Christmas-tree" types, such as spruces, firs, and most pines, occasionally will develop a double leader, usually as a result of shearing or insect damage to the terminal bud. Select the most central or strongest leader and clip the other at its base.

If you shear your pines, keep in mind that shearing before June may result in prematurely stimulating the appearance of part of the next year's growth; shearing after June may inhibit bud set, especially with white pines. The normal bud cluster on an unsheared pine twig consists of a dominant terminal bud and a whorl of about five lateral buds; a sheared twig may develop several codominant buds and a dozen or more lateral buds, so you may have to follow up one season's shearing by thinning weak, surplus, or codominant growth the next year. Remember that once you begin to shear a conifer, you will have to continue the treatment every season, or else contend with a corona of loose growth around a dense core—not a pretty sight, and impossible to correct after the first year. The natural texture and shadowing of an unsheared conifer often is aesthetically superior to the smooth outline of a tightly sheared one, and it requires no annual follow-up to maintain.

When to Prune Trees

Even though many experts claim that the correct time to prune is whenever you have the saw in your hand, there are nonetheless

Pruning

The jump-cut technique is useful for removing a branch that will fall unobstructed to the ground. About a foot from the trunk, make an upward incision halfway through the branch (A). Then make a downward cut an inch or two farther out (B). Afterwards, remove the stump and seal the wound (C).

some inopportune times. Maples, elms, walnuts, birches, yellowwood, and some other trees will "bleed" if cut when the sap is rising in late winter and early spring, inviting unsightly bacterial infections and sooty molds. Oaks are more likely to become infected with the fatal oak wilt disease if pruned in May or June.

If trees are pruned in late summer or fall, wound-closure activity is delayed until the following year, exposing the tree to winter damage. Trees become increasingly brittle and more easily damaged if pruned during extremely cold weather, below about 22° F. The onset of a severe cold snap during or within a few days of a winter pruning job can cause the freshly cut cambium to die back, enlarging the wounds. Pruning when a tree is actively growing in spring removes significant carbohydrate energy, retarding growth and wound closure. Bark becomes very loose and is easily torn, from bud break in the spring through early summer. Heavy late-summer pruning may stimulate the development of succulent new growth with insufficient time for fall hardening, resulting in winter injury. Most pines, except perhaps pitch pine and shortleaf pine, will not develop adventitious buds on old wood, so any shearing or pinching of new

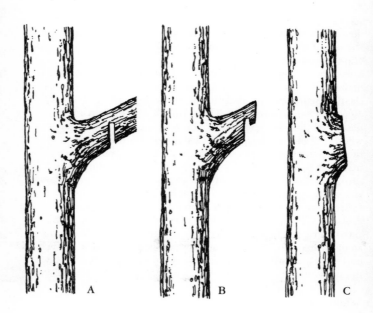

A   B   C

growth must be done in June, when the tree is still capable of setting replacement buds.

With all these precautions, it almost seems as if there is no good time to prune—but it is more accurate to say that pruning at any time of year may introduce some risks and stresses. The advantages of proper pruning, conducted at the least stressful time for the kind of tree involved, far outweigh these risks. In general, most trees respond best to late-winter pruning. You can remove dead or diseased branches, water sprouts, and suckers at any time as soon as you notice them. You might defer heavily pruning those species that bleed until midsummer, when new growth is hardened, or even the following early winter, after the leaves have fallen. You can slow the growth of overly vigorous trees by pruning them in early summer.

Making a Proper Cut

Once you have decided what, where, and when to prune, you must learn to apply the proper techniques. Unless you hire an arborist to perform the work, you should learn a few basics of tree surgery in order to complete the job correctly and safely.

Most, and perhaps all, of your do-it-yourself tree pruning will involve smaller trees and smaller branches that you can remove with a single cut and control with your free hand. If there is any chance, though, of the bark peeling as the branch tears free, use the jump cut (described below). As a rule, the most important part of the structure of a young tree is its top, where future growth begins; when pruning, start at the top and work downward, removing crossing branches, thinning, and cleaning up the crown as you descend.

If you decide to prune large tree limbs yourself, work while standing on the ground, if possible, or from a secure position in the tree or on a ladder. If you climb into the tree, use standard safety rigging if you climb higher than about 10 feet up. Wear sturdy, strong-toed shoes with soft rubber soles for traction; don't wear golf spikes or other cleated shoes or gaffs that will injure the bark. The standard methods for limb removal are the jump cut, the roped cut, and the piece cut.

Jump Cut

Use the jump cut only if you are certain that the limb you are cutting will fall unobstructed to the ground. Start approximately one foot away from the base of the limb you are removing and cut from below for roughly half the limb's thickness, or until the weight of the limb starts to close the cut and bind the saw. Then move about an inch or two farther out and start cutting from above. When the limb snaps, it will jump away from the cut slightly and fall to the ground at about the same angle as it

Pruning

When making a roped cut, thread the butt rope through a branch higher than the one you are removing; secure it near the trunk. The top rope comes over another branch and is secured farther out from the trunk. The ropes will bear the weight of the limb you are removing. Anchor both ropes with a heavy weight.

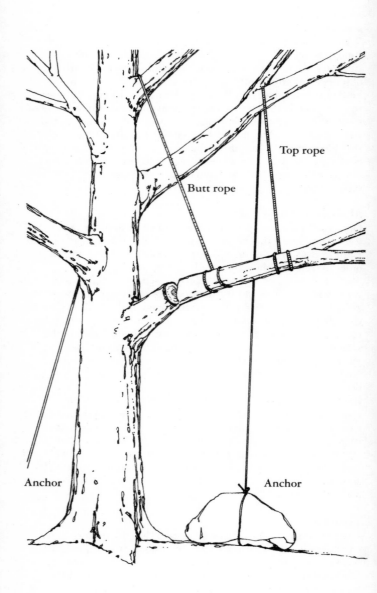

Top rope

Butt rope

Anchor

Anchor

To remove a weak or narrow crotch that has grown up over included (ingrown) bark, first sever the limb above the crotch to remove most of its weight. Then remove the stub of the limb by cutting upward from the outside.

grew in the tree. If you want it to land twigs-first to prevent the butt from gouging the lawn below, make the undercut a narrow V-notch rather than a single kerf. Doing this will allow the branch to tilt downward before it jumps loose. After the branch has fallen, cut the stub back to, but not into, the branch collar, beginning with an undercut to keep bark from peeling as the stub falls.

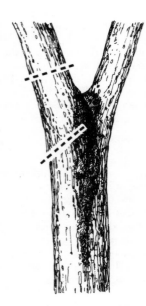

Roped Cut

If a cut limb is likely to fall on other limbs, on shrubs, or on a fence or other structure, you will need to control its descent. Use an adequate rope (not a clothesline), and use two if the limb is large. Tie the limb about two feet past the cut with one rope and well past the apparent center of gravity of the limb with the other, using a secure knot, such as a timber hitch with a half hitch. Then throw the ends of the ropes through separate wide crotch supports or over sturdy horizontal limbs directly above the one being cut, and tie them off to the base of another tree or to some other secure anchor. If you can't run each rope straight up from its attachment on the limb to a support, the limb will sway when it is cut, so use a third rope, controlled by an assistant on the ground, as a guideline. Saw the limb off to a foot-long stub without using an undercut; doing so will allow the limb to sag gradually, without jumping, and put less strain on the rope. Once the limb swings free, climb down and lower it slowly to the ground, asking other people for help if necessary. Then proceed to remove the stub as with the jump cut.

Piece Cut

If you need to take a limb down in sections, or pieces, you can use a jump cut for each piece or, if necessary, a roped cut. If you piece-cut a limb with the aid of an extension ladder, you probably will lean the ladder against the proximal portion of the limb being cut (that is, the portion toward the tree). Remember two things: First, make sure that the ladder is on the correct side of the cut; and second, make sure that the ladder extends far enough above the limb so that it won't fall when the limb rises, which can happen when the portion being cut breaks loose. Take a few moments to tie the ladder into place if it feels shaky or insecure; or use a stable stepladder, if it is tall enough.

Correcting Narrow Crotches
Occasionally you will need to remove half of a narrow fork or crotch. Keep in mind that the branch was forming included (ingrown) bark early in its growth, deep in what is now the heartwood. If the fork has not trapped included bark, you may be able to see a bark ridge extending down from the crotch, and the base of this bark ridge is the start of the fork. This is where you should make the final cut, starting at the outside of the limb. The more vertically a limb is growing, the more dangerous it is to cut, because its direction of fall becomes less predictable and its center of gravity is higher. Use caution or seek expert help for such situations.

Wound Closure
Trees growing in the forest naturally shed their lower limbs as they grow. The limbs detach at the swellings, or branch collars, of wood at their bases. Callus growth then forms wood to cover the abscissions, causing the wound closure that is referred to commonly but misleadingly as healing. Damaged wood does not "heal," or regenerate; the tree simply concentrates metabolic chemical preservatives around the wound to isolate it.
It is helpful to remember this natural shedding and closure process and try to imitate it when you are pruning. By cutting along the natural abscission layer at the outer edge of the branch collar, you will allow the tree to use its inherent closure and decay-resistance mechanisms most effectively. Even if a pruning wound becomes infected with decay before it closes, the tree's chemical defenses will contain the infection, provided the tree is healthy and the wound has not breached the branch collar. In extreme cases, some of these defenses fail, and the tree develops a cavity or becomes completely hollow. In the first year after pruning, the layer of spring wood that forms is extremely resistant to penetration of decay from within, and the hollow will be self-limiting unless that layer is subsequently wounded again. Leave cavity repair to an expert or ignore it completely. A hollow but vigorous tree, left alone, can become stronger each year as the cavity is contained and the cambium continues to add layers to the sapwood.
The value of tree-wound dressings has been debated for decades. Many of the substances used to coat tree wounds do more harm than good, and they are seldom necessary. Some of the newer dressings that contain maleic hydrazide, naphthalene acetic acid,

or chlorofluorenol growth inhibitors in an asphalt emulsion, however, are beneficial for the prevention of water sprout and sucker growth where such problems are likely. Use such preparations with caution so as not to affect wound closure and subsequent tree growth.

Specialized Pruning Techniques

Several pruning techniques have been developed to manipulate the natural forms of plants, chiefly trees. Many of these techniques have evolved into art forms that require considerable training and experience. Some topiary figures, for example, are built around welded frames weighing a ton or more and require skills much beyond routine pruning. Some of the maze gardens of Europe carry hedgework to a precise and exacting level of artistry. Espalier training can create a two-dimensional tree that hugs a warm wall in winter, providing protection from severe cold and spring frosts, but the natural geometry of a tree is not planar, and such designs demand meticulous attention. Pleaching is the process of transforming a row of living trees into a magnificent interlaced archway or pergola.

Artistic pruning also can enhance the natural forms and features of plants. A master pruner can so adroitly convert an overgrown, century-old shrub into a picturesque, knurred small tree that the actual evidence of pruning is almost invisible to the casual observer. The training of a young beech, hornbeam, or crape myrtle at the hands of a clever pruner can mold its smooth, sinuous limbs into a storybook centerpiece. And the applications of ancient Chinese penjing or Japanese bonsai techniques by masters, executed flawlessly over decades or even centuries, have produced some of the most remarkable miniature wonders of the horticultural world. Although you may not have the inclination or the patience to learn such craftsmanship, you will look upon the results with more appreciation, and awe, as you continue to increase your own general pruning knowledge and skill. If you do wish to attempt one of these techniques, visit your local botanical garden and check out a couple of books on the subject so that you can become familiar with what it entails before you start.

Managing

One of the greatest challenges to today's gardener is finding ways to solve pest problems without using toxic materials. Reliance on chemical controls has left a legacy of health hazards, decreasing effectiveness, and threats to wildlife and the environment. In recent years, therefore, gardeners have turned with growing frequency toward a range of less toxic—and often more effective—pest controls. The result is that more and more gardeners are learning about the principles of integrated pest management, for outwitting insects, pathogens, vertebrates such as moles, and even weeds, with little or no use of conventional pesticides.

Integrated pest management (IPM) enables gardeners to analyze the causes of pest problems and to reduce or eliminate conditions that support pest presence. The emphasis on prevention both reduces the occurrence of pest problems and permits effective use of nonchemical controls, or, if necessary, least-toxic pesticides. There are literally thousands of organisms that can, under some circumstances, become pests in the garden; no single reference can tell you how to manage them all. But by learning the principles of integrated pest management, you will develop strategies that can be adapted to suit a wide range of situations, equipping yourself with environmentally sound tactics to control any pest, in any location, under any growing conditions.

Integrated Pest Management and the Garden Ecosystem

Integrated pest management strategies are based on an understanding of the garden as an ecosystem with many interrelated parts. The term "ecosystem" refers to all the components of a garden—plants, animals, climate, and soil—that are bound together with one another in a certain balance. Because everything in an ecosystem is connected to everything else, any action taken in one part of the ecosystem (such as fertilizing or applying a pesticide) affects other parts of the system—often in unimagined ways.

Traditional methods of pest control focus on only one component of the ecosystem: the pest organism alone. If the pest organism is all you consider, your only options are to endure it or to remove it. In contrast, integrated pest management takes into account the ecological relationships of pests with other components of the garden. By looking at your garden as an ecosystem, you can usually find a choice of methods to modify or to remove conditions that support a pest, or to create situations that encourage its natural controls—the predators, parasitoids, and pathogens that attack insects, plant disease organisms, and weeds. The important fact to remember is this: Changing any one of the components in an ecosystem affects all the other components to

Pests Safely

some degree. It follows, therefore, that there is almost always more than one way to suppress pests without falling back on poisons.

What Is Integrated Pest Management?

IPM is a two-level system. The first step in the process is regular monitoring, which can determine if and when treatments are needed. The second step is the application of physical, mechanical, cultural, biological, and educational tactics to keep pest numbers tolerably low. As a last resort, least-toxic chemical controls are used to eradicate pests. With the integrated pest management approach, pests are not "treated" according to a predetermined schedule; instead, treatments are applied only when called for—if monitoring indicates that the pest will cause unacceptable aesthetic or economic damage. The treatments chosen are timed to have the greatest effect while causing the least disruption to other components of the ecosystem.

Basic Parts of an Integrated Pest Management Program

A fully integrated program for managing garden pests starts with a bit of education. First, obtain an accurate identification of the pest and the plant it is damaging, including their scientific (Latin) names. The easiest way is to carry or mail a sample of the pest or the damaged plant to your county Cooperative Extension office or to a local nursery. (You can also consult some of the illustrated books listed in the bibliography at the end of this guide.)

You cannot overestimate the importance of accurate identification. Too often gardeners attribute plant damage to the wrong organism, and subsequent control measures fail to solve the problem. For example, mealybugs (*Planococcus citri*), woolly apple aphids (*Eriosoma lanigerum*), and cottonycushion scale (*Icerya purchasi*) are all white and cottony-looking, indistinguishable to the untrained eye. But effective measures against these species differ considerably. With accurate information about the life cycle and behavior of a pest, you can reduce or eliminate the food, water, and habitat it needs to survive.

Consider the case of the sowbug, the slug, and the strawberry. Strawberries just past the peak of ripeness attract slugs and snails, which feed on them at night, then sleep the day away in a dark, secluded spot. During the day, sowbugs—which feed primarily on decaying organic matter—move into the damaged berries. Often it is the sowbug, not the slug or snail, that a gardener will blame for the damage. Attacking the sowbugs, however, utterly fails to cure the problem.

Thorough familiarity with your plants—their names and preferred growing conditions—will make your efforts against garden pests more effective. You will frequently find, for example, that some chronically pest-ridden plants are growing under less-than-

Managing Pests Safely

optimum conditions such as too much shade or too acid soil. Harsh as it may seem, it is often best to remove these diseased plants and either amend the conditions or replace the plants with others better suited to those growing conditions. Plants growing in the right place seldom have significant pest problems.

Monitoring
Part of having a "green thumb" is being good at noticing the details—the critical connections among various elements of the garden. If you want to be aware of how your own activities affect other organisms in your garden, it is smart to learn how to monitor your garden.

Monitoring is the regular observation and recording of the condition of your plants, the rise and fall of numbers of pests and their natural enemies, garden-management activities, weather conditions, and other relevant events. Through monitoring, you will learn to anticipate, and even to prevent, conditions that can lead to pest problems.

The most crucial thing is to make regular inspections of your plants, initially on a weekly or biweekly basis during the growing season. Once you have become familiar with the identity, life cycles, and behaviors of common pests in your garden and the plants they are attracted to, you can increase or decrease monitoring frequency, depending on season, pest abundance, and other factors. Observe plants at different times of the day and night, since garden organisms operate on a wide range of schedules.

A number of tools will aid you in your monitoring activities. For example, sticky traps in various insect-attracting colors, or traps containing chemical insect attractants called pheromones (discussed later in this chapter) can be used to capture pest insects and give you an early warning of their presence. A magnifying glass or 10-power hand lens helps you to see tiny insects and mites, or small patches of fungi that damage plants. A clear plastic bag or small vial is handy for holding specimens that you wish to examine more closely.

Keep track of weather variations with a maximum/minimum thermometer. High temperatures may speed the development of certain pest populations, or do just the opposite, sending them into a state of suspended activity. An early or late freeze, a spring that is rainier or drier than usual, or a late summer can affect the activity of pest organisms. Through careful observation, you can learn to anticipate these effects and put that knowledge to work in your management program.

What to Look For
Whether you jot informal notes in a garden diary, or enter data on a more formal chart, the important thing is to write down your

observations. Only by comparing pest information from one season to the next can you learn if and when you need to intervene with a pest-control action. When monitoring, learn to keep a sharp eye out for the following variables.

Plant Condition
The overall condition of a plant often determines what kind of a home it will make for a pest. In general, strong, vigorous plants will suffer less damage from pests than will plants under stress. Plants become stressed if they are grown in unsuitable areas with too much sun or shade, or in poorly drained soil, or if they receive improper care (such as too much fertilizer, too little water). Learn to recognize early signs of poor plant condition, including yellowing leaves, dead and dying plant parts, and slowed growth; if you can correct the horticultural causes, you may increase the plant's resistance to pests.

Evidence of Damage and Abundance of Pests
If you notice insects, weeds, or pathogens, look to see if they are causing any damage—check for holes in petals; brown spots in the lawn, and so forth. Note the nature of the damage, and make a record of where the damage is found (for example, on new unfurled leaves, on the lower portion of the tree trunk). Also take note of the microenvironment—is it shady? damp? warm?— and determine how many pests are present. You may record this as precisely as "10 caterpillars on one foot of branch five feet off the ground on the north side of the tree," or as generally as "none," "many," or "very high numbers." The information will be critical later on as you estimate the effectiveness of your pest-management program.

Write down your observations even if there is no apparent damage; record the date, site, or plant, and type of organism. Make a mental note to check again a few days later in hot weather, or in a week in cool weather, to see if the population has gotten larger or smaller and if natural enemies are present.

Natural Enemies
Learn to recognize the natural enemies of the pests you observe—what feeds on the pest or competes with it? If you notice aphids on your roses one day, check again a week later. If the aphids have disappeared altogether, or if their numbers have fallen dramatically, you may find that your rose garden is also host to ladybird beetles, syrphid-fly larvae, or mini-wasps, all of which are natural enemies of aphids. Record any evidence of natural enemies, the date, whether or not the pest population has fallen, and whether any damage was apparent.

Managing Pests Safely *You can help control certain garden pests by importing or encouraging a population of the pest's natural enemies. The adult ladybird beetle (top left) and its larvae (top right) prey on a number of pests. The adult lacewing (bottom left) and its larvae (bottom right) are also effective natural predators.*

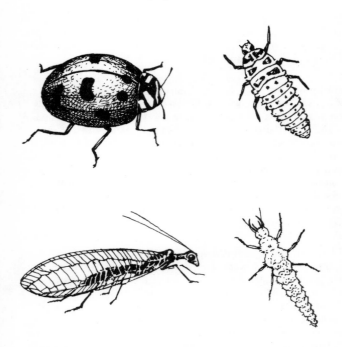

Weather and Microclimate

Some plant problems are the result not of insect pests alone, but of other contributing factors as well, particularly climatic ones. How hot, cold, wet, dry, or windy has it been? How long have these conditions existed? Are there specific local variations, such as poor air circulation, where the problem occurs? You will learn to keep a careful eye out for microclimates that promote the growth of insects, diseases, and weeds.

Too Much of a Good Thing

Some regular garden activities might inadvertently encourage pests or discourage natural enemies. For example, applying too much fertilizer encourages aphids; mowing lawns too short stimulates weed growth; and broad-spectrum pesticides are more deadly to beneficial insects than to many pests. Learn to recognize occasions when benign neglect is called for.

Establishing Pest-Tolerance Levels

Whether an organism is viewed as a pest is really an issue of whether or not its damage or annoyance is tolerable. For example, most people don't mind a few wormy apples on a tree, but if most of the apples have worms, the worms will likely be regarded as a pest. Data collected from monitoring enables you to establish your tolerance level for pests, a central concept of integrated pest management.

All plants can withstand a certain degree of pest presence without requiring treatment. In fact, eliminating pests altogether is impossible as well as undesirable, since pests sustain the natural enemies that feed on them and perform other roles in the ecosystem that we may not fully understand. For instance, golfers regard the little white English daisies (*Bellis perennis*) as out of place on a green, but pest managers know them to be sources of nectar for beneficial insects that attack more serious lawn pests, such as sod webworms.

To determine your pest-tolerance level, first decide how much aesthetic or economic damage your plants or crops can withstand. Second, establish through monitoring how large the pest population can grow before it causes that level of damage. And finally, undertake a treatment that keeps the pest population small enough so that it does not cause an unacceptable amount of damage.

Setting a Tolerance Level: A Case Study

We can apply these three steps to the management of a familiar garden pest: the rose aphid (*Macrosiphum rosae*). Assume that it is early spring and you have just counted 25 aphids on five rosebuds, or an average of five per bud. A week later, the average number of aphids is 40 per bud, but the buds still appear undamaged. By the third week, you note the presence of a few ladybird beetles and their tiny, alligatorlike larvae. Both adult and larval stages of the beetle are voracious aphid predators. On the three rosebushes where you spotted the beetles, the number of aphids has dropped to fewer than 25 per bud, and the blossoms on these bushes appear undamaged. But where no ladybird beetles appeared, there are more than 60 aphids per bud, and the opened blossoms look puckered and disfigured.

By monitoring the aphids, you can estimate the upper limit of your tolerance level; as we saw in this example, the maximum tolerable number of aphids per rosebud is about 40. When numbers approach that level, you may need to intervene with a pest-control action; but you have also learned that just a few ladybird beetles keep aphid numbers low enough to prevent unacceptable damage. Therefore, if aphid numbers rise near the limit of your tolerance next spring, your decision on whether to intervene with a pest-control treatment will be influenced by whether or not ladybird beetles or other natural enemies of aphids are in evidence.

Managing Pests Safely *A strip of concrete between lawn and fences or walls eliminates a prime site for weeds and insects—and gives the lawn a neat edge.*

You can adjust your tolerance levels for pests up or down depending on a number of variables, such as location and overall condition of your plants. Flowers that are in full view of visitors, for example, should be more pristine than those at the back of the yard—and therefore your tolerance for pests here will be lower. Healthy, vigorous lilacs, for instance, can support a fair amount of powdery mildew and still bloom prodigiously, while lilacs in poor condition may fail to bloom at all when attacked by the powdery mildew fungus.

Treatment Strategies and Tactics

In an integrated pest management program, the objective is to use a combination of strategies that attack the pest problem at different vulnerable points. This multifaceted approach increases the likelihood of success because few pests can survive a battery of treatments.

Select strategies that are least disruptive of natural controls and least damaging to the general environment, least hazardous to human health and other organisms, and most likely to reduce the pest population permanently. Your pest-control solutions should be

Some insects can simply be vacuumed up. An ordinary portable vacuum will handle some pests; this Bioclip vacuum is specifically designed for sucking up pests.

easy to execute and cost-effective over the short and long term. Fortunately, many strategies and tactics that meet these criteria are readily available to gardeners.

Habitat Modification

Reduce or eliminate the habitat or environmental conditions the pest needs to survive. For example, spreading dry sawdust on garden paths ties up the soil nitrogen, reducing the habitat for weed growth. Similarly, planting trees on a slightly elevated soil mound prevents the collection of water against the bottom of the trunk. Without a chronically damp habitat at the soil line, disease organisms are prevented from attacking the root crown.

Horticultural Controls

You can prevent or solve many pest problems by changing horticultural practices in the garden. Discourage weeds in lawns by raising the mowing height on temperate-climate grasses such as tall fescue and Kentucky bluegrass to two and a half to three inches. The higher cut helps shade out weeds. Disappoint aphids by substituting slow-release forms of nitrogen such as composted sludge or manure in place of highly soluble chemical fertilizers such as ammonium nitrate. Plants containing excessive nitrogen levels are particularly attractive to aphids and other pest insects.

Managing Pests Safely

Physical and Mechanical Controls

Sometimes it seems as if pests have been deliberately designed into gardens. For example, lawns planted up to the edge of fences or walls create a "weedy" appearance when the grass missed by the mower grows up against the fence. Solve this problem permanently by designing out the intersection of lawn and fence. Pour a six- to eight-inch-wide concrete "mowing strip" between the fence and the lawn. As the wheel of the mower travels along the mowing strip, it creates a neat edge to the lawn.

You can remove or kill many pests by hand. Set traps, including sticky cards and black-light traps, to deter or kill many insects; or try vacuuming up insects such as whiteflies. Exclude birds with netting or fabric row covers, and slugs and snails with sheets of copper around raised beds. Even heat and cold can work for you; for those weeds that you cannot eradicate with a hoe, a controlled use of a garden flame may help.

Biological Controls

Virtually every garden pest has its predators—sometimes more than one. Encourage the growth of parasitoids, those natural enemies, which may also include pathogens, antagonists, and other competitors.

Predators are organisms that feed directly on their hosts. Common insect predators include ladybird beetles and lacewing larvae, which devour a wide array of pest insects; seedhead weevils and certain other beetles, which feed on some rangeland weeds; predatory mites, which feed on pest mites, thrips, and other insects; and assassin and pirate bugs, which consume caterpillars and other insects.

Parasitoids are organisms that lay their eggs in or on their hosts; they include several kinds of tiny wasps, barely visible to the naked eye. The eggs hatch into small wormlike larvae that eat their prey from the inside, often using the prey's body as a cocoon during metamorphosis. When metamorphosis is complete, the adult cuts a hole in the cocoon and flies off to find other prey. Parasitized aphids turn a metallic silver or bronze color when used as cocoons and are called "mummies."

Pathogens are microorganisms (or microbes) such as fungi, bacteria, protozoa, and viruses that cause disease in insects and other pests. A number of such pathogens have been formulated into microbial insecticides widely used against caterpillars, mosquitoes, and beetle pests. These microbial products tend to be highly effective against a narrow range of pests. One strain of *Bacillus thuringiensis* (BT), for instance, the most widely used microbial insecticide, kills only caterpillars. It is harmless to other insects and to mammals, biodegrades quickly, and does not pollute the environment, making

Some garden pests can be controlled by the introduction of parasitoids, organisms that lay their eggs in or on a host. When the larvae hatch, they kill the pest host by eating it from the inside. Shown here is the destruction of an aphid by a parasitoid wasp.

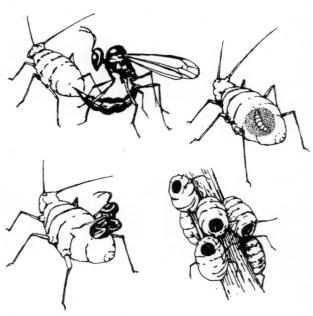

it a very safe and useful pest-management tool. Products made with BT are marketed under a variety of brand names, targeted for specific pests. The BT *israelensis* strain controls mosquito and blackfly larvae, while two other BT strains control Colorado potato beetles (*Leptinotarsa decimlineata*) and elm leaf beetles (*Pyrrhalta luteola*). Another beneficial bacteria is milky spore disease (*Bacillus popilliae*); it kills only the "white grub" stage of Japanese beetles (*Popillia japonica*). Most nurseries and garden centers and many mail-order companies sell microbial pest controls.

Microscopic parasitic nematodes, or roundworms, are also available commercially to control an expanding array of garden pests, ranging from strawberry root weevils (*Otiorhyncus ovatus*) and black vine weevils (*O. sulcatus*), which attack rhododendrons, cranberries, and other plants, to the grubs of Japanese and May beetles and masked chafers in lawns. These beneficial nematodes generally are sold as microbial insecticides even though, strictly speaking, they are parasitoids.

Another effective way to control pests is to introduce strong competition—"antagonists." Commercial preparations and soil amendments containing beneficial antagonistic microbes, such as fungi, bacteria, and actinomycetes, are beginning to reach the market. Among the antagonists preferred by garden experts are beneficial soil microorganisms that win out over plant pathogens for space and nutrients in the soil, thereby limiting their numbers. Other antagonists attack pathogens directly by infecting them with toxins that break down their cell structure. Some of the most well-studied antagonists are the beneficial fungi of the genera *Trichoderma* and *Gliocladium*. Both groups compete with other, pathogenic fungi, including those that cause damping-off diseases of young seedlings, necrotic ring spot and other diseases in lawns, and other problems. You can increase the presence and activity of these beneficial microbes in your soil by adding composted fir bark and amendments made from composted hardwoods.

Least-Toxic Chemical Controls

If the nontoxic strategies and tactics discussed above fail to solve your pest problem, you may need to turn to least-toxic chemical controls as a last resort. The problems and dangers associated with the use of conventional synthetic pesticides have become more widely recognized, and fortunately other, less toxic materials are becoming more readily available. Some, such as insecticidal dusts, horticultural oils, and insecticidal soaps, have been around for many years, albeit in less effective formulations. Others, such as pheromones, insect-growth regulators, and some botanicals, are recent arrivals and herald a new era in more environmentally safe pesticides.

A number of features distinguish these least-toxic pesticides from conventional formulations. Understanding these features is the secret to safe and effective use.

First, these least-toxic materials tend to break down quickly in the presence of sunlight and microbes, they biodegrade fairly rapidly (within hours or days), and they often must be reapplied. This is particularly true of soaps and botanical products such as pyrethrum. Thus, for example, if you treat a plant for aphids with a soap spray, you may have to treat it again if aphid numbers rise, because soaps leave no toxic residues.

Second, some less toxic materials may work more slowly than their common, deadlier counterparts. The microbial insecticide *Bacillus thuringiensis* (BT), for instance, must be ingested by a target caterpillar before it goes into effect. Moreover, the caterpillar must be sufficiently developed to consume enough BT to be affected. When a caterpillar has ingested sufficient BT, it will stop feeding within an hour or so, but it may take up to a week to die.

Third, some least-toxic materials are highly selective in their action against pests. That is, they may be toxic only to a narrow range of pests, or they may inhibit a key function, such as reproduction. The selective effectiveness of these compounds makes them less toxic to the general environment, but also requires greater sophistication on the part of the user.

Safety Precautions

Exercise safe practices when using any chemical control, no matter how benign. There are three basic precautions you should take. First, read the label. Before you use any pesticide—even those considered low in toxicity to humans—read the label. Follow all instructions to the letter, heeding all the manufacturer's precautions. Just like medicines, which can be extremely dangerous in too large a dosage, pesticides must be administered carefully. Over-application can lead at best to damaged plants, and at worst to serious harm to human health and the environment. Furthermore, pests develop resistance to overused substances, whether new products or old standbys.

Second, protect yourself. When applying pesticides, always wear rubber gloves, a long-sleeved cotton or cotton-blend shirt, cotton trousers, and eye protection. A dust mask or a respirator is also prudent, even when you are handling the relatively benign materials described here.

Third, use a spot-treatment approach. Apply pesticides only to those plants or areas of the lawn or garden where pest numbers threaten to exceed tolerance levels. Do not spray an entire plant or area where pests are not yet a problem. Such unnecessary applications will kill off beneficial organisms and leave toxic residues that may be harmful to other non-target organisms, such as pets, wildlife, or people.

There are six main kinds of least-toxic pesticides: soaps, insecticidal dusts, horticultural oils, botanicals, insect-growth regulators, and pheromones. Each is briefly described below.

Pesticidal Soaps

Composed of potassium salts of fatty acids combined with fish or vegetable oil, soaps have been used as insecticides since the late 1700s. When a soap solution is sprayed on an insect, it dissolves the protective waxy coating on the insect's body, causing dehydration and death. Once a soap spray is applied, an insect quickly stops feeding; it may, however, remain paralyzed for hours or even a few days before dying. The principal value of soaps as pesticides is that they are virtually nontoxic to the user unless ingested in large amounts; and even at high doses, they have no serious systemic effects, although they can cause nausea. Soaps biodegrade rapidly in the soil, and affect a relatively select range of insects: soft-bodied mites and sucking insects such as aphids, scale crawlers, whiteflies, and thrips are most susceptible. Slow-moving insects are more vulnerable than are highly mobile insects that react quickly and fly away. The hard-shelled adult forms of many beneficial insects, such as ladybird beetles, rapidly moving lacewings, and syrphid flies, are not endangered, but the flightless, soft-bodied, pre-adult forms of these insects tend to succumb.

Managing Pests Safely

Two companies manufacture pesticidal soaps in the United States: Safer Inc., and Ringer Inc. Safer also makes a soap-based herbicide, and a fungicide/miticide composed of fatty acid salts and sulfur. This latter product is effective against mites, chiggers, and ticks, as well as a variety of fungi that attack ornamental and food plants, including powdery mildew, black spot, scab, brown canker, leafspot, and rust.

Insecticidal Dusts

Insecticidal dusts cling to or are absorbed by the waxy layer on the outside of an insect's cuticle. They destroy the waxy protective coat, and the insect dies of dehydration. Dusts used in garden pest control include diatomaceous earth (DE) and silica aerogel. DE is mined from the fossilized silica shell remains of algae, better known as diatoms. It has both abrasive and absorbent qualities, and is in its natural form virtually nontoxic to mammals. Diatomaceous earth is formulated as a powder or a dust, and is also combined with the botanical insecticide pyrethrin. (Note, however, that swimming-pool-grade DE has been chemically treated and should not be used for pest-control purposes.)

Silica aerogels are amorphous, nonabrasive, chemically inert materials that are used as dehydrating agents and insecticides. Formed by mixing sodium silicate with sulfuric acid, the small particles of these fluffy aerogels are extremely absorbent. Silica aerogels are comparatively safe for people and animals. They are formulated as dusts or aerosols, either alone or in combination with pyrethrin. These two kinds of dusts—diatomaceous earth and silica aerogels—are effective against most insects, killing leaf-feeding types such as aphids, beetles, caterpillars, and mites as well as fleas, ticks, ants, and crickets.

Horticultural Oils

The use of oils to curb pests is an ancient tradition. Written records date from as early as the first century A.D., when the Roman scholar Pliny wrote that mineral oils controlled certain plant pests. Some oils are petroleum-based, meaning that they come from fossilized plants; others are derived from living plants or from animal fat. In general, horticultural oils kill insects at all stages of development by blocking their breathing apparatus and suffocating them. Because oils operate mechanically rather than biochemically on an insect, they pose very little danger to mammals. They also have relatively short residual lives, and they have less impact on natural-enemy populations than do synthetic products. They can, however, irritate skin and eyes, so always wear protective clothing, gloves, and goggles when applying oil sprays.

In the past, heavy horticultural oils, with viscosities ranging from 100 to 220, were used as dormant sprays on fruit and shade trees that had shed their leaves for the winter. Cautious gardeners did not use oils on plants in leaf because heavy oils tend to burn plant leaves. Today there are lighter, more highly refined oils with a lower viscosity range (60 to 80). Under appropriate conditions, these lighter oils can be applied to most plants during the growing season without harm. Nearly all the horticultural oil sprays on the market today are lighter and more highly refined than the oils of the past, although they may retain their old names.

Horticultural oils help control a wide range of insects and mites that attack fruit and ornamental trees, shrubs, and bedding and indoor plants. Such oils often are most effective against aphids, adelgids, cankerworms, leafhoppers, leafrollers, leaftiers, mealybugs, mites, psyllids, plant lice, scales, and tent caterpillars. In addition, oils are used to control the larval stage of mosquitoes, and the heavy oils also work as herbicides against a wide range of weeds.

Botanicals

This group consists of those pesticides that are derived from plants. Common examples include pyrethrum, which is made from a species of chrysanthemum, and nicotine, from the tobacco plant. Other common botanical pesticides are ryania, rotenone, and sabadilla. A new botanical pesticide called neem, extracted from the neem tree (*Azadirachta indica*), has been registered by the EPA for use against leafminers and other ornamental-plant pests. It is effective against a very wide range of pests, and relatively nontoxic to humans and beneficial insects. Extracts from citrus oils known as d-limonene and linalool have also been found effective against many insect pests. Currently, EPA-registered citrus-oil materials are permitted for use only against fleas and ticks, although the materials are also known to work against ants and other garden insects. In the near future, we can expect to see improved formulations of these and other botanicals reaching the market. Do not assume that all pesticides derived from plants are harmless to humans and other animals. The botanical insecticide nicotine is a poison that impedes neuromuscular functioning, causing insects to convulse and die. The same fate can befall humans exposed to higher doses of nicotine.

Like horticultural oils, botanicals are fairly short-lived, breaking down into harmless compounds within hours or days in the presence of sunlight. Furthermore, since they are chemically very close to the plants from which they were derived, they are easily decomposed by a variety of microbes common in most soils.

Pyrethrum-Based Botanicals

The pyrethrum-based botanicals have been used for hundreds of years, pyrethrin being the active ingredient derived from *Chrysanthemum cineraefolium*, grown primarily in Kenya and

Tanzania, and exported throughout the world. The term "pyrethrin" refers to the active compounds in the flowers that are extracted and reformulated for use in commercial insecticides. Pyrethroids are synthetic compounds that resemble pyrethrins in chemical structure but are more toxic to insects and more stable in the presence of sunlight. Some formulations persist in the environment longer than either pyrethrum or pyrethrin, often lasting 10 days or more, compared to a few hours or days for the natural botanicals. Pyrethrum is available as a powder, while pyrethrin and pyrethroids can be purchased in liquid, powder, or spray form. All are toxic to a wide range of garden pests, including ants, aphids, beetles, caterpillars, fleas, flies, leafhoppers, lice, and mosquitoes.

Insect-Growth Regulators
An insect's maturation processes and other vital functions are governed by hormones called insect-growth regulators. Not surprisingly, scientists have found a way to use insect-growth regulators (IGRs) or their synthetic mimics to curb pests, arresting their development before they reach maturity. Since IGRs affect biochemical processes unique to arthropods (such as insects), they are considered relatively benign to non-target organisms. Insect-growth regulators are most commonly marketed for use indoors, where sunlight and microbes are less able to decompose them. IGR compounds such as methoprene or kinoprene are effective in controlling aphids, scale, whiteflies, mealybugs, and other insects that attack plants grown indoors or in greenhouses. Fenoxycarb is an insect-growth regulator used to control fire ants indoors.

Pheromones
Insects produce chemicals called pheromones that, when emitted into the air, serve as communication stimuli. Many of these pheromones have been synthesized and manufactured as lures to attract insects to traps or baits containing insecticides. The most commonly used pheromones are sex-attractant chemicals, such as a chemical secreted by female moths that is placed in a trap to capture males of the same species.

Pheromones are used chiefly to detect the presence of certain insect species, to determine when egg-laying begins, and so on. But large numbers of traps or lures can also be used in pest control. For example, commercial growers confuse tomato pinworm moths (*Keiferia lycopersicella*) by using thousands of small lures containing synthetic sex-attractant pheromones. The prevalence of the synthetic pheromone throughout the crop makes it difficult for male and female moths to find each other and mate, thus keeping the insects within tolerance levels. This technique has completely replaced the use of conventional insecticides in some cotton-growing regions.

Pheromone traps work effectively against many garden insect pests, including the caterpillar stages of codling moths, peachtree borers, Nantucket pine tip moths, navel orangeworms, leafrollers, and armyworms; adult Japanese beetles and European elm bark beetles; and apple maggots and fruit flies.

Integrated Pest Management—Worth the Trouble?

IPM is a new approach to pest control in the garden—one that works hand in hand with nature in producing a successful garden, with room for some of the less lovable creatures that share our garden space. Using the integrated pest management techniques requires more thought and planning than just spraying a pesticide whenever a pest appears. Once you have gained some experience with these methods, however, you will find them easier and more sensible to use. As integrated pest management solutions move your garden into a better balance with nature, the number and severity of pest problems will subside to very low levels, leaving you more time to enjoy your plants and to reap their harvest. Moreover, the knowledge you gain while monitoring the fascinating lives and times of the insects, mollusks, birds, and mammals that inhabit a healthy garden will not only increase your ability but also your enjoyment of gardening. And, after all, isn't the search for such experiences among the important reasons why we garden in the first place?

Lawns

Fashions in lawns have changed in recent years, and we seem to be entering a period when almost anything goes. Gardeners are planting all kinds of lawns—from high-maintenance, crew-cut, weedless surfaces to low-maintenance turfs free of chemical input, to meadows that require only infrequent mowing. Except in the dwindling number of municipalities with stringent lawn regulations, all are perfectly acceptable. It is a matter of individual taste.

Meadows, of course, are modeled after natural situations. Putting greens, by contrast, are not. You can choose anything in between for your lawn, but be forewarned: The closer you approach the putting-green model and the farther you get from the meadow, the more maintenance will be needed.

Low maintenance does not necessarily mean a shaggy, weed-infested lawn. Luckily, new tools, techniques, and grass types make it easier than ever to have a good-looking lawn without a lot of work.

Birth of the Lawn

The first lawns were born on medieval British estates. They were actually no more than patches of sod cut out of meadows and transplanted, complete with wildflowers and weeds, onto the estates. Browsing sheep and an occasional cut with a scythe kept them trim; selective grazing by the sheep meant that some of the flowers survived. These early lawns signified safety, the half-tame area separating a dwelling from the wilds around it.

In the 19th century, two events changed the nature of the lawn forever: the invention of the lawn mower, and the popularization of golf. Early in the century, an engineer named Edward Budding borrowed the principles of a textile cutter and built the first hand-powered reel mower. His mower democratized the lawn, allowing all classes to maintain one without the expense of servants or sheep. No longer the exclusive preserve of the affluent, well-kept lawns became pleasing symbols of comfortable middle-class life. Today, many people still feel strongly about their lawns.

Mowers changed lawns in another way. Because these machines were not as selective as grazing sheep, or even men wielding scythes, most plants fell before their spinning blades, and the lawn became more of a monocrop.

The game of golf, of course, predates the invention of the lawn mower. But golf's requirements—closely mowed grass and a playing area free of weeds and flowers—greatly influenced the study of turf as the game became more popular. The perfect putting green and weed-free fairway were the ideals that professionals pursued. University research, often funded by golf associations and chemical companies, was aimed at maintaining turf to these exacting standards. This ideal trickled down to the masses and became a model for the suburban lawn as well. The putting-green look soon became a style to adopt.

This sloping expanse of lawn shows the effects of careful grooming, efficient watering, and timely fertilizing.

Classic flower borders and trellises surround this lawn with color and fragrance. A ground-level edging around the lawn allows for easy mowing.

*A perennial border is
nicely set off by a close-
cropped, dense lawn.
The neatly cut lawn
edge takes some effort to
maintain, but it is a
perfect foil to the bushy
garden bed.*

*This pattern of lawns
and paths divides the
yard into separate
"rooms." Such an
innovative design can
add considerable interest
to a large, level space.*

Turf alternates with moss in a unique pattern that lends interest to the expansive, level area shown at left. Moss is a good choice for shady spots where grass may be difficult to grow.

A shade-tolerant variety of grass was selected for the sunken lawn area below. Ferns and other woodland foliage plants surround it and add to the cool, green atmosphere.

Another classic lawn-and-border look is achieved with mixed flowers, shrubs, and trees flanking a manicured lawn.

The lawn and
recreation area in this
dry-climate yard was
kept small deliberately
in order to save water.
The plants in the wide
surrounding border are
drought tolerant.

Because it slopes gently toward the patio, this lawn encourages water to stay in the yard and benefit the flowers that have been tucked between the pavers. The grass is allowed to grow fairly high, which also helps it retain moisture in an area of little rainfall.

A ground cover of spring cinquefoil substitutes for lawn in this southwestern yard. Such drought-tolerant ground covers are wise choices for low-traffic areas.

A limited expanse of
relatively tall lawn
grass, complemented by a
large bed of perennials
chosen for their low
water needs, helps save
water and lend beauty
to this front yard.

Low, flowering ground
covers, including sedums,
thyme, and saxifrage,
offer a colorful
alternative to a lawn,
which would have
required much more
water to maintain.

Some gardeners are choosing to plant wildflower meadows in place of high-maintenance lawns. Despite their natural look, meadows do require some attention; this seaside field of African daisies and baby blue eyes is reseeded every winter, after the previous year's growth is turned under.

In shady areas, low woodland plants are excellent ground covers, spreading quickly to fill large spaces. The choices here include sweet woodruff, honesty, and false mitrewort.

Bright green Irish moss substitutes for turf in an area of light traffic. The tufted perennial is also useful to cover the ground between paving stones in a walkway.

Japanese-style designs can help conserve water by incorporating decorative gravel in place of turf. Here, carefully pruned podocarpus, spruce, and false cypress trees combine with gravel and large stones to grace an entryway.

ice plant, a succulent perennial, grew quickly to cover this sandy seaside yard. It requires little water and is helpful in controlling erosion.

Planting bulbs in a lawn can yield a glorious springtime meadow such as the one seen here. Once these daffodil blossoms fade and the leaves begin to yellow, the lawn will be mowed as usual through the remainder of the spring and summer.

High Maintenance or Low Maintenance?

Keeping up the putting-green lawn is a science in itself. A general rule in lawn care is that maintenance begets the need for more maintenance. Heavily fertilized lawns need more frequent mowing. Closely mowed lawns need more irrigation. Well-irrigated lawns are more prone to diseases and weed infestation. What is more, chemicals used to cure diseases or to kill weeds often give rise to new diseases.

But doesn't a good-looking lawn require high maintenance? Not necessarily. Studies have shown that moderate amounts of care—specifically, mowing to two inches, irrigating if there is a critical water shortage, and fertilizing but not applying pesticides or fungicides—produces results just as satisfactory as those obtained through more labor-intensive efforts. In other words, extra work and chemicals lavished on a high-maintenance plot do not necessarily pay off in appearance.

When it comes to lawns, beauty is in the eye of the beholder. If you can tolerate a variety of plants in your lawn, then you can have a very easy lawn to maintain. But as your compulsion about getting rid of weeds increases, so will your costs. A weed, of course, is simply a plant that is not supposed to be where it is. If you decide that dandelions don't belong in your lawn, then they become weeds and you have to spend energy eliminating them. If you also deem clover a weed, you will have to spend additional energy trying to eradicate it.

Preferences with regard to grass height are also a question of personal taste. A look at the traditional American yard may lead you to believe that there is a natural human preference for short grass and scattered trees. But "short" is a relative term: Botanically speaking, short grass may be as long as six inches, but in much of our suburban culture, short grass is one and a half inches long. Happily, that restrictive norm seems to be giving way to more enlightened ideas of lawn design.

Grasses for the Masses

The best way to reduce the maintenance requirements of your lawn is to grow a species of grass suited to your climate and your inclination. Over the past 10 years, there has been an explosion of new grass varieties. Today, you can find varieties that resist drought, insects, and diseases; varieties that stand up to heavy foot traffic; and varieties that need less frequent mowing. (A selection of the most popular is given in the chart later in this chapter.)

Grass Types

The grasses that are most often used in American lawns—very few of which are native to North America—come in several types: fine- or coarse-bladed, sod-forming or bunching, annual or perennial, warm-season or cool-season.

A Selection of Lawn Grasses

Species	*Season*	*Texture*	*Sowing Rate*[1]
Bahiagrass	W	coarse	5
Bentgrass	C	fine	1/2–1
Bermudagrass	W	coarse to fine	1–3
Blue gramagrass	W	medium-fine	1–1-1/2
Buffalograss	W	fine	5–7
Carpetgrass	W	coarse	3–4
Centipedegrass	W	coarse	1/4–1
Creeping fescue	C	fine	3–5
Chewings fescue	C	fine	3–4
Kentucky bluegrass	C	fine	1–2
Perennial ryegrass	C	coarse	4–6
St. Augustine grass	W	coarse	N/A
Tall fescue	C	coarse	5–8
Zoysiagrass	W	coarse to fine	N/A

C = Cool
W = Warm
[1] Pounds per 1,000 square feet
[2] Pounds of actual nitrogen per year

Mowing Height	Fertilizer[2]	Disease Resistance	Comments
2–3	2–4	poor	Establishes slowly, but grows well in shade.
1/2–1-1/2	2–4	poor	A fussy grass best left on the putting green.
1–2	2–3	fair	Very vigorous; hybrid varieties carry some disease resistance.
1–2	1–2	fair	Drought resistant, but may turn brown during extended drought.
2–2-1/2	1–2	poor	Drought tolerant, but may turn brown in mid-summer.
1–2	2–3	good	Grows well in sandy soils.
1–2	2–4	good	Grows slowly; does not require high fertility.
2–2-1/2	1–2	fair	Does not require heavy fertilization; diseases may be problem in South.
2–2-1/2	1–2	good	Good for shade.
2-1/2–3	2–3	fair	Improved, named varieties have resistance to several diseases.
2–2-1/2	2–3	good	Fast growing; some varieties resist insect damage.
2–3	2–4	poor	Grows well in shade; requires heavy fertilization.
2–4	1–2	good	Handles shade, drought, and wear.
1/2–1	2–3	fair	Grows very slowly; prone to thatch.

Lawns

Sod-forming grass shown here grows by spreading horizontal roots called stolons that send up another small plant when the stolon roots. Bunch grass grows only from the basal growth point. The two types of grasses are often mixed.

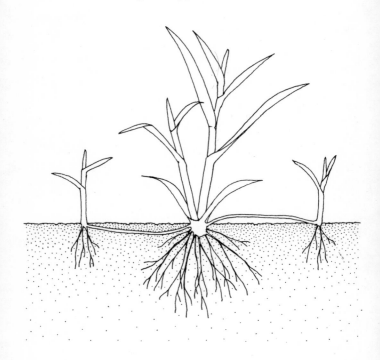

Fine-bladed grass imparts a putting-green look to a lawn, while coarse-bladed grass can look weedy. By definition, fine-textured grass has blades less than a quarter-inch wide. Anything wider is defined as coarse-textured grass. Bentgrass, Kentucky bluegrass, and zoysia are the most common fine-textured grasses, while annual ryegrass, tall fescue, and St. Augustine grass are coarse textured. The quality may vary from variety to variety within a species, and you may find that some coarse-textured grasses are worth planting because of their other redeeming attributes.

Grasses are also classified by the way they grow. Sod-forming grasses send out stolons (horizontal stems that creep above ground), or rhizomes (underground stems). These enable the plant to spread and fill in bare patches, and they will force out weeds and create a thick lawn. Sod-forming grasses include sod-Kentucky bluegrass, bentgrass, Bermudagrass, and zoysiagrass. Bunch grasses, by contrast, grow only from the basal growth point of the plant and do not throw out stolons or rhizomes. They are often fast growers that stand up well to traffic. Bunch grasses can be mixed with sod-forming grasses with good results. Some examples of bunch grasses are perennial ryegrass, tall fescue, and blue grama grass.

Perennial grasses are usually the only types you should consider for a permanent lawn. You might want to plant annual types as a nurse crop, however, or to provide winter color in southern areas.

In grasses, the most basic division of types is warm-season and cool-season. Their names describe their growth habits. Warm-season grasses, such as Bermudagrass and St. Augustine grass, grow most vigorously where the weather is warm, at temperatures of 80° to 95° F. Frost causes them to "brown out" or die back. They are normally planted south of the so-called bluegrass line, which runs approximately along the northern borders of North Carolina, Tennessee, Arkansas, Oklahoma, and Texas, and through New Mexico and Arizona to the Pacific, passing through the southern part of California. Some gardeners south of the line also plant cool-season grasses in the fall to provide winter color.

Cool-season grasses grow best north of the bluegrass line, and they perform most vigorously in cool weather of spring and fall, at temperatures between 60° and 75° F. Cool-season grasses may turn brown or go dormant during high summer heat. The most common cool-season grasses are Kentucky bluegrass, bentgrass, perennial ryegrass, and the fescues (fine, tall, creeping, and Chewings).

Northern Grasses

Kentucky bluegrass is a fine-leaved, sod-forming grass, and nothing makes a better lawn in most parts of the country. Kentucky bluegrass can survive the heat of the middle South, the cold of New England, and the heavy rains of the Northwest. With its fine texture, deep-green color, spreading habit, and rapid sod-forming ability, it grows into a classic lawn. But Kentucky bluegrass does not grow well in shady or moist conditions, and it requires more water than some other types. Some varieties of Kentucky bluegrass are also susceptible to fungal diseases. The best varieties include 'Adelphi', 'Fylking', 'Glade', and 'Merion'.

Bentgrass, which is used for putting greens, is the lowest-growing, finest-textured grass available. Bentgrass is also extremely finicky, however. It needs constant, close mowing (as low as half an inch), requires plenty of water and fertilizer, and is susceptible to several diseases. For the most part, bentgrass is not suitable for home lawns. Velvet bentgrass, however, is a good choice for shady areas where the soil is infertile, and creeping bentgrass grows well in wet soils.

Perennial ryegrass has become more popular for lawns since the advent of the new, finer-leaved "turf-type" varieties. These varieties germinate rapidly and grow quickly. They also mix well with Kentucky bluegrass. Perennial ryegrass is tough and stands up well to foot traffic. Some of the new varieties are resistant to certain insects as well as diseases. Look for 'Manhattan II', 'Repel' (which resists sod webworm, billbug, and chinchbug), 'Citation II', and 'Prelude'.

Growing Zones
The United States is divided into five turf-growing regions based on climate.
•Zone one is the humid Northeast, which supports Kentucky bluegrass, along with bentgrass, fescues, improved turf-type tall fescues, and improved perennial ryegrasses.
•Zone two is the humid South. The best grasses for this area are bermudagrass, zoysia, and in limited areas, carpetgrass, centipedegrass, St. Augustine grass, and bahiagrass.
•Zone three is the Great Plains. You can grow bluegrass here under irrigation. For low maintenance, the best choices are blue gramagrass, buffalograss, and crested wheatgrass.
•Zone four is the dry Southwest. Bermudagrass and zoysia grow best here, while bluegrass and fescues may be grown at high altitudes.
•Zone five is the humid Northwest. Grasses that grow well here are the same as in zone one: Kentucky bluegrass, bentgrass, fescues, and ryegrass.
Once you've decided which grasses grow well where you live, you can consider the qualities best suited to your needs.

Fine fescues are very fine-leaved grasses that make an attractive lawn. They are also the most shade-tolerant of the northern grasses, and have some tolerance to drought. Their disease resistance and low fertilizer requirements make fine fescues a good choice for a low-maintenance lawn. The best varieties include 'Banner', 'Reliant', and 'Flyer'.

Turf-type tall fescue is a coarse-textured bunch grass, very suitable for the well-used lawn because it can withstand heavy traffic, will grow in light shade, and requires little fertilizer. Good varieties include 'Apache', 'Clemfine', 'Houndog', and 'Rebel'.

Creeping fescue spreads rapidly via rhizomes and forms a thick sod. It grows well in cool, humid regions, and can tolerate acid, poor soil. Among the favored varieties are 'Dawson', 'Flyer', 'Fortress', 'Pennlawn', 'Ensylvia', and 'Ruby'.

Chewings fescue is a bunch grass with a more erect growth habit than creeping fescue. It is a good choice for shady areas. Improved varieties include 'Agram', 'Banner', 'Atlanta', 'Waldorf', and 'Jamestown'.

Southern Grasses
There are fewer improved varieties of warm-season grasses available from seed. As a consequence, many have to be planted from sprigs or plugs.

Bermudagrass is the southern counterpart of Kentucky bluegrass; it is the most popular grass from Florida to California, and it makes a turf that will survive even neglect. Bermudagrass is coarse- to fine-textured, depending on the variety, and it is a sod-forming perennial that spreads by stolons and rhizomes. It establishes itself quickly and forces weeds out; in fact, it is so vigorous that you may consider it a weed in some situations. Bermudagrass grows throughout the warmer regions of the United States into the Midwest and New England. In cool weather, though, it turns off-color, and after frost it turns brown. Overall, it is a good, low-maintenance grass that will thrive in poor soil ranging from heavy clay to deep sand. The best varieties include 'Tifgreen', 'Tifway', and 'Tifway II'.

Bahiagrass is a coarse, low-growing, sod-forming grass. It spreads slowly, but in time will form a thick turf that crowds out weeds. One drawback is that the thick-stemmed, dense turf is difficult to cut with a reel mower. Look for the varieties 'Paraguay', 'Pensacola', and 'Tifhi'.

Blue grama grass is a fine-textured, bunch-type grass that grows well in the alkaline soils of the Great Plains. It is drought-resistant, but will go dormant and turn brown in severe droughts. It is best for cool, dry areas.

Buffalograss is a fine-textured, sod-forming, native American grass that spreads by stolons. It is one of the best grasses to grow in the Great Plains because it is very drought-resistant and does well in alkaline, clay soils. It needs less mowing and less fertilizer than do most southern grasses, and so it is a good low-maintenance choice for these areas. Buffalograss turns brown in midsummer and again when growth stops in the fall.

Carpetgrass is a coarse-textured, sod-forming perennial that spreads rapidly. It carries resistance to disease and insect damage, and can tolerate heavy foot traffic. It will also grow well in poor soils. Carpetgrass thrives especially in sandy soils with plenty of moisture—making it a good lawn grass for the southeast coast of the United States.

Centipedegrass is a coarse grass that spreads by creeping stolons. It grows on poor soils and matures to a height of only three to four inches, thus requiring less mowing than does Bermudagrass.

St. Augustine grass is a coarse, sod-forming perennial that spreads both by stolons and by rhizomes, and grows well in the shade. In favorable conditions, it forms a thick, dense turf that crowds out other grasses and weeds. Favored varieties are 'Roselawn', 'Better Blue', and 'Floratine'.

Zoysias are coarse to fine (depending on the species), low-growing perennials that spread by stolons and by rhizomes. Zoysias are tough grasses that form a dense sod and choke out weeds. They grow slowly however, and take as long as two to three years to fill in from plug planting. Zoysias have some drought tolerance, but they are shallow rooted and must be irrigated in dry areas. Because

Lawns

To check the slope of your yard, sink a yardstick to a depth of 1 foot near the house; 100 feet away, sink a 4-foot stake. Tie a line on the first stake and run it to the second; adjust the height of the string at the second stake until the line is level. Tie it off and measure the distance from here to the ground; this is the drop per 100 feet.

they grow slowly, they do not need mowing as often as Bermudagrass. The recommended varieties include 'Meyer', 'Flawn', and 'Midwestern'.

Improved Varieties
No matter what variety of grass you choose, you should always looked for improved, named varieties of a species. You may have to pay a little more, but it will be worth it. Improved varieties may possess increased vigor, a finer texture, and resistance to certain diseases or even insects.

Starting with the Soil
The most carefully chosen grass will not grow well unless the soil beneath it is of good tilth. If you are about to put in a new lawn from scratch, you can start out right with improved grass varieties and good soil. When lawns suffer from diseases or weeds, the odds are that poor, infertile, or compacted soil is to blame. Once a lawn is started, you won't have the chance to improve the soil, so it is best to make sure you do the right thing from the start. Time spent testing the soil, correcting deficiencies, and improving drainage and grading will pay off for years to come. General soil care is discussed earlier in this guide, but all lawns have some specific soil requirements.

Checking Grades
First, check the grading of your yard. It should slope down three to six degrees away from the house in all directions, a grade equal to a one-foot drop for every lateral 100 feet. If the slope is any less, water may stand in the yard, giving rise to diseases and weeds. If the slope is steeper, too much water may run off, leaving dry patches.
It is relatively simple to check the slope of your lot. Start near the house and sink a three-foot stake one foot deep into the ground.

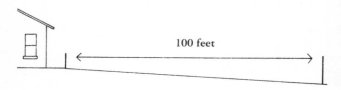

100 feet

Then pace off 100 feet in one direction and sink a four-foot stake one foot into the ground. Return to the first stake and tie a light string to it at ground level. Stretch the string tightly to the other stake and hold it there as your helper fastens a line level to the midpoint of the string. Raise or lower your end of the string until the line is level, and tie it to the second stake. The distance between the point where the string is tied to the second stake and the ground is the rate of drop per 100 feet. Repeat the procedure in all four directions. If the rate of drop in any direction is less than six inches or more than two and a half feet, you should consider regrading if you wish to have a handsome lawn.

Regrading
Changing the grade of your property is a big job that calls for heavy equipment; it is best to leave it to a contractor. If your lot is very steep, you might consider building terraces or berms. Or you may want to leave steep banks in place and plant them with ground covers. If your lot is graded properly but the soil is overly wet, consider installing drain tiles (discussed in the chapter on preparing the soil).

If you are faced with bumps, potholes, or low spots, you can even the soil out yourself with a shovel, rake, and wheelbarrow.

Soil Fertility and pH
After the work of regrading has been done, it is time to analyze the fertility and texture of your soil. Start with a soil test. You can buy a test kit and do it yourself, or send a soil sample off to your local Cooperative Extension office. To collect soil for a test, use a trowel to dig up the soil from a depth of at least four inches in several places around your yard. Mix the samples together, let them dry, then send them off in the package provided by the testing agency. There is nothing mysterious about a lawn's fertility needs. Like other plants, grasses need a soil rich in nitrogen, phosphorus, and potassium. If your soil tests in the normal range, broadcast a starter fertilizer over the area. Use approximately two to three pounds of actual nitrogen, five to eight pounds of phosphorus, and two to three pounds of potash per 1,000 square feet; or use 50 pounds of a 5-10-5 fertilizer. To make an organic mix, combine 25 pounds each of blood meal, bone meal, and greensand, and apply the mixture to 1,000 square feet.

Most grasses prefer a neutral pH, in the range of 6.5 to 7.5. Add limestone to raise the pH to the proper level or sulfur to lower it. The amount of either needed to do the job will vary according to the base pH and the soil type. Generally, to raise the pH from 5.5 to 6.5 in sandy soil, you will need 30 pounds of limestone per 1,000 square feet. It will take 80 pounds of limestone, however, to do the same in loamy soil, and 110 pounds in clay. Conversely, lowering the pH of sandy soil from 8.5 to 7.5 requires 45 pounds of sulfur; clay soils call for about 70 pounds.

Soil Structure

Before adding any amendments, take a close look at your soil's structure. Knowing whether you are working with sand, clay, loam, or something in between will help you gauge your liming or sulfur needs, and will also aid you in choosing grass types and in setting your irrigation schedule.

A simple, but not exactly precise, way to test your soil's texture is described in the chapter "Preparing the Soil." It will tell you approximately what percentages of sand, silt, and clay are present. A clay soil will contain about 60 percent clay, 30 percent silt, and 10 percent sand. Loamy soils are about 20 percent clay, 40 percent silt, and 40 percent sand. Sandy loam is 10 percent clay, 20 percent silt, and 70 percent sand.

If your soil is more than 60 percent clay or 70 percent sand, work at least a two-inch layer of organic matter or a three-inch layer of rich topsoil into it. The organic matter can consist of compost, peat moss, dried manure, rice hulls, or any combination thereof. Sprinkle the lime or sulfur additive over the layer of organic matter; then till to a depth of six inches or make one or two passes with a tractor-mounted disk.

Clearing Weeds

While you prepare your soil, it is also the time to make one last attack on the weeds. To combat perennial weeds, it is best to make several passes over the soil with a metal garden rake to remove weed roots, rhizomes, and stolons. You can kill off annual weed seeds by solarizing the soil or by successive tilling. (To solarize soil, first plow or till it, then water it thoroughly. Then stretch a sheet of clear plastic tightly over the soil. Leave the plastic in place for about four weeks to kill weeds in the top layer of soil.) Successive tilling will bring weed seeds to the surface, where they can germinate. Wait at least two weeks after the first tilling until a solid crop of new weeds sprouts; then you can do them in with another tilling. This time, set the tiller at a shallower setting to chop out the weeds, or slice them with a hoe.

Replanting Existing Lawns

If you have started with bare soil, you are just about ready to sow. But if you are replanting an old lawn, you first have to get rid of the old sod, thatch, and weeds. If your old lawn is in fair shape, with less than 25 percent weeds, the easiest way to start a new lawn is simply to over-seed. If your lawn has more weeds than grass, however, you are going to have to get rid of all the existing vegetation. You can rent a sod stripper (a machine like a lawn mower that slices off the top layer of sod) or hire someone to come in and do the job for you. But be prepared to lose some of your topsoil along with the sod.

Alternatively, the best solution is to hire someone with a plow to come in and turn the whole lawn over. You can do this with a rotary tiller, of course, but tilling sod is a long and arduous process. It can take from five to ten passes to rid your patch of all the sod and weeds.

If your lawn is not too large and time is not of the essence, you can also mulch the vegetation to death. Just cover the lawn with sheets of black plastic. Anchor the plastic down tightly and wait for the grass to shrivel. But be prepared for a fairly long wait. Depending on the type of grass and the temperature, it can take from three to six weeks. Even then, the seedbed won't be ready for planting. You will still have to plow or till.

Finally, if you are chemically inclined, you can zap the entire area with a broad-spectrum herbicide such as glyphosate (sold under the brand names Roundup and Kleenup). It will kill all vegetation within a week or two. But again, the area will still have to be tilled, and, of course, the herbicide won't help you improve the tilth of the soil in the way plowing or tilling would. After the seedbed has been prepared, test the soil for texture and fertility, and add amendments as necessary.

Planting

You can start a new lawn from seed, sod, or sprigs and plugs. Seeding is the cheapest, easiest, and most common method, and—since many new improved turf grasses are available only as seed—it also has the advantage of offering the greatest choice of varieties. Sodding is a slightly faster way to establish a lawn, but it takes more work. The soil must be prepared every bit as carefully as for seeding, and the sod must be laid with precision. Sprigs and plugs (individual grass plants or parts of plants) are less expensive than sod, because you do not plant them in a solid blanket. But they demand patience. It may take years for plugs to fill in and cover an area. In the meantime, keep the soil between them free of weeds.

When to Plant

The first critical task in starting a lawn by seed is deciding when to sow. The theory is to plant at a time when grass has an advantage over weeds. You will be pampering the new grass, and weeds will certainly try to take advantage of that treatment. In the North, the best time to sow a lawn is the autumn. The cool-season grasses are ready to take off once the heat breaks, but most annual weeds are not programmed to germinate in the fall, giving the grass an advantage.

Rotary Tiller

Used for aerating and turning under topsoil, a rotary tiller is useful in preparing a new area as a seedbed, and necessary if you wish to rid your yard of old lawn growth before replanting. Tilling is a big job, but it will improve the tilth of your soil and help in the eradication of weeds.

Lawn Rake

A good lawn rake, made of metal or wood, is your best ally for clearing up leaves, sticks, and surface debris from a lawn. When putting down new seed, rake a thin layer of soil over it; you can use the back of the rake to tamp down the soil afterward.

Lawn Roller

When planting a new lawn, use a roller to firm the soil in the seedbed before you broadcast the seed. If you decide to plant your lawn with sod, you will also need to use a light lawn roller to firm the sod down into the soil once you have put it down.

Sprinkler

Several types of lawn sprinklers are available, each with its advantages and drawbacks. It is critical, when planting seed or laying sod, to make sure the soil is thoroughly damp; the soil surface in a newly seeded lawn should not be allowed to dry out until the new growth has reached a height of 2 inches.

Spreader

Two kinds of spreaders are chiefly used for fertilizing lawns: the drop spreader (shown here) and the rotary spreader. The drop spreader has a gate at the bottom that can be adjusted until the proper amount of fertilizer is deposited on the lawn. Rotary spreaders cover more ground in less time, but they are less precise.

Grass will have plenty of time to become established as long as it is planted six weeks before the first fall frost.

In the North, you can also sow grass in early spring. It is best to get the job done as soon as the ground can be worked, certainly no later than mid-May in most areas. Doing this will give the grass plenty of time to establish itself before the summer heat sets in.

In the South, warm temperatures favor the growth of grass, so the best time to sow is late spring to early summer.

Choosing Seed

The size of individual grass seed varies quite a bit from species to species, and so does its coverage. Refer to the chart on page 370 to determine the amount of grass seed you will need. While you're shopping, take a close look at the grass-seed label. It should list the species and varieties in the bag or box, the percentage of each, and whether they are fine- or coarse-textured. The label will also tell you how much weed seed, crop seed, and inert matter is present. Good-quality grass seed contains no weed or crop seed at all, and it has less than three percent inert matter.

You will also find a germination-rate number for each type of seed in the package. The germination rate should always exceed 80 percent, and the closer it is to 100 percent the better. Look for named varieties of seed whenever possible: 'Merion' Kentucky bluegrass, for example, rather than just a generic Kentucky bluegrass.

Sowing Seed

The easiest and most accurate way to sow grass seed is with a broadcast seeder, but you can also do a perfectly acceptable job by hand. When you are ready to sow, divide the seed into two equal portions. Put half in the seeder, or, if you are sowing by hand, in a bucket. Make one pass over the area with the first batch of seed. Then with the rest of the seed, make a second pass at right angles to the first. This will give you good coverage.

After all the seed has been sown, rake a thin layer of soil over it. Firm down the seedbed with a lawn roller, or tamp it with the back of a rake. To keep the soil moist, which is critical for germination, cover it thinly with weed-free straw. Do not use hay—it contains weed seed. Peat moss and sawdust are also poor choices for mulch because they crust over into an impenetrable layer. The new wide row covers made of spun polyester are excellent mulching material for newly seeded lawns. Use pins made from coat hangers to keep the covers in place, and remove the covers when the grass reaches one inch in height.

Do not allow the soil surface to dry out until the grass is two inches tall, even if you must water it lightly several times a day. But also be careful not to saturate the soil. When the grass emerges, stay off it, and do not mow until it is at least two, perhaps three, inches high.

Sodding

When you need a lawn in a hurry, sod is best; in most cases, it establishes faster than seed. But planting sod is more work. The best time for sodding is the same as for seeding: fall or early spring in the North, spring in the South. Never plant during hot, dry weather—you cannot afford to let the sod dry out before its roots have knitted in the soil.

It will pay to do some shopping around. Sod should be about three-quarters of an inch thick. If it is any thicker than one inch, it may have a tough time getting started. Also, the sod should be deep green, without brown edges or patches.

Sodding is no shortcut to establishing a lawn. You will need to prepare the ground just as carefully as when you plant seed. Once the soil is ready, after all the amendments have been added, give it a final raking and then firm the seedbed with a roller. Before you actually lay the sod, turn on the sprinkler and let it run long enough to wet the soil to a depth of eight inches. This may take a full day, depending on your soil type and the flow rate of your sprinkler. The water should be applied uniformly and gently so that no puddles or mud forms.

Laying Sod

Sodding is not a job to rush, but once you start you must work until you are done. If the sod sits in a pile and heats up, the roots may be permanently damaged.

Laying sod is a precise operation. Begin by establishing a straight line, which you can do by lining the first course of sod against a straight edge such as a two-by-four, a string stretched between two stakes, or the edge of a sidewalk. Lay the sod strips as you would lay brick, fitting them together as tightly as possible without overlap. After you have laid the first course, place a piece of plywood on it, and kneel on this platform while you put down the next course. (Doing so will press the sod firmly down into the soil; the plywood will distribute your weight evenly.) Make sure that the edges of the second course are in good contact with the first, but don't line the patches up exactly. Instead, stagger them like a brick wall. Once the sod is in place, go over it once or twice with a light lawn roller.

If you lay sod on a slope, you will have to use pegs, or staples made from coat hangers, to keep it from slipping down the hill. Push the pegs in just far enough to hold the sod, then pull them out before you roll it. After rolling, replace the pegs and leave them in place until the sod is established.

On a slope or on flat land, the final step is to spread a thin layer of topsoil over the sod, and work the soil into the cracks with a broom

When sodding your yard, put the pieces down as though you were laying bricks, lining up the pieces as closely and neatly as possible. When you finish a row, put down a plank on top of it, and kneel on the plank while you put down the next row; doing this will help evenly distribute your weight and press the sod into the ground.

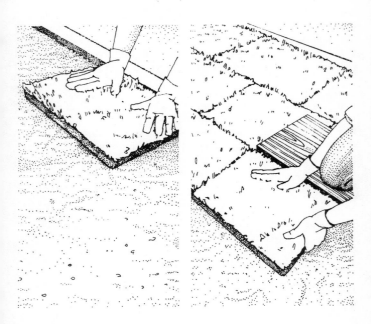

or the back of a wooden rake. Keep the soil moist by watering during the warmest part of each day until the roots have knitted into the soil.

Spot and Strip Sodding
There are other methods of planting lawns, primarily if you plan to plant warm-season grasses. Zoysias and the new, improved varieties of Bermudagrass and centipedegrass aren't readily available from seed; if you wish to use any of these, you will have to plant them by means of spot sodding, strip sodding, or sprigging.

Spot sodding is similar to straight sodding, but rather than covering the lawn with sod, you will plant small plugs or blocks of sod at intervals. Because bare patches are left in the soil (which grass will eventually fill in), you will need less sod and the cost will be lower. The plugs are usually two-inch squares; the blocks are 12 inches square.

If you spot sod, prepare the ground as if you were straight sodding. Then, instead of laying the plugs or blocks on top of the soil, dig two- to three-inch-deep holes, one foot apart, and plant the plugs or blocks firmly in them. For quicker establishment, plant them closer.

Lawns

Strip sodding is a less expensive option. Instead of covering the entire lawn with sod, lay it in strips two to four inches wide leaving foot-wide bare strips in between. As the sod grows, it will fill in the bare strips. This process may take up to one year, however; the bare spots must be kept weed-free in the interim.

Sprigging
Planting individual plants, runners, cuttings, or stolons at regularly spaced intervals is called "sprigging." Set the plants or pieces in furrows three to four inches deep, at intervals determined by the species you are using and on how fast you want to establish a lawn. Sprigs of Bermudagrass, centipedegrass, and St. Augustine grass are usually planted 12 inches apart, while zoysia sprigs are placed six inches apart. Sprigs can also be planted end to end in rows, rather than at intervals.

Although these methods are faster and less expensive than sodding, they involve more work in the long run. You have to keep the bare areas free of weeds until the grass has filled in, which may be only a few weeks for Bermudagrass but up to two years for zoysias. The best tool for controlling weeds in the interim is the trusty hoe.

Reseeding
If you are confronted with a thin, weedy, disease-prone lawn, don't panic—you may not have to tear it up and start from scratch. Regular maintenance may eventually get it back into shape, and in the meantime you can sow an improved grass variety right over the existing lawn. If your lawn drains well and contains less than 25 percent weeds, reseeding is the way to go.

Most new grasses are so vigorous that they will eventually crowd out old, weaker grass. But the new seed must get off to a good start. Sowing time is critical; as with any lawn seeding, the best times are fall and early spring in the North, and spring and early summer in the South.

Preparing the Ground
Before you sow, you have to make the existing lawn receptive to the new seed. In small lawns, doing this will require no tools other than a metal garden rake and a lawn mower. First, mow the lawn closely, at half the normal mowing height and as low as half an inch, depending on the species of grass. Next, rake the lawn thoroughly and vigorously. Remove all the clippings, and as much thatch as you can. Expose and rough up as much soil as possible, and pull up or hoe out all the weeds you find.

If you are reseeding an area larger than 1,000 square feet, the work will go faster with a verticutter or a slice seeder, which you can rent at a tool shop. The verticutter resembles a lawn mower, but the blades are set vertically. It slices through the thatch and soil, exposing the soil and creating a good environment in which grass seed can germinate. Run the verticutter over the lawn in one direction, then run it back again in the opposite direction. A slice seeder is a more specialized piece of equipment that cuts through the sod and sows the seed at the same time.

Sowing the Seed

After you prepare the soil, it is time to plant. Because you are not sowing the seed into bare soil, you will have to spread the seed more thickly, or "over-seed." Use one and a half times the amount of seed recommended on the package. For example, perennial ryegrass is usually planted at a rate of four to six pounds per 1,000 square feet; for over-seeding, use six to nine pounds. Use a drop spreader, or sow the seed by hand, tossing it as you walk slowly over the lawn.

After sowing, rake the entire area lightly. Then top-dress the lawn with a thin layer of sand or topsoil. About half a cubic yard of soil should cover 1,000 square feet. Finally, water the lawn thoroughly, putting down at least an inch of water. Keep the lawn well watered, and stay off the over-seeded area until after grass has come up—some two to four weeks after planting.

Once the grass is up, don't mow until it has reached its maximum mowing height (two to four inches, depending on variety).

Rejuvenating Your Lawn

If your lawn looks a little shabby, you might be able to whip it into shape without replacing it or reseeding. But first, it is a good idea to take a close look at the lawn to find out what the problem is.

Thatch

The first sign of trouble to look for is thatch. Thatch is an impenetrable mat, mainly made up of roots, stolons, and rhizomes of grass plants that fail to decompose normally. Thick thatch prevents water from reaching the grass roots, and it harbors insects and diseases. By blocking light penetration, it also weakens the grass and prevents turf from spreading as it should.

To check your grass for thatch, take a walk on your lawn with a ruler in your hand. First, get a feel for the lawn under your feet. If it is springy rather than firm, or if your feet sink deeply into the turf, you should suspect thatch. Look down at the lawn. You should be able to see soil between the grass plants. If, instead, you see a layer of tan, strawlike organic matter, your lawn has thatch.

Once you have spotted the thatch, it is time to use the ruler. Measure the depth of the thatch. If it is less than one-quarter inch, it is not thick enough to cause any problems. If it is between one-quarter and one-half inch, it has the potential to become a problem.

Lawns

If it is more than one-half inch thick, it is time to do something about it.

How Thatch is Formed

To get rid of thatch and to keep it from coming back, it helps to know something about how it is formed. For years people have blamed grass clippings. The theory was that clippings settle into the lawn, turn brown, and become thatch. Within the past few years, however, turf researchers have exonerated clippings. Several research projects have shown that, in a properly managed lawn, clippings begin to decompose almost as soon as they hit the ground. By tracing nitrogen isotopes, scientists found that nitrogen from clippings shows up in new growth of grass within a week. In some situations, clippings can contribute to thatch—the clippings of bentgrass and red fescue, for example, are especially tough. If too much of the plant is cut at any one time, the long clippings that are left on the lawn will break down slowly, especially if the decomposition process is disrupted.

If thatch is not made of clippings, then what is it? Actually, it is the tougher parts of the grass plants—the stems, stolons, rhizomes, and roots. These wiry, fibrous parts are slower to break down than clippings. In a well-maintained lawn, with healthy soil, these grass parts will break down without forming thatch. Healthy soil is teeming with decomposers—microorganisms, such as fungi, bacteria, and actinomycetes; insects; and earthworms. Earthworms are particularly effective at converting green matter to humus. The presence of thatch is a sign that the decomposition system has broken down somehow. Most often poor maintenance practices cause the problem. If you mow too closely, you will cut off stems and stolons and leave excessively long clippings. Over-watering may drown out the soil's decomposers and drive out earthworms. But most commonly thatch is caused by the excessive use of chemical fertilizers and pesticides. Chemical fertilizers tend to acidify soil and chase out worms, which prefer a neutral pH. Insecticides and fungicides both make the soil inhospitable to microorganisms and earthworms. Tests of two popular fungicides have shown that after three years of applications, worms will no longer live in the soil.

Removing Thatch

If your lawn is plagued by thatch, you will have to develop a strategy to remove it and to keep it from coming back. Your plan will be a function of the size of your lawn and how much time and muscle you are willing to invest.

You can remove thatch manually with a heavy cavex, or thatch, rake. This tool has double-edged, crescent-shaped blades that slice through and pull up thatch. Pull the rake toward you, applying

A thatch problem calls for a thatch, or cavex, rake (D); a verticutter (E) will slice through the thatch and lift it to the surface. A core cultivator (A) can be used for general maintenance of properly aerated soil. A weed popper (C) comes in handy for pulling out weed roots, and a briar hook (B) lets you remove weeds without bending.

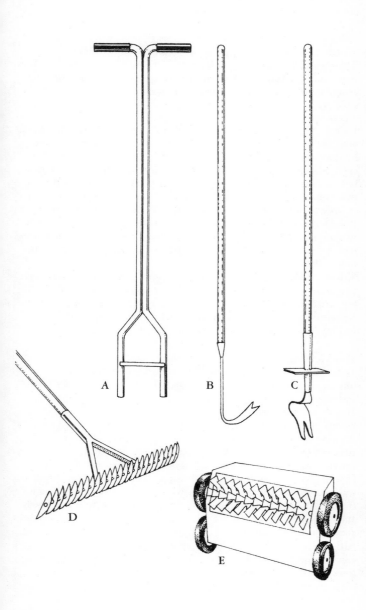

A

B

C

D

E

downward pressure; it will dislodge thatch and debris. Push the rake away from you to clean the thatch from the blades.

A thatch rake will do a good job on small lawns of up to 4,000 to 5,000 square feet. If your lawn is any larger, it pays to rent a gasoline-powered dethatcher, also known as a verticutter or vertimower. These machines operate like lawn mowers with vertical blades. As you guide the verticutter across the lawn, it will slice through the thatch and lift it to the surface, where you can rake it away.

Aerating

Using a gasoline-powered aerator or a manual core cultivator on your lawn, and then top-dressing it, will also remove thatch, and help to cure one of its causes—compacted, poorly drained soil. A core cultivator is a hand-and-foot-operated tool with two or four hollow tines. To operate it, push the tines into the turf and then lift the tool to pull up cores of sod, soil, and thatch. As you push the cultivator down again at the next spot, the cores will pop out of the tines and fall to the surface of the lawn. Continue across your lawn in this way until it is dotted with regularly spaced holes about three inches deep and half an inch in diameter. For large lawns, gasoline-powered aerators are available.

When the job is done, you will be left with soil cores scattered over the lawn. You can rake them up, or leave them in place and pulverize them—either with a rake, or by dragging a length of chainlink fence over them. Aerating revitalizes compacted soil, so you may wish to apply the technique even if you don't have thatch.

Top-dressing

To finish the aerating job, top-dress your lawn with a layer of topsoil, sand, or compost. The topdressing will seep into the holes and help to improve soil structure.

Top-dressing is a practice unfamiliar to most people, although it is widely employed by turf professionals. There is really no mystery to it. Top-dressing merely means spreading a thin layer of soil or compost over an existing lawn. Top-dressing improves the tilth, aeration, and drainage of the soil; and by adding organic matter or fresh topsoil to your lawn, top-dressing increases and encourages soil microorganisms and earthworms, both of which help to reduce thatch. As long as the topdressing material has not been sterilized, and especially if it contains ample organic matter, it will also contain microorganisms.

Although topsoil and sand are used most commonly for topdressing, several other materials will work, including finely screened compost, ground seaweed, rotted sawdust, well-rotted manure, and peat moss.

You don't need much to do the job. Using a fertilizer spreader, or broadcasting by hand, put down a layer no more than three-eighths inch thick over your entire lawn. About three-quarters of a cubic yard of topsoil will cover 1,000 square feet of lawn. The best time to top-dress is in the fall.

Repairing a Lawn

From time to time, even the healthiest lawn will show symptoms of wear, such as thin spots or bare patches. But before you reseed or repair, you should first determine what is causing the problem. You may need to spend time examining the trouble spot, then doing some detective work to decide why the problem has occurred.

The spot may be too wet because of a leaking hose or poor drainage. If you suspect drainage and compaction problems, dig a hole about a foot deep and fill it with water. The water should begin to drain out immediately, and it should be completely gone by the next day. If it is not, consider installing drain tiles.

Trouble spots can be the result of heavy foot traffic. If so, consider sowing a tougher grass, such as tall fescue, or eliminating turf in this area altogether and replacing it with a flagstone or brick walk.

Weak patches of grass may be caused by pockets of extremely sandy or clayey soil. Dig up the turf and analyze its texture according to the instructions in the chapter on soil preparation. If necessary, add organic matter and work it deeply—at least six inches—into the soil.

Your turf may be struggling in the shade, or in competition with tree roots. If so, replace the grass with a more shade-tolerant variety or ground cover.

Finally, determine if your own carelessness could have burned or harmed the grass. Did you spill gasoline, fertilizer, or an herbicide? If so, dig out the topsoil to a depth of six inches. Water the area well to leach the contaminant from the subsoil, then fill in the hole with fresh topsoil and replant.

Reseeding

After you have corrected the problem, it is time to sow. Seed selection is very important. You must choose a variety suited to the conditions, such as shade or traffic, and the new grass must match the surrounding turf. A patch of bentgrass in a Kentucky bluegrass lawn will stick out like a sore thumb.

To prepare the soil for sowing, dig up the bad patch and as much as six inches of the surrounding turf, removing all turf and weeds. Turn the soil to a depth of six inches, eliminating any remaining weeds and grass roots in the process. Then rake the surface well and water it thoroughly.

Spread the seed evenly at the rate recommended on the package, then cover it with a thin (about one-quarter-inch) layer of topsoil, and water. Keep the soil surface evenly moist until the grass is at least one inch high. Also, stay off the area, and don't mow it until

Lawns

the grass has reached its maximum recommended height. You will get the best results if you sow during the preferred planting time for your area—fall or early spring in the North, late spring or early summer in the South.

Mowing the Lawn

There is more to mowing than meets the eye, and its effects on grass are far greater than a mere change in appearance. Grass blades are, of course, connected to roots, and the state of the blades directly affects the state of the roots. The longer the blades, the longer the roots. Also, the grass blade is the photosynthetic surface where food, in the form of carbohydrates, is made. The less surface area a blade has, the less food it will produce. When the blades are kept cut short, or when you make a single drastic cut, the roots cannot grow to their optimum length. If you cut off too much of the blade, the roots may stop growing altogether and die back. This occurrence is a serious problem because grass plants with short, weak roots lack vigor. They are more susceptible to disease and are less able to survive on water deep in the soil when drought strikes.

When to Mow

Mowing causes a severe physical shock to the grass, no matter how high or low the cut. But there are times when the grass plant is better able to withstand the shock of mowing. When it is growing vigorously—in the spring and fall for northern grasses, and in the summer for southern grasses—the plant will bounce right back from the stress. But when times are tough, during heat and drought stress, the grass is not as well equipped to handle the damage inflicted by the mower.

It is therefore best to alter your mowing practices according to the season. Mow low during peak growth periods and high during periods of slow growth. Also, vary the frequency of your mowing according to growth rates. Naturally, you will mow more often during peak growth periods.

There is one general rule for cutting grass: Never take off more than one-third of the grass blade at any one time. If you are cutting your lawn to two inches, for example, mow it when it reaches three inches and no sooner.

Grass Height

There is no one right height for every lawn. Optimal mowing heights vary according to the time of year and the type of grass. Some grass types are naturally low-growing and do best when they are kept short. Let them grow long, and you will get thatch buildup, seedhead formation, and a poor appearance. Creeping and velvet bentgrasses, for example, do best at a height of about half an inch. Colonial bentgrass, Bermudagrass, carpetgrass, centipedegrass, blue grama grass, and zoysias should be cut to between one-half inch and two inches. A medium height of two to two and a half inches is best for buffalograss, creeping fescue, perennial ryegrass, and Chewings fescue. Grasses that should be kept high—between two and three inches—include bahiagrass, Kentucky bluegrass, and St. Augustine grass. Tall fescue can be topped out at a somewhat rangy four inches. (For a complete list of mowing heights, see the chart on pages 370–371.)

In general, most species of grass do best when they are allowed to grow a little longer than you are used to. If there is one piece of universal advice from the experts, it is mow high and mow often. Studies have shown that high and frequent mowing imparts the greatest vigor, making a healthier lawn with fewer weeds. Frequent mowing also means that the clippings are fairly short. If the soil is alive with microorganisms, these clippings will break down quickly and return nutrients to the soil.

Mowing Schedule

Here is a hypothetical schedule for Joe Mower, who cultivates a lawn of Kentucky bluegrass in Pennsylvania. As soon as the lawn has dried in the spring, he gets his mower out, adjusting it to remove about half an inch of the top growth. The lawn is still dormant at this point, but by mowing now he is removing the brown tips from the grass. He then rakes up the clippings, which he must do just this once to get rid of the dried tops. Then he sets the mower aside until the lawn has greened up and started growing actively. Joe knows that the best height for Kentucky bluegrass in the spring is two and a half inches, so he waits until the grass is three inches tall and cuts off half an inch.

Joe continues mowing to that height. He mows whenever the grass reaches three inches, no matter what day of the week. He also watches the weather. He knows that when the temperature reaches the 80s (°F) consistently, or when two weeks pass without rain, the growth of Kentucky bluegrass slows. In such conditions, he waits until the grass reaches three and a half to four inches, and cuts it back to three inches. Gradually, he finds that he is mowing less frequently until cooler weather signals the start of fall. As the grass begins another growth spurt, Joe returns to his spring mowing schedule until his grass has stopped growing altogether. Joe then services his lawn mower and puts it away for the winter.

Other cool-season grasses call for a similar mowing schedule; what will differ is the mowing height. For warm-season grasses, the same principles apply—cut higher during times of stress and more frequently during peak growth periods. But remember that for southern grasses, it is cool weather that causes stress, so in the early spring and late fall, you should let the grass grow a little longer. You should also raise the height of the mower if drought strikes during the mowing season.

Lawns

Power mowers like the one at left are popular and easy to use. The rotary blade sweeps through the grass, whacking off the blades. Many gardeners prefer to use an old-fashioned reel mower (right), either in a power style or a push style. The blades make a cleaner cut, with a scissoring action that is less damaging to grass.

Mower Types

If Joe Mower is like most of us, he uses a rotary mower, the mower of choice these days. Rotary mowers have plenty of advantages: They are easy to maintain; they can be adjusted to many heights; and they toss clippings off to the side, where they can be further chopped up with the next pass. The new mulching-type rotary mowers do an even better job of chopping clippings into fine particles.

A rotary mower is a simple machine. Its whirring blade chops the grass off—not so much slicing through the grass as whacking it. Nonetheless, a dull or nicked blade can leave the grass tattered and bruised. The result is a grayish lawn. For best results, the blade should be sharpened about once a month.

A reel mower cuts grass more kindly. The scissoring action of the blades makes a cleaner cut, damaging less of the grass blade and thus leaving a smaller area open to transpiration in hot weather. But reel mowers are not for every gardener, or for every lawn. They will cut low, but they have trouble with anything longer than two inches or with grasses that send up tall seedheads, such as bahiagrass and St. Augustine grass. They also cannot cut tough grasses, such as ryegrass, cleanly. Tough, stalky weeds, such as plantain, are also troublesome to reel mowers. Finally, reel mowers can be cranky machines, requiring repeated adjustments to keep the blades aligned properly.

Whatever mower you use, be sure to overlap the previous swath of the mower by one-third its width to make a clean cut. Change the pattern of your mowing occasionally, too, to prevent the wheels from making permanent ruts in your lawn.

Watering

When it comes to watering, many people are guilty of killing their lawns with kindness. It is true that grass needs as much as an inch or two of water per week to grow. But in many parts of the country, mother nature does a good job of watering. There are some regions where nature needs some help. The amount needed varies, however, depending on many factors.

Watering According to Soil Type

The first variable affecting water needs is the soil type. Think of the soil under your lawn as a water reservoir. Its capacity is determined by the soil type. Clay soils can store up to two and a half inches of water per foot. So, a typical clay lawn that requires an inch of water per week can survive for more than two weeks on the moisture in its reservoir if the soil is saturated to start with. Loamy soil holds one and a half inches of moisture per foot of depth, while sandy soil holds only three-quarters of an inch per foot. Clearly, a lawn planted in sand will need watering much more frequently than one planted in clay.

How to Water

You should think of watering as refilling the reservoir, rather than sprinkling the grass. The worst thing you can do to your lawn is to give it frequent sprinklings of water. The grass plants won't put down deep roots. Instead, the roots will stay in the top layer of soil, where they can find plenty of water. If the water supply is cut off, the roots will dry out quickly and the plants will surely wilt, and perhaps die.

The trick is to water deeply when you water at all, and to water only when the grass absolutely needs it—when the water reservoir is just about dry. You will know your lawn needs water when it begins to wilt, when the blades turn dull, and when the turf won't spring back. If you want to get water to the grass before it wilts, you can check the level of the reservoir. Dig up a patch of sod. (You'll be able to replace it later without damage.) Look at how deep the roots grow, then check the soil for moisture. If it feels damp to the touch, you can put off watering. But if the soil is bone-dry, it is time to get out the hose and sprinkler.

Sprinklers

When you irrigate a lawn, you should always water slowly so that the water has time to seep into the soil without running off the surface. Use a sprinkler with a low flow rate (less than one-quarter inch per hour), and let it run until is has put down at least an inch of water. You can gauge the amount of water your sprinkler is delivering by placing a number of coffee cans around the lawn as the sprinkler is running, then measuring the height of water in the cans.

Several types of lawn sprinklers are available. Revolving sprinklers are inexpensive, but they don't cover much ground, and their coverage is uneven. Fixed sprinklers usually can be adjusted to water different-shaped areas, from circles to squares. However, their coverage area is limited, too. Oscillating sprinklers irrigate rectangular patterns, and can be adjusted to spray to only one side. Many cover unevenly, and water may puddle up near the ends of the arc. Impulse sprinklers water circular areas with a reliable and even coverage rate. (For more information on in-ground systems, see the chapter on watering your plants.)

There are alternatives to sprinkling. In the North, most grasses will survive a summer without water by going dormant. They may stop growing, and even turn brown, but once the weather cools and the rain returns in the fall, they will come back to life. In the South, Bermudagrass is relatively drought-tolerant. Buffalograss, blue grama grass, and wheatgrass are even more so. (For more on drought-tolerant lawn alternatives, consult *Taylor's Guide to Water-Saving Gardening*.)

Fertilizing

Because the lawn is not a natural system, like a meadow or a prairie, it needs a little help from its friends to survive—specifically, regular feedings. By applying fertilizer with adequate macronutrients—nitrogen, phosphorus, potassium, calcium, magnesium, and sulfur—as well as micronutrients, such as iron, manganese, and zinc, you will help the roots store a good supply of carbohydrates to fuel the growth of the plant.

Grass that doesn't get enough fertilizer grows slowly and sparsely. It loses the battle against weeds that thrive under low fertility, such as plantain. Under-fertilized grass generally is less vigorous, and more vulnerable to damage from insects, disease, and drought. However, over-fertilized grass has problems as well. If you apply too much high-nitrogen, water-soluble fertilizer, roots stay near the soil surface. If you then stop fertilizing, the plant is ill-equipped to survive on its own. Heavy fertilization can also encourage some diseases and inhibit beneficial soil microbes. It's best to use a relatively low-analysis, slow-acting fertilizer that will provide the plant with a steady supply of food rather than a big jolt of nutrients.

When to Fertilize

Turf scientists are now concluding that we feed our lawns too much. The established lawn routine has been to pour on fertilizer spring, summer, and fall. As a result, the lawn grows fast and so do the weeds.

Grass grows best when it receives a slow, steady supply of fertilizer. How much and when depends on the type of grass and the climate. In the North, most turfgrasses can get by with one or two applications of a slow-acting fertilizer annually. In the South, grass grows best with two or three small doses during the growing season.

In the North, the best time to fertilize is September or October. The roots of the grass plant grow well into the autumn, actually continuing after top growth stops. If a grass plant is fertilized in the fall, its roots can store enough carbohydrates to get the plant off to a good start in the spring. Moreover, since annual weeds are gearing down in the fall, the fertilizer does them no good. What is more, if you fertilize the grass in fall, you won't have to feed it in the spring when weeds are hungry and can take advantage of that free food. Alternatively, instead of a one-shot feeding in the fall, you can give northern grass a half-dose in the spring (May or June) and another in the fall.

Fertilizing techniques in the South are different. Warm-season grasses are active photosynthesizers in the heat of summer, and are natural summer feeders. Their requirements vary more than do

Lawns

those of northern grasses. Some varieties can do quite well with two feedings, one in early summer, perhaps June, and one in late summer, around August. Others need feeding every month. But again, the more frequent the feedings, the smaller the dose of fertilizer required.

How Much Fertilizer to Use
Different types of grass need different amounts of fertilizer. Bahiagrass, bentgrass, centipedegrass, and St. Augustinegrass are all heavy feeders, requiring two to four pounds of actual nitrogen for each 1,000 square feet per year. Bermudagrass, Kentucky bluegrass, carpetgrass, perennial ryegrass, and zoysias are moderate feeders, requiring two to three pounds of nitrogen per 1,000 square feet annually. Light feeders, which need only one to two pounds of nitrogen per 1,000 square feet per year, include buffalograss, fine fescue, and tall fescue.

Most bags of fertilizer are labeled with recommendations for application rates; these are usually based on a high-fertility regime. In order to convert them to a low-fertility schedule, you will have to do a little figuring. First, you will need to determine the actual amount of active ingredients in the bag.

Actual nitrogen, for example, is the part of the fertilizer that is made up of nitrogen. It's listed as a percentage; 20-10-5 on a bag means that the mixture inside contains 20 percent nitrogen, 10 percent phosphorus, and five percent potash. Thus, a 100-pound bag of this fertilizer would contain 20 pounds of actual nitrogen. That's enough to cover 10,000 square feet if you're feeding at a rate of two pounds per 1,000 square feet.

What about the other numbers? Nitrogen is the key nutrient for grass, but phosphorus and potash are important too. Phosphorus helps young grass establish itself vigorously. As the grass matures, this nutrient aids in root growth. Potassium makes turf tougher and increases a grass's resistance to cold, disease, drought, and heat. It doesn't take much of either to do the trick—about half a pound of potassium per 1,000 square feet, and one pound of potash for the same area.

Fertilizer Types
Once you have decided how much fertilizer to use, you must select the type. Turf fertilizers come in many different forms: They may be liquid or granular; fast-acting or slow release; synthetic or natural.

Liquid fertilizers are fast-acting. They contain water-soluble nitrogen, and therefore they go right to work greening up your lawn. But they also run out of steam quickly. Liquid fertilizers tend to be a here-today-gone-tomorrow proposition, and at their worst they may be gone today. Many of the nutrients may leach out of the soil before the roots can make use of them. A lawn fed with liquid fertilizers will become hooked on that quick fix and will require repeated applications throughout the year.

It's better to follow the old gardening principle of feeding the soil instead of the plant. For that, you'll want to use dry fertilizers. But not all dry fertilizers are created equal. Some are nearly as fast-acting, and as quick to disappear, as are liquid fertilizers. Check the analysis on the back of the bag. It will tell you what percentage of the nitrogen is water-soluble and what percentage is insoluble. The higher the percentage of water-soluble nitrogen in the fertilizer, the less staying power it will have. Insoluble nitrogen, which isn't actually insoluble at all, is released more slowly through chemical reactions in the soil.

Slow-release synthetic fertilizers include brands called Osmocote and IBDU. Natural fertilizers, such as dehydrated chicken manure, Milorganite, or one of the many new natural blends are good too.

Applying Fertilizer

You can fertilize your lawn by hand, but to achieve an even application without streaking, it pays to use either a drop spreader or a rotary spreader. Rotary spreaders broadcast the fertilizer in a circular pattern as you push them across the lawn and will cover more ground than a drop spreader, but they are less precise. Since precision is important when you are cutting back on fertilizer, it pays to use a drop spreader. Most are equipped with controls that allow you to vary the rate of application. You will need to calibrate your spreader according to the type of fertilizer you are using. Most chemical fertilizers and some organic fertilizers have spreader-setting guidelines on the bag. For Milorganite, for example, you're instructed to set the spreader at number 10.

With many fertilizers, however, you are on your own. You will have to calibrate the spreader yourself in order to apply the proper amount of fertilizer.

First, determine the amount of actual nitrogen you want to spread per 1,000 square feet. Convert that to pounds of fertilizer. If you intend to apply one pound of nitrogen per 1,000 square feet, for example, and you're using composted chicken manure with an analysis of 4-4-2, you'll need 25 pounds. Now, mark off a 1,000-square-foot area on your lawn.

Fill the spreader with more fertilizer than you need—double the amount, if the spreader will hold it. In this case, put 50 pounds of chicken manure in the spreader hopper, set the selector at the lowest setting, and push the spreader over the marked-off area, walking at a normal pace.

When you have finished, determine how much fertilizer you've used. If you have used it all without covering the marked-off area, then you will have to push the spreader faster, to lessen the dose

Lawns

next time. If there is fertilizer remaining in the hopper, weigh it. If you have 25 pounds left, then you have used 25 pounds—exactly the right amount. If you have applied less, go over the marked-off area again until you have applied 25 pounds. Now mark off another 1,000-square-foot area, fill the hopper, set the spreader gate wider, and try again. This time you should be closer to having a perfectly calibrated spreader.

When you use a drop spreader, make sure to overlap each pass slightly so that you don't leave any unfertilized spots. Don't stop the spreader without first closing the gate.

Here are a couple of fertilizing schedules for common lawn grasses in the North and South, using a 10-10-10 fertilizer. Use them as models, varying the amount of fertilizer according to the nitrogen needs of your grass type (refer to the chart on page 370). The listed rates are all based on an area of 1,000 square feet.

For a northern Kentucky bluegrass lawn, apply 20 pounds of fertilizer in the fall, after the grass has stopped growing actively—in September or October, depending on your climate. If you didn't have a chance to fertilize in the fall, apply 10 pounds in the spring, and 10 pounds again in the fall.

For a southern lawn of Bermudagrass, apply 10 pounds every month from May through August.

Weeding

When it comes to weeds, many gardeners automatically reach for the herbicide. If your aim is a completely weed-free lawn you may not have any other choice. But if you are willing to settle for a few weeds, there are ways to grow a good-looking lawn without introducing the risks of chemical weed killers to your property. One of the best methods involves a good dose of old-fashioned elbow

---

Guidelines for Growing a Disease-free Lawn
- Grow the proper type of grass, preferably a variety resistant to diseases common in your area.
- Reduce shade and increase airflow by pruning trees and shrubs.
- Correct compacted or poorly drained soil.
- Top-dress with an organically rich material, such as compost or manure.
- Fertilize lightly.
- Water only when necessary.
- Mow regularly.
- Don't mow or walk over areas that show disease symptoms.

grease. Many gardeners who spend hours weeding or hoeing their vegetable gardens and flower borders never think of weeding their lawns too. But it can be done. The trick is to remove as much of the weed and its root as possible, while disturbing as little of the lawn, as you can. Several long-handled lawn weeding tools enable you to do this without crawling around on your hands and knees. A weed popper has sharp tines for digging under weeds and a spring-loaded foot pedal that propels the weeds, roots and all, out of the ground. A claw weeder grabs the roots below ground level as you pull the weed up. A long-handled asparagus knife will let you cut off the weeds at the roots, then pull them out easily. Long-handled shears can be used to cut off annual weeds before they set seeds.

When weeding, remember that weeds are vigorous invaders. They will take advantage of every opportunity to colonize a bare spot on the lawn. So, after you pull a weed, you must replace it with grass. It is a good idea to carry around a bag of topsoil and some grass seed as you weed. When a weed comes out, fill in the divot with soil, then seed it immediately with grass.

Keeping Weeds Out

General practices can also aid in weed control. The best defense against weeds is a vigorous lawn. If your lawn is thick and healthy, weeds won't have room to make any inroads. Also, switching to a lighter fertilizing schedule will go a long way to ridding your lawn of weeds. Even how and when you mow can have a major effect. A high-growing lawn will shade low-growing weeds, thus weakening them. Shade will also discourage weed seeds from germinating.

Weed Types

For specific controls, it helps to know a little bit about the nature of weeds. Like grass, there are several types—cool-season, warm-season, annual, perennial, broad leaved, and grassy. You can design a weed-control strategy based on the habits of the invader.

The best way to handle cool-season annuals, such as annual bluegrass, chickweed, henbit, and prostrate knotweed, is to remove the weeds early in the year before seedheads appear. Mow high in spring and fall in the North and high in late summer in the South.

Cool-season perennials include quackgrass, plantain, dandelion, and ground ivy. The best way to remove them is by raking them up early in the year.

Crabgrass, foxtail, purslane, and spurge are all warm-season annuals. To keep them under control, mow high during summer, and remove clippings when seedheads are present.

Warm-season perennials include Dallisgrass, nimbelweed, nutsedge, and Bermudagrass (which can be a weed when it springs

Lawn Weeds I: Cool-Season Perennials

Plantain

The best way to control the growth of plantain (*Plantago* spp.) in the lawn is to rake the plants out in early spring. Plantain spreads by seeds; if it becomes established, you may have to resort to using a chemical; the recommended treatment is 2,4-D, sold as Dacamine and Weedone.

Dandelion

One or two pretty yellow flowers may be tolerable in your lawn, but it is best not to let these familiar weeds get too strong a hold. If you mow them, be sure to do so before the yellow flowers turn to white, fluffy seed heads. Some people may wish to apply a formulation of 2,4-D, as for plantain.

Ground Ivy

A pretty, blue-flowered ground cover in the right situation, *Glechoma hederacea* can be a pest in lawns, thriving on rich, damp soil and spreading by runners or seeds. Pull it up if you want your lawn to be a smooth expanse of green. If you allow it to remain, be careful not to let it encroach on shrubs or flower beds, where it can do serious damage.

Quackgrass

Also called witchgrass, couch grass, and quick grass, this species (*Agropyron repens*) can be troublesome, especially in the North. It spreads by persistent stolons and by seeds; if your lawn is invaded, try applying glyphosate (also useful against Johnson grass, *Sorghum halapense*). A black plastic mulch over the area may also work.

Yellow Nutsedge

Also called nutgrass, yellow nutsedge (*Cyperus esculentus*) can be troublesome—although in certain parts of the world it is grown as a food crop. If you decide to use an herbicide, try bentazon (Basagran); apply in late July, repeating 10 days to 2 weeks later if needed.

Bermudagrass

Important as a lawn and pasture grass in many parts of the South, Bermudagrass (*Cynodon dactylon*) is sometimes a pest in other situations. If you wish to eradicate it, the best herbicidal remedy is to apply spot treatments of dalapon (sold as Basfapon B); read the label directions carefully.

Nimbleweed

Nimbleweed, or nimble Will (*Muhlenbergia schreberi*), is a fairly important forage grass in some parts of the continent, but when it appears in lawns it can be unsightly. It grows to 3-feet tall and often flops over, rooting again where it hits the ground. To eradicate, mow high in summer, dig out clumps, and withhold water and fertilizer.

Dallisgrass

Another warm-season perennial grass that can be an eyesore, dallisgrass (*Paspalum dilatatum*) is related to Bahiagrass (*P. notatum*). Like nimbleweed, it is best eradicated by digging and mowing high in summer.

Lawn Weeds III: Warm-Season Annuals

Crabgrass

The stiff rosettes of crabgrass are a familiar and unwelcome sight in lawns everywhere. Once established, crabgrass is very difficult to eradicate; the best treatment is to be sure your lawn has no bare spots where this weed can get a purchase. When it appears, dig it up before it sets seed, or you will have to apply a heavy treatment of herbicides.

Prostrate Spurge

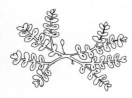

This annual (*Euphorbia supina*) is extremely adaptable, appearing not only in lawns and gardens but also in waste places with thin, poor, gravelly soil. It spreads by seeds so it should be dug before seeds set; if you use an herbicide, experts may recommend dicamba. Follow directions carefully.

Foxtail

This annual (*Alopecurus* spp.) may appear during the warm weather. To keep it under control, mow high during the summer months and be certain to remove all grass clippings if the weeds bear seedheads at the time of mowing.

Purslane

Portulaca oleracea spreads readily by seed, especially in places with freshly tilled soil—such as a new lawn. It stores water in its leaves, making it drought tolerant and likely to reappear and reestablish itself after it has been pulled. If you use an herbicide, experts will recommend 2,4-D.

Annual Bluegrass

Annual Bluegrass (*Poa annua*) can be extremely tough to eradicate. When mowing a lawn where it is present, be sure to capture all the seedheads in a grass catcher, or to carefully rake up all clippings. Some gardeners may wish to use a herbicide such as bensulide on very tough problems.

Chickweed

Chickweed (*Stellaria media*) is a fast-growing, fast-spreading annual that will adapt to a wide variety of situations. It spreads by stolons and by seeds (which are produced all season long); but it can be fairly easily pulled from the ground when it appears. Some gardeners may wish to control it with postemergent applications of mecoprop or dicamba.

Henbit

This plant (*Lamium amplexicaule*) may grow as an annual or a biennial; it spreads by means of rooting stems as well as by seeds. Dig henbit and other cool-season annuals early in the year, before the seedheads appear. In the North, mow high in spring and fall; in the South, mow high in late summer.

Prostrate Knotweed

As the name suggests, prostrate knotweed (*Polygonum aviculare*) is a flat-growing plant. It spreads chiefly by seeds, and if you find that your lawn is badly infested you may wish to try a treatment of herbicides; experts will recommend dicamba or mecoprop.

Common Diseases and Their Symptoms

Here is a short list of some common grass diseases along with notes on what they look like:

•**Brown patch:** Dark or water-soaked patches that turn brown.
•**Dollar spot:** Round, bleached-out spots about the size of a silver dollar.
•**Red thread:** Red threads of fungus that extend from grass blades; grass often affected in circular patches up to two feet in diameter.
•**Pythium blight:** Circular spots of dark, water-soaked grass, growing together to form large irregular clusters.
•**Powdery mildew:** Small patches of white or gray fungus on grass blades.
•**Melting out:** Tan spots with reddish-brown borders.
•**Rust:** Rust-colored spores on grass blades.
•**Stripe smut:** Yellow or brown grass with dark stripes on the blades.
•**Fusarium blight:** Patches two to six inches in diameter turning brown, then tan and yellow.
•**Summer Patch:** Patches of dead grass mixed with live plants.

If your lawn shows any of these symptoms consult an expert about control measures.

up amid other types of turf grass). To control them, mow high in summer, dig out clumps of weeds, and refrain from watering and fertilizing.

Lawn Pests

Insects are rarely serious problems in a healthy lawn. Occasionally, an infestation will require treatment, but before you spray or take any other action, make sure you know exactly what is causing the damage. You will have to do some scouting and take a close look at your lawn to find the culprit. Some lawn pests, such as aphids, mites, and cutworms, are familiar enemies to anyone who grows flowers or vegetables. (For control suggestions, see the chapter on pest management.) Other pests are specific to lawns.

Lawn pests may attack from either underground or above ground. Grubs, for example, attack from below. A common symptom of grub infestation is the incursion of patches of brown grass that you can easily pull up. To check for grubs, dig up a square foot of sod in a suspect area. Turn it over and hunt for grubs, which will appear as white or brown larvae, usually with legs, one-half to one inch long. If you find three or four in the sample, you probably won't need to take any action. If you find more, however, they have exceeded the damage threshold, and it is time to control them. Milky-spore bacteria are effective against Japanese-beetle grubs. Neem or beneficial nematodes can be used against other grubs.

Chinch bugs are lawn pests throughout the country. The adults are one-sixteenth inch long, and are orange or brown. The pinhead-size nymphs do most of the damage, though. If your grass is turning yellow and dying off in patches, you've probably got a problem with chinch bugs. To check, cut both ends off of a coffee can and press one end firmly into the grass. Fill the can with water. If chinch bugs are present, they will float to the surface of the water. If you find more than 20 bugs in the can, it is time to take action. Dust the lawn with sabadilla, a natural insecticide, or use *Beauveria bassiana,* a fungus that infects the pests.

Sod webworms are especially fond of Kentucky bluegrass, as well as the fescues, bentgrass, and zoysia grass. When feeding, they leave irregular brown spots of thin turf. Use a flashlight to check the lawn at night, looking for small larvae with brown heads and brown spots on their bodies. If you find more than 15 per square yard, spray the lawn with insecticidal soap or *Bacillus thuringiensis.*

Billbugs are one-quarter to one-half inch long with a long snout that ends in a set of mandibles. They are usually brown or gray. It isn't the adult bugs that damage a lawn—that task goes to the legless grubs, which are just over half an inch long. White with yellow-brown heads, the grubs emerge in late spring to early summer and feed on grass stems, causing the shoots to turn brown and die. Ten billbug larvae per square foot of lawn can do enough damage to warrant control. Rotenone will kill both the adults and the grubs.

Mole crickets are light brown, an inch and a half long, and commonly found along the southern Atlantic and Gulf coasts. The crickets eat grass roots, and they also disrupt the soil with their tunnels. They can be controlled with the bacteria *Bacillus popilliae,* which is sold as Doom or Milky Spore.

For insecticidal control, consult your extension agent and follow guidelines on packages. Keep in mind that pesticides may be harmful to birds and other wildlife as well as to people.

Lawn Diseases

Disease diagnosis and cure are the most mysterious aspects of lawn care. There are scores of common grass diseases, and all but one (St. Augustine decline virus) are caused by fungi. Many have symptoms so similar that only a plant pathologist can make a definitive identification. Some, however, are easy to spot. And there are some general preventive steps anyone can take to keep a lawn free of disease.

Where do lawn diseases come from? Pathogenic fungi that cause diseases are always present in the soil, but they are not always

Lawn Pests

Grubs

Grubs are detected by patches of brown grass that are easily dislodged. These pests may be brown or white and are generally 1/2–1-inch long. Treat serious infestations with beneficial nematodes or Neem; for Japanese-beetle grubs, use milky-spore bacteria.

Billbug

Just 1/4–1/2-inch long, billbugs are brown or gray with a long snout that ends in a pair of mandibles. The presence of the adult is an indicator that you may have larvae as well; the grubs, which damage lawns, should be treated with rotenone.

Sod Webworm

Using a flashlight, check your lawn at night for infestations of the larvae of this insect. Sod webworm larvae are particularly partial to Kentucky bluegrass. They have brown heads and brown spots on the body. Treat with insecticidal soap or *Bacillus thuringiensis*.

Mole Cricket

Common along the Atlantic and Gulf coasts, mole crickets eat grass roots and disrupt soil by making tunnels. They are 1-1/2-inches long and pale brown. Control them with *Bacillus popilliae*, which is sold under the trade names of Doom and Milky Spore.

Chinch Bug

Found everywhere in North America, chinch bugs are tiny but pestilential. The adults are orange-brown and just 1/16-inch long; the even smaller nymphs will turn your grass yellow in patches. Treat chinch bugs with a dusting of sabadilla (a natural pesticide) or with *Beauveria bassiana*, a fungus that attacks chinch bugs.

active enough to cause damage; other factors also may hold them in check. Most diseases are triggered by poor practices that allow pathogens to get the upper hand. These practices may include improper fertilization, irrigation, or mowing. Diseases may also result from excessive use of insecticides, herbicides, and even fungicides. The primary cause of disease, however, is trying to grow the wrong type of grass in the wrong place.

Growing a grass type in an unsuitable environment—a warm-season grass in a cool area, a water-loving grass in a dry climate, or a delicate grass in a heavily trafficked area—will cause stress to the grass, and stress invites disease. If you have a disease problem, look first at the grass type you're growing. If you need to replace it, take heart: New grass varieties are likely to be much more disease resistant. From 'Midnight Kentucky' bluegrass, which resists leafspot and melting out, to 'Reliant' fine fescue, which resists powdery mildew, there is a type and variety immune to nearly every disease. If you are shopping for grass, it pays to go with the new, named varieties that carry disease resistance.

Treating Diseases

Whether your lawn is old or new, there are ways to handle diseases. First, go easy on the chemicals. Countless studies have shown that a fungicide applied to cure one disease opens the gates for others. The reason is that fungicides (and to some degree herbicides and insecticides too) damage beneficial organisms in the soil. Healthy soil is teeming with fungi, bacteria, and actinomycetes that work to keep the pathogens in check. For a disease-free lawn you should seek to keep the soil alive with these fighters. Cutting down on chemicals will help. You can also increase the life of the soil by fertilizing or top-dressing with manure or compost.

If your lawn looks poor, don't blame disease right off the bat. While diseases generally occur as patches, rings, or spots of discolored grass, there can be other causes of such symptoms, including dog damage, herbicide burning, spilled gasoline or other chemicals, poor drainage, and compacted soils. Make sure you check for all of these first.

If you can find no other probable cause, it is time to consult a professional—your extension agent, a local garden center, or a lawn-service representative. The expert will need a lot of information to make a correct diagnosis. Make sure you have the answers to the following questions: What type of grass is affected? What are the symptoms and when did they first appear? Have the symptoms changed over time? If so, how? Has the area changed shape or grown larger? Do the grass blades in the area look striped or show patterns or lesions? Is the area in sun or shade? The more accurate and complete your answers, the better the chance that the expert will make a correct diagnosis and recommend the proper cure.

Lawns

Undoubtedly, the best course of action is to maintain the vigor of your lawn so that diseases cannot get a foothold.

Growing a Lawn in Shade

A lawn that is too shady is especially prone to disease. However, it is possible to grow a healthy lawn in the shade if you do it correctly right from the start. First, make sure the soil is fertile and well drained, and remove all perennial weed roots from the top six inches of the soil. Then plant a suitable type of grass. In general, fescues handle the shade best. 'Rebel' tall fescue, 'Jamestown Chewings' fescue, and 'Fortress' red fescue are good varieties. Kentucky bluegrass is not a good shade grass, but some varieties of it—'A-34' and 'Nugget'—for example, are better than most. If you insist on using Kentucky bluegrass, mix it with red fescue at a rate of 70 percent fescue to 30 percent bluegrass.

Once the grass is up, you must care for it differently than if it were growing in full sun. Grass growing in the shade has less light available for photosynthesis, of course. But you can increase the photosynthetic activity per plant by increasing the area of each plant. In other words, let the grass grow longer. Allow grass in shady areas to grow up to one inch higher than the same grass in sunny spots.

For the same reason, grass in the shade needs more fertilizer. Since it cannot manufacture as much of its own food (due to the decrease in photosynthesis), a little extra fertilizer will help keep it healthy. Grass in shady areas often must compete with the trees and shrubs casting the shade for nutrients and water. A little more water is called for, but don't water in the evening, when the grass will stay wet and provide a breeding ground for disease. To lessen the chance of disease, it helps to increase air circulation by pruning trees and shrubs whenever possible.

Alternatives to Lawn Grasses

In most cases, grass is an ideal ground cover. It spreads rapidly, knitting the soil in place with thick roots and stolons. It is inexpensive, comparatively free of insects and diseases, and requires little care other than mowing. There are situations, however, in which lawn grass is not the answer for covering the ground. Consider alternatives for spots that are too dry, too wet, or too steep to mow.

Drought-tolerant Gardens

Lawns use a lot of water, perhaps too much for the driest areas of the country. In such regions, you can replace traditional lawn grasses with more drought-tolerant types. Buffalograss and blue grama grass are drought-tolerant warm-season grasses. They can get by on less than half the water that other common grasses require. In cooler areas, tall fescue and red fescue are the most drought-tolerant types of grasses.

You can also do away with grass entirely. In the Southwest, a new school of designers is creating spectacular landscapes using only native plants, stone mulch, paths, and soil itself as a landscape element.

Use your imagination. Combine drought-tolerant ornamental grasses, such as Red Switch grass (*Panicum virgatum*) with drought-tolerant ground covers, such as sedum, and plenty of mulch. Japanese-style gardens are naturals for dry areas. They take a minimalist approach to landscaping, with areas of sand, carefully raked into patterns and dotted with artfully chosen and placed stones. Coniferous shrubs or trees provide a touch of green.

For an extensive selection of drought-tolerant ground covers and other plants, consult *Taylor's Guide to Water-Saving Gardening*. Here is a short list of some of the best ground covers for dry areas:

•Achillea, or common yarrow (*Achillea millefolium*)—A semi-evergreen, creeping plant with gray-green foliage, and flowers ranging in color from white to yellow to pink; grows quickly. Zones 3–10.

•Artemisia (*Artemisia ludoviciana*)—Gray-green foliage; grows to three feet tall with grayish-white flowers; grows moderately. Zones 5–9.

•Juniper (*Juniperus* spp.)—Coniferous evergreen genus with many creeping species and foliage ranging in color from yellow-green to near-blue; grows slowly. Zones 3–9.

•Lantana (*Lantana* spp.)—Herbaceous plant with textured green leaves and bright orange, red, or purple flowers; grows moderately fast. Zones 8–10.

•Sedum, or stonecrop (*Sedum* spp.)—Succulent plant with green leaves on trailing stems and yellow or pink flowers; spreads moderately fast. Zones 4–10.

•Thyme (*Thymus praecox*)—Evergreen, small-leaved plant with purple, white, or red flowers; spreads moderately fast. Zones 3–9.

General Purpose Ground Covers

Even if drought isn't a problem in your area, you may want to shrink your lawn by planting ground covers along its edges, around trees and buildings, and in spots where grass doesn't grow well, such as on slopes, or in shady or wet areas.

Following is a list of some good, general-purpose ground covers. Check *Taylor's Guide to Ground Covers, Vines & Grasses* for more options.

•Crown vetch (*Coronilla varia*)—Finely cut, light-green leaves with pink to white flowers; blooms in summer; grows well on banks and slopes; spreads rapidly. Zones 4–9.

•Green-and-gold (*Chrysogonum virginiar.im*)—Rich green, oval leaves and bright yellow flowers blooming from spring until fall; grows to 10 inches high and spreads rapidly, especially in rich, moist soils. Zones 5–9.

•Hosta (*Hosta* spp.)—Broad leaves in many shades of green, some variegated; grows well in shade; spreads slowly. Zones 3–9.

•Ivy (*Hedera* spp.)—Evergreen vines with rich, shiny leaves; grows well in both shade and sun and performs well on steep slopes; spreads rapidly. Zones 3–9.

•Lily-of-the-valley (*Convallaria majalis*)—Broad, green foliage and white, bell-shaped flowers; blooms in spring; spreads rapidly in shady areas. Zones 4–9.

•Lily-turf (*Liriope* spp.)—A clumping grassy plant with upright clusters of white, blue, or violet flowers; spreads moderately fast; tolerates sun or shade. Zones 5–10.

•Pachysandra (*Pachysandra* spp.)—Rosettes of dark green leaves, with inconspicuous white flowers; thrives in shade and competes well with tree roots; spreads moderately fast. Zones 3–9.

•Vinca minor (*Vinca minor*)—Dark green, glossy foliage on a low-growing, creeping perennial; blue-violet flowers in spring; tolerates moist soils; spreads slowly. Zones 5–9.

Meadows and Prairies

Some people are getting back to original landscapes by planting wildflower meadows and prairies. While they take much less mowing than do lawns, they are not entirely a no-work alternative. Establishing a wildflower meadow or prairie involves more than just throwing a handful of flower seeds on the lawn and watching them burst into bloom. You have to do some preparation to get good germination and coverage, and once the growth is established, you have to maintain it and mow it regularly, though infrequently, to help encourage the flowers.

The most foolproof way to turn a small patch of lawn into meadow or a prairie is to start with flower transplants, either homegrown or store-bought. Mark out your area, mow it as closely as possible, then use a bulb planter or a trowel to dig up patches of sod for the plants. Arrange the plants in a random pattern, clumping groups of the same plants together in some areas.

For larger areas, seed is the only economical way to go. But you cannot merely broadcast it over an existing lawn and expect a meadow to pop up. You will have to prepare the area first. Again, mow as closely as possible. There are several ways to work up the planting area. Rent a sod verticutter, which will slice the sod and expose soil for planting. Or, rototill shallowly, so that the lawn isn't turned under but a good amount of soil is exposed. Or use a metal rake, scratching the lawn deeply to expose soil.

Once the soil has been exposed broadcast seed over the entire area. Then, top-dress with a one-quarter-inch layer of topsoil or finely screened compost, and water it well. Meadows and prairies should be mowed occasionally, perhaps two or three times a year, to reduce shading and help flowers in their competition with the grasses. It's best to mow early in spring, late in fall, and, perhaps, in mid-summer if there is a lull in blossoming.

Here are some recommended plants for meadows and prairies in various areas of the country:

• West—Clarkia, primrose, California poppy, yarrow, blue flax.
• Midwest—Cornflower, coreopsis, purple coneflower, corn poppy, Indian blanket.
• East—Bachelor's button, coreopsis, primrose, corn poppy, black-eyed Susan.
• South—Purple coneflower, Indian blanket, phlox, California poppy, tansy.

Whether you desire a traditional close-cut lawn, or are willing to settle for a more laid-back look, you can take control of your own turf. The key is to treat your lawn as a growing, changing part of your landscape, just as you would a perennial border or a vegetable bed. Introduce improved grass varieties when possible. Vary your mowing, fertilizing, and watering according to the season. Investigate and experiment with cultural controls of weeds, insects and diseases. When problems arise, try to deduce the cause. Chances are good that you'll be able to solve it yourself. And with just a little bit of care, you'll find it's easy to have a healthy, good-looking lawn.

Frost Date Map

This map is based on freeze data tabulations made by the United States Weather Bureau.

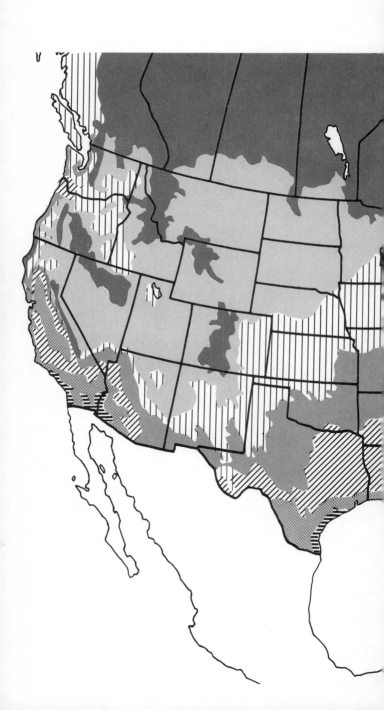

The key below shows the average dates of the last spring frost and the average length of the growing season in seven frost zones. The growing season is the period between the spring and fall frosts, often referred to as the frost-free days.

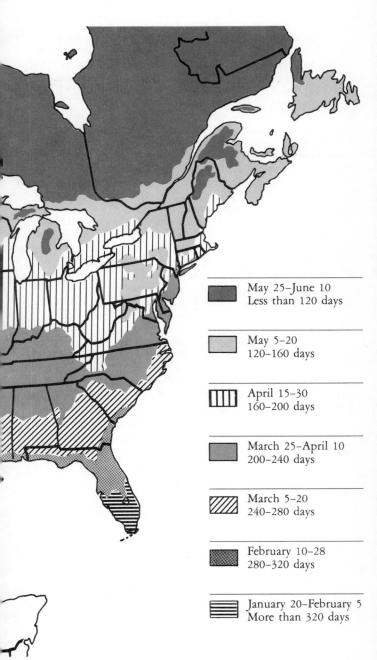

May 25–June 10
Less than 120 days

May 5–20
120–160 days

April 15–30
160–200 days

March 25–April 10
200–240 days

March 5–20
240–280 days

February 10–28
280–320 days

January 20–February 5
More than 320 days

Plant Chart

The plant charts on the following pages will provide you with a carefully selected listing of some of the plants you may want to add to your garden. The charts are divided into six groups, based on plant types: annuals, bulbs, ground covers, perennials, roses, and shrubs. The plants given for each group were chosen for the relative ease with which they can be purchased and grown.

Within each group, the plants are listed in alphabetical order by their scientific (Latin) names; these scientific names appear in italics and are followed by the common, or English, name, in Roman. Next to the name, in the first column, is given the page number of the relevant individual *Taylor's Guide* from which that plant was selected; when you refer to the individual guide, you will find a color photograph of the plant and, in the Plant Encyclopedia, a full description of its growth and cultivation.

The United States Department of Agriculture has divided North America into ten hardiness zones, based on average minimum temperatures. In the plant charts, the zone ratings are provided for the bulbs, perennials, ground covers, and shrubs listed. By turning to the Hardiness Zone Map on pages 36–37, you can quickly decide if the plant in question may be suitable to your region. (Remember, however, that the zone information is an estimated average. Other factors, such as sunlight, exposure to wind, and precipitation, may have an effect on the average minimum temperatures in your garden.)

For the annuals covered in the plant charts, the relative hardiness of each type is indicated. For the roses, the season of bloom is given. These charts are intended to provide beginning gardeners with suggestions about which plants may be best suited for their gardens. The chart listings are by no means exhaustive. For fuller information about any plant or group of plants, turn to the single-subject, full-sized *Taylor's Guides to Gardening* (*Bulbs, Annuals, Trees, Roses, Perennials,* and *Shrubs*), or to the handy-sized *Taylor's Pocket Guides to Gardening.*

	Page Numbers	Zones
Bulbs		
Acidanthera bicolor Sweet-scented Gladiolus	172	7
Agapanthus africanus African Lily	267	9
Amaryllis belladonna Belladonna Lily	249	9
Anemone coronaria Poppy Anemone	203, 258	5
Begonia grandis Hardy Begonia	228	6
Begonia ✕ *tuberhybrida* Tuberous Begonia	213	10
Brodiaea coronaria Brodiaea	261	7–8
Canna ✕ *generalis* Common Garden Canna	214, 215	8
Chionodoxa sardensis Glory-of-the-Snow	260	4
Clivia miniata Clivia	213	9
Colchicum autumnale Autumn Crocus	220	5
Crinum moorei Crinum Lily	176	9
Crocosmia ✕ *crocosmiiflora* Montbretia	208	7
Crocus goulimyi Crocus	221	8
Crocus longiflorus Crocus	254	5
Dahlia pinnata hybrids Dahlia	194, 202	9
Eranthis hyemalis Winter Aconite	197	4–5
Eucharis grandiflora Amazon Lily	177	10
Eucomis comosa Pineapple Flower	186	7
Freesia ✕ *hybrida* Freesia	178, 188	9
Fritillaria imperialis Crown Imperial	211	5
Fritillaria pudica Yellow Fritillary	193	4
Galtonia candicans Summer Hyacinth	181	6
Gladiolus byzantinus Gladiolus	244	5
Gladiolus ✕ *colvillei* Gladiolus	172	7
Gladiolus ✕ *hortulanus* Gladiolus	218, 219	9
Gladiolus tristis Gladiolus	182	7
Gloriosa rothschildiana Glory-Lily	210	10
Haemanthus coccineus Blood Lily	217	9
Hemerocallis fulva Common Daylily	149	3–4

Plant Chart

	Page Numbers	Zones
Bulbs continued		
Hemerocallis hybrids Daylily Hybrids	142, 153	3–4
Homeria breyniana Homeria	207	9
Hymenocallis narcissiflora Peruvian Daffodil	175	8
Ixia maculata Ixia	183, 188	7
Lapeirousia laxa Lapeirousia	206	7
Leucojum autumnale Leucojum	161	6
Lilium auratum Lily	137	5
Lilium canadense Meadow Lily	138, 151	4
Lilium lancifolium Tiger Lily	151	4
Lilium regale Regal Lily	133	4
Lilium speciosum Japanese Lily	128, 131	5
Lilium Hybrid Classes		
American Hybrids	127	4–8
Asiatic Hybrids	131, 146	4–7
Aurelian Hybrids	132, 140	4–7
Candidum Hybrids	136	5
Oriental Hybrids Madonna Lily	126, 129	5
Lycoris radiata Red Spider-Lily	204	7
Milla biflora Mexican Star	169	9
Moraea ramosissima African Iris	187	9
Nerine sarniensis Guernsey Lily	236	9
Ornithogalum thyrsoides Wonder Flower	173	8
Polianthes tuberosa Tuberose	178	9
Puschkinia scilloides Striped Squill	157	4
Ranunculus asiaticus Persian Buttercup	200	8
Scilla siberica Siberian Squill	263	4
Sparaxis tricolor Harlequin Flower	205	9
Tigridia pavonia Tiger Flower	205	7
Triteleia hyacinthina Wild Hyacinth	170	6–7
Tritonia crocata Montbretia	216	7
Vallota speciosa Scarborough Lily	212	10

	Page Numbers	Zones
Watsonia beatricis Bugle-Lily	208	8
Zephyranthes candida Zephyr Lily	166	9
Ground Covers		
Achillea tomentosa Woolly Yarrow	156	3
Acorus gramineus Japanese Sweet Flag	274	6
Ajuga reptans Bugleweed	116, 208	3
Alchemilla mollis Lady's-Mantle	131	4
Andromeda polifolia Bog Rosemary	182	3
Anemone canadensis Canada Anemone	166	4
Antennaria dioica Pussytoes	114, 183	4–5
Arabis procurrens Rock Cress	165	5
Arctostaphylos uva-ursi Bearberry	98, 99	3
Arctotis hybrids African Daisy	150	9
Arenaria montana Mountain Sandwort	162	4
Arenaria verna Irish Moss	79, 164	3
Artemisia stellerana Beach Wormwood	130	3–4
Asarum europaeum European Wild Ginger	123	5
Astilbe chinensis 'Pumila' Chinese Astilbe	187	5
Baccharis pilularis Dwarf Coyote Brush	73, 109	7
Berberis verruculosa Warty Barberry	97	6
Bergenia ciliata Bergenia	135, 136	6
Bergenia cordifolia Heartleaf Bergenia	134, 136	3
Bignonia capreolata Cross Vine	227	7
Bruckenthalia spiculifolia Spike-Heath	187	5
Brunnera macrophylla Siberian Bugloss	132, 207	4
Calluna vulgaris Heather	168, 189	5
Campanula carpatica Carpathian Harebell	167, 198	4
Campanula elatines garganica Bellflower	200	5
Ceanothus gloriosus Point Reyes Ceanothus	206	7
Cerastium tomentosum Snow-in-Summer	81	4
Ceratostigma plumbaginoides Leadwort	199	5
Chamaemelum nobile Roman Chamomile	85	6

Plant Chart

	Page Numbers	Zones
Ground Covers continued		
Chrysogonum virginianum Green-and-Gold	154	5
Convallaria majalis Lily-of-the-Valley	138, 172	4
Cornus canadensis Bunchberry	112, 166	2
Coronilla varia Crown Vetch	183	4
Cotoneaster dammeri Bearberry Cotoneaster	103	5
Cotoneaster horizontalis Rock Cotoneaster	100, 101	5
Daboecia cantabrica Irish Heath	171, 190	5
Daphne cneorum Rose Daphne	182	5
Dianthus gratianopolitanus Cheddar Pink	84, 193	5
Disporum sessile 'Variegatum'	141	5
Duchesnea indica Mock Strawberry	110, 161	4
Epimedium grandiflorum Longspur Epimedium	126	5
Epimedium ✕ *rubrum* Red Epimedium	126	5
Epimedium ✕ *versicolor* Persian Epimedium	125	5
Erica carnea Spring Heath	170, 188	5
Eriophyllum lanatum Woolly Eriophyllum	151	5
Euonymus fortunei Winter Creeper	104, 118	4
Fragaria chiloensis Beach Strawberry	113	5
Galax urceolata Galax	133	5
Galium odoratum Sweet Woodruff	82, 167	5
Gaultheria procumbens Wintergreen	98, 99	5
Gaultheria shallon Salal	94, 95	6
Gaylussacia brachycera Box Huckleberry	96	5
Gelsemium sempervirens Carolina Jessamine	226	7
Genista pilosa Broom	155	6
Geranium endressii Pyrenean Cranesbill	196	4
Geranium sanguineum Blood-red Cranesbill	197	4
Gypsophila repens Creeping Baby's-Breath	185	4
Hedera canariensis Algerian Ivy	133	8
Hedera colchica Persian Ivy	216, 217	8
Hedera helix English Ivy	215, 217	6

Plant Chart

	Page Numbers	Zones
Ground Covers continued		
Opuntia humifusa Prickly Pear	72, 160	5
Pachysandra procumbens Alleghany Spurge	112	5
Pachysandra terminalis Japanese Spurge	114, 115	5
Paxistima myrsinites Oregon Boxwood	97	5
Pennisetum villosum Feathertop	263	9
Phlox stolonifera Creeping Phlox	203	4
Phlox subulata Moss Pink	162, 194	4
Potentilla tabernaemontani Spring Cinquefoil	111, 154	4
Potentilla tridentata Three-toothed Cinquefoil	109, 164	3
Primula × *polyantha* Primrose	146, 147	5
Primula vulgaris English Primrose	192	5
Rhododendron indicum hybrids	177, 178	6
Rhododendron kiusianum hybrids	174–179	7
Rhododendron North Tisbury hybrids	179	6
Rhododendron Robin Hill hybrids	176	6
Rhus aromatica Fragrant Sumac	93	3
Robinia hispida Rose Acacia	176	5
Sagina subulata Irish Moss	78	5
Santolina chamaecyparissus Lavender Cotton	84, 156	6
Santolina virens Green Lavender Cotton	85, 157	6
Sarcococca hookerana humilis Sweet Box	107	6
Saxifraga stolonifera Strawberry Geranium	124, 173	7
Saxifraga × *urbium* London Pride	75, 184	5
Sedum reflexum Yellow Stonecrop	79	5
Sedum × *rubrotinctum* Pork and Beans	77	8
Sedum spurium Two-Row Stonecrop	76, 180	3
Skimmia reevesiana Reeves Skimmia	102	7
Stachys byzantina Lamb's-Ears	128, 129	5
Symphytum grandiflorum Comfrey	170	5
Taxus baccata 'Repandens'	86	5
Taxus cuspidata 'Densa' Cushion Japanese Yew	87	5

Plant Chart

	Page Numbers	Zones
Perennials continued		
Arabis caucasica 'Snow Cap' Wall Cress	238	4
Artemisia schmidtiana 'Silver Mound' Artemisia	89	4
Aruncus dioicus Goatsbeard	263	4
Asarum canadense Canadian Wild Ginger	82	4
Asarum europaeum European Wild Ginger	81	5
Asclepias tuberosa Butterfly Weed	139	4
Aster novae-angliae New England Aster	196	5
Aster ✕ *frikartii* Aster Hybrids	222	6
Astilbe ✕ *arendsii* 'Fanal' Astilbe	144	5
Astilbe chinensis 'Pumila' Chinese Astilbe	191	5
Astilbe tacquetii 'Superba' Astilbe	186	5
Aubrieta deltoidea False Rockress	155	5
Aurinia saxitilis 'Citrina' Basket-of-Gold	116	4
Baptisia australis Blue False Indigo	232	4
Belamcanda chinensis Blackberry Lily	138	5
Bergenia 'Margery Fish' Hybrid Bergenia	177	3
Bergenia cordifolia Heartleaf Bergenia	182	3
Boltonia asteroides 'Snowbank' White Boltonia	244	4
Brunnera macrophylla Siberian Bugloss	206	4
Calceolaria 'John Innes' Calceolaria	115	7
Callirhoe involucrata Finger Poppy Mallow	164	4
Caltha palustris Cowslip	113	4
Campanula carpatica 'Isobel'	214	4
Campanula garganica Adriatic Bellflower	202	6
Campanula glomerata Danesblood Bellflower	213	3–4
Campanula lactiflora Milky Bellflower	226	4
Campanula latifolia Great Bellflower	227	4
Campanula rotundifolia Bluebell	225	3
Catananche caerulea Cupid's Dart	223	5
Centaurea hypoleuca 'John Coutts' Centaurea	198	4
Centaurea macrocephala Globe Centaurea	105	3–4

Plant Chart

	Page Numbers	Zones
Perennials continued		
Galega officinalis Goat's Rue	183	5
Galium odoratum Sweet Woodruff	268	5
Gaura lindheimeri White Gaura	255	6
Gentiana asclepiadea Willow Gentian	212	6–7
Geranium himalayense Lilac Cranesbill	210	4
Geum quellyon 'Mrs. Bradshaw' Chilean Avens	148	5–6
Goniolimon tataricum Tatarian Statice	158	4
Gypsophila paniculata Baby's Breath	156	4
Helenium autumnale False Sunflower	132	4
Helianthus ✕ *multiflorus* Perennial Sunflower	129	5
Helianthemum nummularium 'Fire Dragon'	150	6
Heliopsis helianthoides scabra Orange Sunflower	130	4–5
Helleborus orientalis Lenten Rose	153	5
Hemerocallis 'Bonanza' Daylily	107	4
Heuchera sanguinea Coral Bells	145	4
Hibiscus moscheutos Rose Mallow	162	5
Hosta lancifolia Narrowleaf Plantainlily	228	4
Iberis sempervirens Candytuft	238	4
Inula ensifolia Swordleaf Inula	131	4
Iris Bearded Iris	219	4
Iris cristata Crested Iris	216	4
Iris ensata 'Azure' Japanese Iris	217	5
Iris laevigata 'Variegata' Rabbitear Iris	219	5
Iris pumila Dwarf Bearded Iris	218	4
Iris sibirica Siberian Iris	218	4
Iris tectorum Roof Iris	217	5–6
Kniphofia uvaria Red-hot Poker	143	5
Lamium maculatum Spotted Dead Nettle	250	4
Lavandula angustifolia Lavender	225	5–6
Liatris spicata Gay-Feather	187	4
Ligularia ✕ *przewalskii* 'The Rocket' Ligularia	108	4

Plant Chart

	Page Numbers	Zones
Perennials continued		
Salvia farinacea 'Catima' Mealy-Cup Sage	233	8
Salvia pratensis Meadow Clary	234	6
Salvia ✕ *superba* 'Mainacht' Violet Sage	234	5
Sanguisorba canadensis Great Burnet	263	4
Santolina chamaecyparissus Lavender Cotton	99	6
Saponaria ocymoides Rock Soapwort	155	4
Saxifraga stolonifera Strawberry Geranium	240	6
Scabiosa caucasica Pincushion Flower	200	4
Sedum aizoon Aizoon Stonecrop	104	4
Sedum spectabile Showy Stonecrop	195	4
Shortia galacifolia Oconee Bells	152	5
Sidalcea malviflora 'Loveliness' Checkerbloom	181	5
Smilacina racemosa False Solomon's-Seal	266	4
Solidago 'Gold Dwarf' Goldenrod	117	4
Stachys macrantha 'Robusta' Big Betony	185	4
Stylophorum diphyllum Celandine Poppy	120	6
Symphytum ✕ *uplandicum* Russian Comfrey	227	5
Thalictrum aquilegifolium Meadowrue	194	5–6
Thalictrum rochebrunianum Meadowrue	161	5–6
Thermopsis caroliniana Carolina Thermopsis	109	4
Tradescantia ✕ *andersoniana* 'Pauline'	176	5
Tricyrtis hirta Toad Lily	221	6
Trillium grandiflorum Snow Trillium	249	5
Trollius europaeus Common Globeflower	123	5–6
Valeriana officinalis Common Valerian	193	5
Veronica virginica Culver's Root	190	4
Viola odorata 'Royal Robe' Sweet Violet	204	5
Yucca glauca Soapweed	93	5
Shrubs		
Abelia 'Edward Goucher' Glossy Abelia	131	7
Abelia ✕ *grandiflora* Glossy Abelia	130	5–9

	Page Numbers	*Zones*
Shrubs continued		
Cytisus scoparius Scotch Broom	178, 179	6
Daphne ✕ *burkwoodii* Burkwood Daphne	135	4
Daphne cneorum Rose Daphne	134	5
Daphne odora Fragrant Daphne	135	7
Deutzia gracilis Slender Deutzia	103	5
Deutzia scabra Fuzzy Deutzia	102, 103	5
Dirca palustris Leatherwood	164, 165	5
Enkianthus campanulatus Redvein Enkianthus	98, 99	5
Erica ✕ *darleyensis* Darley Heath	153	6
Exochorda ✕ *macrantha* 'The Bride' Pearlbush	101	5
Exochorda racemosa Common Pearlbush	100	5
Forsythia ✕ *intermedia* Border Forsythia	172, 173	5
Fothergilla gardenii Dwarf Fothergilla	198, 199	5
Gardenia jasminoides Gardenia	123	8
Gaylussacia brachycera Box Huckleberry	153	6
Genista lydia Lydia Woadwaxen	180	7
Genista tinctoria Woadwaxen	181	5
Hamamelis ✕ *intermedia* Hybrid Witch Hazel	170	5
Hamamelis mollis Chinese Witch Hazel	171	6
Hamamelis virginiana Common Witch Hazel	170	4
Hibiscus syriacus Rose-of-Sharon	120	5
Holodiscus discolor Cream Bush	175	4
Hydrangea arborescens Smooth Hydrangea	140	4
Hydrangea macrophylla Bigleaf Hydrangea	141	7
Hydrangea paniculata Panicle Hydrangea	140, 141	4
Hydrangea quercifolia Oakleaf Hydrangea	138, 139	5
Hypericum calycinum Aaronsbeard St. Johnswort	159	6
Hypericum frondosum Golden St. Johnswort	160	6
Itea virginica Virginia Sweet Spire	204, 205	5
Jasminum nudiflorum Winter Jasmine	163	7
Kalmia angustifolia Sheep Laurel	114	3

	Page Numbers	Zones
Kalmia latifolia Mountain Laurel	114, 115	5
Kerria japonica Japanese Kerria	162, 163	5
Kolkwitzia amabilis Beauty Bush	97	5
Leucothoe axillaris Coast Leucothoe	203	6
Leucothoe fontanesiana Drooping Leucothoe	202, 203	5
Ligustrum amurense Amur Privet	276	4
Ligustrum japonicum Japanese Privet	124	7
Ligustrum obtusifolium Border Privet	124, 125	4
Lonicera tatarica Tatarian Honeysuckle	236	4
Loropetalum chinense Loropetalum	174, 175	7
Magnolia quinquepeta Lily Magnolia	90, 91	5
Magnolia stellata Star Magnolia	88, 89	4
Mahonia aquifolium Oregon Grape Holly	188	5
Mahonia bealei Leatherleaf Mahonia	189	7
Nandina domestica Nandina	238, 239	7
Nerium oleander Oleander	122, 123	8–10
Osmanthus heterophyllus Holly Osmanthus	270, 271	7
Philadelphus coronarius Common Mock-Orange	126, 127	5
Phlomis fruticosa Jerusalem Sage	181	7
Physocarpus opulifolius Common Ninebark	142	3
Pieris floribunda Mountain Pieris	200	5
Pieris japonica Japanese Pieris	201	5
Poncirus trifoliata Trifoliate Orange	86, 87	6
Potentilla fruticosa Shrubby Cinquefoil	158	3
Prunus glandulosa Dwarf Flowering Almond	84	5
Rhododendron Exbury Hybrid Azaleas	104, 105	5
Rhododendron yakusimanum Yako Rhododendron	106, 107	5
Rhodotypos scandens Jetbead	122	5
Ribes odoratum Clove Currant	80	5
Ribes sanguineum Flowering Currant	80, 81	6–8
Rosa hugonis Hugo Rose	159	5
Rosa rugosa Rugosa Rose	119	3

	Page Numbers	Zones
Shrubs continued		
Salix discolor Common Pussy Willow	169	3
Sambucus canadensis American Elder	232, 233	4
Skimmia japonica Japanese Skimmia	230, 231	8
Spiraea japonica Japanese Spirea	143	4
Spiraea ✕ *vanhouttei* Vanhoutte Spirea	151	4
Staphylea colchica Colchis Bladdernut	100, 101	5
Syringa ✕ *chinensis* Chinese Lilac	75, 77	4
Tamarix ramosissima Five-stamen Tamarisk	96	3
Viburnum ✕ *burkwoodii* Burkwood Viburnum	227	4
Vitex agnus-castus Lilac Chaste Tree	78, 79	7
Weigela florida Old-fashioned Weigela	82, 83	4

The hardiness ratings for annuals are: hardy annuals (HA), half-hardy annuals (HHA), and tender annuals (TA).

	Page Numbers	Hardiness
Annuals		
Ageratum houstonianum Flossflower	123, 154	TA
Agrostemma githago Corn Cockle	84	HHA
Alcea rosea Garden Hollyhock	109, 254	HA
Antirrhinum majus Common Snapdragon	111, 267	HHA
Arctotis stoechadifolia African Daisy	103	TA
Begonia ✕ *semperflorens-cultorum* Wax Begonia	80, 250	TA
Bellis perennis English Daisy	101	HA
Borago officinalis Borage	140	HA
Browallia speciosa 'Blue Bells' Browallia	128	TA
Calendula officinalis Pot Marigold	236	HA
Callistephus chinensis China Aster	102	TA
Campanula medium Canterbury Bells	138	HA
Carum Carvi Caraway	152	HA
Catharanthus roseus Madagascar Periwinkle	81, 162	TA
Celosia cristata Celosia	268-271	TA
Centaurea americana Basket-Flower	99	HA
Centaurea cyanus Bachelor's Button	124	HA
Cheiranthus cheiri Wallflower	205	HHA
Chrysanthemum carinatum parthenium Feverfew	158, 213	HHA
Chrysanthemum coronarium Crown Daisy	223	HA
Clarkia amoena Farewell-to-Spring	86	HA
Cleome hasslerana Spider Flower	118	HHA
Coleus ✕ *hybridus* Garden Coleus	186, 187	TA
Consolida ambigua Rocket Larkspur	143	HA
Cosmos bipinnatus Garden Cosmos	105	TA
Cuphea ignea Firecracker Plant	264	TA
Dahlia hybrids	102, 220	TA
Dianthus barbatus Sweet William	114	HA
Digitalis purpurea 'Foxy' Annual Foxglove	95, 96	HA
Dimorphotheca pluvialis Cape Marigold	157	TA
Dorotheanthus bellidiformis Livingstone Daisy	100, 243	TA

Plant Chart

	Page Numbers	Hardiness
Annuals continued		
Dyssodia tenuiloba Dahlberg Daisy	228	HA
Echium lycopsis Viper's Bugloss	139	HA
Eschscholzia californica California Poppy	208	HA
Eustoma grandiflorum Lisianthus	137	HHA
Gaillardia pulchella Blanket Flower	224, 240	HA
Gazania rigens Treasure Flower	224, 225	TA
Gerbera jamesonii 'Happipot' Transvaal Daisy	242	HHA
Helianthus annuus Sunflower	155, 230	HA
Helichrysum bracteatum 'Bikini' Strawflower	244	HHA
Heliotropium arborescens Common Heliotrope	145	TA
Hibiscus moscheutos Rose Mallow	163, 218	HHA
Hunnemannia fumariifolia Mexican Tulip Poppy	209	HHA
Iberis umbellata Globe Candytuft	115	HA
Impatiens wallerana Impatiens	80, 251	TA
Ipomoea tricolor Morning Glory	135	TA
Ipomopsis rubra Standing Cypress	265	HA
Lantana montevidensis Weeping Lantana	116	HHA
Lathyrus odoratus 'Mammoth Mixed' Sweet Pea	109	HA
Lavatera trimestris Lavatera	87	HA
Limnanthes douglasii Meadow Foam	201	HA
Limonium sinuatum Statice	266	TA
Linaria maroccana Toadflax	110	HA
Lobelia erinus Edging Lobelia	129	HA
Lobularia maritima Sweet Alyssum	116, 150	HA
Lonas annua African Daisy	212	HHA
Lunaria annua Honesty	88	HA
Matthiola incana 'Annua' Stock	107	HA
Mentzelia lindleyi Blazing Star	201	HA
Mesembryanthemum crystallinum Ice Plant	101, 155	TA
Mimulus guttatus Monkey Flower	206	HHA
Myosotis sylvatica Forget-Me-Not	145	HA

	Page Numbers	Hardiness
Nemophila menziesii Baby Blue-Eyes	130	HA
Nicotiana alata Flowering Tobacco	92, 265	TA
Oenothera missourensis Evening Primrose	203	HA
Oenothera speciosa Showy Evening Primrose	87	HA
Papaver nudicaule Iceland Poppy	252	HHA
Papaver rhoeas Corn Poppy	255	HA
Pelargonium ✕ *hortorum* Zonal Geranium	257	TA
Petunia ✕ *hybrida* Common Garden Petunia	82, 247	A
Phlox drummondii Annual Phlox	246	HA
Platystemon californicus Creamcups	200	HA
Portulaca grandiflora Rose Moss	253	TA
Primula obconica German Primrose	115	HHA
Rudbeckia hirta Gloriosa Daisy	222, 241	HHA
Salpiglossis sinuata Painted-Tongue	248	TA
Salvia farinacea 'Victoria' Mealy-Cup Sage	142	HHA
Scabiosa atropurpurea Sweet Scabious	119	HHA
Scabiosa stellata Starflower	118	HHA
Senecio cineraria 'Silver Dust' Dusty Miller	181	HHA
Tagetes erecta African Marigold	231, 234	HHA
Tagetes patula French Marigold	235, 237	HHA
Tithonia rotundifolia Mexican Sunflower	237	TA
Torenia fournieri Wishbone Flower	133	TA
Trachymene coerulea Blue Laceflower	122	HA
Tropaeolum majus Nasturtium	249	TA
Verbena ✕ *hybrida* Garden Verbena	106, 246	TA
Viola cornuta Horned Violet	207	HA
Viola ✕ *wittrockiana* Pansy	132, 248	HA
Zinnia elegans Common Zinnia	235, 242	TA
Zinnia haageana Mexican Zinnia	238, 241	TA

Plant Chart

The bloom times for roses are: early (E), midseason (M), late (L), and all season (A).

	Page Numbers	Bloom Time
Roses		
Species Roses		
Rosa moyesii	85	E
Rosa rugosa alba	76	A
Rosa rugosa rubra	82	A
Rosa spinosissima	79	E
Rosa spinosissima altaica	87	E
Climbing Roses		
America	103	M
Dublin Bay	104	M
Lawrence Johnston	95	E—M
May Queen	98	M
New Dawn	97	M
Shrub Roses		
Cornelia	112	M
The Fairy	115	L
Margo Koster	126	L
Roseraie de l'Haÿ	123	E
Will Scarlet	126	M
Old Garden Roses		
Boule de Neige	139	M
Gruss an Teplitz	175	M
Maiden's Blush	145	E—M
Tuscany	172	M
Zéphirine Drouhin	166	A
Floribunda Roses		
Apricot Nectar	184	M
Impatient	199	M
Ivory Fashion	185	M
Little Darling	192	M
Sun Flare	185	A

	Page Numbers	Bloom Time
Grandiflora Roses		
Aquarius	209	A
Love	211	A
Prominent	206	A
Queen Elizabeth	208	M
White Lightnin'	211	A
Hybrid Tea Roses		
Kaiserin Auguste Viktoria	214	E–M
Kölner Karneval	225	A
Pink Peace	227	A
Precious Platinum	234	A
Tiffany	222	A
Miniature Roses		
Beauty Secret	284	M
Chipper	268	M
Cricket	279	M
Jean Kenneally	252	M
Starglo	250	M

Buying Plants

Once you know what you'd like to grow in your garden and which plants will grow in your area, you're ready to buy. It may all seem very straightforward from here, but there are still some things you should know. First, you may well be bewildered by the variety of outlets where you can purchase plants. Then, once you decide on where to go, you may find the plant matching the name on your list bears little resemblance to the prototype in your neighbor's yard. In both cases you need to understand the language of gardening before filling your order.

Plant Names

Every known plant has one scientific name consisting of at least two parts. For example, *Acer saccharum* is what you may know as the sugar maple. *Acer,* the genus name, groups this tree with all other maples. *Saccharum,* the species name, distinguishes it as a particular type—the sugar maple.

This system of nomenclature, developed in the eighteenth century by the Swedish naturalist Carolus Linnaeus, provides a standard name for each plant that is accepted worldwide. It clears up confusion not only among speakers of different languages but also among gardeners who may use different names in one language for the same plant. Such common names—like "sugar maple"—are more recognizable and evocative than scientific names, and they can often be used without creating confusion. But to communicate clearly when ordering or asking advice about plants, learn and use the correct scientific names.

Varieties

Sometimes the scientific name of a plant consists of more than genus and species names. Species may also be subdivided into varieties. These are naturally occurring variants of a species, usually with an origin in a different geographical region than the typical species plant. For example, *Allium cyathophorum* var. *farreri* grows wild in Kansu Province of China, while the typical *Allium cyathophorum* is found in central Asia. Some references omit the abbreviation "var.," to create a three-part name: *Allium cyathophorum farreri.*

Cultivars

Bred with the intention of enhancing or minimizing certain inherited traits—color, fragrance, hardiness, size, or habit of growth—the selected plants or groups of plants developed under cultivation are known as cultivars. They are commonly but incorrectly called varieties. The name of a cultivar is added to the end of the scientific name, set off by single quotation marks. For example, *Acer palmatum* 'Dissectum' is a cultivar of the Japanese maple, *Acer palmatum.* It was developed for its deeply cut, fern-like leaves. Cultivars are preserved through vegetative propagation and, in some cases, may be an inbred line of plants that now invariably reproduce from seed.

Hybrids
Seed companies and nurseries are obliged to come up with new selections every year to excite the imaginations of gardeners. The emphasis is on desirable qualities—disease resistance, dwarfness, and new types of fruits and vegetables that freeze or can better than older ones. One way to accomplish this is through hybrids. The offspring of two plants of different species, hybrids are more vigorous than either parent.

This does not mean older types are bad or the new selections better; they may merely be a different color. But sometimes a truly new and useful plant—such as the hybrid poplar tree—comes onto the market. Mail-order nursery catalogues are good textbooks, but remember to choose plants based on your particular conditions.

Sources of Plants
When you are ready to purchase your plants, you can go to either your local nursery or you can order them through the mail. Each option has its advantages and you'd be wise to shop around before making your final decisions.

Ordering Through the Mail
Many mail-order nurseries advertise their catalogues in the classified section of garden magazines. Plants may be available for either spring or autumn shipping. Nurseries frequently dig up plants for early spring delivery the previous autumn, then store them in refrigerators over the winter. This is necessary because field-grown plants cannot be dug when the ground is frozen. Perennials shipped in autumn are freshly dug and packed just as they begin to go dormant. Consequently they can make the transfer into your garden with less shock then plants that have been held out of the ground for long periods of time. Some plants, such as Oriental poppies, lilies (except in the coldest climates), and peonies, are traditionally planted in autumn. Some nurseries, however, do not have a full selection of other perennials available at that time. Whether you order for spring or fall delivery, be sure to send your order in early to get the best selection, since uncommon plants are frequently in short supply. Study the catalogues in advance to become familiar with the suppliers' policy on terms of sale, shipping dates, and plant guarantees. It is helpful to specify a shipping date that coordinates with the best planting time in your area, especially if the mail-order source is located in another section of the country. At present, delivery by United Parcel Service seems to be more reliable than the U.S. Postal Service. The cost may be higher, but plants arrive faster and in better condition.

Buying Plants

If you buy perennials by mail, do not expect too much from your plants initially. You are basically buying rootstock, and the plants you receive won't look like the glowing pictures in the catalogue. Give them some time and proper care, however, and they will soon catch up with established plants in your garden.

It is important for fellow gardeners that you report to the supplier any plants that are unsatisfactory. Most nurseries are honest and anxious to protect their reputations and will replace plants or seeds if they do not produce. Write a letter specifically describing the problem (plant dead, dried out, or unusually small) and indicate whether you want a refund or replacement. But keep in mind that you have the responsibility of choosing wisely and providing good growing conditions. The catalogue should state the firm's policy on refunds.

Shopping at Local Nurseries

Some local retail garden centers or specialty nurseries offer catalogues, too. Try to get one before you visit the nursery, so you can determine what choices will be available. In spring you will find the best selections, but visit your garden center in summer or early fall as well to see plants at their mature height or in flower. Look for plants that appear healthy and well cared for, with no evidence of insects or diseases present. Insect-ridden or diseased plants will not perform well, and they can also introduce problems to the healthy plants in your garden. Look for plants with deep green foliage and dense, compact growth. When buying perennials, choose plants with multistemmed bases instead of ones that have just a few long stalks with single flowers at the tips. When you are not sure what a mature plant will look like or the kind of sun, soil, and water it requires, ask for help. Every nursery should have a knowledgeable staff, whether it is the largest garden center in your area or a "mom and pop" operation selling plants off a back porch. If the salesperson does not answer your questions, or at least offer to find answers, look elsewhere for your plants.

Mail-order Nurseries versus Garden Centers

Is it preferable to buy plants from a local garden center or from a mail-order nursery? Before you decide, consider the advantages of each.

When you buy plants locally, you can see what you are getting and choose the plants individually. Plants are likely to be larger than those bought through the mail, and they will make an instant show in the garden. Since plants in garden centers are usually sold in pots, they may be held in a shady spot until it suits your schedule to plant them.

Mail-order sources frequently offer a wider selection of plants. These plants, however, are usually shipped bare root, have been out of the ground for long periods of time, and demand immediate attention upon their arrival.

Price alone is not a reliable criterion for choosing one plant source over another, since cost is not always an indication of plant size or quality. The cost of a plant also reflects, to some extent, its availability and ease of propagation.

Whether you buy plants from a local garden center or from a mail order nursery, beware of extravagant claims for plant performance. If it sounds too good to be true, it probably is.

Planting

The perfect planting day is cool, cloudy, and calm. Since such days rarely seem to match the gardener's schedule, at least avoid planting on a windy day or during a heat wave. If mail-order plants appear desiccated when they arrive, soak them in a one-quarter strength soluble fertilizer solution for an hour before planting or potting up. Water plants thoroughly after you have planted them. Unless an inch of rain falls in a week, continue to water them every three or four days until they are established.

Plant Sources

The list below includes just a sampling of some of the best sources of plants for your garden. Some suppliers offer large and varied selections of popular forms, others carry rare variations, and a few specialize in certain groups of plants. Catalogues may be free, or the fee may be refunded with your first order.

Abundant Life Seed Foundation
P.O. Box 772
Port Townsend, WA 98368
(206) 385-5660

Andre Viette Farm & Nursery
Route 1
Box 16
Fisherville, VA 22939
(703) 943-2315

Appalachian Gardens
Box 82
Waynesboro, PA 17268
(717) 762-4312

Applewood Seed Company
3380 Vivian Street
Arvada, CO 80002
(303) 431-6283

Bernardo Beach Native Plant Farm
1 Sanchez Road
Veguita, NM 87062
Retail outlet: 520 Montano NW, Albuquerque, NM
(505) 345-6248

Bluebird Nursery, Inc.
521 Linden Street
Clarkson, NE 68629
(402) 892-3457

Bluestone Perennials Inc.
7211 Middle Ridge Road
Madison, OH 44057
(216) 428-7535

Botanical Nursery
219 Concord Road
Wayland, MA 01778
(508) 358-4846

Breck's
6523 North Galena Road
Peoria, IL 61632
(309) 691-4616

Brooks Tree Farm
9785 Portland Road, N.E.
Salem, OR 97305
(503) 393-6300

Busse Gardens
Route 2
Box 238
Cokato, MN 55321
(612) 286-2654

Caprice Farm Nursery
15425 S.W. Pleasant Hill Road
Sherwood, OR 97140
(503) 625-7241

Carroll Gardens
Box 310
444 East Main Street
Westminster, MD 21157
(301) 848-5422

Cedar Lane Farms
3790 Sandy Creek Road
Madison, GA 30650
(404) 342-2626

Clyde Robin Seed Company
P.O. Box 2366
Castro Valley, CA 94546
(415) 785-0425

Cooley's Gardens
P.O. Box 126
Silverton, OR 97381
(503) 873-5463

Crownsville Nursery
P.O. Box 797
Crownsville, MD 21032
(301) 923-2212

DeGroot, Inc.
P.O. Box 575
Coloma, MI 49038
(616) 468-6714

DeJaeger Bulbs, Inc.
188 Ashbury Street
South Hamilton, MA 01982
(508) 468-4707

**D.V. Burrell Seed
Growers Company**
P.O. Box 150
405 North Main Street
Rocky Ford, CO 81067
(719) 254-3318

**Earl May Seed &
Nursery Company**
Highway 59 South
Shenandoah, IA 51603
(712) 246-2780

**Far North Gardens
and International
Grower's Exchange**
P.O. Box 52248
Livonia, MI 48152
(313) 522-9040

Garden Place
6780 Heisley Road
P.O. Box 388
Mentor, OH 44061
(216) 255-3705

Gilbert H. Wild & Son, Inc.
P.O. Box 338
Sarcoxie, MO 64862
(417) 548-3514

Girard Nurseries
Route 20 East
P.O. Box 428
Geneva, OH 44041
(216) 969-1636

Gossler Farms Nursery
1200 Weaver Road
Springfield, OR 97477
(503) 746-6611

Green Horizons
218 Quinlan, Suite 571
Kerrville, TX 78028
(512) 257-5141

Greer Gardens
1280 Goodpasture Island Road
Eugene, OR 97401
(503) 686-8266

**Gurney Seed &
Nursery Company**
Yankton, SD 57079
(605) 665-1671

Harris Seeds
60 Saginaw Drive
Rochester, NY 14623
(716) 442-0410

Harris Moran Seeds
3670 Buffalo Road
Rochester, NY 14624
(716) 594-9411

**Hauser's Superior
View Farm**
Route 1
Box 199
Bayfield, WI 54814
(715) 779-5404

Heaths and Heathers
62 Elma-Monte Road
Elma, WA 98541
(206) 482-3258

Holbrook Farm & Nursery
Route 2
Box 223B, 5025
Fletcher, SC 28732
(704) 891-7790

J. W. Jung Seed Company
335 South High Street
Randolph, WI 53956
(414) 326-3121

Jackson & Perkins
83-A Rose Lane
Medford, OR 97501
(503) 776-2400

Johnny's Selected Seeds
Foss Hill Road
Albion, ME 04910
(207) 437-9294

Kelly Nurseries
P.O. Box 800
Dansville, NY 14437-0800
(800) 325-4180

Lamb Nurseries
East 101 Sharp Avenue
Spokane, WA 99202
(509) 328-7956

Louisiana Nursery
Route 7
Box 43
Opelousas, LA 70570
(318) 948-3696

**Massachusetts
Horticultural Society**
Horticulture Hall
300 Massachusetts Avenue
Boston, MA 02115
(617) 536-9280

Maxalea Nurseries
900 Oak Hill Road
Baltimore, MD 21239
(301) 377-7500

Mellinger's, Inc.
2310 West South Range
North Lima, OH 44452
(216) 549-9861

Milaeger's Gardens
4838 Douglas Avenue
Racine, WI 53402
(414) 639-2040

Musser Forests
Box 340
Indiana, PA 15701
(412) 465-5685

**The National Arbor
Day Foundation**
100 Arbor Avenue
Nebraska City, NE 68410
(402) 474-5655

**Nichol's Herbs and
Rare Seeds**
1190 North Pacific Highway
Albany, OR 97321
(503) 928-9280

Old Farm Nursery
5550 Indiana Street
Golden, CO 80403
(303) 278-0754

Oliver Nurseries, Inc.
1159 Bronson Road
Fairfield, CT 06430
(203) 259-5609

**Otis S. Twilley Seed
Company, Inc.**
P.O. Box 65
Trevose, PA 19053
(215) 639-8800

Park Seed Company
Highway 254 North
Greenwood, SC 29647
(803) 223-7333

Plants of the Southwest
930 Baca St.
Sante Fe, NM 87501
(505) 983-1548

Prairie Nursery
P.O. Box 306
Westfield, WI 53964
(608) 296-3679

Quality Dutch Bulbs
P.O. Box 225
50 Lake Drive
Hillsdale, NJ 07642
(201) 391-6586

Rice Creek Gardens
11506 Central Avenue N.E.
Blaine, MN 55434
(612) 574-1197

Roses of Yesterday & Today
802 Brown's Valley Road
Watsonville, CA 95076
(408) 724-3537

Roslyn Nursery
211 Burrs Lane
Dix Hills, NY 11746
(516) 643-9347

Schichtel Nursery, Inc.
6745 Chestnut Ridge Road
Orchard Park, NY 14127
(716) 662-9896

Schreiner's Gardens, Inc.
3625 Quinaby Road N.E.
Salem, OR 97303
(503) 393-3232

Spring Hill Nurseries
6523 North Galena Road
Peoria, IL 61632
(309) 691-4616

Stock Seed Farms, Inc.
Route 1
Box 112
Murdock, NE 68407
(402) 867-3771

Stokes Seeds Inc.
P.O. Box 548
Buffalo, NY 14240
(716) 672-8844

Thompson & Morgan
P.O. Box 1308
Jackson, NJ 08527
(201) 363-2225

Tranquil Lake Nursery
45 River Street
Rehoboth, MA 02769
(508) 336-6491

Van Bourgondien & Sons
P.O. Box A
245 Farmingdale Road
Babylon, NY 11702
(516) 669-3500

W. Atlee Burpee Company
300 Park Avenue
Warminster, PA 18974
(215) 674-4900

Wayside Gardens
Hodges, SC 29695
(803) 223-1968

Weston Nurseries
P.O. Box 186
East Main Street
Hopkinton, MA 01748
(508) 435-3414

White Flower Farm
Route 63
Litchfield, CT 06759-0050
(203) 567-0801

Tools Suppliers

All you need are a few simple, versatile, and well-made tools to get you started in your garden. As a general rule, buy the best-quality tools you can find. The investment will be well worth the money— and if you take proper care of your tools they will last a long time. To learn more about specific garden tools, consult the essays in this book on creating a garden bed, planting, and pruning. In addition to your local merchants, many mail-order companies carry a full line of tools. You may wish to try one of the following sources:

A. M. Leonard
P.O. Box 816
Piqua, OH 45356
(513) 773-2694

Country Manufacturing, Inc.
P.O. Box 104
Fredericktown, OH 43019
(614) 694-9926

Garden Way Carts
102nd and 9th Avenue
Troy, New York 12180
(518) 235-6010

Gardener's Eden
P.O. Box 7453
San Francisco, CA 94120
(415) 421-4242

Gardener's Supply Company
128 Intervale Road
Burlington, VT 05401
(802) 863-1700

Harmony Farm Supply
P.O. Box 460
Graton, CA 95444
(707) 823-9125

Kinsman Company
River Road
Point Pleasant, PA 18950
(215) 297-5613

Langenbach Fine Tool Company
P.O. Box 453
Blairstown, NJ 07825
(201) 362-5886

Mellinger's
2310 W. South Range Road
North Lima, OH 44452
(216) 549-9861

Peaceful Valley Farm Supply
P.O. Box 2209
110 Springhill Boulevard
Grass Valley, CA 95945
(916) 272-4769

Smith and Hawken
25 Corte Madera
Mill Valley, CA 94941
(415) 383-2000

The Clapper Company
1121 Washington St.
West Newton, MA 02165
(617) 244-7900

The Natural Gardening Company
217 San Anselmo Avenue
San Anselmo, CA 94960
(415) 456-5060

The Walt Nicke Company
P.O. Box 433
36 McLeod Lane
Topsfield, MA 01983
(508) 887-3388

Soil Testing

If you are new to gardening or uncertain about the nature of the soil in your yard, it is a good idea to have your soil tested before you begin planting. A soil-test kit will reveal your soil's texture, nutrient level, and pH (acidity or alkalinity); experts can then describe what steps to take to improve your soil. Although you can evaluate some aspects of your soil at home, for more accurate results you may want to send a representative soil sample to a laboratory. Below is a list of state-run and private soil testing labs. Prices for soil tests are generally lower at state laboratories, but the more expensive private labs can sometimes provide more detailed information. In each case, the laboratory will provide you with a computer printout with the results of your soil test. Contact each laboratory directly to get more information on how to obtain and send soil samples. Soil tests are also performed by some local county extension agencies; ask your state laboratory representative for details.

By State

Alabama
Soil Testing Laboratory
Auburn University
Auburn, AL 36849

Alaska
Soil Testing Laboratory
Agricultural Experiment
Station
University of Alaska
533 East Firewood
Palmer, AK 99645

Arizona
Soil, Water, and Plant Tissue
Testing Lab
Department of Soils, Water,
and Engineering
University of Arizona
Tucson, AZ 85721

Arkansas
Soil Testing and Research
Laboratory
University of Arkansas
Fayetteville, AR 72701

California
No soil testing service is
available through this state.

Colorado
Soil Testing Laboratory
Colorado State University
Fort Collins, CO 80523

Connecticut
Soil Testing Laboratory
Plant Science Department
University of Connecticut
Storrs, CT 06238

Delaware
Soil Testing Laboratory
University of Delaware
Newark, DE 19711

Florida
Soil Testing Laboratory
University of Florida
Gainesville, FL 32611

Georgia
Soil Testing and Plant
Analysis Laboratory
University of Georgia
Athens, GA 30602

Hawaii
Soil Testing Laboratory
University of Hawaii
1910 East-West Road
Honolulu, HI 96822

Idaho
Soil Testing Laboratory
Department of Plant and
Soil Science
College of Agriculture
Moscow, ID 83843

Illinois
No soil testing service is
available through this state.

Indiana
Plant and Soil
Analysis Laboratory
Agronomy Department
Purdue University
West Lafayette, IN 49707

Iowa
Soil Testing Laboratory
Iowa State University
Ames, IA 50011

Kansas
Soil Testing Laboratory
Agronomy Department
Kansas State University
Manhattan, KS 66506

Kentucky
Soil Testing Laboratory
University of Kentucky
Lexington, KY 40546

Louisiana
Soil Testing Laboratory
Department of Agronomy
Louisiana State University
Baton Rouge, LA 70803

Maine
Soil Testing Laboratory
Department of Plant and
Soil Sciences
University of Maine
Orono, ME 04469

Maryland
Soil Testing Laboratory
Agronomy Department
University of Maryland
College Park, MD 20742

Massachusetts
Soil and Plant
Tissue Laboratory
University of Massachusetts
240 Beaver Street
Waltham, MA 02254

Michigan
Soil Testing Laboratory
Michigan State University
East Lansing, MI 48824

Minnesota
Soil Testing Laboratory
University of Minnesota
St. Paul, MN 55108

Mississippi
Soil Testing Laboratory
Mississippi State University
Mississippi State, MS 39762

Missouri
Soil Testing Laboratory
University of Missouri
Columbia, MO 65211

Montana
Soil Testing Laboratory
Plant and Soil Science
Department
Montana State University
Bozeman, MT 59717

Nebraska
Soil Testing Laboratory
University of Nebraska
Lincoln, NE 68583

Nevada
Soil Testing Laboratory
Plant Science Department
University of Nevada
Reno, NV 89507

New Hampshire
Analytical Services Laboratory
University of New Hampshire
Durham, NH 03824

New Jersey
Soil Testing Laboratory
Lipman Hall Annex
Rutgers University
New Brunswick, NJ 08903

New Mexico
Soil and Water
Testing Laboratory
Crop and Soil
Science Department
New Mexico State University
Las Cruces, NM 88003

New York
Soil Testing Laboratory
Cornell University
Ithaca, NY 14853

North Carolina
Soil Testing Laboratory
Agronomic Division
North Carolina Department
of Agriculture
Raleigh, NC 27611

North Dakota
Soil Testing Laboratory
North Dakota State University
Fargo, ND 58105

Ohio
Soil Testing Laboratory
Ohio Research and
Development Center
Ohio State University
Wooster, OH 44691

Oklahoma
Soil Testing Laboratory
Agronomy Department
Oklahoma State University
Stillwater, OK 74078

Oregon
Soil Testing Laboratory
Oregon State University
Corvallis, OR 97331

Pennsylvania
Soil Testing Laboratory
College of Agriculture
Pennsylvania State University
University Park, PA 16802

Rhode Island
Soil Testing Laboratory
University of Rhode Island
Kingston, RI 02881

South Carolina
Soil Testing Laboratory
Clemson University
Clemson, SC 29634

South Dakota
Soil Testing Laboratory
South Dakota State University
Brookings, SD 57007

Tennessee
Soil Testing Laboratory
University of Tennessee
Nashville, TN 37211

Texas
Soil Testing Laboratory
Texas A & M University
College Station, TX 77843

Utah
Soil Testing Laboratory
Utah State University
Logan, UT 84322

Vermont
Soil Testing Laboratory
University of Vermont
Burlington, VT 05405

Virginia
Soil Testing Laboratory
Agronomy Department
Virginia Polytechnic Institute
Blacksburg, VA 24061

Washington
Soil Testing Laboratory
Washington State University
Pullman, WA 99164

West Virginia
Soil Testing Laboratory
West Virginia University
Morgantown, WV 26506

Wisconsin
Soil and Plant
Analysis Laboratory
University of Wisconsin
511 Mineral Point Road
Madison, WI 53705

Wyoming
Soil Testing Laboratory
Plant Science Department
University of Wyoming
Box 3354
Laramie, WY 82071

Independent Laboratories

Freedom Soil Lab
P.O. Box 1144
Freedom, CA 95019
(408) 724-4427

I.F.M.
333 Ohme Gardens Road
Wenatchee, WA 98801
(509) 662-3179

Necessary Trading Co.
P.O. Box 305, 1 Nature's Way
New Castle, VA 24127
(703) 864-5103

Ohio Earth Food
13737 Duquette Avenue N.E.
Hartville, OH 44632
(216) 877-9356

Peaceful Valley Farm Supply
P.O. Box 2209
110 Springhill Boulevard
Grass Valley, CA 95945
(916) 272-4769

Soil-Test Kit Suppliers

E. C. Geiger, Inc.
P.O. Box 285
Route 63
Harleysville, PA 19438
(215) 256-6511

Farnam Companies
P.O. Box 34820
Phoenix, AZ 85067
(800) 528-1378

**LaMotte Chemical Products
Company**
P.O. Box 329
Chestertown, MD 21620
(301) 778-3100

Luster Leaf Products
P.O. Box 1067
Crystal Lake, IL 60014
(815) 455-5160

Micro Essential Laboratory
4224 Avenue H
Brooklyn, NY 11210
(718) 338-3618

Necessary Trading Company
P.O. Box 305
1 Nature's Way
New Castle, VA 24127
(703) 864-5103

Ohio Earth Food, Inc.
13737 Duquette Avenue N.E.
Hartville, OH 44632
(216) 877-9356

**Stuppy Greenhouse
Company**
P.O. Box 12456
North Kansas City, MO 64116
(800) 821-2132

Resources for

Gardeners everywhere are beginning to show greater interest in reducing the use of toxic pesticides and herbicides in the landscape. There are several national organizations that can provide you with written information that will help in your efforts to reduce pesticide use.

The National Resources Defense Council (NRDC) is a national, nonprofit public-interest organization dedicated to protecting the environment and preserving natural resources. The NRDC publishes booklets and brochures; for information, write to the NRDC at 40 West 20th Street, New York, NY 10011; or call (212) 727-2700.

The Bio-Integral Resource Center (BIRC) publishes information on the safe, biological control of pests; a nonprofit organization, BIRC provides information and technical advice on integrated pest management. Members of BIRC receive advice from the technical staff on the least-toxic methods for solving any pest problem found in the home, garden, on pets, or in the community at large. BIRC publishes *Common Sense Pest Control Quarterly* and *The IPM Practitioner,* two magazines that focus on practical integrated pest management methods for solving common pest problems. Also available are a series of instructional publications on the proper use of beneficial organisms to control garden pests. For a comprehensive directory of products compatible with integrated pest management programs, contact the Bio-Integral Resource Center (BIRC), P.O. Box 7414, Berkeley, CA 94707; (415) 524-2567.

Information on the toxicity of pesticides can be obtained by contacting the National Coalition Against the Misuse of Pesticides (NCAMP), 530 7th Street, S.E., Washington, DC 20003; (202) 543-5450. This nonprofit organization maintains an extensive file of toxicology literature on pesticides. They can provide a summary of published data, and also tell you which pesticides lack the full range of toxicological tests.

The National Pesticide Telecommunications Network (NPTN) operates a "Pesticide Hotline" funded by the U.S. Environmental Protection Agency and Texas Tech University. Information on pesticide toxicity as well as on the proper use of pesticides is also available. They are located in the Health Sciences Center, School of Medicine, Department of Preventive Medicine, Texas Tech University, Lubbock, TX 79430; (800) 858-7378.

The following mail-order companies carry some of the products recommended for integrated pest management programs:

Brody Enterprises, Inc.
9 Arlington Place
Fair Lawn, NJ 07410
(800) 458-8727

Gardener's Supply
128 Intervale Rd.
Burlington, VT 05401-2840
(800) 863-1700

Pest Control

Gardens Alive!
P.O. Box 149
Sunman, IN 47041
(812) 623-3800

Growing Naturally
149 Pine Lane
P.O. Box 54
Pineville, PA 18946
(215) 598-7025

Harmony Farm Supply
P.O. Box 460
Graton, CA 95444
(707) 823-9125

Hydro-Gardens
P.O. Box 9707
Colorado Springs, CO 80932
(800) 634-6362;
in CO (719) 495-2266

IFM
333 Ohme Gardens Rd.
Wenatchee, WA 98801
(800) 332-3179

Natural America
Box 7
Brentwood, NY 11717
(516) 435-2380

Natural Farm Products, Inc.
Rte. 2
Box 201A
Spencer Rd. SE
Kalkaska, MI 49646
(616) 369-2465

Nature's Touch
11150 W. Addison St.
Franklin Park, IL 60131
(312) 455-6900

Necessary Trading Co.
8311 Salem Ave.
New Castle, VA 24127
(703) 864-5103

Peaceful Valley Farm Supply
P.O. Box 2209
Grass Valley, CA 95945
(916) 272-4769

Pest Management Supply Co.
P.O. Box 938
Amherst, MA 01004
(800) 272-7672

Plow and Hearth
301 Madison Rd.
Orange, VA 22960
(703) 672-1712

Safer Inc.
189 Well Avenue
Newton, MA 01259
(617) 964-2990;
(800) 527-0512

Reading List

The following list will point you toward other good sources of general gardening information, as well as further reading on specific topics covered in this book.

In addition, the ten other *Taylor's Guides to Gardening* provide in-depth coverage of a single garden subject. Every *Taylor's Guide* has full-color photographs of 200 to 300 different plants; the plant accounts describe each one, with tips on how to plant and care for it. The volumes include *Taylor's Guides* to Annuals; Bulbs; Garden Design; Ground Covers, Vines & Grasses; Houseplants; Perennials; Roses; Trees; Shrubs; Vegetables & Herbs; and Water-Saving Gardening. *Taylor's Pocket Guides* provide a handy-sized, quick-reference resource for many of the topics covered by the full-sized *Taylor's Guides*.

Adriance, Guy W. and Fred B. Brison. *Propagation of Horticultural Plants.* New York: McGraw-Hill, 1955.

All About Fertilizers, Soils & Water. San Francisco, CA: Ortho Books, 1979.

Ball, Jeff and Charles O. Cresson. *The 60-Minute Flower Garden.* Emmaus, PA: Rodale Press, 1987.

Bear, Firman E. *Earth. The Stuff of Life.* Norman: University of Oklahoma Press, 1987.

Bowles, John Paul, ed. *Soils.* New York: Brooklyn Botanic Garden, 1986.

Brady, N. C. *The Nature and Properties of Soils.* New York: Macmillan, 1974.

Browse, P. D. A. McMillan. *Hardy Woods Plants from Seed.* London: Grower Books, 1979.

Carr, A. *Rodale's Color Encyclopedia of Garden Insects.* Emmaus, PA: Rodale Press, 1979.

Curtis, Will C. *Propagation of Wildflowers.* MA: New England Wild Flower Society, Inc., 1986.

Damrosch, Barbara. *The Garden Primer.* New York: Workman Publishing, 1988.

DeBach, P. *Biological Control of Insect Pests and Weeds.* London: Chapman and Hall, 1973.

Dirr, Michael A., and Charles W. Heuser, Jr. *The Reference Manual of Woody Plant Propagation: From Seed to Tissue Culture.* GA: Varsity Press, Inc., 1987.

Dirr, Michael A. *Manual of Woody Landscape Plants: Their Identification, Ornamental Characteristics, Culture, Propagation and Uses.* Champaign, IL: Stipes Publishing Co., 1977.

Donahue, Roy L., and John Miller. *Soils: An Introduction to Soils and Plant Growth.* Englewood Cliffs, NJ: Prentice-Hall, 1983.

Drip Irrigation for the Home Garden and Landscape. Berkeley: University of California, 1976.

Emery, Dara E. *Seed Propagation of Native California Plants.* CA: Santa Barbara Botanic Gardens, 1988.

Esau, K. *Anatomy of Seed Plants.* New York: John Wiley and Sons, 1977.

Fish, Margery. *We Made A Garden.* London/Boston: Faber and Faber, 1956, reprinted 1983.

Flint, M. L., and R. van den Bosch. *Introduction to Integrated Pest Management.* New York: Plenum Press, 1981.

Gardening Techniques. San Francisco, CA: Ortho Books, 1984.

Garner, R. J. *The Grafter's Handbook.* New York: Oxford University Press, 1979.

Golueke, Clarence G. *Composting: A Study of the Process and its Principles.* Emmaus, PA: Rodale Press, 1972.

Harris, Richard W. *Arboriculture—Care of Trees, Shrubs, and Vines in the Landscape.* Englewood Cliffs, NJ: Prentice-Hall, 1983.

Hartmann, H. T., D. E. Kester, and F. T. Davies, Jr. *Plant Propagation, Principles and Practices.* Englewood Cliffs, NJ: Prentice-Hall, 1990.

Hartmann, Hudson T., and Dale E. Kester. *Plant Propagation: Principles and Practices.* Englewood Cliffs, NJ: Prentice-Hall, 1983.

Huffaker, C. B., and P. S. Messenger. *Theory and Practice of Biological Control.* New York: Academic Press, 1976.

Johnson, W. T., and H. H. Lyon. *Insects That Feed On Trees and Shrubs.* Ithaca: Cornell University Press, 1988.

Justice, Oren L., and Louis N. Bass. *Principles and Practices of Seed Storage.* Washington, DC: United States Department of Agriculture, 1978.

Kozlowski, T. T. *Seed Biology. I and II.* New York: Academic Press, 1972.

Kramer, P. J., and T. T. Kozlowski. *Physiology of Woody Plants.* New York: Academic Press, 1979.

Landscaping for Water Conservation: Xeriscape! CO: City of Aurora Utilities Department and Denver Water Department, 1989.

Reading List

Macdonald, Bruce. *Practical Woody Plant Propagtion for Nursery Growers,* Vol. I. OR: Timber Press, 1986.

Marer, P. J. *The Safe and Effective Use of Pesticides.* Berkeley: University of California, 1988.

Mastalerz, J. W. *The Greenhouse Environment.* New York: John Wiley and Sons, 1977.

Matlock, G. *Water Harvesting for Urban Landscapes.* AZ: Tuscon Water Department, 1985.

Mengel, K., and E. A. Kirkby. *Principles of Plant Nutrition.* Worblaufen-Bern, Switzerland: International Potash Institute, 1979.

Mist Propagation of Cuttings of Horticultural and Plantation Crop Plants. UK: Commonwealth Bureau of Horticulture and Plantation Crops, 1980.

Nelson, John O. "Water Conserving Landscapes Show Impressive Savings." *Journal of the American Water Works Association,* March, 1987, pp. 35–42.

Nierling, Arno. *Easy Gardening With Drought Resistant Plants.* New York: Hearthside Press, Inc., 1968.

Nokes, Jill. *How to Grow Native Plants of Texas and the Southwest.* Austin: Texas Monthly Press, 1986.

Olkowski, William, Sheila Daar, and Helga Olkowski. *Common Sense Pest Control for the Home and Garden.* Newtown, CT: Taunton Press, 1991.

Reader's Digest Illustrated Guide to Gardening. Pleasantville, NY: Reader's Digest Association, 1978.

Robinette, Gary O. *Landscaping Planning for Energy Conservation.* Reston, VA: Environmental Design Press, 1988.

Salisbury, F.B., and C.W. Ross. *Plant Physiology.* Belmont, CA: Wadsworth Publishing Co., Inc., 1978.

Schopmeyer, C. S. *Seed of Woody Plants in the United States.* Washington, DC: United States Department of Agriculture, 1974.

Sinclair, W .A., H. H. Lyon, and W. T. Johnson. *Diseases of Trees and Shrubs.* Ithaca: Cornell University Press, 1987.

Smyser, Carol A. *Nature's Design: A Practical Guide to Natural Landscaping.* Emmaus, PA: Rodale Press, 1982.

Soil. Washington, DC: U.S.D.A. Yearbook of Agriculture, 1957.

Soils and Men. Washington, DC: U.S.D.A. Yearbook of Agriculture, 1938.

Thompson, J. R. *An Introduction to Seed Technology.* Great Britain: Leonard Hill, 1979.

Thompson, L. M., and F. R. Troeh. *Soils and Soil Fertility.* New York: McGraw Hill, 1973.

Turf and Garden Fertilizer Handbook. Washington, DC: The Fertilizer Institute, 1983.

Wells, James S. *Plant Propagation Practices.* New York: Macmillan, 1961.

Young, James A., and Cheryl G. Young. *Collecting, Processing and Germinating Seeds of Wildland Plants.* Portland, OR: Timber Press, 1986.

Appendices

Glossary

Acid Soil
Soil with a pH value of less than 7.

Adventitious
Growing or arising in an abnormal location.

Alkaline Soil
Soil with a pH value of more than 7.

Alternate
Arranged singly along a twig or shoot, and not in whorls or opposite pairs.

Annual
A plant whose entire life span, from sprouting to flowering and producing seeds, is encompassed in a single growing season. Annuals survive cold or dry seasons as dormant seeds. *See also* Biennial and Perennial.

Anther
The terminal part of a stamen, containing pollen in one or more pollen sacs.

Apical
Borne or arising from the growing tip of a leaf, branch, or plant.

Apical dominance
Inhibition of the growth of lateral buds or shoots by the presence of a terminal bud or shoot.

Axil
The angle formed by a leafstalk and the stem from which it grows.

Axis
The central stalk of a compound leaf or flower cluster; the main stem of a plant.

Balled and burlapped
Having the roots of a plant encased in a ball of soil and tied with burlap and string for transport.

Bare-rooted
Dug out of a loose growing medium with no soil around the roots. Some shrubs are sold in this condition by nurseries.

Basal
Appearing at the base of the stem.

Berry
A fleshy fruit with one to many seeds that is developed from a single ovary.

Biennial
A plant whose life span extends to two growing seasons, sprouting in the first growing season and then flowering, producing seed, and dying in the second. *See also* Annual and Perennial.

Bisexual
In horticulture, having both stamens and pistils present.

Bolting
The premature or unwanted production of flowers and seeds, often triggered by heat, excessive day length, drought, or nutrient deficiency.

Bonsai
The Japanese art of pruning and shaping trees and shrubs that produces long-lived miniature container plants.

Broadleaf evergreen
An evergreen plant that is not a conifer (also broad-leaved evergreen).

Bud
A young and undeveloped leaf, flower, or shoot, usually covered tightly with scales.

Bulb
A short underground stem, the swollen portion consisting mostly of fleshy, food-storing scale leaves.

Bulbil
A small bulblike structure, usually borne among the flowers or in the axil of a leaf, but never at ground level like a true bulb.

Bulblet
A small bulb produced at the periphery of a larger bulb.

Calyx
Collectively, the sepals of a flower.

Cambium
The thin formative layer between the xylem and phloem that gives rise to new cells and is responsible for secondary growth.

Cane
A long, woody, pliable stem.

Chlorophyll
The green pigment in plant leaves necessary for the process of photosynthesis.

Clay soil
Soil with extremely small particles, less than 0.00008 inch in diameter, with a large capacity for water and plant nutrients.

Cloche
A glass or rigid plastic cover used to protect plants from frost, wind, or rain.

Conifer
A cone-bearing tree or shrub, often evergreen, usually with needlelike leaves.

Corm
A solid, vertical, underground stem, resembling a bulb, with a bud on top and often with a membranous coat of dried leaf bases.

Cormel
A small corm that is produced by and develops alongside of its parent corm. Also called a cormlet.

Corolla
Collectively, the petals of a flower.

Corona
A crownlike structure on some corollas, as in daffodils and the Milkweed family.

Creeping
Prostrate or trailing over the ground or over other plants.

Cross-pollination
The transfer of pollen from the flower of one plant to the pistil of another plant.

Crown
The part of a plant between the roots and the stem, usually at soil level. In roses, the region of the bud union.

Cultivar
An unvarying plant variety, maintained by vegetative propagation or by inbred seed.

Cutting
A piece of plant without roots; set in a rooting medium, it develops roots, and can then be potted as a new plant.

Cyme
A branching flower cluster that blooms from the center toward the edges, and in which the tip of the axis always bears a flower.

Dead-heading
Removing blooms that are spent; dead-heading removes seedpods that sap the bulb's strength and encourages the growth of the flower at the tip of the stem.

Deciduous
Of a plant, dropping its leaves at the end of the growing season; not evergreen.

Dieback
Death of a plant's stems, beginning at the tips; caused by lack of water, nutrient deficiency, disease, or injury from pruning.

Dioecious
Bearing staminate and pistillate flowers on different plants of the same species.

Disbudding
The pinching off of selected buds to benefit those left to grow.

Division
Propagation by division of crowns or tubers into segments that can be induced to send out roots.

Dormancy
A state of rest and reduced metabolic activity in which live plant tissues do not grow.

Dripline
The circular area under a tree, extending from the trunk to the outside tips of the branches.

Dwarf
A plant that, due to inherited characteristics, is shorter and/or slower-growing than the normal forms.

Espalier
A plant that has been trained to grow flat against a wall or framework.

Evergreen
Retaining green leaves for most or all of an annual cycle of growth.

Everlasting
Describing a plant whose flowers can be prepared for dried arrangements.

Eye
A bud on a cutting, tuber, or tuberous root.

Family
A group of plants in related genera, all of which share characteristics not found in other families.

Fertile
Bearing functional stamens or pistils, and therefore able to produce seed.

Fertilizers
Substances that contain one or more of the necessary plant nutrients (nitrogen, phosphorus, and potassium).

Filament
The threadlike lower portion of a stamen, bearing the anther.

Fruit
The mature, fully developed ovary of a flower, and anything that matures with it, usually one or more seeds.

Genus
A group of closely related species; plural, genera. The first word in a plant's botanical or scientific name is the name of the genus to which the plant belongs.

Germinate
To sprout (applied to seeds).

Hardening off
The process of acclimating seedlings gradually to their permanent place in the garden.

Hardiness
The ability of a plant to withstand winter cold; often expressed in terms of geographic zones.

Heeling in
Laying a plant sideways in a trench so that roots are covered.

Herb
A plant without a permanent, woody stem, usually dying back during cold weather.

Herbaceous perennial
An herb that dies back each fall but sends out new shoots and flowers for several successive years.

Horizon
A layer of soil in the soil profile.

Horticulture
The cultivation of plants for ornament or food.

Humus
Partly or wholly decomposed vegetable matter; an important constituent of garden soil.

Hybrid
The offspring of two parent plants that belong to different clones, species, subspecies, or genera.

Invasive
Spreading aggressively from the original site of planting.

Lateral
Borne in the axil of a leaf or branch, but not at the tip.

Layering
A method of propagating plants in which a stem is induced to send out roots by surrounding a section of it with soil.

Leaf axil
The angle between the petiole of a leaf and the stem to which it is attached.

Leaf margin
The edge of a leaf.

Leaflet
One of the subdivisions of a compound leaf.

Lime
A soil amendment containing calcium; provides increased alkalinity and nutrient content.

Loam
A humus-rich soil containing up to 25 percent clay, up to 50 percent silt, and less than 50 percent sand.

Meristem
The formative or growing layer of plant tissue.

Microclimate
The climatic conditions of a particular garden or site, taking into account degree of sun, shade, wind, humidity, and rainfall.

Monoecious
Having both staminate (male) and pistillate (female) flowers on the same plant.

Mulch
A protective covering spread over the soil around the base of plants to retard evaporation, control temperature, or enrich the soil.

Naturalized
Established as a part of the flora in an area other than the place of origin.

Needle-leaf evergreen
An evergreen plant that has needlelike foliage; usually a conifer.

Neutral soil
Soil that is neither acid nor alkaline, having a pH value of 7.

Node
The place on a stem where a leaf, bud, or branch is attached.

Offset
A short, lateral shoot ending in an erect bud, and arising at or near the base of a plant; an offset readily produces new roots.

Opposite
Arranged along a twig or shoot in pairs, with one on each side, and not alternate or whorled.

Organic matter
A substance derived from plant or animal material.

Ovary
The swollen base of a pistil within which seeds develop.

Ovule
The immature seed in the ovary that contains the egg.

Panicle
An open flower cluster, blooming from bottom to top, and never terminating in a flower.

Peat moss
Partly decomposed moss, rich in nutrients and with a high water retention, used as a component of artificial soil mixtures, as a soil amendment, and sometimes as a mulch.

Penjing
The Chinese art of dwarfing trees and shrubs, similar to Japanese bonsai.

Perennial
A plant whose life span extends over several growing seasons and that produces seeds in several growing seasons, rather than only one. *See also* Annual and Biennial.

Permanent wilting point
The point of soil dryness at which plants can no longer obtain water from the soil.

Petal
One of a series of flower parts lying within the sepals and next to the stamens and pistils, often large and brightly colored.

Petiole
The stalk of a leaf.

pH
A symbol for the hydrogen ion content of the soil, and thus a means of expressing the acidity or alkalinity of the soil.

Pinching
The use of the fingers or finger and thumb to remove a flower, stem tip, or bud to promote dense, stocky growth and more blossoms.

Pistil
The female reproductive organ of a flower, consisting of an ovary, style, and stigma.

Pistillate flower
A female flower having one or more pistils but no functional stamens.

Pod
A dry, one-celled fruit, with thicker walls than a capsule.

Pollen
Minute grains containing the male germ cells and released by the stamens.

Pollination
The transfer of pollen from an anther to a stigma.

Propagate
To produce new plants, either by vegetative means involving the rooting of pieces of a plant, or by sowing seeds.

Prostrate
Lying on the ground; creeping.

Prune
To cut, pinch back, or otherwise inhibit or control the growth of a plant to maintain vigor, shape the plant, or spur growth.

Radicle
The primary root of a plant, developed in a seedling; the embryonic root of a seedling.

Rhizomatous
Having rhizomes, or underground stems.

Rhizome
A horizontal underground stem, distinguished from a root by the presence of nodes, and often enlarged by food storage.

Root
The underground portion of a plant that serves to anchor it and absorb water and minerals from the soil.

Rootstock
The swollen, more or less elongate stem of a perennial herb; sometimes refers to a rhizome.

Rosette
A crowded cluster of leaves; usually basal, circular, and appearing to grow directly out of the ground.

Runner
A specialized stem that develops from the axil of a leaf in the crown of the plant; also, a prostrate shoot, rooting at its nodes.

Sandy soil
Soil with large particles, ranging in diameter from 0.08 to 0.002 inch, that drains quickly and hold nutrients poorly.

Scarified seeds
Seeds that have been scratched or sanded in order to induce them to absorb water and germinate.

Scree
An accumulation of rocky detritus on a hillside or at the base of a slope.

Seed
A fertilized, ripened ovule, almost always covered with a protective coating and contained in a fruit.

Semi-evergreen
Retaining at least some green foliage well into winter; or, shedding leaves only in cold climates.

Sepal
One of the outermost series of flower parts, arranged in a ring outside the petals, and usually green and leaflike.

Shrub
A woody, perennial plant, smaller than a tree, usually with several stems or trunks.

Silt
Soil with medium-sized particles, ranging in diameter from 0.002 to 0.00008 inch.

Softwood
The immature stem or stems of woody plants.

Soil
A mixture of solids, liquids, and gases that serve as a growing medium for plants.

Soil amendment
Any bulk material incorporated into the soil; usually intended to improve drainage, soil structure, or soil aeration.

Species
A population of plants or animals whose members are at least potentially able to breed with each other, but which is reproductively isolated from other populations. The second word in a plant's botanical or scientific name designates the species to which it belongs.

Spine
A strong, sharp, usually woody projection from the stem or branches of a plant, not usually from a bud.

Stamen
The male reproductive organ of a flower, consisting of a filament and a pollen-containing anther.

Staminate flower
A male flower, that is, one that bears anthers and lacks pistils.

Sterile
Lacking functional stamens or pistils, and therefore not capable of sexual reproduction.

Stigma
The tip of the pistil where the pollen lands and develops into the style.

Stolon
A modified aerial stem that grows along the ground, often rooting at the nodes; also, an unthickened rhizome.

Stomata (singular, stoma)
Microscopic pores, located mainly on the undersides of leaves, through which a plant takes in and releases oxygen, carbon dioxide, water vapor, and other gases.

Style
The elongated part of a pistil between the stigma and the ovary.

Subshrub
A partly woody plant.

Subspecies
A naturally occurring geographical variant of a species.

Succulent
A plant with thick, fleshy leaves or stems that contain abundant water-storage tissue.

Sucker
A secondary shoot arising from the underground buds or the roots of a plant, and which forms its own leaves and roots.

Symbiotic
Existing in mutually beneficial and cooperative relationship; usually said of two unrelated or dissimilar organisms.

Tap root
The main, central root of a plant.

Terminal
Borne at the tip of a stem or shoot, rather than in the axil.

Topiary
The art of shearing trees and shrubs into unusual shapes.

Transpiration
The release of water vapor or other gases through the stomata.

Tuber
A swollen, mostly underground stem that bears buds and serves as a storage site for food.

Variegated
Marked, striped, or blotched with some color other than green.

Variety
A population of plants that differ consistently from the typical form of the species, either occurring naturally or produced in cultivation.

Vegetative propagation
Propagation by means other than seeds.

Whorl
A group of three or more leaves or shoots, all emerging from a stem at a single node.

Whorled
Arranged along a twig or shoot in groups of three or more at each node.

Winter-kill
To be killed by harsh winter weather.

Woody
Producing hard rather than fleshy stems and having buds that survive aboveground in winter.

Xylem
Microscopic "veins" or tubular passageways that carry water and dissolved nutrients from the roots of a plant to other plant parts.

Index

*Numbers in boldface
refer to pages on
which color plates or
illustrations appear.*

Chanticleer Press

Publisher: Andrew Stewart
Senior Editor: Ann Whitman
Editors: Jane Mintzer Hoffman,
  Carol M. Healy
Editorial Assistants: Katherine Jacobs,
  Micaela Porta
Managing Editor: Barbara Sturman
Production: Kathy Rosenbloom,
  Deirdre Duggan
Project Design: Diana M. Jones
Photo Library: Tim Allan
Frost Date Map: Paul Singer
Hardiness Zone Map: Mapping
  Specialists, Ltd.

Founding Publisher: Paul Steiner